The History of Anglo-Japanese Relations, 1600–2000

The History of Anglo-Japanese Relations, 1600–2000

General Editors: **Chihiro Hosoya** and **Ian Nish**

The five volumes which make up the series *The History of Anglo-Japanese Relations, 1600–2000* cover the relationship between these two island communities from the first contacts at the start of the seventeenth century through to the end of the present millennium. While the studies cover the Anglo-Japanese relationship over the past four centuries, they tend to concentrate on features of the past 150 years. The volumes have been prepared independently over the past five years by Japanese and non-Japanese scholars who have met to debate and discuss their papers. These studies analyse the rise and fall of these relations in four dimensions: political and diplomatic; economic and business; military and naval; and social and cultural.

Titles in the series:

Volume 1: THE POLITICAL–DIPLOMATIC DIMENSION, 1600–1930
Ian Nish and Yoichi Kibata (*editors*)

Volume 2: THE POLITICAL–DIPLOMATIC DIMENSION, 1931–2000
Ian Nish and Yoichi Kibata (*editors*)

Volume 3: THE MILITARY–NAVAL DIMENSION
Ian Gow and Yoichi Hirama (*editors*)

Volume 4: THE ECONOMIC–BUSINESS DIMENSION
Janet Hunter and S. Sugiyama (*editors*)

Volume 5: THE SOCIAL–CULTURAL DIMENSION
Gordon Daniels and Chushichi Tsuzuki (*editors*)

The History of Anglo-Japanese Relations, 1600–2000
Series Standing Order ISBN 0–333–79224–6
(*outside North America only*)

You can receive future titles in this series as they are published by placing a standing order. Please contact your bookseller or, in case of difficulty, write to us at the address below with your name and address, the title of the series and the ISBN quoted above.

Customer Services Department, Macmillan Distribution Ltd, Houndmills, Basingstoke, Hampshire RG21 6XS, England

The History of Anglo-Japanese Relations, 1600–2000

Volume 4

Economic and Business Relations

Edited by

Janet E. Hunter

and

S. Sugiyama

palgrave

First published 2002 by
PALGRAVE
Houndmills, Basingstoke, Hampshire RG21 6XS and
175 Fifth Avenue, New York, N.Y. 10010
Companies and representatives throughout the world

PALGRAVE is the new global academic imprint of St. Martin's Press LLC Scholarly and Reference Division and Palgrave Publishers Ltd (formerly Macmillan Press Ltd).

ISBN 0–333–79197–5 hardback

This book is printed on paper suitable for recycling and made from fully managed and sustained forest sources.

A catalogue record for this book is available from the British Library.

Library of Congress cataloging-in-publication data has been applied for.

10 9 8 7 6 5 4 3 2 1
11 10 09 08 07 06 05 04 03 02

Printed and bound in Great Britain by
Antony Rowe Ltd, Chippenham, Wiltshire

Contents

List of Tables

List of Figures

List of Photographs

Notes on the Contributors

Marie Conte-Helm is Director of the Daiwa Anglo-Japanese Foundation, and Visiting Professor at the University of Northumbria at Newcastle.

Janet Hunter is Saji Senior Lecturer in Japanese Economic and Social History at the London School of Economics and Political Science.

Kanji Ishii was formerly Professor in the Economics Department of Tokyo University, and now teaches at Tokyo Keizai University.

Christopher Madeley teaches at Chaucer College, Canterbury.

Bunji Nagura is Professor in the Department of Social Sciences of Ibaraki University, Mito City.

John Sharkey was formerly British Academy Research Fellow in the Department of History, School of Oriental and African Studies, London.

Shinya Sugiyama is Professor in the Economics Department of Keio University, Tokyo.

Toshio Suzuki is Professor in the Economics Department of Tohoku University, Sendai.

Norio Tamaki is Professor in the Faculty of Commerce at Keio University, Tokyo.

John Weste teaches in the Department of East Asian Studies at the University of Durham.

Editors' Note

Japanese names are given in the Japanese order, with family name preceding given name, except where the reference is to a Japanese author writing in English.

Romanization is according to the modified Hepburn system, but macrons to indicate long vowels have been omitted.

Acknowledgements

This volume consists of an overview of the history of business and economic relations between Japan and Britain, followed by eight more specialist essays, four by Japanese scholars, and four by British scholars. The chapters as a whole have benefited from support from a number of organizations and individuals. We would like to express our gratitude to the funders and organizers of the Anglo-Japanese History Project. For research and editing assistance, and help with the organization of workshops, we would like to thank Kishida Makoto, Helen Macnaughtan, Miki Sayoko, Anna Spadavecchia, Peter von Staden and Washizaki Shuntaro. Participants at the workshops at which draft versions of the chapters were presented offered valuable comments and advice. Responsibility for the content of the papers naturally lies exclusively with the editors and authors, but we hope that this volume will help to stimulate further research and a greater understanding of this aspect of the history of Anglo-Japanese relations.

We would like to thank the Museum of British Road Transport for permission to reproduced photographs 1–5 in chapter 6, and the Institute of Mechanical Engineers for permission to reproduce photographs 6 and 7 in chapter 8.

Janet Hunter and S. Sugiyama
2001

1

Anglo-Japanese Economic Relations in Historical Perspective, 1600–2000: Trade and Industry, Finance, Technology and the Industrial Challenge

Janet Hunter and S. Sugiyama

Introduction

This chapter gives an overview of Anglo-Japanese economic relations from the early seventeenth century to the present time, focusing on the key terms of 'trade and industry', 'finance', 'technology' and 'the industrial challenge'. In so doing, it also describes the background to the eight chapters that comprise the rest of the book. For ease of analysis, we have divided the 400-year story of Anglo-Japanese commercial and economic relations into the following four periods, although we recognize that these divisions cannot be exact.

The first period covers British relations with the Tokugawa regime, from *c.*1600, when William Adams came to Japan, up to the conclusion of the 'unequal' commercial treaty between Britain and Japan in 1858, which marked the beginning of close relations between the two countries. The following century saw great changes in Anglo-Japanese economic relations and is therefore subdivided at several points. The second period is the time from the implementation of the 'unequal' treaty, with the first opening of treaty ports in 1859, to the end of the treaty port system in 1899. At first, particularly for the newly established Meiji government, Britain was the model for Japanese modernization. Japan's industrialization could not have been achieved without help from Britain in terms of materials, technology and human capital. However, Japan's rapid industrialization changed the character of its relationship with Britain from dependence to self-reliance. In the 1890s the attainment of treaty revision, victory in the Sino-Japanese War, and the establishment of the gold standard led to the formation of a partnership between the two countries.

The third period ranges from 1900 to the end of the Pacific War in 1945. This period combines two aspects: prior to the First World War, Anglo-Japanese relations involved both cooperation and competition; in particular, against the background of the Anglo-Japanese Alliance of 1902, the City played a crucial role in raising foreign loans for Japan. After the First World War and the establishment of a new international order by the Washington Conference, however, Anglo-Japanese relations were placed in a wider international system. Increasing Japanese competition, which became apparent in the mid-1920s, caused economic conflicts over cotton textiles exports and shipping on the world market, in which Britain had previously enjoyed unchallenged supremacy. Anglo-Japanese competition became ever more important, particularly in the 1930s after the economic depression and Japan's military takeover of Manchuria, leading to the complete suspension of the trade relationship with the outbreak of the Pacific War.

The final period was the postwar period, characterized more by friendship and mutual understanding. The Anglo-Japanese relationship could only exist in the context of an international order dominated by the United States and by the formation of an integrated Europe. In the 1960s and 1970s, Japan developed a trade surplus with Britain, and Japanese capital investment in Britain increased. However, the relationship changed in the 1990s as Japan entered the period of economic stagnation after the collapse of the 'bubble' economy, while Britain experienced a period of relative growth.

Anglo-Japanese trade relations in the Tokugawa period

The period before the treaties, 1600–1854

Trade relations between England and Japan can probably be said to date from the arrival in Japan of the Elizabethan pilot William Adams. Adams left Rotterdam in June 1598 on board the Dutch ship *de Liefde*, and in April 1600 was shipwrecked off the coast of eastern Kyushu. At the end of the same year the English East India Company was founded; a trading station was established at Bantam two years later.[1] In June 1613 the *Clove*, an East India Company ship captained by John Saris, entered Hirado in northern Kyushu. Hirado was already an important port for Dutch and Portuguese ships, playing a crucial role in East Asian trade.[2]

When Saris arrived, William Adams was at Sunpu (Shizuoka), where the first Tokugawa Shogun, Tokugawa Ieyasu, was spending his nominal retirement. Saris called Adams to Hirado and met Ieyasu at Sunpu, with Adams acting as interpreter. Saris gave Ieyasu a letter from James I with gifts, and then proceeded to Edo, where he paid his respects to the second Shogun, Hidetada. Ieyasu had a positive attitude to trade, and when Saris visited Sunpu again on the way back to Hirado, the East India Company was duly given a licence. The licence contained the following privileges: exemption from tariff duties, the freedom to visit any port in Japan, the freedom to erect houses, reside and trade at Edo, and extraterritoriality. The company's main object was to obtain 'a connection with the Chinese through Japan, and to carry on a General Trade between India, China and Japan'.[3] The chief attraction for outsiders lay in the fact that since China had prohibited direct trade with Japan, intermediaries were needed in order to obtain imports of necessities such as raw silk.

In June 1613 Saris founded the English factory at Hirado and Richard Cocks was appointed Chief Merchant. The Hirado factory had several English members of staff under Cocks and traded in raw silk and silk fabrics. Acting on instructions from Saris, who left Hirado in December 1613, Cocks set up branches at Edo and Osaka, with sub-agencies at Kyoto and Sakai, and an agency at Nagasaki. The policy of the East India Company was to sell to big merchants, whereas the Dutch organized a large credit business among retailers.[4] After the death of Ieyasu in 1616, the trade privileges granted to the English factory were gradually reduced, and limits were placed on the number of ships. As a result they had to withdraw from Edo and Osaka.

In 1622 the Hirado factory was doing so badly that the Batavia branch of the East India Company decided to reduce its size and running costs. In December 1623, the English factory at Hirado was closed, and all the staff left for Batavia. The losses were mainly caused by advances totalling 12821 taels (about £4000) made to family members of the local daimyo (domain-lord), Matsuura, and to merchants in Nagasaki and Hirado. There was another large debt amounting to 6636 taels owed by Andrea Dittis, the Captain of the Chinese colony at Hirado, who had been advanced this sum to act as a middleman in gaining access to the Chinese market. The East India Company entrusted its buildings and warehouses to the safe keeping of a Japanese feudal lord, and Cornelis van Neijen-Roode, chief of the Dutch factory at Hirado, was given power of attorney to collect the advances. The closure of the factory has been attributed variously to disagreements between Saris/Cocks and William Adams, to the death of Ieyasu, or to the deaths of indispensable members of the factory staff including Adams in 1620.[5] However, it should be remembered that the activities of the East India Company in the East were largely dependent on the Netherlands for both military and commercial support. When the Amboyna Massacre of 1623 and the increasing antagonism between the two countries created an unfavourable business environment for the East India Company, there was an inevitable decline in British influence in East and Southeast Asia.

The Council of the English East India Company at Batavia twice proposed the reopening of the Hirado factory, in 1627 and 1633, but their plans were not realized. In 1639 the Tokugawa Bakufu decided to restrict formal diplomatic relations to the Dutch and Chinese only, prohibiting any relations with Portugal. Two years later, the Dutch factory at Hirado was moved to Dejima, and Nagasaki became the only official harbour for trade with the Netherlands and China.[6] The East India Company considered the question of trade with Japan in 1653 and in the 1660s, and sent two ships on an investigatory trip in 1672, but neither ever returned. Finally, in June 1673, the *Return* was sent to Nagasaki with a cargo including raw silk, silk fabrics, chintz, refined leather, medicine, spices, and white sugar. However, the Bakufu refused to reopen trade with the company because of the marital links between Charles II and the Portuguese royal family.[7]

This was the last substantial attempt to restore the trade with Japan until the nineteenth century. Britain became heavily involved in India, and the start of official trade with China on the opening of the port of Canton in 1757 made it possible to import tea directly, which greatly reduced interest in restoring trading links with Japan. In 1792 Lord Macartney was despatched to China as a plenipotentiary, but a planned visit to Japan did not take place because of the outbreak of the Napoleonic Wars. In 1797, owing to the lack of Dutch ships, the Dutch at Batavia were compelled to charter the English ship *Eliza* to make the annual visit to Nagasaki. In 1803, as the result of this voyage, the East India Company was persuaded to send a ship to Japan, but it was refused admittance.[8]

In October 1808, during the Anglo-Dutch War, the English frigate *Phaeton* entered Nagasaki under a Dutch flag in search of a Dutch ship. This forced the Bakufu to strengthen Japan's naval defences. In 1811, when Java was placed under the protection of the East India Company, Thomas Stamford Raffles was appointed Lieutenant Governor of Java and its Dependencies. He was keen to take the Dutch factory at Nagasaki into British management for the following reasons:

> To establish a British Factory in Japan, and furnish a population of not less than 25 Millions with the staple Commodities, and with the Manufacturers of Great Britain is in itself a grand national object; but it may be of more particular consideration to the Honorable Company from its relative importance to China, and the apparent facility of eventually supplanting the Commerce which at present exists between that Country and Japan.[9]

In 1813 he despatched two ships, the *Charlotte* and the *Maria*, to Nagasaki, loaded with goods such as sugar, tin and spices, but Hendrik Doeff, the then head of the Dutch factory at Nagasaki, refused to hand control over to Britain. While woollens, hardware and glass manufactures were expected to be the main export articles from Britain, moreover, it seemed likely that Japan would only have copper and camphor to offer in return. On the whole, it seemed that 'a direct trade with that Island [Japan] is not likely to be attended with those beneficial consequences which are expected by the Government of Java'.[10]

Meanwhile, industrial development in Britain was changing the role and significance of the East India Company in Asian trade. 'Country traders' who conducted opium trading began to play a crucial role in the settlement of trade between Britain, India and China, and the company lost its monopoly in trade other than tea in 1813.[11] Despite Raffles' enthusiasm, therefore, the East India Company declined to make any further efforts to trade with Japan, stating that 'We have no grounds to presume that the Japanese have any particular predeliction for British Manufactures, or that the supply which they at present obtain through China, is inadequate to the demands of their market.'[12] As free trade developed after the company's monopoly was abolished in 1833, interest in trade with Japan increased, particularly among manufacturers and merchants. British survey ships occasionally visited the Japanese coast, but no substantial change occurred until 1854.

Britain and the opening of Japan

British government officials and merchants were both attracted by China as a potential market, but did not place any great urgency on trade with Japan. British policy towards Japan followed the United States, which took the initiative in opening the country.[13] Following the Treaty of Peace and Amity between Japan and the United States signed in March 1854, however, John Bowring, the then Superintendent of Trade in China, urged the British government to start its own negotiations. The expansion of the Taiping Rebellion and the commencement of the Crimean War prevented immediate action. However, in early September 1854, Sir James Stirling, Commander-in-Chief of the East Indies Squadron, visited Nagasaki to investigate the possible presence of Russian warships, and on 14 October 1854, a convention for regulating the admission of British ships into the ports of Japan was signed at Nagasaki between Sir James Stirling and the Bakufu. This convention was limited to British naval activities relating to the Crimean War, and did not contain any clauses which would facilitate actual trade between the two countries.

In 1857 the Earl of Elgin received instructions from the Foreign Secretary, Lord Clarendon, to visit Japan in order to negotiate a commercial treaty after he had settled matters concerning the Arrow War in his capacity as a plenipotentiary to China. In August, following the Tianjin Treaty of June 1858, Lord Elgin visited Nagasaki and then proceeded to Edo, meeting Townsend Harris, the American Consul, at Shimoda on the way. On 26 August 1858, a Treaty of Peace, Friendship, and Commerce was concluded between Britain and Japan, on lines similar to the commercial treaty with the United States which Japan had signed that July.[14]

The treaty consisted of 24 articles, and additional trade regulations. It was based on the principle of free trade, stipulating the opening dates of ports and cities (Article 3), extraterritoriality (Article 5), the free use of currencies (Article 10), tariffs (Articles 16 and 17), and a 'most-favoured nation' clause (Article 23). The treaty was fundamentally 'unequal' in its main provisions. It stipulated that Japan was to open to foreign trade the ports of Hakodate,

Kanagawa (Yokohama) and Nagasaki in July 1859, Niigata in January 1860, Hyogo (Kobe) in January 1863, and the two cities of Edo and Osaka in 1862 and 1863 respectively. Major differences in the Anglo-Japanese commercial treaty compared with the United States–Japan treaty were as follows: first, the 'most-favoured nation clause' was not included in the latter; secondly, import tariff rates for cotton and woollen manufactures, major potential imports from Britain, were reduced from 20 per cent to 5 per cent; and, thirdly, a clause allowing for the revision of tariff rates five years after the opening of Kanagawa was revised to read 'if either the British or Japanese Government desires it' rather than 'if the Japanese Government desires it'. In effect this amounted to a denial of Japanese tariff autonomy.[15]

The commercial activities of western firms were strictly confined to the treaty ports. Western merchants were not allowed to go into the interior of Japan for commercial purposes, although they were in principle allowed to go freely within the limits of 10*ri* (24.4 miles) in any direction. Tariff rates for all articles were stipulated in the additional trade regulations. All export duties were set at 5 per cent ad valorem. Import duties were in general set at 20 per cent ad valorem with 5 per cent ad valorem for cotton and woollen manufactures, steam-machinery, rice, coals, and minerals, such as zinc, lead and tin, and 35 per cent for liquor. The import of opium was prohibited. Later in 1866, in response to renewed foreign pressure (chiefly concerning imperial ratification of the 1858 treaties and the promised opening of Hyogo), Japan consented to tariff revision, which came into effect in July 1866. Both export and import duties were then fixed on a basis of 5 per cent ad valorem.[16]

The commercial treaties further set exchange rates between currencies of the same metallic base. Three hundred and eleven *ichibu* (Japanese silver coins) were to be equivalent to 100 Mexican dollars, which had been circulating widely in Southeast and East Asia as a standard trading currency since the early sixteenth century. Japanese and foreign currencies were to circulate freely for trade purposes. Both exports and imports of gold and silver, coined or uncoined, were duty-free. Relative to gold, silver had a much higher value in Japan than outside. The first British Minister to visit Japan, Rutherford Alcock, claimed that western merchants were making large amounts of money from exchange transactions which exploited this difference, but the outflow of gold coins from Japan should not be exaggerated.[17]

For Japan, the commercial treaties of 1858 signified the end of a period of over two hundred years during which the government had exercised almost total control over all relationships with the outside world. The opening of the ports meant the incorporation of Japan into the world economic system, and a shift from a closed to an open economy. Taken literally, the treaties contained 'unequal' items; however, as will be shown, the system which they created was not without its attraction to the Bakufu and the Meiji government.

From Japan's dependence on Britain to equal partnership: trade under the 'unequal' treaties, 1859–1899

The advance of British firms to Japan

The 'opening' of China and Japan, in 1842 and 1859 respectively, signified a new phase in East Asian trade. The development of ocean shipping routes for steamers and the extension of telegraphic communication was bringing the area closer to the European and American markets. As trade increased, the necessary infrastructure, such as shipping, banking and other facilities, was gradually created. Regular shipping routes by steamers were opened one after another. The Peninsular and Oriental Steam Navigation Co. (P&O) commenced a regular service between Shanghai and Nagasaki in 1859 which was extended to Yokohama in 1864. Other British shipping companies, such as the Blue Funnel, Castle, and Glen lines, followed in the 1860s and 1870s. The opening of the Suez Canal in 1869 encouraged the shift from sailing ships to steamers, so that by the late 1870s almost all China trade was carried by steamers through the canal. As we will see later, British shipping companies played a crucial role in Japan's external and coastal trade. Increasing competition among shipping companies and the consequent rapid fall in freight rates forced the formation of shipping conferences in order to control competition and allow concerted measures against non-members.[18]

The growth of the telegraphic network was revolutionizing established commercial patterns and the nature of financial procedures, through making possible both telegraphic transfers and the reception of immediate information on the European and American markets. In the early 1870s, both the Eastern Extension Australasia and China Telegraph Co. (British) and the Great Northern Telegraph Co. (Danish) constructed telegraphic cables to East Asia, and the latter made an extension to Nagasaki.[19]

Western banks which had been established in India and China also advanced to Japan in the 1860s. The main role was played by British colonial banks. The Chartered Mercantile Bank of India, London and China, which was founded in London in 1854, opened its Yokohama branch in 1863; the Oriental Bank Corporation, founded in London in 1842, opened its Yokohama branch in 1864; the Hongkong and Shanghai Banking Corporation, which was founded in Hong Kong in 1865 to serve British business interests, opened its Yokohama branch in 1866. The Chartered Bank of India, Australia, and China, which was founded in London in 1858, also wanted to open a branch in Japan but was not able to do so until 1880. Such banks played a crucial role in providing the finance for foreign trade, either by buying and selling bills of exchange drawn on London, Hong Kong and Shanghai, or by providing Mexican dollars and issuing their own banknotes. Of these banks, the Hongkong and Shanghai Banking Corporation was particularly influential and financed most foreign trade with Japan until the mid-1880s. Western banks were essential to early stages of Japan's industrialization, but their business activities were gradually restricted as the Japanese monetary system was formed in the late 1880s.[20]

Western firms already engaged in the China trade advanced to Japan. They included the British firms of Adamson, Bell & Co. (later Dodwell & Co.), Aspinall, Cornes & Co., Butterfield and Swire, Dent & Co., Gilman & Co., Jardine, Matheson & Co., and Macpherson & Marshall. There were also small, locally-based British firms, such as Glover & Co. and Alt & Co. in Nagasaki and E.H. Hunter in Kobe and Osaka. The opening of regular shipping routes and the entry of commercial banks ready to provide funds made it possible for independent merchants with small capital, generally young men in their twenties, to join in the trade and compete with the larger western firms which were already established in the area. In most cases offices were small. Independent western merchants worked together in partnership agreements of two to three years' duration, generally with one to four staff members in addition to local employees.[21] If a partnership was profitable it would be renewed, and therefore most continued until interrupted by bankruptcy.

Table 1.1 shows the number of western firms and residents in the treaty ports and open cities from 1870 to 1895. Yokohama and Hyogo were the two ports where western firms and residents tended to congregate, although the role of Nagasaki was crucial in the 1860s and 1870s. Western firms located in Yokohama accounted for 46 per cent of the total number of western firms in Japan in 1870; this had grown to 60 per cent in 1895. The corresponding figures for Hyogo and Osaka are 29 per cent and 34 per cent, and for Nagasaki 9 per cent and 6 per cent. The number of British firms remained more or less constant at about a hundred up to 1890, accounting for over 40 per cent of the total number of western firms. British residents varied from 800 to 1200 up until 1890, forming just under 50 per cent of the total number of western residents.

Activities of British firms and 'treaty port trade'

The Japan trade developed within an institutional framework known as the treaty port system which continued until 1899. Western trading firms were commission, or agency, houses and engaged in the buying and selling of commodities either on their own account or on commission for the European and American markets, while providing other facilities for trade, such as shipping insurance, banking and warehousing. They were more interested in exporting rather than importing. This was partly because exports of raw silk and tea yielded a greater profit, but also because their commercial activities were strictly confined to the treaty ports.[22]

According to the archives of Jardine, Matheson & Co., branches and agents of this company were situated at treaty ports and engaged in export and import activities in accordance with instructions from the partners,

Table 1.1 Number of British firms and residents in Japanese treaty ports, 1870–95

Firms

Year	*British*								*European & America*	*Total*
	Kanagawa	*Hyogo & Osaka*	*Nagasaki*	*Hakodate*	*Niigata*	*Edo*	*Total*	*(%)*		
1870	54	31	9	2	0	5	101	(39.5)	155	256
1875	65	32	9	2	0	1	109	(42.4)	148	257
1880	53	47	4	3	0	1	108	(41.9)	150	258
1885	53	26	7	n.a.	n.a.	n.a.	86	(42.2)	118	204
1890	64	40	5	4	0	0	113	(43.6)	146	259
1895	85	56	5	2	0	0	148	(41.7)	207	355

Residents

Year	*British*								*European & American*	*Total*
	Kanagawa	*Hyogo & Osaka*	*Nagasaki*	*Hakodate*	*Niigata*	*Edo*	*Total*	*(%)*		
1870	513	134	91	16	6	22	782	(49.3)	804	1586
1875	620	235	129	13	0	285	1282	(49.6)	1301	2583
1880	567	228	75	23	8	156	1057	(44.8)	1302	2359
1885	587	250	73	n.a.	n.a.	n.a.	910	(45.3)	1101	2011
1890	748	361	100	27	0	0	1236	(44.0)	1571	2807
1895	806	473	121	24	0	0	1424	(44.1)	1803	3227

Sources: *Commercial reports* for Japan for 1870, 1875, 1880. *Diplomatic and consular report on trade and finance*, nos 47, 961, 1727, 1758, 1779, 1786.
Note: There are no figures for females at Kanagawa in 1870. Figures for 1890 do not give one British national known to be at Kushiro.

mainly sent from Shanghai.[23] They imported cotton and woollen manufactures, sugar, rice, metals, and peas, and exported silk, tea, and marine products. Branches and agents worked according to the 'agency house system'. This meant that they were generally given instructions about the type and quantity of goods, as well as price limits, in which to deal. However, this system did not work efficiently in the case of raw silk and tea because price fluctuations were so rapid.

Figures for Japanese exports and imports handled by British firms at Yokohama are available only for certain years. In the mid-1860s, British merchants accounted for 60 per cent of exports and 75 per cent of imports.[24] In 1889, British firms had a near monopoly, or at least a large share, in imports of cotton manufactures, sugar and iron; in exports, British firms controlled only 21 per cent of silk exports but two-thirds of tea exports.[25]

During the early 1860s, western firms were eager to lend money to daimyo and Japanese merchants. However, the foreign debts of the domains grew to ¥4 million, comprising unpaid imports of ships, weapons, rice and other goods, advances on exports of products such as raw silk and tea, cash loans to cover normal domain expenditure, and loans to provide commercial capital. When the domains were dissolved in 1871, the Meiji government assumed responsibility for the debts amounting to ¥3.7 million.[26]

Since western merchants were dependent on Japanese merchants for market information, they could only hope to penetrate the inland market by sending their Japanese employees, or by offering advances to Japanese merchants to obtain export articles such as raw silk in the interior market. There are several known cases of British firms engaging in the latter type of business activity. For example, in the 1860s Jardine, Matheson & Co. made advances of 870000 Mexican dollars to Takasuya Seibei, a silk merchant, for 'country purchase'. When the silk did not materialize, this led to a diplomatic dispute between the British delegation and the Bakufu.[27] An alternative was for western firms to provide funds for Japanese merchants who were suffering from a shortage of capital. One instance of this is the close financial relationship between the Oriental Bank and the house of Mitsui in the early Meiji period. In the 1870s Jardine, Matheson & Co. provided loans to Goto Shojiro, merchant and politician, for the running of the Takashima coal mine. Here, as with Takasuya, the experience was not successful, since Goto's failure to repay them eventually led to a court case.[28]

Western firms also attempted to make direct investments in export-related industries such as tea, coal, raw silk, shipbuilding, and shipyards. In treaty port areas, for example, they founded tea-refiring places employing Japanese workers. In 1867 there were six tea-refiring places in Nagasaki operated by western merchants, and in 1873 there were 15 in Yokohama and 11 in Kobe. At the busiest season, it was reported, one tea-refiring place might employ 1500–2000 workers. As we shall see later, Glover & Co. provided funds to the Saga domain for the development of the Takashima coal mine and constructed a slip dock in Nagasaki. In 1869 Jardine, Matheson & Co. planned to operate a new filature as a joint concern with the Maebashi domain. However, all attempts by western merchants to invest or advance money resulted in eventual failure.[29] From the mid-1860s, western firms came to concentrate on developing stable commercial relationships with reliable Japanese export and import merchants at the treaty ports, rather than attempting to form their own independent networks using Japanese employees or non-established Japanese merchants.

In addition to the inflexibility of the agency house system, which was an internal structural problem, western firms faced a severe external business environment. First, they encountered severe competition from other foreign merchants, both western and Chinese. Small western merchants who were provided with funds by western commercial banks threatened the agency house system. Chinese merchants who already had established business links with China remained strong competitors in textile importing and tea exporting. Western merchants found it particularly difficult to compete with them. The second difficulty experienced by western merchants was the well-organized Japanese commercial and distribution system which dated back to the Tokugawa regime. The trade and distribution of goods for both selling and buying within Japan were in the hands of Japanese merchants. Western firms were entirely dependent on these merchants' detailed knowledge and understanding of Japanese business methods. Moreover, as Ishii Kanji points out in chapter 2 of this volume, western firms soon began to face severe competition from Japanese firms such as Mitsui Bussan, which had become involved in foreign trade. Similarly, in the 1880s western banks suffered such a challenge from the financial system set up by the Yokohama Specie Bank and other Japanese firms that some had to withdraw from the country. In 1880, Japanese firms accounted for 16 per cent of exports and 7 per cent of imports; by 1900 this had increased to 36 per cent and 39 per cent respectively. In the 1890s, Japanese firms were dominant in exports of rice and coal, and in imports of raw cotton and machine tools.[30]

One might assume that it was easy for individual western merchants to function profitably under the privileged institutional and legal protection afforded by the 'unequal' treaties. However, western business in Japan was generally far from stable. The mortality rate of western firms was high, reaching as much as 62 per cent in Yokohama in the second half of the 1860s. For the two decades of the 1860s and 1870s, western merchants suffered severely from decreasing profits, particularly in product transactions. While reducing their dealings in commodities and increasingly carrying out produce trade on joint accounts with other firms in order to decrease the risk, they also became more concerned with shipping, insurance, banking and the provision of treaty port utilities. Imports of western goods were hit by the decline in the gold price of silver from the mid-1870s. This discouraged western firms from importing goods into Japan, while at the same time encouraging exports. Western merchants were also severely hit by the rapid decrease in the purchasing power of consumers during the deflation of the first half of the 1880s. As a whole, it was more obviously in the interests of western firms to concentrate on exports, favoured as these were by the worldwide increase in international trade, than to try to improve the unprofitable and unpromising import business.

In this way, trade developed under the control of Japanese export and import merchants. The treaty port system helped to isolate Japanese from both western people and western influence, and also gave the Bakufu and the Meiji government the opportunity to control and restrict trade with the West, and so offset to some extent the lack of tariff autonomy. It acted as a non-tariff barrier to economic penetration by the industrialized West and protected the domestic market from western manipulation. Western merchants were prevented from extending their activities beyond the treaty ports, and Japan's domestic markets were protected from the excessive entry of foreign capital.

British merchants in Japan: T.B. Glover and E.H. Hunter

The many small and medium-sized merchants played an extremely active role in development at a local level. However, because of a lack of archival sources, their contribution to the modernization of Japan has been completely overshadowed by that of foreign government employees. This section is therefore devoted to an examination of two such merchants: the relatively well-known T.B. Glover, whose activities centred on Nagasaki, and the little-known Edward H. Hunter, who was engaged in shipbuilding in Kobe and Osaka.

The case of Thomas Blake Glover (1838–1911) is a negative example which indicates how difficult it was for independent western firms having small capital.[31] Glover seems to have been typical of the independent western merchants operating in East Asia in the mid-nineteenth century, since he operated on a small capital, engaged in speculative business, and had what one might call 'a mid-Victorian business mind'.[32] Glover was born at Fraserburgh in Scotland and arrived at Nagasaki via Shanghai in 1859, soon after the opening of Japan to foreign trade. He worked first under Kenneth R. Mackenzie, a Scottish merchant and agent to Jardine, Matheson & Co. In 1861, however, Glover established himself as a general commission agent and took over Mackenzie's work as agent for Jardine, Matheson & Co. and other firms, and in February 1862 he formed Glover & Co. At first Glover & Co. mainly exported refired Japanese tea to England, but despite financial help from Jardine, Matheson & Co. this business was not profitable.

Glover experienced a temporary upturn in his fortunes from late 1863, when he took advantage of the critical political situation to expand his business activities. The firm increased its holdings of land leases and used them as security for obtaining funds from Jardine, Matheson & Co. to finance plans for expansion. With the help of these funds, he switched his major interests to more speculative activities, such as the sale of ships, and arms and ammunition. He used this type of business to strengthen his political and economic relations, not only with the Bakufu and Bakufu-related domains, but also with the potentially anti-Bakufu domains of southwest Japan. Glover and Co. became the largest western firm in Nagasaki, and set up branches in Shanghai and Yokohama. In 1865 Glover ordered munitions from Armstrong & Co. on behalf of the Shogunate; he sold ships and even arranged for some domains to have ships built in Britain. Such orders were generally made through Glover Brothers, the Aberdeen firm of his brother Charles. Glover's links with the Satsuma domain grew closer as it developed an increasingly pro-trade and pro-British stance, particularly after the Kagoshima bombardment in 1863. He promoted business between Satsuma and Shanghai, arranged for young samurai from Satsuma, some of whom were to play prominent roles in the early Meiji government, to study in England in 1865, and persuaded Sir Harry Parkes to visit the capital of Satsuma in July 1866.

However, Glover soon faced serious financial difficulties, the result both of the rapid expansion of his business, and of the great changes in domestic Japanese politics which followed the Meiji Restoration of 1868. Glover was forced to review his approach, and to find other sources of profit, in order to make up for the decrease in sales of ships, arms and ammunition. First, at Nagasaki, he attempted to change from a trader into an entrepreneur, by constructing a patent slip dock and developing the Takashima coal mine. Second, he opened branches in the newly opened ports of Hyogo and Osaka, in anticipation of good trading prospects. However, neither attempt proved as successful as he had hoped. His debts to both the Netherlands Trading Society and Jardine, Matheson & Co. increased, and almost all the funds which he raised were invested in fixed capital. In August 1870, the company's financial difficulties were so great that it had to be declared bankrupt. The total debts amounted to 87400 Mexican dollars, even when Glover's property assets were included. After the bankruptcy he continued to work at the Takashima coal mine, which was eventually bought by Mitsubishi, the firm founded by Iwasaki Yataro, who had had business dealings with Glover before the Restoration. Glover acted as a consultant for Mitsubishi in various ways, playing a crucial role in the founding of what became the Kirin Brewery Co. Glover's son, Kuraba Tomisaburo (1870–1945), is renowned for introducing trawler fishing into Japan in 1908.

Edward Hazlett Hunter (1843–1917) is a contrasting example of a successful Japan-based British businessman.[33] He was born in Londonderry, and arrived at Yokohama in 1865, joining the British firm of Edward C. Kirby & Co. Hunter worked for Onohama Ironworks (Onohama Tekkosho) in Kobe, the shipyard founded by E.C. Kirby with two compatriots in 1868. In 1874 Hunter established his own firm, E.H. Hunter & Co., in Kobe, handling building machinery, machine tools and paints. At the time of the Satsuma Rebellion in 1877 he was able to make profits dealing in military goods. In 1881, with help from Japanese friends, he completed the construction of a shipyard, Osaka Ironworks (Osaka Tekkosho). It employed two hundred Japanese and built steamers as well as doing ship repairs. It also produced steam engines and boilers on order from paper-manufacturing and cotton-spinning factories in the Osaka area. Hunter faced financial difficulties during the deflation of the early 1880s. He tried to export antimony and establish a mill to prepare rice for export, but both enterprises resulted in failure. In 1884 Osaka Ironworks was taken over by a Japanese friend, but in the following year Hunter was able to take control again when the friend was unable to make payments. In the late 1880s he started to build iron and steel steamers.

In 1895, his eldest son Hirano Ryutaro (1871–1936) (later Hanta Ryutaro), who had been educated in civil engineering at the University of Glasgow, took over the business. During the Sino-Japanese War he built steamers for military use, and after the Shipbuilding Encouragement Act of 1896, he expanded by constructing a new shipyard in Osaka for large ships in 1899. This built large steamers of light draft, for instance on order from Osaka Shosen, for the Yangzi and South China coastal trade. The firm also built dredgers which were widely used for the construction of harbours, including the one at Osaka. It further expanded into trawlers and whalers as well as producing cast iron water pipes and steel frames for bridges. In 1900 a factory was founded in Jilong, which had close links with the Government General of Taiwan and played a crucial role in constructing the harbour of Jilong. Osaka Ironworks was even appointed as a factory for the Japanese Navy and built naval ships, including destroyers. In the economic depression following the Russo-Japanese War, however, the firm experienced growing financial difficulties. It was still classed as one of the three biggest shipyards in Japan in the early 1910s, but it was difficult for Hanta himself to produce the capital required for expanding and equipping his facilities so that he could continue to produce large ships. Trawler construction had been very important, but new orders dried up after amendments made to the fishing regulations in 1911. Three years later, Hanta had to turn Osaka Ironworks into a limited company with a nominal capital of ¥6 million, half of which was paid up. In the period from 1888 until 1913 it had built 57 cargo-passenger and cargo ships, three whalers, 48 trawlers, 35 dredgers and three naval vessels. After this, it passed through the hands of Osaka Shosen, Kuhara Kogyo and Nihon Sangyo and in 1936 came under the management of Hitachi Seisakusho, being given the name of Hitachi Zosen KK in 1943.

Anglo-Japanese trade and Japan's external economic policy

In the changing world economy of the second half of the nineteenth century, Japan featured alongside China as a supplier of raw materials and as a market for manufactured goods. British manufacturers and merchants were optimistic about the vast possibilities of the China market, but less sanguine about Japan. In 1870 China accounted for 4.8 per cent and 3.2 per cent of Britain's total exports and imports respectively, while Japan took a negligible share. By the turn of the century, however, while both China and Japan had only a negligible role in Britain's total imports, Japan's share of British exports had risen to 3.4 per cent and China's had fallen to only 2.9 per cent.[34]

Table 1.2 shows Japan's import and export trade for the 1860s and 1870s.[35] Like many other latecomer countries, Japan's trade structure after the opening of the ports was that of a typical monoculture economy: primary products such as raw silk, tea, coal and marine products were exported in return for imports of manufactured goods such as cotton and woollen manufactures from the already industrialized West. Exports of raw silk and tea accounted for over 60 per cent of total exports, and cotton and woollen manufactured goods, mainly from Britain, accounted for about 50 per cent of total imports in an average year. This trade pattern persisted throughout the nineteenth century.

Table 1.3 shows Japan's balance of payments by region in the prewar period. During the period under consideration, Japan's trade balance tended to suffer from an excess of imports. In the official Japanese statistics, figures for the distribution of trade by country are available after 1873, but figures for separate trade goods are not available until the late 1870s. Figure 1.1 shows Japan's trade with Britain and the British Empire in the prewar period. The British Empire, which included Hong Kong, India, the Straits Settlements, Canada, Australia, New Zealand and East and South Africa, played a crucial role in prewar Japanese trade. Figures 1.2 and 1.3 show shares of Britain and the British Empire regions in Japanese export and import trade, and Table 1.4 shows the major trade commodities by partner. In exports from Japan for the period up until 1899, the share of Britain and the British Empire accounted for 25 to 30 per cent, since Hong Kong probably played a crucial role as a transhipment port for Japanese exports even before 1889, when it first appears in the Japanese official trade statistics. As Britain gradually lost her importance as a destination for Japanese exports, compensation appeared in the form of growing trade with other parts of the British Empire. Britain and the British Empire played a more important part in Japan's import trade, taking an average share of over 50 per cent during the period under consideration. In this area Britain was the most important single player, taking a 45 per cent share of Japan's total imports in the 1880s and 28 per cent in the 1890s.

Britain, Hong Kong and India were Japan's three major trade partners in the British Empire. Britain was the largest partner, with a continuing excess of imports to Japan. At first Britain was the chief destination of exports of raw silk and green tea, Japan's two main export articles after the opening of

Table 1.2 Japan's import and export trade, 1865–75 (by value, in thousand dollars)

Major export articles	*1865*	*1870*	*1875*	*Major import articles*	*1865*	*1870*	*1875*
Silk	14843 (80.3)	5310 (35.1)	5993 (33.4)	Cotton yarn	875 (6.2)	3700 (11.9)	4058 (14.4)
Silkworm eggs	727 (2.6)	3473 (22.9)	475 (2.7)	Cotton manufactures	4308 (30.6)	3574 (11.5)	4893 (17.4)
Tea	1935 (6.9)	3848 (25.4)	6916 (38.6)	Woollen manufactures*	6701 (47.6)	1995 (6.4)	4777 (17.0)
Copper	n.a.	461 (3.0)	425 (2.4)	Metals	527 (3.7)	320 (1.0)	1043 (3.7)
Coal	13 (0.0)	159 (1.0)	859 (4.8)	Arms and ammunition	1067 (7.6)	207 (0.7)	45 (0.2)
Dried fish	95 (0.3)	329 (2.2)	664 (3.7)	Sugar	208 (1.5)	2482 (8.0)	3483 (12.4)
Total	18491 (100)	15143 (100)	17918 (100)	Total	14077 (100)	31121 (100)	28174 (100)

Sources: Commercial report, Summary of foreign trade in Japan for the year 1878, pp. 26, 27.
Note: *Cotton and woollen mixtures are included. Figures in parentheses are percentages.

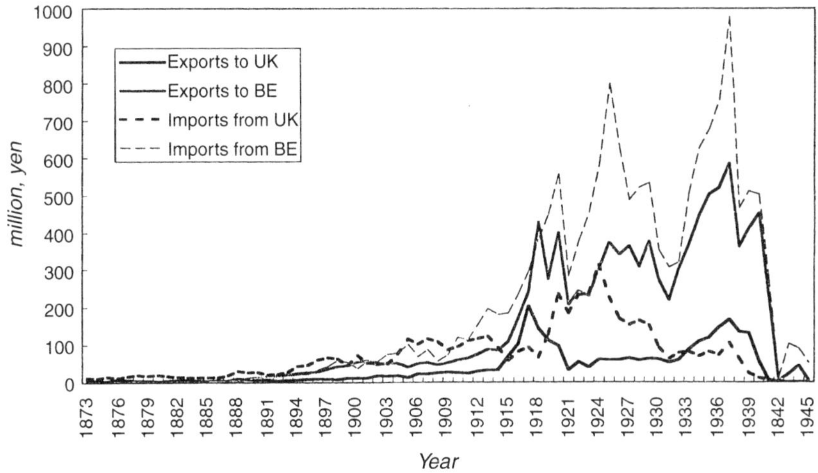

Sources: Nippon Ginko Tokei-kyoku, *Meiji-iko honpo shuyo keizai tokei* (Tokyo, 1966), pp. 278–9, 290–7; *Showa kokusei soran*, vol. 1 (Tokyo, 1980), pp. 638–45.

Figure 1.1 Japan's trade with Britain and the British Empire

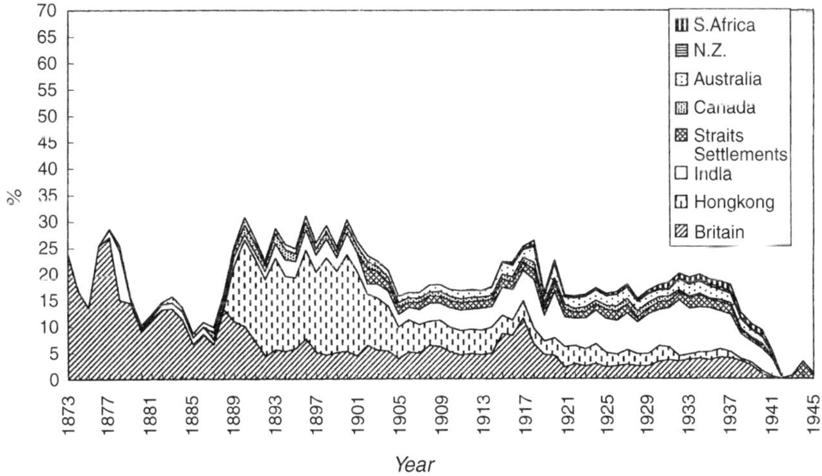

Sources: *Meiji-iko honpo shuyo keizai tokei*, pp. 278–9, 290–7; *Showa kokusei soran*, vol. 1, pp. 638–45.

Figure 1.2 Japanese exports, showing the share held by Britain and the British Empire

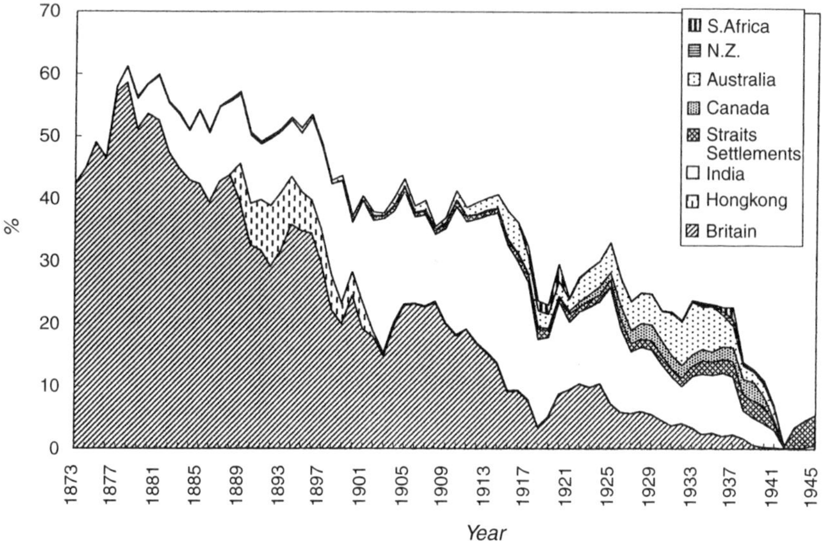

Sources: As Figure 1.2.

Figure 1.3 Japanese imports, showing the share held by Britain and the British Empire

the ports, since London was the distribution centre of the world silk trade and Britain was the biggest tea-importing country. However, as the United States became the main export market of Japanese raw silk and tea in the 1870s, exports of these two articles to Britain sharply decreased.[36] By the mid-1880s Japan was exporting rice, copper and silk manufactures to Britain, and importing cotton yarn and manufactures, woollen manufactures, steamers, iron and steel and machinery. Grey shirting was the most important cotton manufacture, while imports of cotton satin and prints also increased in the late 1890s. Cotton-spinning machines accounted for nearly half of the machinery imported in 1890. Hong Kong was an entrepôt for Japanese export articles. Japan sent copper, coal, matches and marine products and imported primarily refined sugar. In its trade with India, Japan exported coal, matches and silk manufactures, and imported first cotton yarn, and later raw cotton, as well as rice and indigo. In the case of Australia, Japan exported rice and imported wool. Canada emerged as an export market for Japanese green tea, which faced severe competition from India, Ceylon and China in the United States market throughout the 1880s and 1890s.

Since Britain was on the gold standard and Japan was fundamentally on the silver standard until 1897, the continuing depreciation in the gold price of silver from the early 1870s was of great importance. The decline of silver was extremely severe in the early 1890s, the average gold price of silver falling by over 50 per cent between 1872 and 1894. This situation made it

Table 1.3 Japan's balance of payments by region, 1876–1940 (five-year aggregate value in million yen)

Year	Asia				North America	Britain	Other Europe	Latin America	Africa	Oceania	Total
	Korea & Taiwan	China	India	Asia total							
1876/1880	n.a.	–1	–1	–2	28	–59	9			1	–22
1881/1885	0	2	–18	–9	54	–49	25			2	23
1886/1890	–4	6	–29	–29	87	–83	20			6	2
1891/1895	–4	4	–32	–54	162	–128	49			8	37
1896/1900	9	92	–129	–105	74	–256	–34		1	10	–310
1901/1905	44	228	–280	–134	144	–264	–3	0	2	15	–240
1906/1910	54	255	–286	–76	331	–383	–1	–2	3	27	–100
1911/1915	16	481	–573	–115	388	–312	42	–6	–5	6	–2
1916/1920	–302	846	–701	157	5	53	446	15	–87	3	592
1921/1925	–1071	1002	–1141	–1511	517	–945	–587	23	10	–288	–2781
1926/1930	–799	952	–618	–666	685	–426	–771	46	79	–367	–1419
1931/1935	139	253	–28	921	–938	53	–505	191	405	–617	–491
1936/1940	3689	941	–162	4505	–2786	362	–728	–113	300	–249	1293

Source: I. Yamazawa Ippei and Y. Yamamoto, *Boeki to kokusai shushi* (Tokyo, 1979), pp. 206–13.

Table 1.4 Major articles of Japan's trade with Britain and the British Empire (in thousand yen)

		Articles	*1885*	*1890*	*1895*	*1900*
Britain	Exports to	Silk manufactures	n.a.	431	1 477	2 699
		Rice	102	194	1 686	129
		Straw plaits	n.a.	3	858	1 956
		Copper	192	1 815	520	780
		Total	2 412	5 639	7 883	11 263
	Imports from	Woollen manufactures	1 567	3 510	5 342	7 599
		Cotton yarn and thread	2 902	6 433	7 014	7 351
		Cotton manufactures	2 816	4 018	6 740	16 090
		Steam vessels	637	616	3 493	2 227
		Railway materials	109	1 173	3 219	1 796
		Iron and steel	1 888	3 646	4 795	13 505
		Machinery	393	2 177	3 414	4 028
		Total	12 415	26 619	45 172	71 638
Hong Kong	Exports to	Cotton yarn	n.a.	n.a.	8	3 544
		Camphor	n.a.	604	1 154	1 018
		Marine products	n.a.	1 792	1 783	1 945
		Rice	n.a.	123	1 315	445
		Copper	n.a.	1 939	3 516	9 709
		Coal	n.a.	1 861	2 406	4 772
		Matches	n.a.	1 150	2 422	2 781
		Total	n.a.	9 366	18 363	39 177

	Imports from	Sugar (white/refined)	n.a.	5 100	7 014	9 449
		Total	n.a.	5 496	8 078	10 660
India	Exports to	Matches	n.a.	27	864	1 175
		Silk manufactures	n.a.	23	706	1 820
		Coal	n.a.	84	779	3 145
		Total	494	591	4 359	8 704
	Imports from	Rice	n.a.	3 422	390	974
		Raw cotton	n.a.	1 114	7 693	17 696
		Cotton yarn	n.a.	3 543	393	11
		Indigo	n.a.	155	581	2 380
		Total	3 399	8 911	12 002	23 516
Australia	Exports to	Silk fabric	5	50	118	761
		Rice	216	524	824	746
		Total	284	795	1 281	2 531
	Imports from	Wool	32	299	805	760
		Total	72	334	1 032	2 456
Canada	Exports to	Tea	n.a.	879	1 324	1 694
		Total	n.a.	1 023	1 986	2 951
	Imports from	Total	n.a.	26	14	317

Sources: Okura-sho, *Dai-Nihon gaikoku boeki nenpyo*, corresponding years.

possible for Japan to increase her exports to European and American markets and compete on easier terms with Britain and Australia in coal, for instance, as well as discouraging imports from those countries.

Anglo-Japanese capital movements should be considered as well as trade itself. Until the end of the nineteenth century, Japan was not an attractive market for British capital exports. According to estimates by Feinstein, capital exports from Britain, including foreign holdings, amounted to £2610 million by the turn of the century. China absorbed only £50 million, 1.9 per cent of the total, but at £10 million Japan absorbed even less.[37] In any case, the newly established Meiji government was reluctant to raise foreign loans, from fears of being 'colonized' through financial dependency, although Japan had a high country risk for investments. In the period to 1897 Japan raised only two foreign loans, both in the early 1870s, and both from Britain. One was a £1 million government loan at 9 per cent interest for the purpose of repurchasing the railway construction rights which the government had granted to Horatio Nelson Lay, a British citizen. The other was a £2.4 million government loan at 7 per cent interest which was used to abolish the stipend system of the samurai class.[38]

The Meiji government's opposition to foreign capital can also be seen in its refusal to grant mining concessions to non-Japanese. It responded swiftly and decisively to the plan drawn up by Thomas Glover and the domain of Saga for the joint development of the Takashima mine in 1868. In 1872 and 1873 respectively, it took legal steps to prohibit foreigners from holding any rights in mines located in Japanese territory by issuing mining legislation.[39] In 1874 it bought up all rights in the Takashima coal mine from the Netherlands Trading Society, which had taken over responsibility after the bankruptcy of Glover & Co.

Japanese business in Britain

The Japanese trading firms of Mitsui Bussan, Takata Shokai and Okuragumi opened overseas branches to deal in imports and exports with Japan. The overseas branches of Mitsui Bussan, the largest of the three, played a crucial role in importing machinery to Japan and introducing technology. Following the establishment of its Shanghai branch in 1876, Mitsui Bussan sent Robert W. Irwin, a partner in the American firm of Edward Fischer & Co., on an agency contract in order to export rice to Britain and import woollen blankets and cloth. In 1879, the London branch of Mitsui Bussan was established to take over Irwin's business. Mitsui expanded its reputation in the London market by utilizing the connections with merchant bankers such as Baring Brothers and Martin & Co. that Irwin had established. However, the London branch ran at a loss because of the high salaries of the non-Japanese staff. Mitsui Bussan exported rice, raw silk, wax and copper to Britain and imported ship's fittings, bricks, machinery, blankets, sheeting, coal, and iron and copper manufactures, for which it earned a commission. The most profitable activity of the London branch was trade in Japanese government exports of rice, but it also dealt with irregular shipping charters, including charters for the export of coal from the Miike mine to the East Asian market.

From the mid-1880s Mitsui Bussan began to import machines to Japan, and these replaced rice as its main source of income for the London branch. The bulk of the imports were spinning machines from Platt Brothers & Co. Relations with Platt Brothers began with the sale of mule spinning machines to Osaka Boseki (Osaka Spinning Co.) in 1882, and in 1886 Mitsui Bussan became Platt's main agent in Japan. Mitsui Bussan defeated its competitors, H. Lucas & Co. and C. Illis & Co., by taking an 85 per cent share in imports of these machines. It also had dealings with manufacturers of spinning-related machines such as Joseph Sykes Brothers, Mather and Platt, and Dronsfield Brothers, and with shipping and marine insurance firms, including chartering agents and freight brokers such as H.D. Blyth & Co. and Gellatly Hankey Sewell & Co. The fact that merchant bankers Kleinwort Sons & Co. provided credit to the London branch suggests that the influence of the City was behind the rapid expansion of its activities.[40]

The British role in Japan's industrialization: the Iwakura Mission and foreign employees

In the late Tokugawa period, the Bakufu and domains such as Satsuma, Saga and Mito had attempted to introduce modern western technology in the form of iron foundries, cotton-spinning machines and shipyards. For example, in the late 1860s Satsuma set up western-style cotton mills in Kagoshima and Sakai, using throstles and mule spindles from Platt Brothers. The purchase of this machinery was arranged by the young Satsuma samurai who had travelled to Britain illegally in 1865 with the help of Thomas Glover. However, these early attempts at industrialization were not successful.[41]

The urgent task of the newly established Meiji government was to consolidate the nation into a unified state, while maintaining political and economic autonomy in the face of the western threat. Taking over the ironworks, shipyards, and mines owned by the Bakufu and the domains, the government adopted policies for rapid political, economic and social modernization on a western model by introducing institutions, industries, and scientific techniques in the form in which they had developed in the West. In 1870, acting on the advice of Edmund Morell, a graduate of King's College, London, the Meiji government's first step in introducing western industry and technology was the establishment of the Kobusho (Public Works Department). The aim was to promote a wide range of industries including railways, steelmaking, telegraphic communications, shipbuilding and lighthouse construction. However, since these early attempts did not follow any coherent plan or take account of industrial or economic conditions in Japan at the time, it is not surprising that they did not produce any substantial results.

It was only after the return of the Iwakura Mission in 1873 that properly organized steps were taken, under the leadership of Okubo Toshimichi. The Iwakura Mission had set out in November 1871 in order to prepare treaty revision and investigate western institutions. It spent nearly two years visiting the United States and 14 countries of Europe including Britain, the most important country on the mission's list.[42] This is clear from the fact that the time devoted to investigating Britain, from July to November 1872, was longer than elsewhere. They visited shipyards, ironworks, cotton mills, sugar refineries and other institutions, and their investigations made it possible to draw up a realistic blueprint for industrialization. In this sense, the mission was crucial economically as well as politically.

Okubo was extremely impressed by the way in which the navigation acts from 1650 had provided a foundation for British industrialization and also enabled Britain to replace the Netherlands as the dominant maritime nation. He therefore decided that it was essential for Japan to develop a strong shipping industry. The programme initiated by Okubo was given momentum by a growing anxiety that the outflow of specie that had accompanied the increase in imports ever since the late 1860s might completely destabilize the economy, and in time threaten Japan's independence from the West. Since the commercial treaties deprived Japan of tariff autonomy, it was not possible to nurture infant industries through putting up protective tariff barriers. The only way of overcoming the crisis caused by the continued outflow of specie therefore lay first in promoting exports, by encouraging traditional export-related industries, and second in restricting imports, by the development of import substitution through introducing and nurturing modern industries.

Japan's early industrialization was very much a process of trial and error presided over by the Kobusho. The greatest expenditure incurred by the Kobusho, which lasted from 1870 to 1881, was in the period from 1873 to 1877. The fact that railway construction took 48 per cent of the total, mining 31 per cent, and telegraphic construction 12 per cent shows the importance that the government placed on these three industries.[43] Foreign employees, mainly engineers, played a great role as human capital in introducing western technology into Japan and constructing the necessary infrastructure. In the 1870s over 50 per cent of foreign employees were British, and 70–80 per cent of these belonged to the Kobusho. Out of a total of 580 foreign engineers employed by the Kobusho, 450 (78 per cent of all its foreign employees) were British. Of these, 233 belonged to the Railway Bureau, 53 to the Telegraph Bureau, 47 to the Lighthouse Bureau, 40 to the Education Bureau, 35 to the Mining Bureau, and 25 to the Workshop Bureau.[44]

As was shown above, the great majority of British engineers were engaged in railway construction, a major activity of the Kobusho, mainly because it was regarded as a symbol of westernization. The railway between Shinbashi and Yokohama was completed in 1872, and that between Kobe and Osaka in 1874, but the total length of rail constructed by the end of the 1870s was only 76 miles. Almost of all the facilities, including rails, bridges, locomotives, carriages, buildings and storage facilities, were imported from Britain. Dubs & Co., Neilson Reid & Co., the North British Locomotive Co. and Beyer Peacock & Co. were major British suppliers of locomotives, and these materials were imported by both Japanese and British trading firms such as Mitsui Bussan, Okuragumi, Takata Shokai and Jardine, Matheson Co. Almost all the engineers and assistants were British and the operation was also under British management. Edmund Morell is particularly well known for his contribution as the first chief engineer.[45]

The development of mining was the other major field of the Public Works Department, since coal and other minerals were important resources for exporting and coinage. Two British engineers, J.G.H. Godfrey, head of the Mining Bureau 1871–77, and his deputy, Joseph Waters, played an important role in investigating and developing mines such as the Kamaishi iron mine and the Miike coal mine. In the mid-1860s, Erasmus H.M. Gower, who had already worked for the Bakufu in developing the Kayanuma coal mine in Hokkaido, was appointed by the Meiji government, initially to supervise the gold and silver mines at Sado Island. After his contract expired in 1873, he was privately employed to work for coal and copper mines. Frederick Antony Potter was also important as a mining engineer, particularly in developing the Miike coal mine from 1876 to 1882.[46]

Richard Henry Brunton (1841–1901), born at Kincardine, Aberdeen, constructed 28 lighthouses during his period of service from 1868 to 1876. These lighthouses, including the one at Inubosaki in Chiba prefecture, were indispensable to the expansion of trade. George M. Gilbert, a British telegraph engineer, was in charge of telegraphic construction. Telegraph communication between Tokyo and Yokohama began in 1869 and the government hastened the construction of a link between Nagasaki and Yokohama in order to forestall moves by the Great Northern Telegraph Co., which had reached Japan in 1871. On the other hand, Japan's modern postal system, while modelled on the British 'penny postal' service, was introduced by a Japanese, Maejima Hisoka.[47]

The introduction of the modern banking and financial system into Japan was also crucial. Alexander Allan Shand (1844–1930), a Scot, came to Japan to work for the Yokohama branch of the Chartered Mercantile Bank of India, London and China in 1864 and became a consultant and lecturer to the Ministry of Finance in 1872. He published several books on book-keeping and banking which were widely used to train bankers, and proposed the need for a central banking system. After returning to Britain, he joined the

Alliance Bank, which was absorbed by Parr's Bank in 1892, and was the manager of the head office of the latter from 1902 to 1908, remaining on the Board until 1918. From 1898 he helped Takahashi Korekiyo, the then vice-president of the Yokohama Specie Bank, to raise foreign loans in both London and New York.[48]

The high salaries enjoyed by foreign employees became a heavy burden on government finances, and as soon as possible, foreign engineers were replaced by Japanese ones. In 1877 the Imperial College of Engineering (Kobu Daigakko) (absorbed into the Imperial University of Tokyo in 1886) was founded to train and educate Japanese engineers. The first principal of the college was Henry Dyer (1848–1918). He had studied civil engineering at the University of Glasgow under Professor W.J.M. Rankine and was recommended to the Japanese government by Professor Rankine and Hugh Matheson of Matheson & Co. in London. The latter had been a friend of Ito Hirobumi when he was a student in London before the Restoration. When Ito met Matheson again, as deputy head of the Iwakura Mission in 1872, he had asked him to recommend suitable personnel for the College.[49] A number of the other teachers employed at the college were found through the network of Scottish scientists at the universities of Glasgow and Edinburgh. They included William Edward Ayrton (1847–1908) in the field of electricity, Charles Dickinson West (1848–1908) in shipbuilding, and James Alfred Ewing (1856–1935) in mechanical engineering.

Japanese engineers educated in Britain

Before the Meiji Restoration 92 students were sent to study abroad either by the Bakufu or by individual domains. Of these 40 were sent to Britain. During the period 1868–74, 550 students were sent to study abroad; 168 of these (31 per cent) were despatched to Britain. However, Britain's significance as a destination for Japanese students gradually became overshadowed by that of the United States and Germany. In the period 1875 to 1897, the number of students sent to Britain for study by the Ministry of Education declined to 35 out of a total of 159.[50] As Tamaki Norio points out with regard to Fukuzawa Yukichi later in this volume, there were others who did not actually become students, but who were influenced by the British model. Fukuzawa introduced British business thinking to Japan and founded a school which produced many economic leaders who have contributed to Japan's modernization.

Many Japanese with British connections had a crucial role in the early industrialization of Japan. Among them were Inoue Masaru and Yamao Yozo. Both went to Britain illegally in 1863 with Ito Hirobumi and Inoue Kaoru. Inoue Masaru studied mining and civil engineering at University College, London. On his return to Japan he joined the Meiji government and was in charge of mining and railways in the Kobusho. He became head of the Railway Bureau in 1877, and minister at the Kobusho in 1881. Inoue stressed the importance of railway construction and the need to gain independence from foreign engineers. He was the main force behind the construction of the crucially important Tokaido line, which was completed in 1889. Yamao Yozo also studied in London and Glasgow, and worked for the Napier shipyard. After returning from Britain in 1870, he first joined the Civil and Finance departments, and then the Kobusho, where he finally became minister in 1880.[51]

Knowledge of cotton spinning was an obvious prerequisite for the successful operation of the cotton industry, which was a typical case of import substitution. Yamanobe Takeo (1851–1920) had a vital role in its development. After studying 'English learning' in Japan, in 1877 Yamanobe went to Britain, initially as a student of economics. In 1879, however, supported by Shibusawa Eiichi, who intended to start a modern cotton industry in Japan, Yamanobe changed to mechanical engineering and studied spinning technology at King's College, London. Keen to gain actual experience in purchasing raw cotton and marketing cotton products, he also worked at a cotton-spinning mill in Blackburn. Returning to Japan in 1880, he was involved both in selecting the location of the mill and setting up the machinery of what became Osaka Boseki. Osaka Boseki was founded in 1882 with 10500 spindles run by steam power. The initial capital of ¥250000 was raised mainly from merchants and ex-daimyo in the Kansai area under the strong leadership of Shibusawa Eiichi. When the company actually began to operate in 1883 Yamanobe became the first manager. He adopted a two-shift system with electric light for night time operation; later he changed from traditional mule to ring spinning machines and introduced a new type of weaving machine. The success of the Osaka company stimulated the establishment of several other firms on a similar scale in the late 1880s. The Japanese cotton industry was able to oust imported British and Indian cotton yarns from the Japanese domestic market and even began to export cotton yarn to China and Korea after 1890. In 1898 Yamanobe became president of Osaka Boseki, and in 1914 the first president of Toyo Boseki, founded through a merger between Mie Boseki and Osaka Boseki.[52]

Competition on the Japanese import market: cotton and sugar

For the British cotton industry the Asian market was a more important market, taking a share which rose from 31 per cent in 1850 to 58 per cent in 1896.[53] Table 1.5 shows imports of cotton yarn and cotton piece-goods into Japan as well as figures for Japanese domestic production. After the opening of the ports Japanese cotton growing was severely hit by increasing imports of cheap British cotton piece-goods, but the Japanese weaving industry managed to survive. Some weaving districts were able to respond quickly to the new situation by changing from domestically produced hand-spun cotton yarn to imported machine-spun cotton yarn. As a result of increasing demand from the domestic weaving industry, imports of cotton

Table 1.5 Imports of cotton yarn and cotton piece-goods into Japan and their production in Japan

Year	*Cotton yarn (in million lb)*					*Production in Japan*	*Cotton piece goods (in million square yards)*			
	Imports						*Imports*			*Production in Japan*
	Britain	*(%)*	*India*	*(%)*	*Total*		*Britain**	*(%)*	*Total*	
1870	n.a.		n.a.		11816	17	n.a.		37	113
1875	17	(97)	0	(0)	17991	21	29	(45)	65	154
1880	34	(88)	4	(11)	38129	38	47	(59)	79	298
1885	16	(57)	12	(43)	28529	34	31	(48)	64	245
1890	24	(56)	19	(44)	42543	61	33	(57)	59	405
1895	18	(91)	2	(9)	19454	178	51	(68)	76	727
1900	12	(100)	0	(0)	12068	284	82	(61)	134	769

Sources: *Nihon boeki seiran* (Tokyo, 1935), pp. 230, 237–9; *Nihon boeki tokei* (Yokohama, 1980), pp. 266–7; S. Nakamura, *Meiji ishin no kiso kozo* (Tokyo, 1968), appendix table 3.
Note: *Total of grey and bleached shirting.

yarn increased much more rapidly than imports of cotton piece-goods in the period up to the late 1880s.[54] Britain was a chief supplier of cotton yarn, although India took an important position in the 1880s. Imports of cotton yarn into Japan reached a high point in 1888, but rapidly decreased after this date as the Japanese cotton industry developed.

By contrast, cotton piece-goods, mainly grey shirting from Britain, were only able to make limited headway in the Japanese market. When we consider that there was an overall increase in imports of manufactures in which Britain had a comparative advantage, such as machinery, metals, electrical goods and chemicals, this seems strange. In 1886, the British Vice-Consul, J.H. Longford, made a detailed report on the causes behind the decline in imports of British cotton goods.[55] In the 1860s, he wrote, British shirtings had been superior in appearance to domestically produced Japanese hand-woven goods, and almost equal in their wearing capacity. Since British goods were entirely free from sizing and withstood all rough usage, they were able to find a significant Japanese market despite their high prices. Throughout the 1860s and 1870s, however, quality had gradually deteriorated. After the late 1870s, British goods were much cheaper than similar Japanese products, even though there was no great decline in their appearance, but they were inferior in texture quality and durability. Heavily sized, British cloth tore easily and was said to have only a third or a quarter of the wearing power of Japanese fabrics. The gradual decline in sales after 1881 was 'attributable to the disgust produced in the minds of all consumers by the unvarying bad quality of nine tenths of the cotton piece-goods imported in recent years'. In the 1870s, while the quality of Manchester goods deteriorated, the Japanese cotton-weaving industry recovered through using imported cotton yarn, until it reached a level where it was competing with imported cotton piece-goods. The coarser, and medium types of cotton yarn, including Bombay yarn, were used for manufacture into cloth. To Longford, therefore, the decline in quality and the failure to vary patterns were two of the elements which limited the penetration of British cotton piece-goods into the Japanese market.

From the mid-1890s, however, the expanding demand for various types of fabrics which were not competitively produced in Japan led to a general increase in fine yarn and textile imports. Imports of cotton piece-goods increased again from the mid-1890s. Cotton yarn imports suffered a temporary decrease, but in the mid-1890s Japan was the next most important buyer after India of cotton yarn from Britain.[56]

Along with cotton yarn and manufactures, sugar, both brown and refined, was the main import article into Japan in the late nineteenth century.[57] After the opening of the ports, Japan was exposed to increasing imports of cheap sugar and, as a consequence, Japan's traditional sugar industry was greatly affected. The development of the domestic sugar industry was, therefore, one of the urgent tasks of the Meiji government, which made

Table 1.6 Imports and production of sugar (in million piculs)

Year	*Imports*			*Domestic*
	Brown	*White/refined*	*Total*	*production*
1870	527	90	618	n.a.
1875	623	116	740	n.a.
1880	559	122	681	467
1885	612	417	1028	675
1890	835	827	1662	1366
1895	1119	1298	2417	693
1900	2092	1954	4046	1013

Sources: For imports, *Nihon boeki seiran* (Tokyo, 1935), pp. 163–4; for domestic production, Noshomu-sho, *Noshomu tokeihyo*, corresponding years.

an unsuccessful effort to substitute imports by facilitating beet sugar production in Hokkaido. Table 1.6 shows imports of sugar, brown and white/refined, into Japan and the domestic sugar production of Japan. Imports of sugar, both refined and brown, rapidly increased as western-style food became popular. At first 'brown' sugar was unrefined sugar from China, but after 1895 'brown' sugar was raw sugar mainly from Taiwan for use in manufacturing refined sugar.

As Table 1.6 shows, imports of refined sugar from Hong Kong grew rapidly after the mid-1880s. Refined sugar was supplied exclusively by two British firms in Hong Kong. One was Jardine's China Sugar Refining Co., and the other Butterfield Swire's Taikoo Sugar Refining Co. The former was established in 1878 with an initial capital of 600000 Hong Kong dollars, taking over the China Sugar Refinery which had been under the control of Jardine, Matheson & Co. since 1872. The latter was established in 1881 with an initial capital of 600000 Hong Kong dollars, taking over the China Sugar Refinery which had been under the control of Jardine, Matheson & Co. since 1872. Established with an initial capital of £198000, the Taikoo Sugar Refinery aimed to challenge Jardines' monopoly of the sugar market. The two refineries shared a very strong position in the Japanese market in the late nineteenth century, thanks to a concerted agreement on the minimum selling price. According to official annual average figures on sales of refined sugar in Yokohama and Kobe by each company from 1891 to 1894, the China Sugar Refining Co. sold 342400 piculs and the Taikoo Sugar Refinery 597000 piculs.[58] Since the cooperation between the two British refineries meant higher selling prices, however, their sugar could not compete against cheaper brown sugar imported from Taiwan.

The modern Japanese refining industry began with the establishment of a refinery by Suzuki Tozaburo in 1889. This expanded into Nihon Seiseito KK (Japan Sugar Refining Co.), established with an initial capital of ¥300 000 in 1896. Nihon Seito KK (Japan Refining Co.) was founded with an initial capital of ¥1.5 million in 1886. The Sino-Japanese War, and the consequent cession of Taiwan to Japan in 1895, changed the structure of the sugar market. With the advent of partial tariff autonomy in 1899, the Japanese sugar industry developed into a strong competitor of the British refineries. Both the Taikoo and Jardine refineries in Hong Kong were gradually ousted from the Japanese market; as a result, from the early twentieth century they had to concentrate on sales to China.

Trade rivalry in the Asian coal market

Coal played a crucial role in Anglo-Japanese trade relations.[59] Together with raw silk and tea, it was a major export article for Japan, taking an average of 6 per cent of total exports during the period from 1868 to 1899. Unlike raw silk and tea, Japanese coal exports focused on the East Asian market, where they competed with British and Australian coals. The coal market in East Asia was formed in the mid-nineteenth century, facilitated by the evolution of marine transportation and communication which took place particularly after the opening of the Suez Canal in 1869. The coal industry in Japan was strategically placed to take advantage of the growing demand from steamers engaged in Eastern trade. This development was achieved by the introduction of western mining technology, the intensification of labour, and the reduction of freight rates. Coal exports from Japan increased rapidly, competing with British and Australian coals. Behind the increase were the depreciation in the value of silver, and the fact that Japanese coal was suitable for use in both steamers and factories and could be supplied at a low price as against other imported coal.

Table 1.7 shows the coal markets in Shanghai, Hong Kong and Singapore, to which Japanese coal was sent. In the Shanghai coal market imports of Japanese coal began to increase in the mid-1860s. During the period from the late 1860s to the early 1870s there was keen competition between imports from Britain (mainly Cardiff), Australia (Newcastle (NSW), Sydney) and Japan. Japanese coal gained control of the Shanghai market in the mid-1870s. In the late 1870s, however, the Shanghai coal market became sensitive to fluctuations in the quantity of supply and the price of Japanese coal. In the case of Hong Kong, over three-quarters of the coal imported in the 1870s came from Britain and Australia. Japanese coal was first brought there in the early 1870s and increased to a great extent in the early 1880s, when the market price of Japanese coal was fixed at a lower level than other major foreign coals, including those from Britain and Australia. In the late 1880s it established a dominant position in the Hong Kong market. In Singapore during the 1880s, over 70 per cent of all coal came from Britain. As imports

Table 1.7 Annual averages of coal imports into Shanghai, Hong Kong and Singapore by country (in thousand tons and percentages)

Year	*Shanghai*				*Hong Kong*				*Singapore*			
	Britain	*Australia*	*Japan*	*Total*	*Britain*	*Australia*	*Japan*	*Total*	*Britain*	*Australia*	*Japan*	*Total*
1866/70	43 (35)	43 (35)	16 (13)	122 (100)								
1871/75	20 (15)	36 (27)	51 (39)	134 (100)	65 (47)	64 (46)	3 (2)	138 (100)				
1876/80	10* (6)	29 (17)	104 (59)	176 (100)	79 (44)	61 (34)	26 (14)	179 (100)				
1881/85	8* (3)	25 (10)	174 (71)	246 (100)	84 (30)	91 (33)	90 (32)	278 (100)	287 (93)	18 (6)	2 (1)	309 (100)
1886/90	2* (1)	21 (7)	243 (77)	315 (100)	32 (9)	48 (13)	276 (76)	361 (100)	246 (75)	33 (10)	38 (12)	326 (100)
1891/95	16 (4)	23 (5)	319 (73)	436 (100)	30 (6)	16 (3)	432 (80)	541 (100)	174 (46)	50 (13)	123 (32)	382 (100)
1896/99	16 (3)	15 (2)	398 (66)	604 (100)	59 (8)	27 (4)	527 (72)	730 (100)	82 (15)	55 (10)	301 (56)	540 (100)

Sources: S. Sugiyama, *Japan's Industrialization in the World Economy*, pp. 175, 183, 188.
Note: *Figures for imports from the United States are not included.

from Australia and Japan increased, however, Britain's market share gradually decreased to 60 per cent. The Japanese market share was less than 20 per cent until the early 1890s, but it had assumed an important position in the Singapore market by the mid-1890s. The advance of Japanese coal exports into the Asian market was in line with a gradual shift in the focus of Japan's foreign trade as a whole from Europe and the United States to Asia.

Japanese coals were able to overcome keen competition and expand their market share overseas by maintaining low production costs and reducing freight rates. After the Russo-Japanese War, however, increasing domestic consumption led to a shortage of coal for export and a subsequent price rise. This is turn led to a rise in the selling price of Japanese coal on overseas markets and made competition with Chinese and Australian coals fiercer. At more and more of a disadvantage overseas, Japanese coal was gradually directed solely towards the domestic market.

While the trade in silk and tea was exclusively in the hands of western merchants and shipping lines, the development of Japan's coal industry and maritime transportation was closely connected with the formation of the *zaibatsu*, especially Mitsui and Mitsubishi. Mitsubishi's interest in the Takashima coal mine arose from its shipping concerns and expanded to the Chikuho mines in the 1890s. Mitsui's opportunity to become involved in coal exports and the coal industry came when Mitsui Bussan was appointed sole agent for Miike coal in 1876. Its involvement was increased by its purchase of the Miike mine in 1888. The coal industry became a very important field of activity for both firms.

Shipping competition in Japanese coastal waters: P&O and NYK's Bombay line

From 1859, foreign ships engaged in both ocean shipping and in coastal trade between the open ports. Table 1.8 shows British shipping's overall supremacy in Japan's external trade. They took over a half-share of all shipping both in number and tonnage, carrying import articles such as cotton and woollen manufactures and sugar. On the other hand, the American Pacific Mail Steamship Co., which began a regular service between San Francisco and Hong Kong in 1867, extended a regular line between Shanghai and Yokohama in 1870 and dominated the coastal trade between Japan's open ports.

The Meiji government had to establish and promote a Japanese shipping industry in order to compete with foreign shipping. There were two Japanese shipping companies: the government-assisted Yubin Jokisen Kaisha (Mail Steamship Company) and the privately-owned Mitsubishi Shokai. Mitsubishi was originally founded by Iwasaki Yataro in 1870, taking over from a firm owned by Tosa domain. From the mid-1870s the government decided to support Mitsubishi too, as part of Okubo Toshimichi's economic

Table 1.8 British and other foreign shipping entered into Japanese ports, 1860–1890 (in thousand tons)

Year	*British*				*Other foreign*		*Total*	
	Ships	*(%)*	*Tonnage*	*(%)*	*Ships*	*Tonnage*	*Ships*	*Tonnage*
1860	122	(50.6)	45	(51.2)	119	43	241	88
1865	264	(63.6)	99	(59.7)	151	67	415	167
1870	661	(42.3)	319	(27.5)	902	842	1563	1161
1875	350	(42.1)	252	(26.4)	481	699	831	952
1880	493	(67.2)	420	(60.4)	241	276	734	695
1885	568	(58.3)	732	(64.5)	407	403	975	1135
1890	1042	(66.9)	1737	(71.9)	515	679	1557	2417

Sources: For 1860–75, summary of foreign trade in Japan for the year 1878; for 1880, General report on the foreign trade of Japan; for 1885, DCRTF no. 47; for 1890, DCRTF, no. 961.

policy of *mingyo shinko* (facilitating the development of the private sector). Mitsubishi was given an opportunity for growth at the time of the Formosan Expedition in 1874, when it was used to transport military personnel and goods. In the following year, it was ordered by the government to open a regular shipping line to Shanghai. Backed by government subsidies and transfers of government ships, it competed fiercely with the Pacific Mail by cutting freight rates. After informal negotiations between the Japanese government and the Pacific Mail, Mitsubishi purchased ships and port facilities from the latter at a total cost of 810000 Mexican dollars.

After its victory over the Pacific Mail, Mitsubishi embarked on cut-throat competition with P&O, which had started a regular service between Shanghai and Yokohama in February 1876. Once again with the benefit of government support, Mitsubishi reduced freight rates, partly by cutting expenditure, and introduced a new credit system of exchange bills in order to attract consigners. In August of the same year P&O withdrew from the Shanghai–Yokohama line. This left the way clear for Japan to dominate its coastal trade.[60]

The close link between the establishment of the NYK's Bombay line and Japan's need to import raw cotton shows another aspect of the Anglo-Japanese commercial relationship. In November 1893 NYK, which was founded through the amalgamation of Mitsubishi and Kyodo Unyu (Union Transport Co.) in 1885, started a regular service between Japan and Bombay in order to open a direct route for raw cotton imported from India. This reflected the rapid development of the cotton industry in the 1880s. Raw cotton produced in Japan was insufficient in quality, quantity and price. At first Japan imported raw cotton from China, but since this was not suitable for the production of medium cotton yarn (counts of over 20), Japan turned to India. Japanese cotton manufacturers hoped that Indian cotton would be cheaper. However, the shipping route between India and Japan was dominated by a shipping conference comprising P&O and two European companies, and the freight rate for raw cotton from India to Japan was set as high as 17 rupees per ton. With support from cotton-spinning companies and cotton trading firms, including Kanegafuchi Boseki and Osaka Boseki, NYK started a regular service between Japan and Bombay in cooperation with Tata & Sons of Bombay. The shipping conference soon began to compete by dropping its freight rate from 17 rupees to 5 rupees in December 1893, and to $1\frac{1}{2}$ rupees in January 1894. NYK struggled against this fierce competition, strongly backed by the Japan Cotton Spinners Association, but Tata & Sons suffered from large losses and withdrew. In 1896, NYK, P&O and the two other shipping companies agreed on a joint accounting system of freight rates, in which NYK took a 23.3 per cent share and P&O 50 per cent. Ten years later, however, the NYK attained an equal share with the P&O of 32.5 per cent. In 1913 Osaka Shosen (Osaka Mercantile Steamship) also joined the shipping agreement of the Japan–Bombay line. Japanese shipping gradually increased its influence; in 1915, the actual share of freight carried by conference members was 51 per cent for NYK, 24 per cent for Osaka Shosen, and 25 per cent for P&O.[61]

The establishment of the gold standard and the end of the 'unequal' treaties

The possibility of transferring to the gold standard was investigated by the Committee on Currency Systems (*Kahei Seido Chosakai*), which began work in 1893, but insufficient gold reserves and the fact that the silver standard acted as a protective tariff barrier at a time of falling silver values, prevented any final decision from being taken. However, Japan's negative attitude to overseas finance was reversed by the changing international political situation in East Asia after the Sino-Japanese War. It had been possible for private capital investment, primarily in railway construction and cotton spinning, to fund economic development in the late 1880s. However, the economic policy of the post-Sino-Japanese War period involved a series of moves towards the expansion and strengthening of military armaments, the development of heavy industries, and the expansion and consolidation of transport and communication networks. Since it was difficult to find funds to support all of this from within Japan, government support and foreign capital were necessary, but the western countries that were the potential lenders were all on the gold standard. To attract foreign capital, Japan had to move on to the gold standard, and give the yen a stable international value. The indemnity payments made by China as a result of the Sino-Japanese War, which totalled 231.5 million taels (£38 million), provided the necessary gold reserves, and the move was made in 1897. A substantial part of Japanese currency reserves were kept in sterling to enable payment of foreign bills in London.[62]

The attainment of tariff autonomy and the abolition of extraterritoriality were the main targets of treaty revision. Britain was the last of the western powers to agree after a long struggle, and in July 1894, a new commercial treaty was agreed. This treaty stipulated 'full liberty to enter, travel, or reside in any part' of Japan for British citizens, along with 'full and perfect protection for their persons and property' (Article 1), and 'reciprocal freedom of commerce and navigation' (Article 3), but it would 'not take effect until at least five years after its signature' (Article 11).[63] Overall, the Japanese attitude to treaty revision and its consequence, *naichi zakkyo* (mixed residence), was very ambivalent, since the desire for the 'equal' relationship with western countries which would be achieved by the removal of 'unequal' clauses was balanced by the desire to confine foreign capital to the foreign settlements through the continuation of 'treaty port trade'.[64] However, it is likely that Japanese business circles worried about the penetration into the interior of Chinese rather than western merchants. True enough, even after the treaty port system was abolished in 1899 and 'mixed residence' became possible, the established behaviour patterns of British and other western merchants showed little change.[65]

Japan obtained partial tariff autonomy in 1899, when the Fixed Tariff Law was enacted, but this still left conventional tariff rates from 5 per cent to 15 per cent on many items such as cotton and woollen manufactures and iron and steel. It was not until 1911 that Japan finally recovered complete tariff autonomy. However, Japan's move to the gold standard and the linkage between the yen and sterling meant that the former had gained credibility as an international currency. Moreover, the abolition of extraterritoriality and the partial achievement of tariff autonomy were clear signs that, 40 years after the signing of the unequal treaties, Japan had achieved political and economic equality with the West.

From cooperation to competition and conflict, 1900–1945

Anglo-Japanese trade relations

Japan's adoption of the gold standard (until 1917), the revision of the 'unequal' treaties, and the signing of the Anglo-Japanese Alliance in 1902, made the relationship between the two countries into a partnership, albeit a short-lived one. This brought great changes to Japan's external economic policy, and to trade conditions. Meanwhile Japan developed a severe trade deficit from 1896 onwards as a result of its post-Sino-Japanese War economic policies, and began to import capital. The balance of trade grew even worse with the expenses incurred by the Russo-Japanese War and the economic policies adopted in its wake, including payments for foreign technological licences as well as foreign capital loans. Japan's total outstanding foreign debts increased from ¥1410 million in 1905 to ¥2000 million in 1913, and Japan's international balance of payments reached crisis point. Given these circumstances, the outbreak of the First World War was nothing less than 'divine assistance' (*tenyu*) as far as Japan was concerned.[66]

The First World War had a dramatic effect on the Japanese economy, but it did not immediately cause substantial changes in the Anglo-Japanese trade relationship. Exports to Europe and to western colonies in Southeast Asia rose, and enabled Japan to switch from debtor to creditor status, with a favourable trade balance of ¥1396 million and invisible trade receipts of ¥1339 million over the entire 1915–18 period, a combined total of ¥2735 million. Import substitution in the heavy and chemical industries made great progress, the shipping industry expanded rapidly, and Japan's commercial interests in Asian countries, in particular as an exporter of manufactured goods such as textiles, became much greater than before. However, once the war boom had finished, Japan reverted to its previous trade structure, concentrating on exports of raw silk and textiles and imports of primary products and heavy and chemical industrial goods. Its trade balance went into the red once more, and the situation became even worse after the Great Kanto Earthquake of 1923, because the demand for reconstruction materials caused a surge in imports. From the mid-1920s to the mid-1930s the trade deficit exceeded the favourable balance in invisible earnings, leading to a sharp drop in currency reserves (Table 1.9).

Seen in the long term, however, the economic changes which had occurred during the war did affect the Anglo-Japanese relationship. Japan's export trade fell in the 1920s with the return of western goods to the Asian market. However, this was a period in which free trade ideals were pursued in an atmosphere of international cooperation, and Japan's trade relationships diversified. In particular, the US replaced Britain and Europe as Japan's major trade partner. In spite of the overall decline in trade, Japan's deficit vis-à-vis Britain and Europe increased, which adversely influenced Japan's balance of payments until 1930 (Table 1.3). This suggests that the development of heavy and chemical industries had in fact increased Japan's dependence on Britain and Europe, primarily for means of production such as machinery.

During the period from the end of the nineteenth century to 1930, with the exception of the years covered by the First World War, Japan ran a trade deficit with Britain and the British Empire taken as a whole. The share of Britain and the British Empire in Japanese exports decreased after 1905, but continued to reach 15–20 per cent up until 1937, again with the exception of the First World War period (Figures 1.2 and 1.3). While shares of Britain and Hong Kong declined after 1918, India became Japan's most important export market in the British Empire, maintaining a 5–11 per cent share up until 1937. In imports into Japan, the share held by Britain and the British

Table 1.9 Japan's international balance of payments (five-year aggregate current value) (in million yen)

Year	*Current account*				*Capital account*			*Overall balance*	*Currency reserves*
	Commodity trade	*Invisible trade*	*Transfers*	*Total*	*Long-term*	*Short-term*	*Total*		
1891–95	0	–1	141	142	–7	–140	–147	–5	
1896–1900	–356	–46	284	–117	132	–8	125	7	
1901–05	–243	–221	43	–421	716	105	821	400	97
1906–10	–130	–91	60	–161	441	–287	154	–8	446
1911–15	–47	–46	6	–87	32	50	82	–5	341
1916–20	763	1871	183	2817	–1993	956	–1036	1781	2045
1921–25	–2737	780	153	–1804	–194	1274	1080	–666	1501
1926–30	–1390	868	48	–474	–827	845	18	–456	1343
1931–35	–546	536	272	262	–1662	816	–846	–584	495
1936–40	1311	–2388	319	–758	–4157	2361	–1796	–2554	586

Sources: I. Yamazawa and Y. Yamamoto, *Boeki to Kokusai Shushi* (Tokyo, 1979), pp. 218–31.
Notes: (1) Figures of exports prior to 1903 and those for imports prior to 1898 are revised according to f.o.b. and c.i.f.
(2) Figures for currency reserves are as of the end of each period.

Empire remained at 40 per cent until the First World War, and then declined gradually to 28 per cent in the 1920s. It maintained a level of over 20 per cent until 1937, but decreased rapidly after the start of the Sino-Japanese War in 1937. India overtook Britain as a major importer to Japan in the 1910s, but gradually lost ground in the 1920s and 1930s. By contrast Australia's importance as a trade partner, both in exports and in imports, increased in the 1910s and continued to be important until the late 1930s.

Table 1.10 shows major export and import articles of Japan's trade with Britain and the British Empire for the period from 1905 to 1935. Japan exported silk fabrics and copper to Britain and imported manufactured products, but there was a clear shift in major import items from cotton textiles to iron and steel and machinery. In 1933 the balance of trade between the two countries changed from an excess of imports to Japan to an excess of exports from Japan. Hong Kong continued to be an entrepôt for Japanese exports, but the major export items changed from coal and copper to cotton textiles, whose final destination was Southeast Asia. Japan's trade with India was entirely in cotton, raw cotton being imported from India in return for exports of cotton manufactures. Japan ran a large trade deficit with Australia owing to its large imports of wool. On the other hand, its trade with the Straits Settlements and with Canada was relatively limited. In the case of the former, Japan exported first coal, then cotton textiles in return for rubber and iron ore. From Canada, Japan imported wheat, timber and minerals, while exporting silk manufactures. Japan's trade with South Africa increased gradually in the 1930s, with exports of cotton textiles and imports of wool.[67]

Along with the other major economic powers, Japan had suspended the gold standard in 1917 and it was the last to return, in January 1930. However, the timing was unfortunate, as it made Japan acutely vulnerable to the effects of the economic collapse of 1929 and the ensuing Depression. The outflow of gold increased, and rural areas were severely hit by a fall in agricultural prices. In September 1931 the Manchurian Incident occurred; three days later Britain left the gold standard. These events led to speculation that Japan would reimpose an embargo on gold exports. In the face of the continuing economic recession, gold exports from Japan were in fact suspended in December 1931. After this, under Finance Minister Takahashi Korekiyo, the government adopted a more interventionist and spending policy to recover from the Depression. By 1933, the year in which Japan withdrew from the League of Nations, production had returned to pre-Depression levels. This feat was accomplished externally by increasing exports, particularly of cotton textiles, at relatively low selling prices that were aided by the rapid depreciation of the yen. The increasing exports from Japan forced her main overseas markets, including India and the Dutch East Indies, to take protective measures such as the introduction of import quotas and increased import duties on Japanese goods. Japan attempted to preserve

Table 1.10 Major articles of Japan's trade with Britain and the British Empire (in thousand yen)

		Articles	*1905*	*1910*	*1915*	*1920*	*1925*	*1930*	*1935*
Britain	Exports to	Silk fabric	5006	7785	11939	31288	17171	7163	13499
		Copper	390	4445	9228	970	0	10785	0
		Total	13039	25782	68494	97797	59716	61793	119458
	Imports from	Woollen manufactures	20783	15974	4953	44521	86470	10747	9212
		Cotton fabric	15181	12966	4573	14196	8519	3738	909
		Iron and steel	20311	17218	14971	55369	32625	14155	12049
		Machinery	16376	13520	8132	37199	43788	26749	24503
		Total	115380	94701	58084	235353	227292	92557	82160
Hong Kong	Exports to	Cotton yarns	909	2649	7964	28936	20753	2592	945
		Cotton fabric	1358	1731	2171	11223	21753	8607	11055
		Coal	4620	4999	4484	7789	5038	3881	4079
		Total	20215	23460	27401	74066	73629	55646	49732
	Imports from	Total	1129	675	1594	2232	476	538	2838
India	Exports to	Matches	599	1111	5494	10419	1791	12	105
		Silk fabric	3294	5849	7011	13252	13451	6817	21222
		Cotton fabric	1154	4838	7809	77029	81628	20422	95276
		Artificial silk fabric	n.a.	n.a.	n.a.	n.a.	n.a.	10526	23141
		Total	7998	18713	42202	192249	173413	129262	275637
	Imports from	Rice and paddy	32959	1708	648	311	48624	1	200
		Raw cotton (cotton ginned)	53552	101218	139705	357581	475517	147684	259037
		Iron (pig iron & waste)	n.a.	n.a.	1289	5340	4484	11163	12728
		Manures	398	633	884	9849	6509	1312	940
		Total	90227	103361	147585	394930	573319	180424	305645
Straits Settlements	Exports to	Cotton fabric	248	379	945	8276	16242	4545	11616
		Coal	1731	1994	3269	7866	2210	2538	2320
		Total	4424	6550	12690	35749	44904	26930	48536

	Imports from	Rubber and gutta percha	327	1 246	1 727	8 852	26 772	11 615	24 125
		Tin	1 537	1 006	1 430	3 863	3 413	2 728	9 795
		Iron ore	n.a.	n.a.	n.a.	n.a.	3 141	10 401	53
		Total	3 398	4 616	5 356	17 137	37 004	28 918	40 648
Australia	Exports to	Silk fabric	1 493	2 518	5 419	19 932	24 910	13 862	7 490
		Cotton fabric	137	350	1 197	12 414	10 887	2 217	18 211
		Artificial silk fabric	n.a.	n.a.	n.a.	n.a.	n.a.	n.a.	22 323
		Total	4 073	6 552	18 098	58 115	47 495	25 486	74 793
	Imports from	Wheat	1 230	432	99	10 103	31 242	8 689	30 936
		Wool	1 530	5 177	23 979	31 819	96 825	72 335	182 007
		Total	6 001	7 602	28 571	62 459	149 969	94 215	235 149
Canada	Exports to	Silk fabric	973	528	1 515	9 942	10 774	4 452	343
		Total	3 240	4 262	7 024	21 669	20 838	17 903	7 979
	Imports from	Wheat	n.a.	n.a.	n.a.	n.a.	13 507	14 856	6 258
		Pulp for paper-making & wood	162	70	799	3 714	7 715	12 188	12 371
		Lead	51	195	n.a.	n.a.	6 545	5 049	6 929
		Total	732	850	1 063	5 051	37 132	46 259	52 531
Cape Colony & Natal	Exports to	Cotton fabric			277	1 516	2 372	2 746	7 200
		Silk fabric			183	3 135	5 017	5 323	5 955
		Total			1 000	8 206	9 538	14 196	32 769
	Imports from	Wool			n.a.	72 975	272	19	1 872
		Total			0	73 895	1 325	1 615	4 762

Sources: Okura-sho, *Dai-Nihon Gaikoku Boeki Nenpyo*, corresponding years.
Note: Re-exports are excluded. 'Woollen manufactures' includes wool and woollen yarns. Steamers and railway locomotives and carriages are included in 'machinery'.

smooth trade relations by bilateral trade negotiations, for example, with Britain, India, and Australia in the 1930s. However, the outbreak of the Sino-Japanese War in 1937 led to a further increase in direct government control of political and economic activities. The increasing hostility of the international community was making Japan more dependent on China and Southeast Asia both as a market for exports and as a source of such essential raw materials as iron ore, rubber, and petroleum.

Japan's imports of foreign capital

As Table 1.9 shows, the second half of the 1910s and the 1930s were periods of capital exports. During and after the First World War, the value of Japan's capital movements increased, and a deficit in the long-term capital account contrasted with a surplus in the short-term capital account. Japan had to raise capital for export because it was unable to raise funds on the domestic Japanese market.

The establishment of the gold standard in 1897 had enabled Japan to issue foreign loans abroad, but only after the Anglo-Japanese Alliance of 1902 was it able to do so with great success, particularly in London. The period from then up until the beginning of the First World War is known as the first period of capital imports. During the period from 1897 to 1914 the Japanese government issued ¥2121 million in foreign bonds, 28 per cent being raised completely in London and 60 per cent jointly between London and other cities such as New York, Paris and Berlin. The total sum raised in London amounted to about 21 per cent of all government loan issues in London for the period from 1900 to 1913. In particular, over 50 per cent (£82 million in total) of the ¥1560 million in war bonds which were issued at the time of the Russo-Japanese War were raised in Britain and the US. In the majority of cases, whether public or private, foreign loans were issued through the Hongkong Shanghai Banking Corporation, the Chartered Bank of India, Australia and China, and Parr's Bank. All this shows the importance of links with the City to Japan's foreign loans.[68]

Government loan issues were crucial for the Japanese government, especially in order to raise capital for the economic development following the end of the Russo-Japanese War in 1905. However, since borrowing had reached the limit allowed by Japan's country risk, from around 1908–9 it gradually became harder to issue further government bonds. In these circumstances, great significance was attached to the bonds raised by Tokyo, Yokohama, Osaka and other large cities to finance the construction of infrastructure such as electricity, water and gas utilities. Recalling this period, Wakatsuki Reijiro, a Finance Ministry official who later became Prime Minister, revealed that the government had encouraged these local bonds as a sort of escape route to prevent the country's being declared bankrupt. The funds gained were used to maintain government reserves; in return local public bodies received convertible banknotes.[69] Of the ¥178 million in local bonds issued in the period 1902–1912, 88 per cent were raised between 1909 and 1912, and 36 per cent of those were raised completely in London.[70]

Private concerns, including the South Manchurian Railway, the Industrial Bank of Japan, the Kansai Railway, and Hokkaido Tanko Kisen, also raised foreign bonds. The first such company bonds were issued by the Kansai Railway in 1905. By 1913 a total of ¥200 million had been raised, 80 per cent completely in London. In particular, the South Manchurian Railway, established in 1906 with capital of ¥200 million, half of which had been provided by the government, issued sterling company bonds on four occasions from 1907 to 1911 to a total amount of £14 million (¥136.7 million).[71]

The First World War situation encouraged the export of capital from Japan, for example through the purchase of foreign bonds, in what is known as the first period of capital exports. Annual capital exports rose from ¥530 million in 1914 to ¥1910 million in 1919, and the capital account reached a deficit of ¥1430 million for the entire 1915–18 period (see Table 1.9).

The 1920s are called the second period of capital imports, since foreign loans were actively sought in order to obtain sources of revenue and prevent an outflow of foreign reserves. As discussed in Suzuki's chapter in this volume, the government issued foreign bonds on only two occasions in the interwar period – in 1924, after the Kanto earthquake, and in 1930; the total amount was ¥809 million. On the other hand, imports of capital in the form of company bonds issued by private Japanese companies and direct investment by foreign firms became more important than before. At the end of 1928 the balance of foreign bonds issued by Japanese private companies amounted to ¥458 million. Of this total, 76 per cent of the bonds had been issued by electricity companies, which raised ¥523 million during the period 1923–31, 80 per cent on the American market, and less than 20 per cent on the British market. From 1931 Britain ceased to be involved in Japanese government loan issues, the last issuing of bonds on the British market being in connection with Nihon Denryoku (Japan Electricity Co.).[72]

Japan's commodity trade with Britain thus experienced a relative decline from the 1900s, with the exception of the period covered by the First World War. However, one could argue that this decline was offset by the closer relationship with the City, which resulted from the various issues of foreign bonds. In other words, from the British point of view, the focus of economic links with Japan had shifted from 'trade' to 'financial services'.[73] However, as a result of the establishment of the new world order through the Washington Conference and the consequent suspension of the Anglo-Japanese Alliance, Anglo-Japanese economic relations in the 1920s must be considered overall in the context of post-First World War international relations, rather than on a purely bilateral level.

British investment in Japan: the licensing of British technology

Foreign capital played a variety of roles in Japanese firms, from direct investment to technological cooperation, patents and licensing. Foreign business was confined to particular fields of industry such as electrical engineering, and car and rubber manufacturing. In the case of British capital, direct investment was of relatively minor importance. British firms which did make direct investments in Japan during this period include the Rising Sun Petroleum Co. (a subsidiary of Royal Dutch Shell Co., 1900), Nihon Bakuhatsubutsu Seizo (Armstrong Whitworth, Chilworth Gunpowder, and Nobel's Explosives, 1905), Dunlop Far East (Japan Branch) (Dunlop Far East, 1909, becoming Nihon Dunlop in 1917), and Lever Brothers (Lever Brothers, 1913). Joint Anglo-Japanese ventures included Nihon Seikosho (Japan Steel Works, a joint venture between Armstrong, Vickers and Hokkaido Tanko Kisen, 1907), and Teikoku Seishi (J.&P. Coats and Murai Kyodai Shokai, 1907). As in the case of Nihon Seikosho, discussed in Nagura Bunji's chapter in this volume, the main element of direct investment was technological cooperation. In 1906 the Anglo-Japanese Bank was established in London with initial capital of £2 million, but in fact Japan was not a very attractive investment market for British multinationals. Cooperation between British and Japanese firms did not play as important a role as that between American and Japanese firms, for example in the tie-up between General Electric Co. and Shibaura Seisakusho (Shibaura Engineering Works), or Westinghouse Electric Co. and Mitsubishi Denki (Mitsubishi Electric Manufacturing Co.).[74]

After the First World War American capital such as Ford Japan, General Motors Japan and Victor came to play an increasingly central role. There was British investment in joint venture firms such as Nihon Chikuonki Shokai (later known as Nihon Columbia) in 1927, and Toyo Babcock in the following year,[75] but the scale was small in comparison with the prewar period. Teikoku Kagaku Kogyo was a joint sales organization for Brunner Mond & Co. and ICI. Since Ford and General Motors were dominant in the car manufacturing industry until government regulation was introduced in 1936, the entry of Wolseley, through technological cooperation with Isuzu Jidosha,[76] should perhaps therefore be seen as something of an exception.

In 1931, there were 82 firms in Japan which had received some form of foreign investment. British capital was involved in 21 firms, putting it in second place after the US (36 firms). Of these, four were machine-parts manufacturers, four hosiery manufacturers, and three made iron and steel, and iron products. However, Britain left the gold standard in that year and Japan once again passed a law forbidding gold exports. Following these moves came a law preventing the flight of capital abroad in 1932 and exchange control regulations in 1933, both of which provided obstacles to the movement of capital into and out of Japan. The business of western firms was further restricted as the Japanese economy went onto a war footing. Even firms in receipt of foreign direct investment had to introduce Japanese capital in order to survive. In 1941 it seems that foreign investment in Japan, in the form of factory buildings, cash, deposits, stocks and so on, was only ¥400 million.[77]

Anglo-Japanese trade rivalry in China: cotton, shipping, sugar and investment

During the period under consideration, while Britain and Japan cooperated in the areas of finance and technology transfer, trade rivalry shifted away from the Japanese market to markets overseas. China in particular became the focus of Anglo-Japanese diplomatic and economic relations.[78] Table 1.11 shows the main economic indices for British and Japanese activities in China. After the First World War there were clear signs that Japan was overtaking Britain in terms of direct trade and the number of companies involved, but Britain had the upper hand in investments and shipping.

While in some respects commercial circles in both countries had a common interest in the establishment of order and stability in China, trade rivalry erupted in particular in relation to cotton, shipping and sugar.

Table 1.11 Britain and Japan in China

	Year	*Britain*	*Japan*
Direct trade (in million Haikwan taels)	1899	53.9 (11.7)	53.1 (11.5)
	1913	113.3 (11.4)	184.9 (19.0)
	1930	170.9 (7.8)	543.7 (24.7)
Number of firms	1899	401 (43.0)	195 (20.9)
	1913	590 (15.0)	1269 (33.3)
	1930	1027 (12.4)	4633 (55.9)
Shipping (tonnage in million)	1899	23.3 (59.4)	2.8 (7.2)
	1913	38.1 (40.8)	23.4 (25.0)
	1930	57.2 (36.8)	45.6 (29.3)
Investments (in million US dollars)	1902	260.3 (33.0)	1.0 (0.1)
	1914	607.5 (37.7)	219.6 (13.6)
	1930	1189.2 (36.7)	1136.9 (35.1)
Number of spindles (in thousand)	1902	80.5 (16.2)	23.9 (4.8)
	1913	138.0 (16.8)	111.9 (13.6)
	1930	169.2 (7.2)	1587.8 (67.7)

Sources: C.F. Remer, *Foreign Investments in China* (New York: Macmillan, 1933), pp. 407, 553. Z. Yan, *Zhongguo Mianfangzhi Shi Gao* (Beijing: Kexue Chubanshe, 1963), p. 355.
Note: Figures in parentheses are percentages of the total in each case. Misprints are revised.

Competition on the Chinese cotton market and the development of cotton mills in China

The development of the Japanese cotton industry as an export sector turned cotton yarn and cotton piece-goods into a source of Anglo-Japanese competition in the Chinese market. Table 1.12 shows the market shares in imports of cotton yarn into China by country. Imports increased mainly to satisfy demand in the domestic handicraft weaving industry, but decreased rapidly as domestic cotton mills developed after the First World War. Britain dominated the Chinese market for imported cotton yarn up to the early 1890s, when imports of Indian yarn rapidly replaced those from Britain. Imports of Japanese cotton yarn were facilitated by Japan's abolition of the export duty on cotton yarn in 1894, and of the import duty on raw cotton in 1896. This led to fierce competition between Indian and Japanese cotton yarn. The yarn trade was confined to coarse counts of yarn. Indian yarn had overwhelming predominance in south and central China, while Japan replaced Indian yarn in North China and Manchuria. Indian yarn was inferior in quality but its low price made it attractive to poorer Chinese, who purchased coarse yarns as warp for fabrics woven on their own handlooms. Indian yarn was sold through Indian importing houses, which were branches of Bombay firms, and made long-term loans at low interest rates available to buyers, while Japanese firms such as Mitsui Bussan handled most of the Japanese yarn.[79]

Britain competed with America over exports of cotton piece-goods to China, but by the end of the nineteenth century Britain was dominant in fine goods and the latter in coarse goods. Sheetings and drills were the main imported cotton piece-goods. During the period 1905–13, Britain kept a

Table 1.12 Cotton yarn imports into China by country (%)

Year	*Britain*	*India*	*Japan*	*Total (mil. lb)*
1892	4	96	–	174
1900	2	66	32	198
1910	0	57	41	304
1920	1	50	46	177
1928	–	2	98	38

Sources: Chinese Maritime Customs, *Decennial Reports*, 1892–1901, Appendix xxviii; 1902–11, p. 343; 1912–21, vol. 2, p. 438. For 1928, B.L. Reynolds, 'The East Asia "textile cluster" trade, 1868–1973', in E.R. May and J.K. Fairbank (eds), *America's China Trade in Historical Perspective* (Cambridge, MA: Council on East Asian Studies, Harvard University, 1986), p. 143.

stable 50 per cent share of Chinese imports of cotton piece-goods, while the US decreased from 36 per cent to 8 per cent, and Japan increased from 3 per cent to 20 per cent.[80] However, 73 per cent of cotton cloth was produced by the domestic handicraft weaving industry,[81] leaving Britain, Japan and the United States to compete against each other for the limited market that remained. Domestic cloth was not in fact cheaper than imported goods, but was 'far more durable and suitable for all seasons'.[82]

Mitsui Bussan played a crucial role in exporting and marketing cotton yarn and cotton textiles in addition to imports of cotton machinery and raw cotton. For the period 1897–1912 it was responsible for 32 per cent of all cotton yarn exports from Japan and its share of exports of cotton piece-goods reached 36 per cent for the years 1906–12.[83] Around the turn of the twentieth century, Mitsui Bussan slackened the limits on overbuying and overselling to allow branches to operate more effectively and increase their direct business with Chinese merchants. It also abolished the comprador system at its Chinese branches, steadily replacing compradors with Japanese staff trained in Chinese trading methods and in the Chinese language. In the late 1900s 50 per cent of Mitsui Bussan's transactions in cotton goods was carried out directly with Chinese retailers.[84]

After the Treaty of Shimonoseki of 1895 made it possible to set up factories in China's treaty ports, foreign firms began to found cotton-spinning mills at Shanghai. Table 1.11 shows the number and spindles of cotton mills in China. Jardine, Matheson & Co. founded the Ewo Cotton Spinning & Weaving Co. in 1895. Another British firm, Ilbert & Co., founded Laou Kung Mow Cotton Spinning & Weaving Co. in the same year. Japanese trading firms were also interested such activities. For instance, Mitsui Bussan founded the Shanghai Cotton Spinning Co. in 1902 by taking over a Chinese-owned cotton mill. However, these first Japanese attempts were not successful. By 1911 there were 31 cotton mills in China, with 831 000 spindles and 3440 looms. Seventy per cent of the spindles were located in Shanghai. The 31 mills spun coarse yarn from counts of 10s to 20s, with annual production 200–250 million lbs a year, and 40–50 million yards of cloth.[85]

After the First World War, increases in Chinese tariffs further stimulated a shift from exports to actual production in China. Large spinning companies, including Dainihon Boseki, set up cotton mills in quick succession. However, while Chinese and Japanese cotton mills developed, British mills declined. Foreign cotton mills in China (*zaikabo*) were able to produce cotton goods at low cost due to the abundant supply of cheap labour and the easy access to raw cotton and a large consumer market. In 1928 there were three British cotton mills with 153 000 spindles, 43 Japanese mills with 1 397 000 spindles, and 74 Chinese mills with 2 088 000 spindles. These figures seem to show the supremacy of Chinese-owned mills; however, if substantial ownership through actual loan relations is considered, Japanese cotton mills owned 45 per cent of the total spindles, compared to the 44 per cent held by Chinese mills.[86] Meanwhile, the growth in domestic Japanese demand and rising wages increased the domestic and export prices of cotton goods produced in Japan, weakening the overseas competitiveness of both yarn and textiles. This hindered exports of cotton goods to China. Consequently, Japan's export market shifted from China to India and Southeast Asia, and products changed from coarse to medium and fine goods.

Shipping competiton: the Yangzi river and the Taiwan lines

Trade on both the upper and lower parts of the Yangzi river had been conducted according to pooling agreements between the Chinese government-sponsored China Merchants Steam Navigation Co., Swires' China Navigation Co. and Jardines' Indo-China Steam Navigation Co. The China Merchants Steam Navigation Co. was originally founded as a government enterprise in 1872 under the leadership of Li Hongzhang with a capital of 470000 taels. The China Navigation Co. was formed in 1872 in London with a nominal capital of £360000 to serve Swires' expanding shipping interests on the Yangzi river in cooperation with Alfred Holt's Blue Funnel Line, and Butterfield & Swire was appointed general agent. The Indo-China Steam Navigation Co. was formed in 1881 after the amalgamation of Jardines' two shipping companies, the Yangtze Steamer Co. and the China Coast Steam Navigation Co.

The Shimonoseki Treaty opened the port of Chongqing on the upper Yangzi to foreign shipping and also gave Japan navigation rights on the river. As a consequence, in 1896, Daito Shinri Yoko was founded to operate triangular shipping lines between Shanghai, Suzhou and Hangzhou. In 1898 it became the Daito Kisen KK, and was provided with subsidies by the Japanese government. Osaka Shosen, which was founded in 1884 with an initial capital of ¥1.2 million, started a regular service between Shanghai and Hankou in 1898, and between Hankou and Yichang in 1899 with the support of long-term government subsidies. In 1903 the NYK, which had been involved in the formation of Konan Kisen Kaisha the previous year, purchased the Shanghai-based British firm of McBain & Co. for ¥2.5 million (1.35 million taels). This allowed them to link their Henan line with ocean shipping, but did not make it possible for them to run right up to Hankou as they had hoped, since McBain's facilities were located in the British concession at Hankou and this was closed to non-British concerns.[87]

By the middle of the first decade of the twentieth century, Japan had emerged as a serious competitor on the Chinese river trade. On the Yangzi there was fierce competition between 11 shipping firms under five national flags (British, German, French, Chinese and Japanese) with a total tonnage of over 100000 tons.[88] The situation became particularly serious with the entry into the Yangzi trade of the Nisshin Kisen Kaisha in 1907, at a time when established shipping companies were already suffering from a depression in the aftermath of the Russo-Japanese War. Nisshin Kisen had been formed by the four Japanese shipping companies mentioned above, with an initial paid-up capital of ¥8.1 million. Osaka Shosen took 46 per cent of the total shares issued, and NYK 41 per cent. Nisshin Kisen operated nine shipping lines along the Yangzi with an annual government subsidy amounting to ¥800000 for five years. These subsidies played a crucial role in the operation of Nisshin Kisen; for the period from 1907 to 1936 they amounted to 12 per cent of total revenue and 84 per cent of total profits.[89] Nisshin Kisen was not completely opposed to the pooling agreement on the Yangzi, although Swires and Jardines had hostile intentions towards the Japanese company. However, the inefficiency of the China Merchants Steam Navigation Co. made their plan unworkable. The Yangzi Pool Agreement had convinced both Chinese and British companies of the advantages of coexistence in removing cut-throat competition, but their association with the Chinese company handicapped the British firms in responding to the Japanese. Nisshin Kisen demanded a four-party pool agreement and, in 1913, eventually reached an agreement over freight rates with the pool companies. After the end of the First World War, Nisshin Kisen started coastal lines, for instance between Shanghai and Guandong and Shanghai and Tianjin, in addition to its Yangzi routes.

Table 1.13 shows the shares by nationality and total tonnage of cargoes on the most important line of the Yangzi, Shanghai to Hankou, which took 70–80 per cent of the total Yangzi shipping tonnage. Japanese shares decreased faster than British, while Chinese shares increased rapidly. The overall decline in the Japanese shares was first caused by the start of the Chinese boycott of Japanese goods in protest again the Japanese military expedition to Shandong in 1927. It was further accelerated by the increas-

Table 1.13 Shares of cargo carried on the Yangzi by nationality (%)

Year	*British*	*Japanese*	*Chinese*	*Total tonnage (1000 tons)*
1927	50.6	38.7	6.9	1096
1930	39.4	36.0	18.6	1059
1933	41.4	13.5	36.8	736
1936	33.2	23.3	38.6	1408

Sources: *Nisshin Kisen Kabushiki Kaisha Sanjunen-shi*, pp. 106–7.
Note: 'British' means the China Navigation Co. and the Indo-China Steam Navigation Co., 'Japanese' means Nisshin Kisen. The main Chinese firms are China Merchants Steam Navigation Co. and Sanbei Gongsu.

ing Chinese resistance to Japanese military expansion after the Manchurian Incident in 1931 and the Shanghai Incident of the following year.

The second phase of Anglo-Japanese shipping rivalry in the period under consideration was concerned with shipping lines centring on Taiwan. The Douglas Steamship Co., a Hong Kong-based British firm, which had been founded in 1883 by Douglas Lapraik, a British merchant, dominated the South China coastal trade and the trade between mainland China and Taiwan. However, Japan wanted to cut the economic links between Taiwan and mainland China. Osaka Shosen started a regular service between Japan and Taiwan in 1896, with government subsidies, in order to carry sugar and salt to Japan. Subsequently Osaka Shosen was given support by the Government General of Taiwan to open the Taiwan–South China and the South China coastal lines, starting with the Danshui–Hong Kong line in 1899 in competition with the Douglas Steamship Co. As a result of fierce competition over freight rates and Osaka Shosen's generally aggressive business strategies, Douglas & Co. suspended its Danshui–Hong Kong service and finally withdrew from the South China–Taiwan line in 1904, in order to specialize in South China coastal shipping. The Government General of Taiwan attempted to oust Douglas and Co. from the South China coastal trade as well, but without success.[90] Japanese ships were more successful in North and Northeast China, but Britain maintained its dominance in Chinese coastal trade until the outbreak of the Japan–China War, with a 54 per cent share of all commercial shipping along the Chinese coast from treaty ports such as Tianjin in 1936 as opposed to 44 per cent for Chinese shipping and 2 per cent for Japanese.[91]

Competition in the Chinese refined sugar market[92]

Trade rivalry in the Chinese refined sugar market was another major ingredient in the Anglo-Japanese commercial rivalry of the interwar period. In the Chinese market, refined sugar was mainly supplied by two British firms in Hong Kong, the Taikoo Sugar Refining Co. and the China Sugar Refining Co., and two Japanese firms, Dainihon Seito KK and Meiji Seito KK. As mentioned earlier, after the Sino-Japanese War and the consequent cession of Taiwan to Japan in 1895, the two British refineries were gradually ousted from the Japanese market, and from the early twentieth century they had to concentrate on sales to China. Meiji Seito was established in 1906, encouraged by the success of Taiwan Seito, the first large modern sugar factory in Taiwan. Dainihon Seito was formed in 1906, after the merger of the refinery companies of Nihon Seiseito in Tokyo and Nihon Seito in Osaka. Soon after the end of the Russo-Japanese War, Japanese companies such as Dainihon Seito started to challenge the British domination of the refined sugar market in China. When Japan finally obtained complete tariff autonomy in 1911, this further aided the development of the Japanese sugar industry, and exports to the China market grew. In 1912 Meiji Seito attempted to develop outlets for its refined sugar in Korea, Manchuria and China. The Hong Kong refineries began to feel the pressure of Japanese competition again, but they were given a respite by the expansion of the market for East Asian sugar during and immediately after the First World War, which provided them with fresh opportunities.

In the 1920s, as a whole, the sugar market in China expanded, but towards the end of the 1920s there was a gradual decline in the market for refined sugar. This reinforced the competition between the four major refineries in Hong Kong and Japan. Increasing imports of Java white sugar further strengthened the competition, and the market share of refined sugar decreased to 32 per cent of the total imports of sugar into China in the period 1925–30.[93] The Chinese boycott of British goods after 1925 had an unfavourable effect on the sales of the Hong Kong refineries.

The contrast between the business performance of the Hong Kong and the Japanese refineries is obvious. Dainihon Seito and Meiji Seito gained relatively high and steady returns through sales in both Japan and China, while the British refineries depended heavily on sales in China and their profits decreased drastically from the mid-1920s, owing to the growing political unrest in China and the severe competition from Japanese refineries and Java white sugar. Jardines' China Sugar Refining Co. was the first victim of the four-way rivalry, being voluntarily liquidated in May 1928.

China was the major export market for Japanese refined sugar. Throughout the 1920s and 1930s, 30 per cent of total Japanese domestic production of refined sugar was for export. The market situation did not change in the 1930s. In the early part of the decade, consumption of refined sugar was limited, mainly owing to financial restrictions and general poverty throughout the country. The Chinese boycott against Japanese sugar, which began in July 1931, combined with the Sino-Japanese hostilities in Shanghai, caused a gradual shift in Japan's major export market for refined sugar from South and Central China to North and Northeast China. Japan's dependence on Taiwan as a supplier of raw sugar, and on Northeast China as an export market, increased in the late 1930s.

Japanese refineries faced almost the same business environment as British refineries in China. Marketing methods were of crucial importance when competition was keen. While Dainihon Seito sold refined sugar through its China branches, Japanese importing companies like Mitsui Bussan tended to do business directly on a commission basis, without relying on the Chinese compradors who were used by British refineries to market their products. This was a crucial factor in the keen Anglo-Japanese competition. In 1931 the Taikoo Sugar Refinery shifted to direct transactions with Chinese dealers, eliminating the comprador and his various commissions, and speeding up deliveries.

Unlike cotton in the 1930s, as will be shown, sugar rivalry never developed into a diplomatic problem. However, this was not because foreign markets were insignificant. Rather, it was because political conditions in China deteriorated so greatly that the market itself was endangered, and because the related shift of Japanese operations to Northeast China reduced the level of competition.

Anglo-Japanese capital investment in China

As we saw from Table 1.9, large-scale movements of capital in Japan did not begin until the period covered by the First World War. This, like the 1930s, was a time of capital export for Japan. In both cases, a short-term positive balance contrasted with a long-term capital deficit. The greatest problem which Japan faced in overseas capital export was the fact that it had to procure the actual funds outside Japan since there was not a sufficient domestic supply. Britain's share of the estimated world total accumulated foreign direct investment was 45 per cent in 1914, and even in 1938 it was 40 per cent, making Britain the world's largest investor nation. By contrast, while Japan's total exports of capital rapidly increased, its estimated share of accumulated foreign investments was less than 3 per cent even in 1938. China was a major destination for investment, with an estimated share of accumulated foreign direct investment of 8 per cent in 1914, and 6 per cent even in 1938.[94]

Although Japan's role as a foreign investor was negligible in world terms by comparison with that of Britain, even in the late 1930s, in China it was a fierce competitor. Japanese investment in China began with its links with Hanyeping in 1899.[95] Yawata Seitetsusho, founded by the Japanese government in 1897, imported iron ore from there, but there was a gradual shift to a financial relationship dominated by Japan. The involvement became more serious from the World War period, as is suggested by the notorious Nishihara loans of 1918.

Table 1.11 shows that Britain was the main country of origin for investment in China, followed until the First World War by Russia and Germany. By 1914 Japan had acquired a 14 per cent share in foreign investment in China. Since Japan's total export of capital for that year was ¥530 million ($260 million), it follows that 85 per cent of this was destined for China, 55 per cent being marked out for the South Manchurian Railway.[96] In 1931, Japan's share had grown to 35 per cent, closely rivalling that of Britain. At that time, three-quarters of all foreign investment in China went directly to industry, and 77 per cent of this to the four sectors of transport, imports and exports, manufacturing and property.

British and Japanese investments in China were focused on different areas. While British investment in transport was mainly shipping-related, Japanese investment in this sector was involved in the South Manchurian Railway. In manufacturing, British interests were varied, but Japan concentrated on textiles and on the expressing and marketing of soybeans and other vegetable oils. Britain was dominant in the property sector. A similar contrast can be found in the geographical spread of their direct investment in China in 1931. Shanghai and Manchuria were the main areas, but while British investments were concentrated in the former, at 77 per cent, with zero investment in Manchuria, Japan had only 25 per cent in Shanghai as opposed to 63 per cent in Manchuria.[97]

Anglo-Japanese trade rivalry in the Asian cotton market: Britain, Japan and India

During the interwar period various changes occurred in the Japanese cotton industry. There was a shift in yarn production from coarser counts to medium and finer ones, and in textile production from coarse grey to finer printed and dyed goods. Piece goods replaced yarn as the main export, while India and the Dutch East Indies replaced China as the main export markets. From the late 1920s into the early 1930s, Japanese cotton mills carried out a successful programme of rationalization through the introduction of higher technology. The lower selling prices of Japanese textiles resulting from the reduction in production costs and the depreciation of the yen facilitated the increase in exports to India and the Dutch East Indies after 1932. However, the overall trend in the 1930s was towards a diversification in the export markets for Japanese textiles, with an attempt to shift to the more neutral markets of Africa and Latin America, which imposed fewer import restrictions.

Table 1.14 shows the annual average shares of exports of cotton textiles from Britain and Japan for the period from 1909 to 1938. Japan's share in the world textile market increased gradually, reaching 31 per cent in the early 1930s, while Britain's share showed a steady decline. From the mid-1920s cotton textile exports from Japan rapidly increased. Britain faced competition from Japanese textiles in the British colonies, first in East Africa, and then in India. At first, Lancashire did not feel seriously threatened,

Table 1.14 Annual average share in the world market of exports of cotton and cotton piece-goods from Britain and Japan (%)

Year	*Britain*	*Japan*
1909/13	72.5	1.4
1921/25	57.0	12.3
1926/28	46.1	16.9
1931/33	33.3	31.0
1936/38	27.0	38.9

Sources: 'The position of the Lancashire cotton trade', Manchester Chamber of Commerce, *Monthly record* (January 1927); Nihon Menpu Yushutsu Kumiai, *Nihon Mengyo Boeki-shi* (Osaka, 1959), p. 5.

attributing Japan's advancement into the world textile market to a combination of long working hours and low wages resulting from a low standard of living. Manchester's perception of the Japanese cotton industry in the 1920s is discussed in John Sharkey's chapter in this volume. In this context two reports are worthy of mention: one by W.B. Cunningham, British Consul in Osaka, and the other by A.S. Pearse, General Secretary of the International Federation of Master Cotton Spinners' and Manufacturers' Associations. Cunningham pointed out the excellent methods of organization and management and the strong financial foundations of industrial firms in Japan. Pearse pointed out the virtual absence of hedging in raw cotton, the strong financial foundations of industrial firms, the efficient organization of marketing, the technology for blending cotton, and the fact that wages were lower than in Britain.[98]

By the early 1930s, Japanese cotton textiles had penetrated both neutral markets and British spheres of influence. Up till now, Britain had been the dominant exporter, India being her single most important market. It is therefore not surprising that the increase in exports of Japanese textiles to the latter became a focus of Anglo-Japanese commercial conflict during this period. Table 1.15 shows the cotton market in India. The increase in Anglo-Japanese competition at this time was exacerbated by a shrinking of the import market for textiles, owing to the development of the Indian cotton industry. In the early 1930s in particular, however, while Britain experienced a rapid loss of markets, Japan was able to retain its market to a certain extent. The rapid increase in competition damaged Japanese relations with Britain and India, causing the latter to reinforce its restrictions against imports of

Table 1.15 India's domestic production and imports of cotton piece-goods (in million yards and %)

Fiscal year	*Imports from*			
	Britain	*Japan*	*Total imports*	*Domestic production*
1910/14 (average)	2809 (97.3)	5 (0.2)	2886	2096*
1923/24	1319 (88.8)	123 (8.3)	1486	2707
1926/27	1457 (82.5)	244 (13.8)	1767	3591
1929/30	1248 (65.0)	562 (29.2)	1919	3777
1932/33	551 (47.6)	552 (47.6)	1156	4671
1935/36	439 (46.4)	496 (52.4)	946	5160

Sources: For 1911/14–1926/27, F. Utley, *Lancashire and the Far East* (London: Allen & Unwin, 1931), pp. 258–9, 286; For 1929/30–1935/36, Gaimusho (ed.), *Tsusho Joyaku to Tsusho Seisaku no Hensen* (Tokyo: Gaimusho, 1951), p. 895.
Notes: Figures for domestic production in India are a total of mill and handloom production.
* means the annual average for 1909/10–1913/14.

Japanese textiles. In March 1930, faced with increasing imports, the government of India increased the duties on cotton textiles originating in countries outside the British Empire. In April and September 1931, and in August 1932, the minimum specific duty on plain grey goods was further increased to 50 per cent ad valorem or 5 annas per lb. In April 1933 the government of India issued the Safeguarding of Industries Act, and gave Japan notice that it was going to terminate the Indo-Japanese commercial treaty of 1904; in June it increased the duties on all foreign cotton goods to 75 per cent ad valorem. These measures were aimed primarily against Japan, and the Japan Cotton Spinners' Association reacted with a boycott against the purchase of Indian cotton.[99]

Meanwhile in Britain, a 'Special Committee on Japanese Competition' had been formed by the Manchester Chamber of Commerce in December 1932. This recommended that the government should denounce the Anglo-Japanese commercial treaty of 1911. Even so, Britain planned to hold 'tripartite conversations' on the world textile market in conjunction with both India and Japan, but the actual negotiations took place on a bilateral basis. In September 1933, official negotiations between India and Japan opened in Simla. The British Foreign Office instructed G.B. Sansom, then commercial counsellor at the British Embassy in Tokyo, to proceed to India to advise the government there.[100] The Indo-Japanese negotiations were completed early in January 1934, and an agreement was signed in London that July. The agreement, which was valid until March 1937, was on a barter basis: Japan could export 400 million yards of cotton textiles to India, provided that she imported 1.5 million bales of Indian cotton in return. The ad valorem duty on Japanese piece goods was to be reduced from 75 per cent to 50 per cent. The Japan Cotton Spinners' Association suspended its boycott of Indian cotton, and, in March 1934, the Japan Export Association of Cotton Textiles to India was set up as a control organization to supervise the agreement.

In April 1933 the British government had proposed a meeting of British and Japanese industrialists in London to discuss their competition in cotton textiles on a world scale. T.M. Snow, British Ambassador to Tokyo, felt that the real solution would be to stabilize the political situation in China; this would provide an assured market for Japanese goods and diminish competition from them elsewhere.[101] Formal Anglo-Japanese negotiations took place in February and March 1934.[102] The fundamental difference in approach between Britain and Japan had already become clear at an informal meeting of Anglo-Japanese industrialists held at Simla in November 1933. Negotiations became deadlocked at the start on the question of the geographical area to be covered by the discussions. The British delegation emphasized that the increasing volume of low-priced Japanese exports was destabilizing the world market, preventing other countries from restoring their purchasing power. The Japanese side replied that the British proposal was 'very one-sided', and insisted that the economic stability of the world textile market could not be restored merely by restricting Japanese exports; Japan's success was 'the natural outcome of Japan's ability' to reduce production costs in order to adjust to its reduced buying power. The response of the Manchester Chamber of Commerce's Special Committee to this fiasco was to urge the government to introduce import quotas immediately. The Association of British Chambers of Commerce also called upon the British government to take action against Japanese competition. Early in May the British government announced that import quotas on foreign cotton and artificial silk textiles were to be introduced in British colonies and Protectorates.[103]

Trade negotiations also started between Japan and Australia at the beginning of 1935, but the lack of progress put a strain on commercial relations between the two countries. The Australian government imposed high tariffs on Japanese goods, including cotton cloth, in May 1936, and Japan responded in the following month by introducing a system of import permits for Australian wool and wheat. At the end of that year a commercial agreement was signed, but trade did not return to its former volume.[104]

The increased protectionism that Japan was encountering was a natural response to the successful export drive that had brought her so rapidly out of the Depression. Its failure to consider the effect of the push to increase exports of cotton textiles on other producer countries inevitably provoked protective measures against Japanese goods from the very countries which formed her main markets. In time, therefore, the very vigour of the export drive paradoxically had the effect of limiting her exports.

Shipping competition in Asia

Shipping rivalry was another major issue in the trade disagreements between Japan and western countries. Legislation for the expansion of shipping routes and ship construction in 1896, and the provision of shipping subsidies in 1910, resulted in an expansion of regular shipping services by Japanese ships to Europe and North America. Up until the First World War, the two regular shipping companies of NYK and Osaka Shosen led the Japanese shipping industry. Following the commencement of its Japan–Bombay line in 1893, NYK expanded its network to Europe, North America and Asia. In 1896 it started a regular service to Antwerp via London, opening a London office. NYK concluded a temporary agreement with the Far Eastern Conference led by British shipping firms including P&O, but NYK ships were not allowed to call at the port of London on the way back to Japan until 1899.[105] In 1896 NYK also opened lines to Seattle and to Australia, followed by a line to Calcutta in 1911, to New York via the Panama Canal in 1916, and to Hamburg in 1919. Osaka Shosen, which became overall leader of the Japanese shipping industry in the interwar period, expanded its long-distance routes, opening a Hong Kong–Tacoma line in 1909, and a line to Bombay in 1913. The former was extended to Singapore in 1918, when a line joining Yokohama to London was also begun. In 1904, 53 per cent of the vessels entering Japanese ports were British and only 10 per cent Japanese, but by 1914 these proportions had been reversed, with Japan dominant at 54 per cent and Britain reduced to 28 per cent.[106]

During the First World War, the Japanese shipping industry rapidly developed and expanded its shipping routes. For instance, a shortage in tonnage belonging to the Blue Funnel Line, which had up till now monopolized sea cargoes between the British west coast and the Far East, led the British government to propose that NYK call at ports along the west coast such as Liverpool and Birkenhead. In 1920, the Blue Funnel Line proposed a suspension of this carrying trade, but finally agreed with NYK that it should continue.[107]

Table 1.16 shows the number and gross tonnage of ships by nationality from 1905 to 1939. Britain continued to have the largest share, although her share gradually declined. During the interwar period world trade declined, causing a global surplus of shipping capacity. Despite this, Japan consolidated provision along its most important trade routes and also increased the number of vessels. In this field, therefore, Anglo-Japanese competition took on the guise of a Japanese challenge to British domination of major shipping routes. Gross tonnage of Japanese vessels increased, although even in 1939 Japanese tonnage was only a third of Britain's. A 1939 report of the Imperial Shipping Committee named *British Shipping in the Orient* gives a vivid picture of Anglo-Japanese shipping competition during this period. The report pointed to the decline in value of the yen and the low standard of living in Japan, and to the efficient organization of the Japanese economy, but also stated that it was virtually impossible to calculate the extent to which Japan had contributed to the decline of British shipping in Asia.[108]

During the period under consideration Japan's main trade partner was the United States, with raw silk as the main export and iron, raw cotton and machinery as the main imports. A breakdown of ships engaged in Asian–American trade around 1930 by country of origin shows that Britain, Japan and the United States had equal shares of around 30 per cent, but that Japanese ships had a dominant share of 60 per cent in trade with Japan.[109] The British firms with shipping networks from Britain and the European continent to Japan and China via Southeast Asia were P&O, Alfred Holt, Glen & Shire, Ben, Ellerman and Blue Star. Their main Japanese rivals, such as NYK, Osaka Shosen and Kokusai Kisen, belonged to various overlapping shipping agreements, but even in areas where there were price arrangements, fierce competition apparently still existed. British vessels had complete dominance in trade between Britain and its colonies and in the China trade. Even on routes between Japan and Europe, of a total tonnage

Table 1.16 Number and gross tonnage of vessels by nationality (in thousand tons)

Flag	*United Kingdom*			*British Dominions*			*Japanese*			*Total*	
Year	*No.*	*Gross tonnage*	*Percentage by tonnage*	*No.*	*Gross tonnage*	*Percentage by tonnage*	*No.*	*Gross tonnage*	*Percentage by tonnage*	*No.*	*Gross tonnage*
1905	9348	15 803	45.7	2017	1207	3.5	691	871	2.5	29 120	34 601
1910	9417	17 516	44.2	2078	1496	3.8	846	1147	2.9	29 337	39 628
1915	9285	19 541	41.6	2068	1733	3.7	1155	1826	3.9	30 043	46 923
1920	8561	18 330	33.3	2270	2252	4.1	1940	2996	5.4	30 992	55 073
1925	8559	19 441	31.2	2430	2781	4.5	2087	3920	6.3	32 380	62 273
1930	8238	20 438	30.5	2516	2943	4.4	2060	4317	6.4	32 138	67 049
1935	7349	17 400	27.9	2483	3111	5.0	2145	4086	6.6	30 409	62 303
1939	7009	17 984	26.9	2479	3231	4.8	2337	5630	8.4	30 649	66 901

Sources: *Lloyd's Register of Shipping*, corresponding years.
Notes: Vessels include steam, motor and sailing vessels of 100 tons gross and upwards; United States (Great Lakes) and Japanese sailing vessels are not included.

of 1556000 gross tons in 1937, the breakdown worked out at 284000 gross tons for Blue Funnel, 236000 for NYK and 206000 for P&O.[110]

The routes of the greatest concern to the Imperial Shipping Committee were the India–Japan and Japan–Australia lines.[111] The two most important routes to India, the lines to Bombay and Calcutta, came second to the United States in Japanese trade. The main return cargo on the Japan–Bombay line was raw cotton. In 1896, NYK joined a shipping agreement for the Bombay line, which P&O had formed with two other companies, and Osaka Shosen also joined in 1913. The share of the British members fell from 68 per cent in 1888 to 50 per cent in 1896, and to 28 per cent in 1913, while the Japanese share rose from 18 per cent in 1896 to 40 per cent in 1913, and 92 per cent in 1937. On the Japan–Calcutta line, the British India Steam Navigation Co. and the Indo-China Steam Navigation Co. (also British) were dominant until 1911, when the entry of NYK led to a price war. In 1918, the three companies formed the Calcutta shipping agreement and in 1921 they were joined by Osaka Shosen. The main cargoes to Japan were pig iron and jute. In 1914 the ratio of British to Japanese vessels was 66:34 per cent, but by 1937 the share of Japan's vessels had risen to 53 per cent.[112]

Japanese trade with Australia comprised mainly imports of wool, wheat and zinc in return for exports of textiles such as cotton and silk cloth. Routes to Australia were served by the (British) Eastern and Australian Line (E&A), but in 1895 it was joined by NYK, and in 1916 by Osaka Shosen and the Japan Australian Line (JAL), which had been formed under the joint management of Yamashita Kisen, Kawasaki Kisen and Kokusai Kisen. Disputes arose over the share of cargoes of Australian wool carried by the members of the shipping agreement between NYK, Osaka Shosen, JAL and E&A. An understanding was finally reached in 1938, according to which the three Japanese firms obtained a joint share of 77.5 per cent and E&A the remaining 22.5 per cent.[113] Japanese shipping firms made great efforts to develop the routes, but the collapse in prices and sharp fall in cargoes caused by the Great Depression forced them to run at a loss. In 1937, however, Japanese ships carried 85 per cent of the traffic on Japan–Australia routes.[114]

Another element noted as a threat to the position of English shipping was the appearance of third-party carriers such as Japan in the transport of crude rubber from the Straits Settlements to the United States. Six British firms, including Alfred Holt and Ellerman, had concluded an agreement with the American firm of Dallar, but in 1934 two Japanese firms, the shipping division of Mitsui Bussan and Kokusai Kisen, applied for membership. Immediately after becoming members, the Japanese firms only carried around 10 per cent of America-bound cargoes of rubber, but Mitsui Bussan seized control of the rubber trade by buying up rubber at high prices and selling it cheaply in the United States. At the end of 1935, therefore, the Japanese share of cargoes had reached around 50 per cent. Not surprisingly, this led to friction with other members of the agreement.[115]

The weakening of economic relations, 1937–1941

These sources of tension mainly revolved around competition in third markets. Throughout the decade up to the commencement of war in December 1941, direct economic and business links between the two countries remained relatively limited. In the case of commodity trade, for example, Britain's share of Japan's total imports declined steadily from just over 5 per cent in 1931–2 to less than 3 per cent in 1936–8. From 1939 it was less than 1 per cent. Over the same years Britain's share of Japanese exports fluctuated between 3 and 5.5 per cent, again declining dramatically in 1940–1. Such figures paled into insignificance besides the 30 per cent share of the US in Japan's imports, and its 21 per cent of the country's exports.[116] The significance of direct trade with Japan for the British economy was even less. By the early 1930s exports to Japan were accounting for less than 1 per cent of total British exports, and were down to just over 0.2 per cent by 1938.[117] The activities of British business in Japan and its empire underwent a relative decline as the Japanese regime moved towards more overt restrictions and economic controls, and as Britain failed to offer Japan the new technology that the country increasingly sought in its overseas links. As we have seen, after 1931 the UK no longer served as the avenue for Japanese government loan issues, and a loan raised on the London market for the South Manchurian Railway in 1933 was the last to a Japanese corporation. Japanese corporations represented in London declined from a 1927 peak, and while some British locations continued to play host to a small Japanese commercial community, their prominence declined over the 1930s.[118] Such direct links, however, were only a relatively small part of Anglo-Japanese economic relations during the decade. It has been demonstrated that what pushed these relations in the direction of friction and disagreements was conflict over economic issues in other regions, notably the British Empire, China and Manchuria. Anglo-Japanese economic and business relations during the 1930s developed against the broader backdrop of rising protectionism in the international economy, Japan's rapid recovery from depression and her increasing dominance in Asia, and the declining international competitiveness of large parts of British manufacturing.

The political and economic environment in the 1930s was essentially hostile to western business involvement in the Japanese economy, and this resulted in a diminution of activity on the part of British firms even from the relatively low levels of investment that had existed previously. Restrictions on foreign business activity included the passing of exchange control laws that made it impossible to repatriate to Britain the proceeds of any sale of equity in a Japanese subsidiary.[119] Legislation of 1936 stipulated that only companies with over 50 per cent Japanese-owned equity were permitted to assemble or manufacture motor cars in Japan,[120] indicative of the growing wish to retain control even when desirous of acquiring foreign technology. Whereas in 1937 over half of all Japanese marine and fire reinsurance was placed in London, by 1941 almost all had been redirected to the domestic market.[121] By the latter half of the 1930s British investment in Japan was almost as insignificant as Japanese investment in Britain. As Manchuria, formerly a significant destination for foreign investment (and one where the Japanese had positively encouraged such investment), came under tighter Japanese control, there too western businesses found themselves gradually squeezed out. Restrictive Japanese policies combined with a perceived inability on the part of Britain to offer new technological expertise rather than old, weakened the attraction of Japan for the British and discouraged Japanese business from seeking stronger links.

For related reasons the decade also witnessed a decline in the activities of British banks in Japan. Financial and commercial exchanges diminished over time, with an accelerated decline in 1939–40, although many merchant banks were unwilling to distance themselves from Japan even when business became more difficult. Although Japan made use of the facilities of the London market to support its commercial and shipping activities in the mid-1930s, that use declined, and after the conclusion of the Tripartite Pact in September 1940 the London discount market was regarded as virtually closed to Japan.[122] By the end of 1940 the four remaining private Japanese banks with London branches had closed them, leaving their affairs to be handled by the Yokohama Specie Bank.[123] Even before the imposition of sanctions in the summer of 1941, therefore, financial interaction had been in decline. One factor in this was the altered situation in world trade, and the implications that this had for both the British and Japanese balance of payments. Notwithstanding the import of a considerable volume of raw materials from empire territories such as British India and Malaya, Japan had growing trade surpluses with the sterling bloc, and there was concern in Britain that the spending of these surpluses in the dollar area would lead to a destabilization of sterling.[124] It proved impossible to conclude a Payments Agreement between the two countries, but as late as June 1941 the Japanese authorities sought to establish a new exchange arrangement to encourage trade between Japan and the sterling area, which had fallen off considerably in 1939–41, an arrangement identified as 'a typical compromise' between Japan's desire for increased trade and her concern not to prejudice her position vis-à-vis her Axis partners.[125] Such concerns over the significance of Japanese trade for the position of sterling were to re-emerge even more strongly in the early postwar years. It should be noted, however, that the blocking of Japanese assets later in 1941 as one of the countermeasures to Japanese aggression was closely related to these concerns. While it is the embargo on oil and other supplies implemented at the same time that has invariably received attention, it was recognized at the time that freezing the assets was essentially

> to submit to the control of the American and British authorities the financial machinery through which trade between Japan and the sterling and dollar areas must be financed. Control of that machine provides the quickest and most effective method of controlling that trade. It renders unnecessary the promulgation of specific embargoes on the export of this or that commodity.[126]

The freezing of the assets was therefore aimed at laying the basis for a commercial embargo on Japan, and was supplemented by orders freezing Chinese dollar and sterling assets. As expected, the Japanese government immediately responded with a similar blocking of British assets in territories under its control, which were considerably greater.

Public opinion and government response

While currency and financial concerns were an issue in Anglo-Japanese economic relations, however, the exchange issue was essentially thrown into prominence by the growth of Japan's export trade. While in 1937 Japan still accounted for only 6.9 per cent of world manufactured exports, compared with the 20.9 per cent of Britain,[127] it became apparent that Japanese competition was making itself felt in relation to particular commodities and particular regions. In terms of direct trade between the two countries, 1933 marked a major transition, as the surplus on commodity trade with Japan that Britain had consistently enjoyed since the 1870s (with the exception of the First World War years) was transformed to a deficit. More serious in its implications, because of the greater volume of trade, was the impact on British interests of competition in third markets. The main conflicts over Japanese export success in parts of the British Empire and other markets have been discussed above. What is evident is that during the 1930s the growth in Japanese exports of a range of commodities, from cotton piece-goods through to bicycles, lightbulbs and a number of others, threatened the British share in a number of markets. The growth in Japanese exports was supported by productivity increases, a devalued currency and, in some instances, close government-private sector cooperation.[128] The availability of cheap Japanese goods was particularly appealing to populations whose already low purchasing power had been further reduced by depression. From the 1930s the Board of Trade in Britain began to receive complaints from manufacturers of commodities as disparate as wool, rayon, wires, cutlery, bicycles, electric fans, soap and cement.[129] Among the businesses damaged by the Japanese devaluation of the early 1930s was the hardware manufacturing firm of Kenricks, which faced competition from Japanese rice bowls, tumblers and chamber pots.[130] Concerns were also expressed that Japanese goods were underselling British ones in UK markets. Disquiet was again felt among a wide range of producers, of toys, telescopes, rubber footwear, electric lamps, brushes and hosiery. While the amount of imports was not, as we have seen, enormous, the low prices offered by the Japanese rang alarm bells among British manufacturers, who felt that they could never hope to compete with such prices.[131]

In British eyes the advance of Japanese cotton exports into third markets hitherto dominated by British products appeared to be at the cost of a British industry that had long enjoyed enormous political influence. The result was a systematic campaign to increase measures of protection and exclusion against Japanese goods, whether through quotas, tariff barriers or other means, and, when such pressures were unsuccessful, attempts to vilify Japan's 'unfair competition' and 'cheap labour' policies. In Britain's colonial territories the earlier 'open door' policy was progressively abandoned in favour of tariff and quota barriers, while in other areas, such as the Middle East, Britain exerted considerable pressure to have tariff and other barriers set in Lancashire's favour. In most cases, however, such measures, where introduced, tended to favour indigenous producers rather than work in the interests of Lancashire. In some cases British colonies promoted restrictions on Japanese imports for their own interests. It has been noted how British India in 1933 requested denunciation of the Indo-Japanese Commercial Treaty of 1904, while other parts of the empire sought to impose tariffs, in line with the Ottawa agreements on imperial preference of 1932.[132] The continuation of substantial Japanese trade with Britain's Asian empire reflected not just Japan's need of Asian raw materials, such as rubber and cotton, and the attractiveness of Japanese goods to the inhabitants of these countries, but also Britain's declining ability to sacrifice the welfare of its colonial territories to the interests of its own domestic producers. Consistently the British government failed to unite against pressures from British business for stronger protective measures. Although Japanese trade consistently shifted towards its own empire during the decade, trade with the British colonies continued to play a major role through to 1939. In 1935 nearly one-third of Japan's import–export trade was with the British Empire, while British India alone accounted for over 11 per cent of Japanese exports and over 12 per cent of the country's imports.[133] Shipping, as we have seen, was the other major concern. By 1939 it was estimated that over two-thirds of British–Japanese trade in the east was carried in Japanese ships.[134]

It should be noted that these British concerns mainly revolved around the issue of the balance of visible trade, in which Japan enjoyed a bilateral surplus from 1933. The Japanese were more inclined to emphasize the significance of invisibles, in which Japan did not enjoy a similar advantage. This British emphasis on the importance of commodity trade was also to characterize the relationship between the two economies in the latter half of the twentieth century.

Conflicts over economic interests in China and Manchuria, though not British spheres of interest in the same way as the empire, were, as we have seen, similarly fractious. British capital had been dominant in China, particularly in the Shanghai international settlement, and was threatened by Japanese efforts to assert dominance. The instability of the Chinese currency was a major factor in the lack of international currency stabilization. The China market remained to many businesses the 'holy grail' of the large unexploited market, notwithstanding the internal unrest and international conflicts of the decade, and both countries had invested heavily there. The Japanese takeover of Manchuria ultimately led to some British firms being eased out of Manchuria. Among those excluded were leading oil companies and the Jardine engineering group.[135]

Attempts to find an amicable solution to these disagreements were present, but ultimately proved unsuccessful. The 1933 World Economic Conference in London could not be regarded as a success. In 1934 the Federation of British Industry sent a mission to Japan and Manchukuo to discuss cooperation over Chinese economic issues. The mission was supported by British producers interested in the Manchurian market, but encountered a mixed Japanese response on whether the British should be welcomed in the territory, and engendered few concrete results. The 1936 Leith-Ross mission marked a further failure of cooperation.[136] In 1937 Japanese industrialists sent a mission to the West for discussions with British financial and industrial leaders, but progress was halted by the almost immediate occurrence of the Marco Polo Bridge incident.[137] In both government and private attempts at cooperation textiles acted as a major impediment to agreement. The cotton trade was far from being the only bone of contention, but it was invariably the one most vociferously debated.

In general British government policy failed to deliver on Lancashire's demands. While the Board of Trade invariably campaigned in favour of Britain's producers, the Foreign Office and other members of the Cabinet tended to take a more moderate stance. It is apparent that there existed similar tensions and cases of intransigence on the Japanese side, and it has been suggested that after around 1934 Japanese officials and industrialists accepted that trade discrimination was not a critical priority in foreign policy; economic questions were essentially neutralised due to British moderation and Japanese acceptance of it.[138] Nor was British opinion outside government united in support of the Lancashire line. Even within Lancashire there were those who understood that Japan's competitiveness was in part due to technological advances and improved organization. From the publication of Arno Pearse's above-mentioned report for the International Cotton Federation in 1929, through the 1930s a number of attempts were made to 'rehabilitate' the reputation of the Japanese cotton industry as a 'fair' competitor.[139] Platt & Co. of Oldham had in 1929 purchased Toyoda Sakichi's patents on the automatic loom in Europe for £83 500,[140] while in May 1932, Sir Walter Preston, who had visited Japan the same year, publicly recommended that Lancashire be remodelled on Japanese lines.[141]

Those who had taken the trouble to find out more about Japan tended to be more sympathetic to Japan's need to export in the light of the growth of its population and its lack of raw materials.[142] In an address to Chatham House in early 1934, the economist T.E. Gregory warned against being alarmist about Japan undercutting Britain everywhere, emphasizing that Japan was doing a favour to some populations by making very cheap goods available, for example rubber boots in India. He strongly criticized the FBI for issuing a misleading pamphlet entitled 'The Menace of Japanese Capitalism' the previous year, and urged his audience to remember that Japan was an importer as well as an exporter. Under such circumstances, Gregory argued, protectionism was both ineffective and undesirable and what was needed was trade agreements over market shares.[143] Efforts to acquaint British and other foreign businessmen with the Japanese perspective included the publication by the Japanese Foreign Office of the journal *Contemporary Japan*. In April 1937 the Birmingham Chamber of Commerce's monthly journal printed large extracts from an Osaka Mainichi publication entitled *Japan Today and Tomorrow*, though without comment.[144] Receipt of this publication by the Birmingham authorities suggests that Japan was making a serious effort to reach business opinion in the United Kingdom. Later the same year the same journal discussed an article analysing the strains placed on Japan's economy by the war in China,[145] while subsequent issues reported on articles published in the *Journal of the Kobe University of Commerce* and the *Japan Trade Review*.[146]

Other commentators went further by implicitly criticising Britain in the light of the Japanese experience. W.L. Hichens, a member of the Imperial Shipping Committee, speaking in 1939, attributed Japanese competitive success to subsidies, 'scrap and build' policies, currency depreciation, a lower standard of living, better organization, government backing, and merchants and shippers working together. The British, he believed, should learn from Japan. His concluding remarks were reported as follows:

> What he had said about the Japanese he had not meant in any critical spirit. On the whole they had done what they were perfectly entitled to do. Occasionally, perhaps, they had done what many business men were sometimes apt to do, namely observe the letter of an agreement and use all their ingenuity to get round the spirit of it. Their success was due to their great activity and superior organisation. The British Empire could not hope to meet Japanese competition in the future unless it had a more active and vigorous organisation than it had had in the past.[147]

In the climate of the 1930s, however, such statements were open to criticism as being excessively pro-Japanese. Nor was Japanese opinion on the conduct of economic relations with Britain by any means uncompromising and monolithic. In January 1937 Yuki Toyotaro, President of the Tokyo Chamber of Commerce and Industry, called for cooperation in China between the Japanese and British business communities. Yuki subsequently served as Finance Minister in the shortlived Hayashi cabinet later in the year. His cabinet colleague, Foreign Minister Sato Naotake, was reported as believing that economic friction resulted from large exports of cheap Japanese textile products to British colonies, so Japan needed to have greater respect for Britain's traditional interests in China.[148] Such conciliatory views, particularly when held by somewhat transient politicians, made little headway in the face of mounting political tensions.

The start of Britain's conflict with Germany imposed new pressures on the already strained economic relationship with Japan. Although Japan was not yet a member of the Axis pact, Britain's policy of economic warfare against Germany required both restrictions on the ability of neutrals to trade with Germany and more control over raw materials from the Empire. Britain had already considered sanctions against Japan in the summer of 1939 in response to the Tianjin crisis, and the moves adopted as part of this policy restricted Japan's already limited access to raw materials.[149] On the Japanese side it was felt that British economic support of China was helping to postpone Japanese victory over Chiang Kai-shek. Talks aimed at resolving the issue during the summer of 1940 failed to deliver agreement, and in the autumn of that year a cabinet committee was established to enforce restrictions on trade, but with a view to avoiding anything so drastic as might provoke Japan to stronger action. The measures included prohibitions on the supply to Japan of some crucial items such as nickel, and restrictions on some others.[150] From the time that the possibilities of sanctions were first discussed there was an awareness in Britain that they could be counterproductive. Sir Robert Craigie, Britain's ambassador, noted in the spring of 1941 that 'to extend restrictions on Japanese imports to an extent that would force Japan to draw on her reserves on any considerable scale would at present be liable to produce those very actions we wish to avoid'.[151] These reservations were shared by Neville Chamberlain:

> If economic sanctions were ineffective they amounted to nothing more than pinpricks. If, on the other hand, they were effective, then the country against whom they were applied might be stung to retaliate. In effect, the kernel of the position as he saw it was that, before deciding to apply sanctions, one must be prepared if necessary to use force.[152]

The sanctions of July 1941 were a major departure on the previous more conservative British policy, and, as is clear, helped to generate precisely that response. The sanctions did not of themselves preclude the possibility of any trade between the two countries, but limited it both through licensing and through the availability of funds. However, the volume of trade had declined to almost nothing well before the outbreak of war in December, 1941.

It is not the function of this introduction to identify the role played by economic pressures in the path to war, which has been analysed by more than one of the papers in volume 2 of this series. Historians' views of their significance have ranged from identifying them as no more than a background irritant, to the key issue that symbolized Japan's position as a 'have-not' nation and the West's inability or unwillingness to address the problems that provoked Japan's quest for autarky and economic security.[153] What is apparent is that many Japanese felt that Britain was unwilling to understand its aspirations and the pressures that it faced. Deputy Foreign Minister Amau, for example, complained in September 1941 that 'the spontaneous expansion of Japanese people or goods always encounters opposition from the British', while two years earlier, in March 1938, Ishibashi Tanzan had argued that Britain was a 'have' nation unwilling to open her territories to 'have-nots' like Japan.[154] On the British side there is likewise evidence of a persistent reluctance to make concessions to Japan, and an unwillingness to acknowledge the legitimacy of Japanese competition, the increasing dominance of the United States in Asian affairs, and the declining economic and political power of Britain herself. While the outbreak of war suspended these frictions by causing a cessation of economic and business interaction, these same issues re-emerged as the backdrop to Anglo-Japanese economic relations in the years after 1945.

The long postwar in Anglo-Japanese economic and business relations, 1945–2000

Britain and occupied Japan, 1945–1952

The economic links between Britain and Japan that had been severed during the years of war were only slowly rebuilt after Japan's defeat. Issues such as reparations, payment mechanisms, currency exchange rates, as well as shortages and problems in both economies, were compounded by restrictions placed on Japan's international economic activities by the Occupation authorities. Without some trade, though, any rebuilding of the Japanese economy appeared a forlorn hope, and even during the first two years of Occupation, when reform and demilitarization rather than recovery were the watchwords, Japan had begun to exchange commodities with a number of countries. Initial trade was tightly controlled, and it was not until August 1947 that a reluctant SCAP agreed to reopen Japan to private foreign trade, and then only under strict conditions. With such a prospect in view *The Economist* noted:

> There does not seem to be any economic reason why there should not be a considerable trade between this country and Japan, but if the conditions of commerce are to remain as now laid down, a business trip to Japan will be almost as much of a hazard as it was in the time of Queen Elizabeth.[155]

The belief that a revival of trade with Japan was 'hampered by complicated procedure' better suited to the needs of US businessmen than to Britons anxious to revive their prewar interests was echoed elsewhere.[156]

Later in 1947 a party of British businessmen visited Japan under the auspices of the Board of Trade,[157] and a year later Japanese exporters were permitted to conclude direct contracts with foreign buyers. In May of that year a UK Chamber of Commerce in Japan opened in Tokyo, and the British government made considerable efforts to support British traders anxious to re-enter the Japanese market.[158] Not until the beginning of 1950, however, were imports returned to a private basis, and with foreign exchange restricted a tight import programme continued to operate. For much of the Occupation period dealing with Japan remained problematic at a basic level. A review of commercial conditions in Japan published by British representatives in Tokyo in 1950 recounted the bureaucratic barriers to businessmen wishing to visit Japan, the limited availability of accommodation and the problems imposed by travelling on crowded railway trains, although it was noted that 'business men are permitted to travel on the special coaches operated by the Allied Forces against payment in yen'.[159] Prior to the stabilization of the yen in 1949 much of the little trade that existed took place on a barter basis, and while a series of payments and trade agreements sought to iron out exchange difficulties, they were no more than short-term measures, as will be shown below. Not until 1950 did the Foreign Investment Law permit foreign investment in Japan. This law gave the government powers to screen international licensing agreements to ensure conformity with national policy goals.[160] It was the same year that the London market resumed offering credit to Japanese borrowers or agents.[161] The first British bank to re-establish itself in Tokyo was the Hongkong and Shanghai Bank, in 1947. By 1950 it had been joined by the Chartered Bank of India, Australia and China, and the Mercantile Bank of India, but the Japanese banks did not return to London until the early 1950s.

As before the war, direct trade with Britain remained relatively small (Figure 1.4). Japanese trade accounted for well under 1 per cent of Britain's total trade during the Occupation years, and British exports to Japan – most importantly woollen fabrics, motor vehicles and ships – never accounted for more than 1.5 per cent of total Japanese imports (Figures 1.5 and 1.6). The one exception was Japanese exports to Britain, most significantly cotton textiles and wood products, which in 1948–50 accounted for 6–7 per cent of all Japan's exports.[162] A major reason for this upsurge was, ironically, the

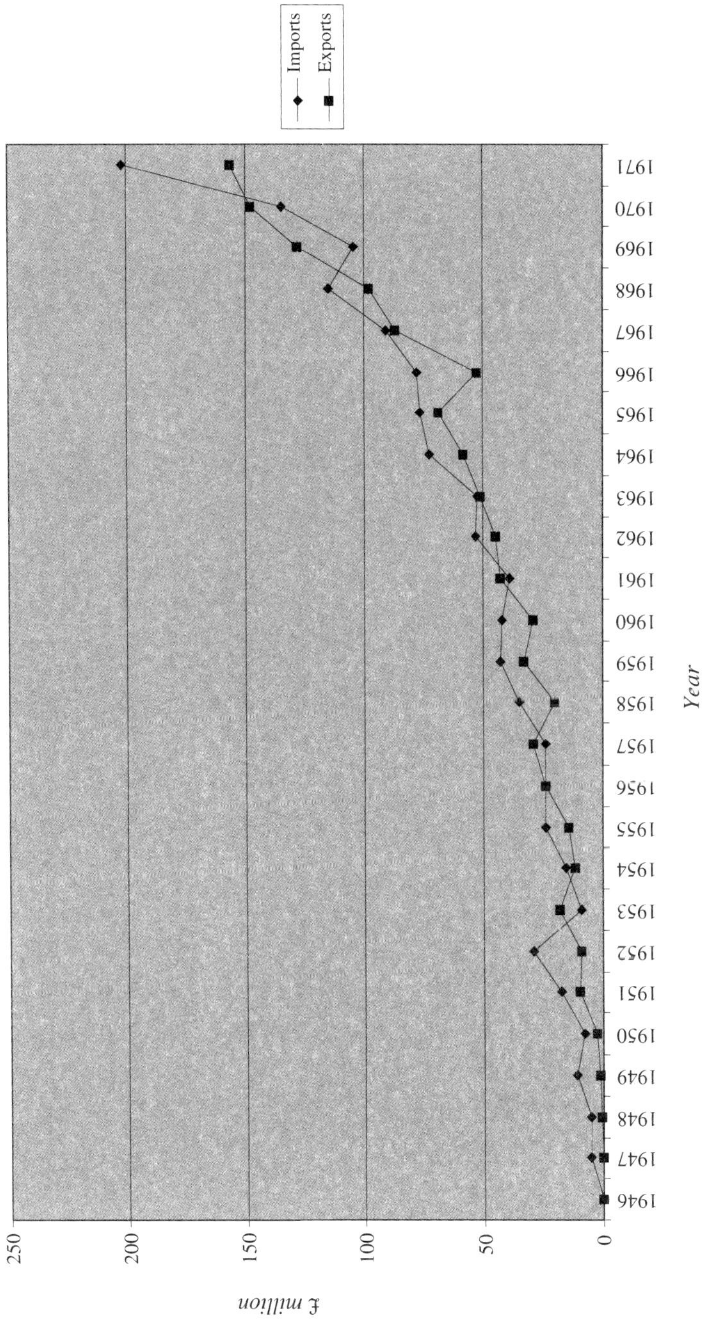

Sources: B.R. Mitchell, *British Historical Statistics* (Cambridge: Cambridge University Press, 1988), p. 514; HMSO and Office for National Statistics, *Annual Abstract of Statistics* (London, annually).

Figure 1.4 British trade with Japan 1946–1971 (by value, current prices)

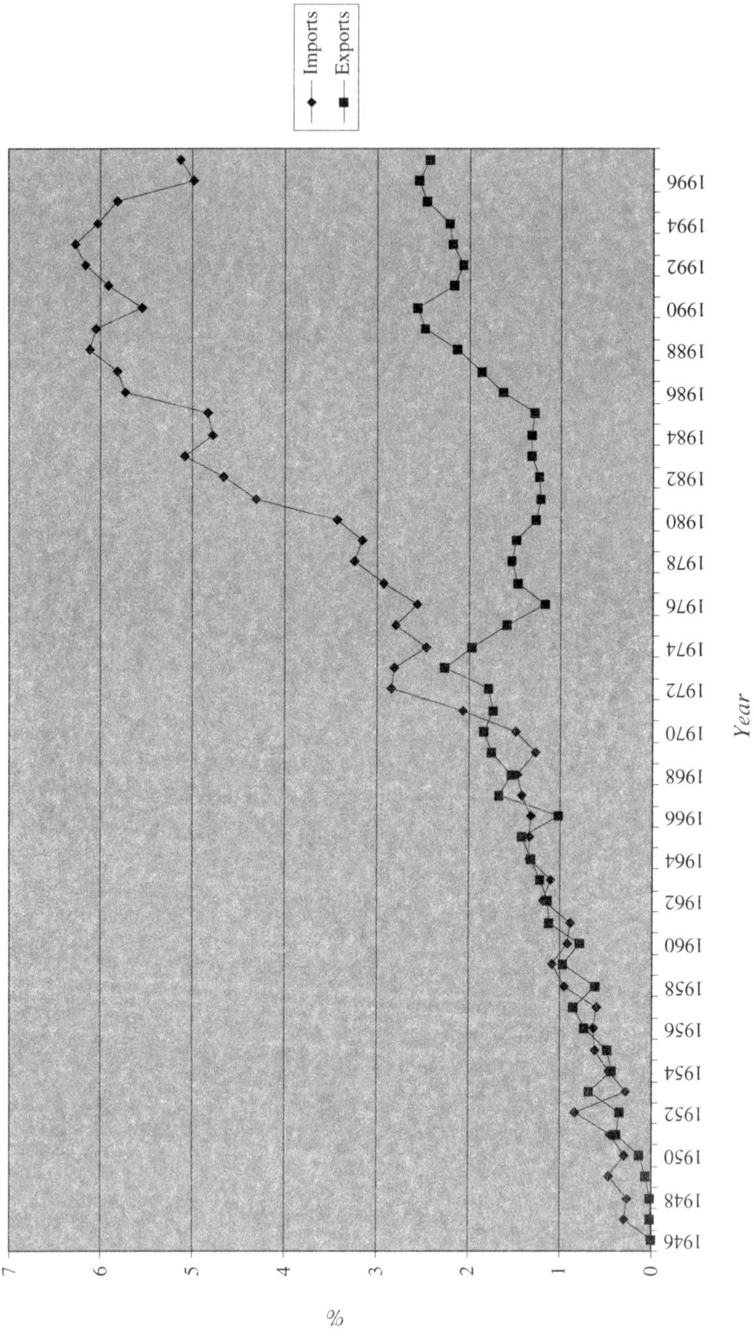

Sources: Calculated from B.R. Mitchell, *British Historical Statistics* (Cambridge: Cambridge University Press, 1988); HMSO and Office for National Statistics, *Annual Abstract of Statistics* (London, annually).

Figure 1.5 Japanese share of British imports and exports, 1946–1997 (by value, current prices)

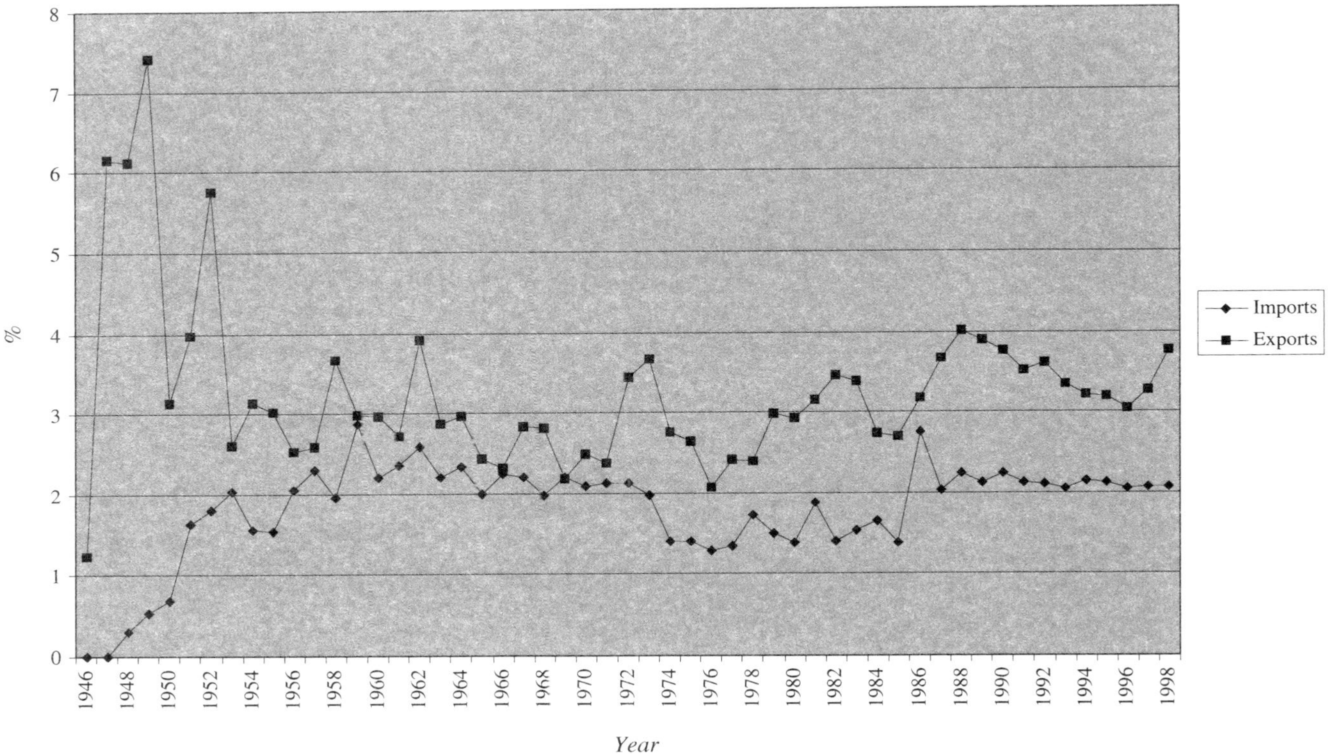

Sources: Calculated from Nihon Tokei Kyokai, *Nihon Choki Tokei Soran* (5 vols, Tokyo: Nihon Tokei Kyokai, 1988), vol. 3, pp. 77–86; Japan Tariff Association, *The Summary Report on Trade of Japan* (Tokyo, annually); Japan Tariff Association, *Japan Exports and Imports* (Tokyo: Japan Tariff Association, Dec. 1997 and Dec. 1998).

Figure 1.6 British share of total Japanese imports and exports, 1946–1998 (by value, current prices)

inability of the Lancashire cotton industry to produce and finish sufficient cloth for colonial export markets due to fuel and other shortages. Following a Cotton Board mission to Japan in 1946, a substantial amount of Japanese cloth was imported for finishing in Lancashire.[163] That the price of these finished textiles was higher than that of similar products finished in Japan itself was of major concern, and threatened serious problems once colonial markets were able to purchase direct from Japan.[164] Payment was, moreover, made in dollars, which raised currency issues that will be returned to below. Overall, Japan enjoyed a surplus on commodity trade with Britain during these years, but in services Britain retained an edge. It is estimated that in 1946–7 British ships carried around two-thirds of the commercial cargo imported into Japan.[165]

Far more significant for bilateral relations, though, was the resumption of Japanese trade with other countries of the sterling area, notably British colonies in Asia. During the years 1945–8 around one-quarter of Japan's exports went to sterling area countries, but these countries provided less than 10% of Japan's imports, well over half of which came from the dollar area.[166] With an inconvertible yen expenditure on foreign currencies had to be avoided, and special arrangements had to be made to cope with this pattern of trading. When in August 1946 Britain suspended the convertibility of sterling, any surplus enjoyed by Japan could no longer be converted into dollars. This posed a dilemma for SCAP, since it meant that Japanese products (especially textiles) sold in Southeast Asian sterling countries were no longer a source of dollars to pay for raw materials.[167] Initial demands that Japan's textile exports to the sterling area be paid for in dollars to cover these raw materials purchases were eventually withdrawn after negotiation, and November 1947 witnessed the first of a series of agreements designed to counter this problem. The commercial press sought to explain these agreements and their implications for trade to the business community.[168] As the Economic Adviser to the UK Liaison Mission in Tokyo put it, among the chief difficulties were

> on the one hand Japan's huge adverse trade balance and the desirability for her to become self-supporting as soon as possible, and on the other hand the need for the sterling area countries to protect themselves against any undue liability for the payment of dollars and against any resumption of excessive price cutting as an aid to expanding Japanese exports.[169]

The situation initiated a long-running battle between British authorities anxious to preserve the influence of sterling and Japan's US rulers, who were not only keen to promote the dollar but who were also anxious that the export trade deemed necessary to Japan's survival should not be unduly hindered. Multilateral payments agreements between Japan and the sterling area were concluded regularly from 1948 to facilitate trade, but these debates over Japan's trade with the sterling area remained a bone of contention through into the 1950s, which remained a decade of inconvertible currencies.[170]

The balance of trade and currency issues symbolized more fundamental concerns relating to the resumption of economic relations between the two countries, and the British response to these dilemmas was far from unanimous. Nor was it consistent over time. On the one hand the legacy of bitterness both from trade frictions in the 1930s and from the war itself was a powerful one, resulting in calls for punitive reparations, harsh restrictions on the rebuilding of war-related industries, and attempts to curb potential Japanese competition to British industries in third markets. Hostile wartime views at the Foreign Office had initially advocated that Japan's heavy plant should be dismantled, her merchant shipping surrendered and large-scale reparations handed over, but had been toned down later in the conflict.[171] Even so, the Labour government in power during the period 1945–51 was in favour of a tough peace treaty. Hugh Gaitskell, as Chancellor of the Exchequer, was a leading critic of Japan within the Cabinet towards the end of the Occupation, resisting the return to Japan of gold deposits held by the allies.[172] Representatives of opinion in pottery and cotton textile districts, such as Staffordshire, Cheshire and Lancashire, campaigned for restrictions on Japanese production and exports of these commodities, and voted against the 1951 peace treaty in protest at the absence of any such measures.[173] There was a persistent concern with hindering the re-emergence of what had been viewed as Japan's prewar commercial malpractices. On the other hand there was a widespread recognition that production for export was an integral part of Japanese economic recovery, and that Britain was unable to provide economic support for a Japan unable to recover. Moreover, many perceived that not only did the inhabitants of Britain's colonies benefit from receiving cheap Japanese goods, but that a demoralized and impoverished Japan would continue to provide fertile ground for unrest and potentially support for communist ideology. The Japanese economy should be rebuilt, but with a view to preventing the resurgence of what had been regarded as unfair trading methods, perhaps in conjunction with substantial reparations.[174] The extent to which one or other of these points of view dominated largely depended on the degree to which national or sectional interest was concerned.

Initial views regarding Japanese economic recovery tended to be pessimistic. The pessimistic view continued well into the 1950s, and was shared by many in Japan. The most optimistic initial belief was that the Japanese economy might be self-supporting by around 1951, but only if a lower standard of living was accepted.[175] This pessimism tended to colour attitudes to specific issues and generate a broader view among diplomats that the impediments to Japanese recovery should not be made too overwhelming.[176] Such conciliatory views were not universal within government circles, however. G.C. Allen noted that the Board of Trade was far more concerned than the Foreign Office with future markets for British products, and hence the potential of Japanese competition, while one senior Treasury official proposed limiting the Japanese merchant marine to sailing ships, partly because of the moral value that operating such ships might endow.[177] It is apparent, however, that notwithstanding the concerns expressed over the implications of Japanese recovery, the British government was for the most part unable or unwilling to take concrete action to protect British business interests against a resurgence of Japanese competition.[178] This is not to say that Britain had no input into Occupation policy regarding the economy. It has been suggested that British input to land reform via the Far East Commission was considerable, and effective opposition was mounted to the Shoup mission's proposals regarding the taxing of foreign residents in Japan.[179] However, policy had to accord with the new reality. The Economic Adviser's Office of the British Liaison Mission in Tokyo noted in 1950 that 'Japan's economic position is basically similar to that of Great Britain, in that she must export in order to pay for her essential imports; in order to keep alive in fact'.[180] Britain could not help to support an unresurgent Japan. Britain's own economic and financial straits meant that such support was untenable. It was also accepted that the US had replaced Britain as the dominant influence in Asia, and particularly in Japan, and that since it was the US that had borne the burden of supporting Japan during the early Occupation years it was not for Britain to take a stand against it.

Well before the end of the Occupation not just cotton producers, but manufacturers of other textiles, such as rayon and wool, were expressing concerns over Japanese competition, but doubts were also surfacing over the desirability of protecting industries that could not sustain international competitiveness. Even before the end of the war *The Economist* had commented caustically that

> The doctrine appears to be growing up, almost unawares, that British industry cannot hope to compete on an open basis with other countries. It is a curious doctrine, and is maintained with the utmost inconsistency against both low-wage and high-wage countries. Where we are not undercut by the low wages of the Japanese – so runs the argument – we are undercut by the high productivity of the Americans. This is pure defeatism.[181]

Its comment on hearing Lancashire's reported response to the new arrangement for sterling trade with Japan in 1948 was:

> If, as is reported, it has been received with 'very mixed' feelings in British cotton circles, that is a sad commentary on the parochialism with which

> world events are now viewed from Lancashire and on the defensive timidity that besets an industry which once thrived on free trade and bestrode the markets of the world.[182]

Five years later the same journal noted that a statement by Lancashire that Japan was beating them on delivery times, though 'intended as a complaint, would be taken by many people as a damaging admission'.[183]

Even before the end of the Occupation attempts were made to reach agreement on the fraught issue of cotton textile competition. An Anglo-American cotton mission to Tokyo in the spring of 1950 held extensive discussions with Japanese cotton producers, and seemed to suggest the possibility of collaboration. However, support for the restrictive policies often called for by Lancashire was limited. It seemed to many that Lancashire either had to address its fundamental problem of high and rigid costs, and sustain its competitiveness by investing in new technology and the production of high-quality goods, or go under. 'The world', it was commented, 'does not owe Lancashire a living.'[184] Through the Occupation and the 1950s Lancashire continued to generate a certain amount of sound and fury, but it achieved few concrete results. The most that could be achieved was the prevention of anything amounting to unfair competition, the eradication of 'sharp commercial practices' and guarantees against unfair trading methods.[185] The Liaison Mission tried to reassure businessmen by telling them that 'the Japanese Government have expressed their determination to set their faces against a recurrence of the unfair practices which characterised Japanese selling methods before the war'.[186]

That Britain was not out to do the Japanese economy down was not always accepted by the dominant US. The head of SCAP's Intelligence Section, General Willoughby, wrote in his memoirs that 'a principal bar to Japan's attempt to build up its competitive position in the world under the occupation was the attitude of the British, who sought by one means or another to bring Japan under the control of the sterling bloc'.[187] One US diplomat was reported as believing that British concern to have Japan recognize Beijing rather than Taipei was based on the British fear that in the event of restrictions on trade with the Chinese mainland 'increased Japanese trade with Southeast Asia must necessarily be at British expense'.[188] The Japanese, for their part, while forcibly drawn into trade with the western bloc, which enhanced their potential threat to British interests, saw it as in their own interest both to recognize US dominance of the international economy and the US championing of free trade. For some Britons, particularly those fearful of Japanese competition, this recognition and all it implied offered a threat to British interests. The strong US–Japan economic links were believed to restrict the commercial prospects of Britain still further. It was in any case symbolic of the waning of British monetary and export influence in the international economy, particularly east of Suez, that was to become conspicuous in the 1950s. The Occupation period re-established the mediation of Anglo-Japanese economic relations through Empire and Commonwealth interests, but this time in the context of the overwhelming dominance of the United States.

Economic reintegration in the shadow of the past, 1952–1973

Efforts to integrate Japan into the western trading community continued after the end of the Occupation, but such an integration threw into greater prominence the potential threat posed by renewed Japanese competition. While it was widely acknowledged that Japan needed to rebuild its export trade, and that this must in due course mean both equal access to the markets of the 'free' world and participation in international economic and trading organizations, moves in this direction were opposed by those fearful of Japanese competition. The Japanese, for their part, needed to work to dispel the stereotype of unfair and fraudulent trading practices that persisted in the mind of many Britons, particularly in the business world.

By comparison with the Occupation period, the significance of Britain as an export market for Japanese goods declined. While the value of direct trade between the two countries rose, particularly during the expansionary period of the 1950s and early 1960s, Britain never accounted for more than 3 per cent of Japan's imports, or more than 4 per cent of Japan's exports throughout the period 1952–73.[189] Except for 1972–3 Japan's share in Britain's trade remained under 2 per cent of the total value (see Figures 1.4–1.6). For most of the 1950s and 1960s Britain tended to run a deficit on commodity trade with Japan, but in a number of years the balance of trade went the other way, giving Britain a surplus. The composition of commodity trade, however, underwent a considerable change over these two decades. Whereas in the early 1950s Japanese exports to Britain had consisted primarily of items such as textiles and china, by 1966 machinery (including ships) was the largest single export category, closely followed by foodstuffs, notably canned fish and mandarin oranges. Also important were some metal products, chemicals and optical instruments. Textiles, though still significant, had declined in relative importance. By this time British exports to Japan were dominated by chemicals, machinery and non-ferrous metals.[190] This shift not only reflected structural change in the Japanese economy, but also suggested its potential for new areas of direct competition with Britain.

While there is evidence of changing British perceptions of Japan during the 1950s, economic relations between the two sides remained bedevilled by the legacy of the 1930s, and import restrictions on both sides impeded commerce. Firstly, the currency problem continued to dominate relations when it came to Japan's trade with the sterling area, particularly Southeast Asia, as is abundantly clear from Noriko Yokoi's work,[191] and from John Weste's chapter in this volume. A succession of trade and payment agreements failed to establish a stable framework, and sporadic crises arose. A general context of currency inconvertibility generated problems over bilateral balancing of the sterling account and a reluctance to settle sterling debts by payment in dollars. Japan's sterling holdings fluctuated between deficit and surplus. The holding of large sterling balances by Japan was felt to act as a possible impediment to sterling convertibility. In 1953, by contrast, Japan's movement towards a deficit with the sterling area led to a run-down of her holdings, and triggered pressure to permit additional imports of Japanese goods into the UK. This resulted in the February 1954 Payments Agreement's establishing a quota system for commodities that were felt could easily be absorbed into the British market, most of the quota values being issued to prewar importers of Japanese consumer goods.[192] The agreement evoked little response in Japan, but aroused considerable hostility in some quarters of British industry. The tension between the interests of some commercial sectors and attempts to sustain the national currency was palpable.

These concerns were sustained despite the fact that around the end of the Korean War in 1953 the general prospects for Japan's rapid recovery and regaining of competitiveness were viewed in Britain as being weak. It was largely in response to business fears of Japanese competition (fair and unfair) at home and abroad that Britain consistently opposed Japan's admittance to GATT during the first half of the 1950s. In 1953 a cabinet committee on policy towards Japan concluded that the British industries most vulnerable to renewed Japanese competition were cotton and rayon textiles, pottery, toys, textile and other machinery, finished steel, bicycles, cables, clocks, cameras and glassware. However, since the total value of trade was relatively small, the main implications had to be seen in terms of the position of sterling. It was realized that the convertibility of sterling would mean that the balance of payments could no longer be used as a reason for restricting Japanese imports in traditional areas. The British opposition to Japan's entry into GATT was due to the belief that it offered no equivalent safeguards in this respect. The wider impression created by this attitude was that Britain was unwilling to help Japan re-enter the western trading community.[193]

Even when Japan's entry into GATT became a foregone conclusion in the summer of 1955 both Britain and Australia were among those members invoking Article 35 of the GATT treaty, which meant that Japan was not granted 'most-favoured nation' status in trade with the UK, nor obliged to concede such treatment to Britain. The wool industry was one that supported this stance:

> It is very important, from the point of view of the wool-textile industry, that cast-iron assurances and safeguards should be obtained with regard to fair trading and a discontinuance of misleading making of goods,

> wherever they may be sold, before the United Kingdom should consent to the application of the General Agreement to trade between the two countries.[194]

Instead a series of bilateral agreements was concluded relating to quotas and restrictions on certain commodities, with the hope that these matters would eventually be found a solution through a fully commercial treaty. Although Britain was over time increasingly uncomfortable with invoking GATT 35, and the annual negotiation of short-term trading agreements with Japan that resulted, it was only after many years of negotiation that a treaty was finally concluded. The negotiations for a commercial treaty started in 1955 when the British government invited the Japanese government to enter into negotations for a long-term commercial treaty 'embodying mutual undertakings with respect to shipping and establishment matters, protection of industrial designs and tariff matters',[195] but it was not until November 1962 that a full commercial treaty was signed between the two countries. Business missions to Japan around this time, notably by the Confederation of British Industry, the President of the Board of Trade, and Chamber of Commerce representatives, may also have played a part in diffusing recognition of the possibilities of the Japanese market and the dispelling of prewar and wartime assumptions and prejudices.[196] The treaty, according to which Britain ceased to invoke Article 35 of the GATT treaty, came into force in spring 1963. It provided for Britain to remove import controls on Japanese goods by 1968 or earlier, but incorporated general safeguards for when imports from Japan were considered excessive, and provided for some voluntary export control on key items, including textiles, clothing, some radio apparatus and some pottery.[197] The treaty did not, however, mean the cessation of all efforts to restrict Japanese imports into the UK, providing as it did for voluntary export controls by the Japanese. As more signs of Japan's increasing economic power emerged, concern about low-wage competition continued.[198] Import quotas in the form of voluntary export restraints persisted. The spectre of flooded domestic markets re-emerged with even greater force during the 1970s and 1980s.

What is significant at this time, however, is that such lively fears were evoked in the context of the limited significance of direct trade between the two countries. One major reason for this is the assistance given to Japan's export activities in Asia and Africa by the weakening competitiveness of Britain and the decline of Commonwealth preference. As was commented in March 1958,

> Shunned by much of Europe, Japan is bound to look for markets mainly in the Afro-Asian world. Here the withering of commonwealth preferences is working in its favour. India, Pakistan, Ceylon and West Africa, though protecting their own industries, treat the Japanese on equal terms

> with other exporters as far as quota restrictions are concerned.... Last year a major shift in Australia's policy took place. Hitherto it has allowed Japan scarcely a taste of the feast which many European exporters of consumer goods have been enjoying in the past ten years. Australia has now recognised the importance of this growing market in the Far East, and has virtually extended most-favoured-nation treatment to the Japanese.[199]

By the early 1960s the Japanese were only marginally disadvantaged by mutual preferences granted to Commonwealth countries.[200]

British concerns over Japanese exports

Initially the business pressure to restrict Japanese access to both British and third markets came primarily from the textile and pottery industries that had suffered from Japanese competition in the prewar years. The vociferous comments of Sir Raymond Streat of the Cotton Board, and of many of his colleagues, are well documented in Streat's diaries, and in the records of the Manchester Chamber of Commerce, and are discussed elsewhere. Some other industries also felt the chill wind of Japanese competition, or were concerned that they might do so. An alert representative of the Yorkshire-based woollen industry visiting Japan in 1955 noted:

> ... of one thing I am convinced: neither the textile industry nor any other industry must underestimate what is happening. Japan is working very hard indeed, and is rapidly acquiring the technical skills and export marketing techniques so that, before long, I believe that Japanese competition will be on a scale which will be far greater than it is today.[201]

The industry subsequently mounted intense opposition to the 1962 commercial treaty with Japan, despite Japan's being a major export destination for British woollen cloth, an opposition that one writer called 'a reflection of the severe reverse that British wool has suffered in the United States as a result of the inroads made by Japanese exporters into what used to be a predominant British market'.[202] Another major industry exposed to Japanese competition was shipbuilding. From as early as 1950 competition from the increasingly efficient Japanese shipbuilding industry mounted a major challenge not just to Britain, but to the world's other major shipbuilders as well, and it was apparent from early that decade that British shipbuilders were losing the race. The overwhelming dominance of Japanese shipbuilders in world markets continued over the next two decades, offering a stark contrast to their British counterparts.[203]

It is important, however, to distinguish clearly between sectional and national interest in the British response to Japan's economic growth. Where indigenous British production or export markets were perceived to be under threat from the Japanese hostility was often vocal, and demanding of protection. Where it was not there appears at this time to have been rather less concern over the implications of any Japanese export success. The journal of the Birmingham Chamber of Commerce, reflecting much more the interests of the engineering and machinery trades, seems to have made some efforts to keep its readership informed about Japan, but nowhere is there apparent the kind of alarmist views on Japanese competition found in its Manchester counterpart.[204] The London Chamber of Commerce, not surprisingly, appears to have been more concerned with the effects of imports from Japan on sterling balances, rather than on British industry.[205] In the Bradford area, while competition from the Japanese wool industry clearly was a cause of considerable concern, as noted above, opinion seemed as inclined to try and understand and correct, as to restrict.[206] The relative absence of concern among large parts of the British business community no doubt contributed to the gradual erosion of protective measures against Japan for a number of commodities, and an increasing recognition that it was inappropriate and unwise to deny Japan access to a wide range of markets, as well as a growing tendency to blame British industry for its own failures, rather than the 'unfair' Japanese.

This is not to say, however, that British business and economic decision-makers were content to forget the past. That perceptions changed but slowly is discussed in a 1956 article by a British correspondent in Tokyo:

> The truth is that serious misconceptions about each other persist in both Britain and Japan. The British stereotype of Japan is a low-standard country run by unscrupulous monopoly capitalists who ruthlessly exploit their working class and ally themselves with militarists: . . . an unfair competitor who floods the market with cheap goods, and a bad customer who buys goods only to copy them and then undercut their original manufacturers . . .
>
> The Japanese, for their part, have considerable respect for the British way of life and especially for British political institutions . . . On the other hand, Japan shares the widespread delusion that both the Commonwealth and the sterling area are . . . designed to conceal effective British economic control of large parts of the earth. Colonies and Dominions remain indistinguishable still in Japanese eyes, and it is popularly believed that if, say, Australia restricts the entry of Japanese goods, it does so on orders from Whitehall.[207]

In some respects Japan continued to remain excluded from many markets of the world, and something of an international trading pariah, well into the 1960s. Over time, however, as Japan's economy continued to grow, the British, as already mentioned, started to compare Japanese business and official management of the economy favourably with what they found at home.

Efforts made by the Japanese to curb unethical trading practices and improve the image of Japanese goods were reported in the British press, and appear to have made some headway at least on popular perceptions. As early as 1952 it was reported of the Japanese that 'they are winning a reputation for fair trading, prompt deliveries and superior salesmanship. Their goods are equal to their samples and up to specifications – which has by no means always been the case with British products since the war'.[208] Shortly after it was noted that the Japanese government had taken a number of steps to prevent the abuse of foreign designs and copyrights, with the patent office instructed to take up any complaints made against Japanese firms for infringement of trade marks and designs registered in Japan.[209] Efforts in this direction appear to have been ongoing. At the International Chamber of Commerce congress held in Tokyo in May 1955, one Japanese representative stressed that the Japanese government had established a commission with a view to improving Japanese patent and trade mark laws to conform to international standards.[210] Others acknowledged that unfair trade practices had caused problems, but made assurances that vigorous countermeasures were being taken against this.[211] However, concerns were expressed about things such as concealed export subsidies deemed contrary to the spirit of GATT,[212] and complaints did not disappear overnight. In March 1955 the question of misleading marking of Japanese wool exports, including the phrase 'Made as in England', with the 'as' in minuscule letters, was raised in the House of Lords.[213] Foreign Minister Fujiyama was confronted with evidence of illegal Japanese copying of British ball bearings on a visit to London in 1957,[214] and in 1962 Ronson Products won a case brought against Japanese firms copying Ronson's gas lighter technology, design and trade mark. Complaints about copyright infringement and patenting continued through the 1960s.[215]

Technology transfer and the Japanese market

Significantly in the Ronson case it was noted that the Japanese copies were of reasonably high quality. *The Economist* noted acerbically in this context that 'It has not been unknown for a British manufacturer to complain about a Japanese copy which on examination proved better than its model'.[216] It is clear that the quality of Japanese products was improving, and as domestic production costs rose the cheap and shoddy image was no longer tenable or desirable. Representatives of the shipbuilding and steel industries, both of which faced fierce Japanese competition in the late 1960s, were compelled to recognize the superior organization and technology of their Japanese competitors. To achieve this advance Japan had been importing technology on a large scale since before the end of the Occupation. For many Britons, however, the realization that Japan was moving forward in technological terms appears to have come relatively slowly, and they were often unable or unwilling to participate in the technology transfer. While some producers, for example those in automobiles and nuclear power, had in the early 1950s seen considerable mileage in technical tie-ups with Japan,[217] such ventures had, for a variety of reasons, not proved to be of lasting success. Many other areas of business failed to pursue technological links with Japan. This relatively low profile of Britain in Japan's very high level of technology imports during the 1950s and 1960s is in part the result of the major share played in this by the United States, building on its ascendancy during the Occupation, and as part of its attempts to integrate Japan into the capitalist camp of the Cold War world. While Britain in general supported the principle of Japanese recovery, the British government was, as we have seen, reluctant to oppose US dominance in Japan, which was often used unashamedly in support of US business interests. In the case of technology transfer, Britain accounted for only 7.5 per cent of Japan's total contracts 1950–70, compared with the 57.8 per cent of the United States.[218] This proportion was, nevertheless, behind that of Germany, which suggests that US dominance was not the only factor. A British business group visiting Japan under the auspices of the London and Birmingham Chambers of Commerce in 1965 reported:

> It is only during the past three or four years, during which over 1000 more technical agreements have been arranged, that British manufacturers have appreciated the wisdom of selling 'know-how' to Japan (in the knowledge that if they do not, others are willing to) and the number of Anglo-Japanese technical agreements have risen to around 150 and there are many others known to be in the pipeline.[219]

With the somewhat abortive attempts to work together on advanced technology projects, US dominance in Japan, as well as failure on the British side to appreciate sufficiently opportunities in Japan and the country's needs, the earlier respect for British technology does not appear always to have been upheld. Japan, by contrast, moved into technology transfer to Britain. While technology exports by Japan at this time remained limited, up to one-quarter of the total went to Europe over the period 1950–71, some of it to Britain.[220] By the late 1960s not just shipping, but industries such as steel and car components manufacturers were very clear that they needed to learn from the technologically advanced Japanese firms with which they found it difficult to compete in the marketplace. Methods of technology acquisition from the Japanese could be as unorthodox as those earlier adopted by the Japanese that had come in for heavy British criticism. In 1965 Mr Donald Stokes (later Lord Stokes) of Leyland was reported as having come back from the United States 'with a bagful of door-handles, window winders, rear-seat controls for car radios and the like from Japanese cars, which are now being studied for possible use in British cars'.[221] Consideration of purchasing such Japanese-made components was potentially highly threatening for the traditional suppliers of the British automotive industry. It is evident from such examples, therefore, that the relative technological strength of the two economies was shifting, and that this was to be one of the keys to the 'invasion' of the British market by Japanese commodities from the 1970s.

Britain appeared no more successful at securing a niche in the Japanese market for commodities. Writing in the mid-1960s, the economist G.C. Allen criticized British business for its lack of interest in Japan:

> In recent years the rate of increase shown by Japan's exports has been much faster than that of any other country, and this increase has been especially rapid during the latest period of recession. In these circumstances it might have been expected that British and other European manufacturers and traders would have displayed a keen interest in Japan both as a market and as a source of supply. In fact their interest until very recently has been tepid. This is particularly true of the British.[222]

Considerable official efforts were made to promote trade and to penetrate the Japanese market, with the organization of events such as trade fairs in Tokyo. 'British weeks' were organized at intervals from the mid-1960s. However, results were often only short term. While such promotions may have benefited export products like biscuits and Scotch whisky, they were less successful with non-consumer goods.[223] By the 1960s the prominent British exports to Japan had a rather traditional profile, focusing on consumer goods, and perhaps reinforcing Britain's image in Japan as a nation looking to the past rather than to the future. It would be inappropriate to attribute the blame for this situation entirely to British manufacturers and exporters. There is no doubt that restrictions at the Japanese end made penetration of the Japanese market particularly difficult. The Japanese government and bureaucracy had a reputation in Britain of hostility to foreign business, and in 1954, for example, Britain complained formally about the country's preferential treatment of its own shipping companies.[224] Restrictive import quotas or punitive taxation in the late 1960s clearly restricted imports of many products, including whisky and wool, and even when tariff barriers were relaxed other obstacles remained, not least cumbersome bureaucratic practices.

Commercial and financial relations between the two countries were also firmly re-established during this period. Japanese banks reopened branches in London during the 1950s, often primarily to serve Japanese customers. A Japanese chamber of commerce was established in London in 1959. Japanese borrowing in London accelerated in the 1960s as the possibilities for investment in Japan grew, while Japanese brokers started business in London in 1964. British bankers saw possibilities in the Japanese leadership of the new Asian Development Bank in 1966. Until around 1970, however, there were considerable restrictions on Japanese investment abroad, so the money flow was into Japan, rather than out of it.[225] Moreover, while British banks and financial houses did operate in Japan, the restrictions on financial activity in the Japanese market during these decades imposed considerable limitations on their activities. The number of British banks operating in Tokyo remained almost static up to the early 1970s.[226] Much British activity in the Japanese market took the form of joint ventures, and capital inflow was relatively insignificant.[227]

The shifting balance of economic power: trends in trade

In 1973 the Japanese government announced that the Japanese market had been 100 per cent liberalized, the culmination of progressive removal of tariff and other barriers to imports. Two years earlier the ¥360 = $1 exchange rate that had prevailed since 1949 had finally been abandoned, and the appreciation of the yen's value suggested that exports might be restrained and imports encouraged. Both factors, as well as the dislocation caused by the 1973 Oil Shock, had potentially major implications for Anglo-Japanese trading and business relations, appearing to remove some of the advantages hitherto possessed by Japan. What happened, in fact, was that although the overall rate of Japanese growth slowed considerably, the efforts to respond to energy constraints with increasing productivity, and to sustain export levels, not only generated a substantial increase in the volume of trade between the two countries, but also marked the start of a consistently growing Japanese surplus in commodity trade with Britain. Japanese exports to Britain became more important for both countries. From under 2 per cent in 1973 Japan grew to provide around 6 per cent of Britain's total imports in the early 1990s. While Japan's share of British exports also grew from the mid-1980s it failed to exceed 3 per cent of the total (Figure 1.5). On the Japanese side change was less apparent. Britain continued to account for under 2 per cent of Japan's imports, while her share of Japanese exports fluctuated from 2–4 per cent (Figure 1.6).

Thus while Japanese commodities became more important for Britain, the reverse was far from being the case. The net result was, notwithstanding the rising value of the yen, a widening bilateral trade gap, which constituted just one element in Japan's global trade surplus during this period. The imbalance widened consistently from the early 1970s. By the mid-1980s Japan was exporting to Britain roughly four times as much as it imported from Britain (Figure 1.7). The imbalance was maintained through a decline in the real value of trade in the early 1990s, and has persisted through to the present. In 1997 Britain imported from Japan goods to the value of well over £9 billion, but exported only just over £4 billion worth of commodities.[228]

Analysis of the composition of commodity trade between the two countries also demonstrates considerable shifts. Tables 1.17 and 1.18 show the increasing significance of machinery and equipment in Japanese exports,

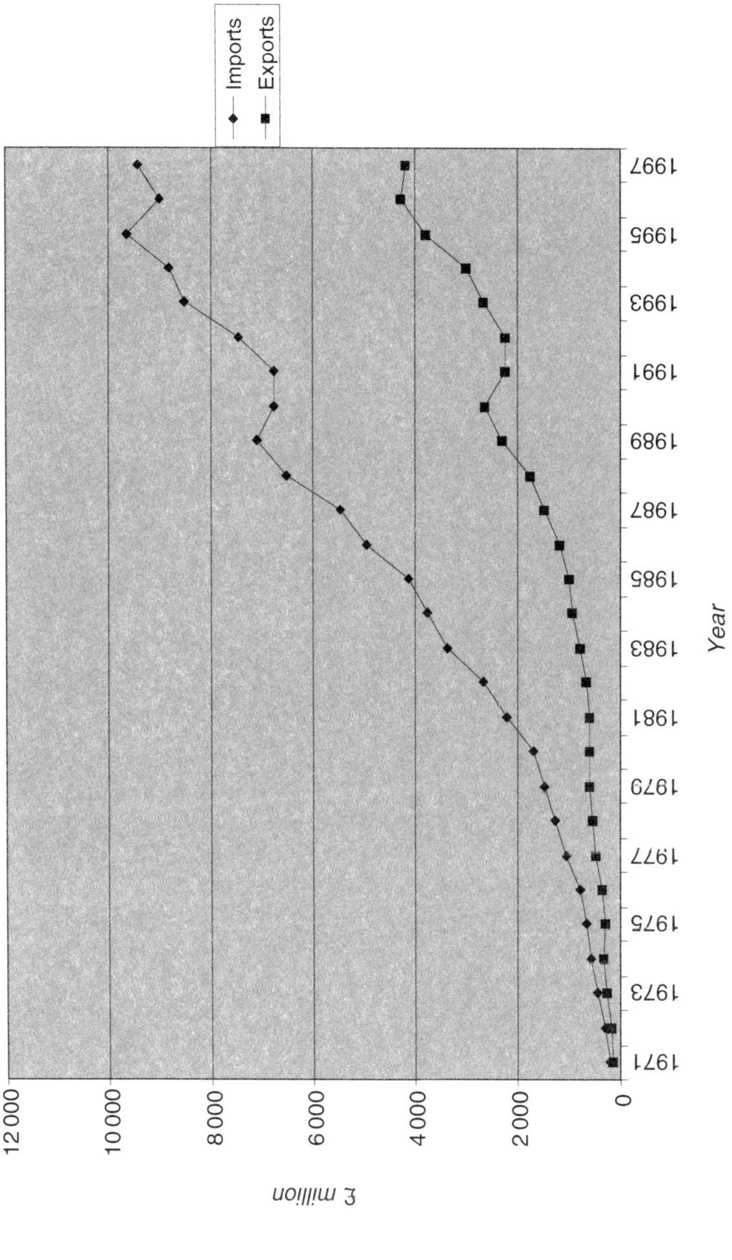

Sources: HMSO and Office for National Statistics, *Annual Abstract of Statistics* (London, annually).

Figure 1.7 British trade with Japan 1971–1997 (by value, current prices)

Table 1.17 Japanese exports to the United Kingdom, 1966–1996: share of major commodities in total exports by value (%)

	1966	*1976*	*1987*	*1996*
Foodstuffs	22.5	3.8	0.2	
Textiles	9.1	3.2	2.7	
Chemicals (organic & inorganic)	7.7	3.8	2.7	6.7
Metal products	7.5	8.5	1.9	3.7
Machinery and equipment, of which:	29.3	71.6	83.3	81.5
Ships/boats	15.9	8.8		
Transport equipment		23.6	34.1	21.2
Office and data processing			11.7	17.0
Electrical equipment				27.5

Source: Japan Tariff Association (Nihon Kanzei Kyokai), *Summary Report on Trade of Japan (Gaikoku Boeki Gaikyo)*, Dec. 1987, pp. 142–9, 158–65 and Dec. 1986, pp. 105–9, 115–19; Bureau of Statistics, Prime Minister's Office, *Japan Statistical Yearbook*, vol. 18 (1967), pp. 310–11 and vol. 28 (1978), pp. 296–7.

Table 1.18 British exports to Japan, 1966–1996: share of major commodities in total exports to Japan by value (%)

	1966	*1976*	*1987*	*1996*
Foodstuffs	4.8	13.4	8.6	7.8
Chemicals/medical products	15.0	16.1	19.5	16.3
Machinery & equipment, of which:	39.9	31.1	26.7	48.5
Office machinery				14.2
Vehicles				10.8
Metal ores and scrap			2.0	
Non-ferrous metals		10.9	6.5	
Textiles & textile raw materials		7.3	10.3	5.5

Source: As Table 1.17.

with a shift away from ships in favour initially of other transport equipment, particularly cars and motorbikes, electronic equipment, and then towards office and data processing machines and components. In the mid-1960s the significance of Japanese textile exports had already declined substantially, but foodstuff exports, particularly canned fish, remained very significant. However, exports of both these commodities had become negligible by the mid-1970s. It was at the start of this decade that the Japanese takeover of markets in commodities such as transistor radios, forklift trucks, ball bearings and colour televisions became cause for concern. In terms of trade the other way, there was a less obvious shift. The proportional significance of foodstuffs as a British export to Japan declined after the mid-1970s. Machinery and equipment remained significant exports to Japan throughout the period, as did chemicals and medical products, but worthy of note is the extent to which, by the mid-1990s, Britain was exporting both office machinery and vehicles to Japan. This was a function both of increasing Japanese investment in the UK, and the growing importance of the European community, as will be shown below.

The imbalance of trade between the two countries provided the context for mutual perceptions. In Britain it generated a degree of public hostility and official attempts to restrict the inflow of Japanese goods or lever concessions in the Japanese market, hindering the removal of economic tensions that had persisted for decades. Frictions arose over a range of goods, and in many cases led to open disagreement and reluctant compromises. Just one of many was Japan's agreement in the late 1970s to commit to a voluntary restraint arrangement, under which Japanese car imports would not take more than an agreed share of the UK market.[229] By 1984 voluntary restraint agreements covered nearly half of Japan's exports to Britain.[230] Pressure for such arrangements continued during the 1980s and 1990s in a context of frictions caused by the persistent surplus, the pain felt by British firms in the context of Japanese competition, and the persistent difficulty of penetrating the Japanese market. Even in the absence of tariffs and quotas, the complexity of Japanese distributional networks, bureaucratic procedures and tax systems could impose very real obstacles. In Japan the process of even formal liberalization remained slow.

Learning from Japan[231]

Despite its souring effect on Anglo-Japanese relations more broadly, Japan's export success and sustained growth was a major factor in a 'learn from Japan' movement that took hold in Britain as in the United States, particularly during the Thatcher years of the 1980s. British managers showed an interest in Japanese management practices, particularly Japanese industrial relations, from the mid-1970s. Alan Berry, a member of the West European Metal Trades Employers' Organization labour relations study tour to Japan in 1978, wrote of Japan's 'enviable record of industrial relations', which he linked to enterprise basis organization and an absence of demarcation disputes.[232] By the early 1980s, particularly given the British government's policy on trade union power, some attempts to emulate Japanese labour practices were causing considerable alarm among labour representatives, and one treatise aimed at labour organizers and representatives cautioned against blanket acceptance of an ill-understood imported philosophy that might well fragment labour further. 'We cannot wish Japan away, but neither can we obligingly accept all the management consultants' and government's rhetoric about "going Japanese".'[233] It was widely recognized, however, that such was the economic influence of Japan that it was imperative to move beyond the more simplistic stereotypes that had long dominated British perceptions of Japan's economy and business. The plethora of writings that resulted showed both increasing sophistication, but on some occasions also fundamental flaws that did little to dispel misconceptions. In fact, in the high unemployment climate of the 1980s sensitive emulation of Japanese management practices appears to have generated positive results and relatively little resistance, and in other cases became incorporated into management thinking more broadly. There is no doubt whatsoever that the Japanese influence on the operation of businesses in Britain has been an enduring one.

Japanese investment: Britain in Europe

Apart from the rapid increase in Japanese products, probably the most obvious facet of Japan's growing presence in Britain during this period was the growth in Japanese investment (see Figure 1.8), Japanese businesses with branches in the UK, and Japanese-owned production facilities. The story of this investment is covered in some detail by Marie Conte-Helm in chapter 9 of this volume, and only a few summary points will be made here. The first Japanese manufacturing facility in Britain was established as early as 1966, and a number of Japanese firms set up sales subsidiaries in Britain – for example, that established by Mitsubishi to sell minicomputers in 1971.[234] More serious interest was shown in the 1970s, for example with the setting up of Sony's plant in south Wales, but it was essentially during the 1980s that Japanese investment in Britain really took off. Production facilities covered a range of goods from ball bearings to zip fasteners, but over time were increasingly concentrated in consumer electronics, industrial electronics and electronic components, in addition to major automobile facilities such as those operated by Nissan and Toyota. By 1994 there were an estimated 41 Japanese-affiliated manufacturers in electronic products, 31 in chemicals, 21 in electronic components and 21 in car parts operating within Britain.[235] The significance of these firms' locating in the UK for the operation of the manufacturing sector has been considerable. The Nissan plant in the North East and its suppliers in the locality, for example, have been credited with revitalizing a region suffering from industrial decline. By 1990 employment in the UK in Japanese sales and manufacturing subsidiaries in electronics alone was already in excess of 30 000, and five years later Japanese firms were believed to be employing around 80 000 personnel.[236] The cars produced by Japanese manufacturers were exported in large numbers; by 1995 Nissan UK was exporting over 70 per cent of its production to the European Union.[237] Car exports also found their way back to Japan itself, an export pattern that is reflected in Table 1.18, and has arguably had some impact on the trade imbalance between the two countries. It should be noted, however, that in some cases the historical legacy continued to cast a shadow over investment decisions. Protests at Hitachi's

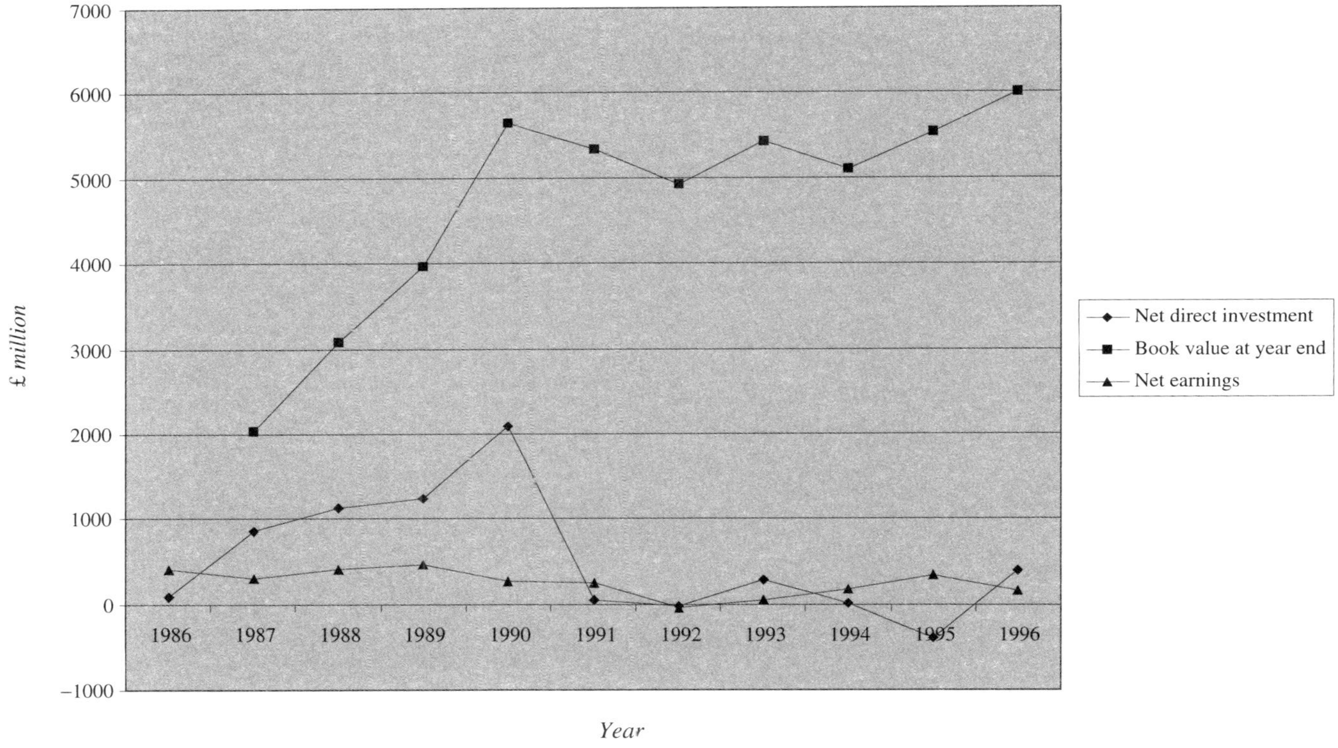

Sources: HMSO and Office for National Statistics, *Annual Abstract of Statistics* (London, annually).

Figure 1.8 Japanese direct investment in the UK, 1986–1996 (current prices)

proposal to invest in the North East, for example, resulted in a decision by the company to invest in Wales instead.

The reasons why Britain received a major part of all Japanese investment in Europe during these years are numerous. A 1991 JETRO survey identified some of the most important reasons for Japanese locating in Britain as being the existence of a good infrastructure for transport and distribution, the relatively low cost and high quality of labour, the English language and the presence of other Japanese manufacturers.[238] Government incentives, lower tax rates and a friendly welcome from the regions also played a part. Most important, perhaps, was the growing significance of the European common market and the European Union as a whole. The formation of what might potentially be a protectionist economic bloc sounded a strong resonance with prewar experience, and until the early 1970s Japan's approach to European economic integration through the EC and EFTA was a cautious one.[239] Trade with the European Economic Community remained relatively small by comparison with Japan's American links. In 1973 Japan's trade with the EEC was only 3 per cent of total EEC trade, and only 10 per cent of total Japanese trade. Compared to four years previously, however, Japanese exports to the EEC had risen by over 200 per cent. By contrast, Japanese imports from the EEC had risen only 87 per cent.[240] During the 1970s, as Japanese exports to Europe increased, along with the potential for friction over the increasing imbalance of trade, the spectre of 'fortress Europe' became one factor that lay behind the growth of the Japanese economic presence.[241]

Britain's entry into the EEC in 1973 was welcomed by the Japanese, who saw Britain as being more supportive of their economic aspirations than some other European countries. Given the other advantages mentioned above, Britain's incorporation into the process of European economic integration was a key factor in Britain's attracting the largest share of Japanese investment in Europe of any one country. Highly significant in historical terms is the fact that whereas many aspects of the Anglo-Japanese economic relationship were formerly mediated through the Empire and the Commonwealth, that mediating role was in the 1980s and 1990s taken over by Europe, in the form of the European Economic Community and the European Union. In the case of trade, for example, the former bilateral arrangements were subsumed by multilateral ones between Europe and Japan. Japan has dealt with Britain through Europe, as it were. At the same time, as Japan's economic ties with the United States weakened in the face of Japan's growing economic might and its attempts to reintegrate itself into Asia, the Asian dimension of Anglo-Japanese economic relations likewise became important for both countries. As in earlier periods, it is only possible to comprehend the complexity of these relationships by locating them in the context of shifts in international economy as a whole.

The Japanese presence in Britain was also felt in technological and financial terms. It was apparent that in the 1950s Britain's reputation as a potential supplier of advanced technology to Japan had declined, and Britain's role in the licensing and sale of technology to Japan through to the 1970s was relatively weak. From this time, too, Japan increased exports of technology, usually in the applied field. The spread of Japanese investment from the 1970s and 1980s, however, brought with it greater collaboration in science and technology. Not only was Japan seen as a potential source of research funding; some Japanese also took the view that Britain's traditional strength in basic research was something that could be usefully tapped. British research activities in Japan were more limited. It was not easy for British companies to access centres of Japanese technological advance due to the existence of strong corporate research links and research rigidities, and most collaborative research in Japan took the form of applied laboratories designed to support imports from outside Japan, hence the strength in pharmaceuticals and fine chemicals. In 1994 an agreement was concluded between the two countries designed to promote interchange in this area.[242]

Particularly significant, perhaps, was the Japanese presence in the field of finance, especially in London. By contrast with the case of commodity trade, Britain had long enjoyed a surplus on invisibles with Japan. In 1997 Britain's exports of services to Japan were more than twice the amount of imports, generating a net surplus of £356 million.[243] As the economic power of Japan grew, however, Japanese financial agents became increasingly involved in international markets. After 1972 there was a substantial growth in the Japanese financial community in London, with activities broadening out from the earlier dominance of trade finance to include investment flows both ways, insurance activity and brokerage.[244] The growth of the Eurobond market acted as a channel for investment in Japan, and indirect investment through channels such as unit trusts also increased. London was attractive to Japanese financial interests. It was regarded as a centre for the acquisition of skills in this area. The market was less regulated than the weaker Japanese market, and its position as one of the major international financial markets made it a crucial conduit for Japanese capital exports. It became the focal point for globalizing Japanese banks in Europe and Japanese securities houses with representation on the Stock Exchange, a relationship that went far beyond bilateral Anglo-Japanese financial relations. As early as 1983 it was estimated that the London market was taking 38 per cent of Japan's international banking business. Further openings for Japanese institutions were provided by the 1986 'Big Bang'. Japanese banks were still accounting for nearly one-quarter of all London's banking business at the end of the decade, when there were an estimated 107 Japanese financial institutions in the City of London.[245]

This expansion of Japanese business was not without its frictions. Many questioned a lack of reciprocity in the welcome afforded by Japan to British financial institutions. While foreign merchant banks and stockbrokers gained access to the Tokyo market during the 1970s, and those markets were further liberalized the following decade, many British businesses felt their activities constrained by government-imposed regulations, the close links between Japanese financial institutions and the Japanese business community, and the imposed division between banking and securities business. Disagreement over British firms' representation on the Tokyo Stock Exchange was eventually solved through a series of bilateral negotiations in the mid-1980s.

Britain in Japan: exports and investment

The collapse of the Japanese 'Bubble economy' and the difficulties faced by many Japanese financial institutions in the 1990s served to restrain but not halt Japanese involvement in financial markets in Britain. More striking, perhaps, have been the changes taking place in the 1990s in the pattern of British financial activity in Japan. With Japan experiencing its own 'Big Bang' and the deregulation of financial markets, the possibilities for greater activity in Japan have obviously been enhanced. Combined with the pressure on financial institutions to globalize, the price falls and restructuring that have occurred in Japan, links between Japanese financial institutions and multinational groups have been forged, something in which British-based groups have been able to participate. As financial institutions and markets become transnational, Anglo-Japanese economic relations again become enmeshed in the wider process.

The same factors have helped to enhance the importance of foreign direct investment in Japan, which has historically been far lower than the OECD average. It has not just been financial institutions that have complained of obstacles to free operation in the Japanese market. During the 1970s and 1980s in particular, as the Japanese economy was nominally 'liberalized', British businesses continued to have difficulties not only in exporting to Japan, but also in investing in and engaging in joint ventures there. G.C. Allen's complaints in 1966 that British businesses needed to exploit more the potential of the Japanese market were equally apposite through the following two decades. On occasions the authorities did what they could to promote British interests in Japan. In the early 1970s the British Overseas Trade Board produced a series of booklets on aspects of the Japanese economy and doing business there. One publication in this series noted that due to transport costs and tariff and non-tariff barriers the best way to advance in the Japanese market was probably through licensing and joint ventures, especially where smaller firms were concerned, since the Japanese tended to discourage wholly-owned subsidiaries of foreign firms. It noted that British companies had been slower than some others to enter licensing agreements with Japan, and that in 1972 only 49 British companies had a stake of more than 20 per cent in the equity of a Japanese company – a figure that contrasted poorly with those of countries such as France and Germany.[246] The booklet did acknowledge, however, that concluding such agreements was not easy, and should be undertaken with caution:

> It is extremely important for a British company to take particular care when selecting a partner in Japan. The selection process will probably entail a longer visit to Japan by the representative of a British principal than would normally be expected, but the extra time and trouble should prove well worth while in view of the initial problems presented by the particular nature of the organisation of Japanese industry and the way in which business is conducted. . . . Above all, the British principal must guard against Japanese companies which agree to form a join venture for the purpose either of their own prestige or to try to ward off an attack by a British company on the Japanese market, or to unload unwanted personnel from the parent Japanese company.[247]

The British authorities continued to make considerable efforts to encourage British business to increase their activities in Japan. In the late 1980s-early 1990s a series of campaigns were launched by the Department of Trade and Industry under the successive titles of 'Opportunity Japan', 'Priority Japan' and 'Action Japan'. The last of these sought to focus efforts on sectors considered particularly attractive to the Japanese, such as healthcare equipment, pharmaceuticals, electrical and car components, and fashionable textiles and items of clothing, such as Doc Marten's boots. Large trade missions went on a regular basis to Japan.[248] There were advances. Pharmaceuticals enjoyed particular advantages, and Rolls Royce, for example, was conspicuously successful in the Japanese market. For much of the period, however, large parts of British business failed to make much impact on the Japanese market. While a small number of luxury and fashion goods, including Scotch whisky, had a high profile and generated considerable profits, many British firms were either unable or unwilling to make the costly efforts required to make much headway in what remained a difficult market. Even although the sustained rise in the value of the yen during the 1980s made imports proportionately cheaper, it was not until the early 1990s that there was some evidence of greater success in British exporting to and investment in Japan. As we have noted, for a variety of reasons cars, chemicals and pharmaceuticals were conspicuous in this rise, and this was in part due to the effects of Japanese investment in Britain. Over time, too, the rise in the value of the yen had made some Japanese corporations keener to import components to retain their competitiveness, and some British businesses were the beneficiaries of this pressure. In the year to March 1993, Japan was the tenth largest market for UK exports, while the UK was the ninth largest for

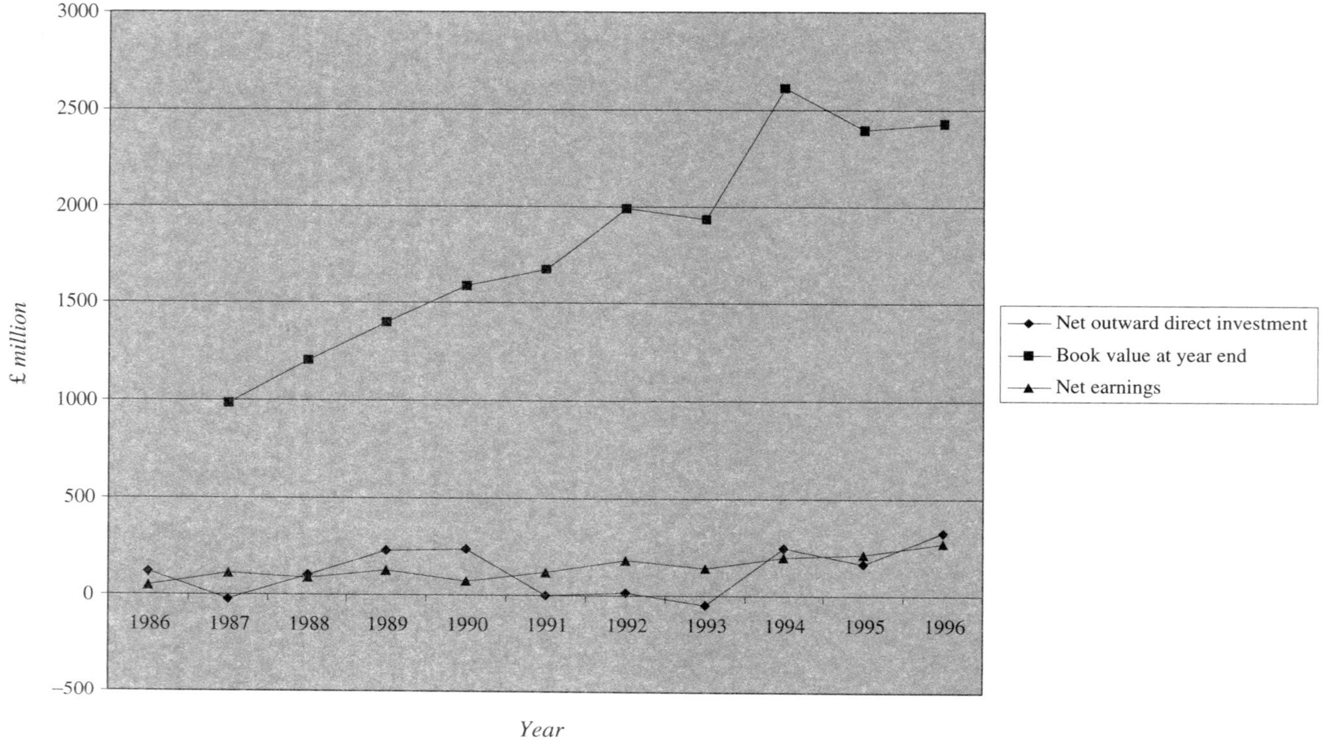

Source: HMSO and Office for National Statistics, *Annual Abstract of Statistics* (London, annually).

Figure 1.9 British direct investment in Japan, 1986–1996 (current prices)

Japan.[249] British investment in Japan, while increasing, continued to lag. The same year Britain accounted for only 5 per cent of the cumulative total of foreign investment in Japan. This share has remained relatively small in subsequent years.

The extent to which British business has made only limited advances both in exports to Japan and in investment there during the postwar years has been much debated. There is no doubt that for much of the postwar period it was not easy to overcome the restrictions placed on penetrating the Japanese market, and that non-tariff barriers in the form of organizational and distributional structures, for example, remain, as well as factors such as consumer taste and personal contacts which take more than legislation to change. Particularly in the context of the widening trade imbalance of the 1970s complaints about exclusion from the Japanese domestic market became widespread. Many commentators, however, have identified the causes of the imbalance in both trade and investment as lying with Britain rather than with Japan. In general, it has been suggested, British firms failed to make the most of the opportunities open to them. They often failed to prepare adequately, or to acquire the necessary understanding of Japanese business. Some efforts were characterized by poor marketing and low-quality goods. British business consistently failed to offer the new technologies and skills needed by Japan, particularly in the earlier decades after the war. British businessmen frequently failed to acquire the Japanese language skills that some have considered essential for successful operation in the country, while their Japanese counterparts often took the view that a knowledge of the English language was a prerequisite for penetrating European and third-country markets.[250] The success of the pharmaceuticals industry, that engaged in technical collaboration in the 1950s that led to continuing investment and cooperation, showed the possibilities, and highlighted the broader failure to act upon them.[251] This too, one can argue, is a story of the relative strengths of Britain and Japan in the international economy.

Conclusion

Economic relations between Britain and Japan have evolved through a number of phases since their inception at the start of the seventeenth century. The century and a half since contacts were renewed in the mid-nineteenth century have witnessed many fluctuations in the extent of business and economic interaction, and the nature of that interaction. Before the First World War Japan sought to industrialize and preserve her independence in the context of a British-dominated international economy. In the interwar years achievement of this goal brought tensions and uncertainties as Britain's supremacy was eroded by the rise of the United States, and depression and protectionism undermined the freedom of international trading activities that had been so crucial to the economic expansion of both nations. Rebuilding the ruptured relationship that was the culmination of these tensions was never going to be easy, and was rendered more difficult by the shifting balance of economic power between the British and Japanese economies in the second half of the twentieth century.

The business and economic relationship between the two countries has never been a simple bilateral one. Even in the seventeenth century it was influenced by the broader context of the countries' relationships with Portugal and Holland. Later on the relationship was mediated by the imperialist interest of both economies, as well as regional concerns – Japan as part of Asia, and Britain as part of Europe. Increasingly the context of the relationship has become one of international economic activity, and globalization. The political and strategic dimension, too, has been ever-present in shaping the economic and business relationship.

It is within these shifting parameters that trading, industrial and financial contacts have developed, that capital has flowed, and technology and know-how have been transferred. The terms of the industrial challenge have been transformed. Japan's industrial challenge in the nineteenth century was to 'catch up' with Britain. By the last quarter of the twentieth century a different kind of industrial challenge had been mounted, in which Japan appeared to be throwing down the gauntlet to Britain and other industrial economies by the success of much of her manufacturing and export activity. That relative shift in income levels, productivity and status in the international economy generated, as we have tried to show, tensions as well as collaboration between the two economies.

The events of the 1990s have undermined the perception in Britain of Japan as an unstoppable economic power. By realizing that the Japanese economy embraces weaknesses it has perhaps become easier for Britain to see the advantage of cooperating with Japan. It should be noted, however, that British perceptions of the Japanese economy have since the 1930s consistently depicted Japan as a potential threat to British interests. While it is now accepted that Japan has as much right to operate freely in the international economy as any other country, it is hard to dispute that this ongoing focus on Japan as the problem has hindered many in Britain from addressing very real problems within Britain itself. By the same token, it may be suggested that an ongoing perception of other players in the international economy, including Britain, as actual or potential threats to Japan's prosperity, may also have served to defer consideration of very real problems within Japan's own economy. Mutual perceptions of Britain's and Japan's economic place in the world tell us more about those who hold those perceptions than about those concerning whom they are held.

For a general survey of Anglo-Japanese economic relations, the following English-language books are useful: E.M. Gull, *British Economic Interests in the Far East* (Oxford: Oxford University Press, 1943); G.C. Allen and A.G. Donnithorne, *Western Enterprise in Far Eastern Economic Development: China and Japan* (London: Allen & Unwin, 1954); F.E. Hyde, *Far Eastern Trade, 1860–1914* (London: A. & C. Black, 1973). A recent comparative survey of the economic history of the two countries which touches in particular on the shifting balance of economic power is K.D. Brown, *Britain and Japan: a Comparative Economic and Social History since 1900* (Manchester: Manchester University Press, 1998).

Notes

1. For trade in the early modern period, see M. Paske-Smith, *Western Barbarians in Japan and Formosa in Tokugawa Days, 1603–1868* (Kobe: J.L. Thompson & Co., 1930, repr. New York: Paragon, 1968); C. Muto, *Nichiei Kotsushi no Kenkyu* (Kyoto: Naigai Shuppan, 1937, repr. Tokyo: Dohosha, 1978), and *A Short History of Anglo-Japanese Relations* (Tokyo: Hokuseido, 1936); M. Takeda, 'Hirado Igirisu Shokan Nikki' in Y. Nagazumi and M. Takeda (eds), *Hirado Oranda Shokan/Igirisu Shokan Nikki* (Tokyo: Soshiete, 1981). For William Adams, see W. Corr, *Adams the Pilot* (Folkestone: Japan Library, 1995).
2. For the role of Hirado as an international port see, for instance, M. Anno, *Koshiron* (Tokyo: Nihon Edyita Sukuru, 1992).
3. Stamford Raffles, *Report on Japan to the Secret Committee of the English East India Company* (Kobe, 1929, repr. London: Curzon, 1971), p. 192.
4. Paske-Smith, *Western Barbarians in Japan and Formosa*, p. 29.
5. Muto, *Nichiei Kotsushi no Kenkyu*, pp. 42, 44, 51; Muto, *Short History of Anglo-Japanese Relations*, pp. 23, 34.
6. Recent studies show that during the Tokugawa era there were three more outlets for trade in addition to the official port of Nagasaki: the Tsushima route between Japan and Korea, the Satsuma–Ryukyu Islands route to China, and later the Matsumae route (Hokkaido) to Russia. See, for example, Y. Nagazumi (ed.), *'Sakoku' o Minaosu* (Tokyo: Yamakawa Shuppansha, 1999).
7. Muto, *Short History of Anglo-Japanese Relations*, p. 56.
8. Raffles, *Report on Japan*, p. 8.
9. Letter from Stamford Raffles to the Secret Committee of the East India Company, 11 February, 1814, in Raffles, *Report on Japan*, p. 89.
10. Letter from Dr Ainslie on the Japan trade, and Report of the Accountant General on the results of the first expedition, both in *Report on Japan*, pp. 162, 165–7, 198.
11. For country trade, see M. Greenberg, *British Trade and the Opening of China, 1800–42* (Cambridge: Cambridge University Press, 1951); W.E. Cheong, *Mandarins and Merchants* (London: Curzon, 1979).
12. Raffles, *Report on Japan*, 5. August 1814, p. 203.
13. W.G. Beasley, *Great Britain and the Opening of Japan* (London: Luzac, 1951), pp. 54, 85.
14. 'Treaty of peace, friendship, and commerce, between Her Majesty and the Tycoon of Japan', in *British Parliamentary Papers* [hereafter *BPP*], 1860m LXIX [Cd 2589].

15. T. Ishii, *Nihon Kaikokushi* (Tokyo: Yoshikawa Kobunkan, 1972), pp. 380–1.
16. Correspondence respecting the revision of the Japanese commercial tariff, in BPP, 1867 LXXIV [Cd 3758].
17. See R. Alcock, *Capital of the Tycoon* (London: Longman & Green, 1863), vol. 1, pp. 281–4. Since the Tokugawa Bakufu adjusted the value of Japanese currency to the international standard in 1860, the outflow of gold from Japan was limited both in quantity and in period.
18. For shipping conferences in the Far Eastern trade, see F.E. Hyde, *Blue Funnel* (Liverpool: Liverpool University Press, 1956), ch. 4; Hyde, *Far Eastern Trade,* pp. 24–41; S. Marriner and F.E. Hyde, *The Senior John Samuel Swire, 1825–1898* (Liverpool: Liverpool University Press, 1967), chs 8, 9; B.M. Deakin (with T. Seward), *Shipping Conferences* (Cambridge: Cambridge University Press, 1973), pp. 29–36. For shipping companies see also B. Cable, *A Hundred Year History of the P.&O, 1837–1937* (London: Nicholson & Watson, 1937); G. Blake, *The Ben Line* (London: Thomas Nelson & Sons, 1956).
19. J. Ahvainen, *The Far Eastern Telegraphs* (Helsinki: Suomalainen Tiedeakatemia, 1981).
20. K. Ishii, *Kindai Nihon Kinyushi Josetsu* (Tokyo: University of Tokyo Press, 1999), ch. 1. See also F.H.H. King, *The History of the Hongkong and Shanghai Banking Corporation* (4 vols, Cambridge: Cambridge University Press, 1987–91); S. Muirhead, *Crisis Banking in the East: the History of the Chartered Bank of India, London and China, 1853–1953* (Aldershot: Scolar Press, 1996); T. Hamashita, 'A History of the Japanese Silver Yen and the Hongkong and Shanghai Banking Corporation, 1871–1913' in F.H.H. King (ed.), *Eastern Banking* (London: Athlone Press, 1983).
21. See Hongkong Daily Press, *The Chronicle and Directory for China, Japan, and the Philippines.*
22. For the nature of 'treaty port trade' see S. Sugiyama, *Japan's Industrialisation in the World Economy, 1859–1899* (London: Athlone, 1988), pp. 52–76.
23. For business activities of western merchants, see K. Ishii, *Kindai Nihon to Igirisu Shihon* (Tokyo: University of Tokyo Press, 1985); Sugiyama, *Japan's Industrialisation,* esp. ch. 3.
24. Yokohama-shi (ed.), *Yokohama-shi Shi,* vol. 2 (Yokohama: Yurindo, 1959), p. 570.
25. *Commercial Report* (hereafter *CR*) for Yokohama for 1889.
26. Okurasho (ed.), *Meiji Zenki Zaisei Keizai Shiryo Shusei,* vol. 9 (Tokyo: Kaizosha, 1933), pp. 40–1, 123–4, 138–9.
27. On the Takasuya affair see Ishii, *Kindai Nihon to Igirisu Shihon,* pp. 31–44; Sugiyama, *Japan's Industrialisation,* pp. 56–64.
28. Ishii, *Kindai Nihon Kinyushi Josetsu,* ch. 2; J. McMaster, 'The Takashima Mine: British Capital and Japanese Industrialisation', *Business History Review,* 37, 3, 1963; Ishii, *Kindai Nihon to Igirisu Shihon,* ch. 3.
29. *CR* for Nagasaki for 1867; 'Reports on the Production of Tea of Japan', p. 9, in *BPP,* 1873. See Sugiyama, *Japan's Industrialisation,* pp. 54–5.
30. Okurasho, *Dai Nihon Gaikoku Boeki Nenpyo,* 1880, 1900; K. Matsui (ed.), *Kindai Nihon Boeki Shi* (Tokyo: Yuhikaku, 1959), vol. 1, pp. 134, 137.
31. The following description of Glover is based on S. Sugiyama, 'Thomas B. Glover: a British Merchant in Japan, 1861–1870', *Business History,* 26, 2, July 1984. For Scots overseas see R.A. Cage (ed.), *The Scots Abroad, 1750–1914* (London: Croom Helm, 1985).
32. W.E. Houghton, *The Victorian Frame of Mind* (New Haven: Yale University Press, 1957).

33. Hitachi Zosen Kabushiki Kaisha, *Hitachi Zosen Kabushiki Kaisha Nanajugonen Shi* (Osaka: Hitachi Zosen KK, 1956), pp. 1–13, 24–80, chronology; Hitachi Zosen Kabushiki Kaisha, *Hitachi Zosen Hyakunen Shi* (Osaka: Hitachi Zosen KK, 1985), pp. 4–13, 17–59. See also H. Saegusa *et al.* (eds), *Kindai Nihon Sangyo Gijutsu no Kindaika* (Tokyo: Toyo Keizai Shinposha, 1960), pp. 73–4.
34. *Annual Statement of the Trade of the United Kingdom with Foreign Countries and British Possessions* for 1870, 1900.
35. For the problems of using official Japanese trade statistics, see I. Yamazawa and Y. Yamamoto, *Boeki to Kokusai Shushi* (vol. 14 of *Long Term Economic Statistics of Japan*) (Tokyo: Toyo Keizai Shinposha, 1979), pp. 125–56.
36. Sugiyama, *Japan's Industrialisation*, chs 4, 5.
37. C.H. Feinstein, 'Home and Foreign Investment' (unpublished PhD thesis, University of Cambridge, 1959), p. 21.
38. T. Tanaka, *Meiji Ishin no Seikyoku to Tetsudo Kensetsu* (Tokyo: Yoshikawa Kobunkan, 1963), chs 2–4. For Lay see also J.J. Gerson, *Horatio Nelson Lay and Sino-British Relations, 1854–1864* (Cambridge MA: East Asian Research Center, Harvard University, 1972). These loans had been redeemed by 1882 and 1897 respectively.
39. See 'Report by Mr. Plunkett on the Mines of Japan', *BPP* 1875 [*c*.1335] LXXIV, pp. 484ff.
40. M. Kasuya, 'Sogyoki Mitsui Bussan no Eigyo Katsudo: Rondon Shiten o Chushin ni', *Keiei Shigaku*, 32, 3, October 1997; Mitsui Bunko (ed.), *Mitsui Jigyo Shi* (Tokyo: Mitsui Bunko, 1980), pp. 284–6; Mitsui & Co., *Hundred Year History of Mitsui & Co. Ltd., 1876–1976* (Tokyo: Mitsui & Co., 1977), pp. 31–2, 38, 45–6.
41. T. Kinugawa, *Honpo Menshi Boseki Shi* (Osaka: Nihon Mengyo Kurabu, 1937), vol. 1, p. 24ff.
42. For the Iwakura Mission see K. Kume (ed.), *Tokumei Zenken Taishi Beio Kairan Jikki* (5 vols, Tokyo: Iwanami Shoten, 1977–82); A. Tanaka, *Iwakura Shisetsudan* (Tokyo: Kodansha, 1977); I. Nish (ed.), *The Iwakura Mission in America and Europe* (Richmond: Curzon Press, 1998), ch. 2.
43. M. Kobayashi, *Nihon no Kogyoka to Kangyo Haraisage* (Tokyo: Toyo Keizai Shinposha, 1977), p. 56.
44. N. Umetani, *Oyatoi Gaikokujin* (Tokyo: Kajima Shuppankai, 1965), pp. 211–22; H. Ishizuka, *Nihon Shihonshugi Seiritsu Shi Kenkyu* (Tokyo: Yoshikawa Kobunkan, 1973), pp. 166–7. For foreign employees see H.J. Jones, *Live Machines* (Tenterden, Kent: Paul Norbury, 1980); O. Checkland, *Britain's Encounter with Meiji Japan* (London: Macmillan – now Palgrave, 1989), chs 3, 5. The figures given in H.J. Jones, 'The Griffis Thesis and Meiji Policy towards Hired Foreigners', in A.W. Burks (ed.), *The Modernizers: Overseas Students, Foreign Employees and Meiji Japan* (Boulder CO: Westview Press, 1985), have not been used, since the sources are not clear.
45. Nihon Kokuyu Tetsudo, *Nihon Kokuyu Tetsudo Hyakunen Shi*, vol. 1 (Tokyo: Nihon Kokuyu Tetsudo, 1969), pp. 315–44; Checkland, *Britain's Encounter with Meiji Japan*, pp. 48–51; M. Sawai, *Nihon Tetsudo Sharyo Kogyo Shi* (Tokyo: Nihon Keizai Hyoronsha, 1998), pp. 24–32; N. Nakamura, *Nihon Tetsudogyo no Keisei* (Tokyo: Nihon Keizai Hyoronsha, 1998), pp. 28–40.
46. M. Yoshida, *Oyatoi Gaikokujin: Sangyo* (Tokyo: Kajima Shuppankai, 1969), pp. 128–35; Saegusa et al. (eds), *Kindai Nihon Sangyo Gijutsu no Kindaika*, pp. 22, 36–8, 49; Y. Yamamoto, 'Sannin Gower', in M. Yoshida (ed.), *Jukyu Seiki Nihon no Joho to Shakai Hendo* (Kyoto: Kyoto Daigaku Jinbunkagaku Kenkyujo, 1985).

47. K. Imazu, 'Oyatoi Gaikokujin Gishi to Kobusho no Gijutsu Kanryo ni tsuite', in T. Shimada *et al.* (eds), *Za Yatoi* (Kyoto: Shibunkaku, 1987). For Maejima, see J. Hunter, 'Maejima Hisoka, 1853–1919: Founder of Japan's Postal System', in I. Nish (ed.), *Britain and Japan: Biographical Portraits*, vol. 1 (Folkestone, Kent: Japan Library, 1994).
48. T. Tsuchiya, *Oyatoi Gaikokujin: Kinyu/Zaisei* (Tokyo: Kajima Shuppankai, 1969). See also O. Checkland and N. Tamaki, 'Alexander Allan Shand, 1844–1930', in I. Nish (ed.), *Britain and Japan: Biographical Portraits*, vol. 2 (Richmond: Japan Library, 1997).
49. M. Kita, 'Kobu Daigakko Token Henry Dyer' in Shimada *et al.* (eds), *Za Yatoi*; M. Kita, *Kokusai Nihon o Hiraita Hitobito* (Tokyo: Dobunkan, 1984), chs 2, 5. See also H. Dyer, *Dai Nippon, the Britain of the East* (London: Blackie & Son, 1904).
50. M. Ishizuki, 'Overseas Study by Japanese in the Early Meiji Period', in Burks (ed.), *The Modernizers*, pp. 169, 180. See also M. Ishizuki, *Kindai Nihon no Kaigai Ryugakusei Shi* (Kyoto: Mineruva Shobo, 1972), appendix, pp. 301ff.; M. Watanabe, *Kindai Nihon Kaigai Ryugakusei Shi*, vol. 1 (Tokyo: Kodansha, 1977), appendix table 2.
51. Y. Yamamoto, 'Inoue Masaru: "Father" of the Japanese Railways', in Nish (ed.), *Britain and Japan*, vol. 2; Kita, *Kokusai Nihon o Hiraita Hitobito*, ch. 2.
52. Kinugawa, *Honpo Menshi Boseki Shi*, vol. 2, ch. 12.
53. D.A. Farnie, *The English Cotton Industry and the World Market, 1815–1896* (Oxford: Oxford University Press, 1979), p. 91.
54. N. Takamura, *Nihon Bosekigyo Shi Josetsu* (Tokyo: Hanawa Shobo, 1971) vol. 1, pp. 182–7, 210–14; M. Tanimoto, *Nihon ni okeru Zairaiteki Keizai Hatten to Orimonogyo* (Nagoya: Nagoya University Press, 1998).
55. F.O. Miscellaneous Series no. 49, 'Reports on the Native Cotton Manufactures of Japan' in *BPP* 1887, LXXXII [*c*.4924–19], pp. 11–13, 27–30. Also Miscellaneous Series no. 7, 'Report on the Import Trade of Great Britain with Japan' in *BPP* 1887, LXXXII [*c*.4294].
56. 'European and American Exports of Cotton Yarns and Piece Goods to Africa and the East', *Board of Trade Journal*, August 1896, p. 141.
57. S. Sugiyama, 'Jukyu-seiki Kohanki ni okeru Higashi Ajia Seito Shijo no Kozo', in A. Hayami, O. Saito and S. Sugiyama (eds), *Tokugawa Shakai kara no Tenbo* (Tokyo: Dobunkan, 1989); Marriner and Hyde, *The Senior John Samuel Swire*, ch. 6. For the development of the sugar industry in Japan see T. Nakajima (ed.), *Gendai Nihon Sangyo Hattatsu Shi: Shokuhin* (Tokyo: Kojunsha, 1967); Togyo Kyokai (ed.), *Kindai Nihon Togyo Shi* (2 vols, Tokyo: Keiso Shobo, 1962, 1997).
58. 'Refined Sugar Sales in Japan (All Grades), 1891–1894', Archives of John Swire & Sons Ltd., SOAS, University of London (JSSI 2/7).
59. Sugiyama, *Japan's Industrialisation*, ch. 6.
60. W.D. Wray, *Mitsubishi and the N.Y.K., 1870–1914* (Cambridge MA: Harvard University Press, 1984), pp. 87–99; Nippon Yusen Kabushiki Kaisha, *Yusen Nanajunen Shi* (Tokyo: Nippon Yusen KK, 1956), pp. 6–15; Nippon Yusen Kabushiki Kaisha, *Nippon Yusen Kabushiki Kaisha Hyakunen Shi* (Tokyo: Nippon Yusen KK, 1988), pp. 9–19; K. Yamaguchi, *Ryutsu no Keiei Shi* (Tokyo: Nihon Keieishi Kenkyujo, 1989), pt 2, ch. 1; N. Takamura, *Saihakken Meiji no Keizai* (Tokyo: Hanawa Shobo, 1995), ch. 3; H. Kokaze, *Teikokushugika no Nihon Kaiun* (Tokyo: Yamakawa Shuppansha, 1995), chs 3, 4.
61. NYK, *Yusen Nanajunen Shi*, pp. 40–7; NYK, *Hyakunen Shi*, pp. 71–4; Osaka Shosen Mitsui Senpaku Kabushiki Kaisha, *Sogyo Hyakunen Shi* (Osaka: Osaka Shosen

Mitsui Senpaku KK, 1985), pp. 142–3; Wray, *Mitsubishi and the NYK*, pp. 400ff. For the Far Eastern shipping conference see W.D. Wray, 'NYK and the Commercial Diplomacy of the Far Eastern Freight Conference, 1896–1956', in T. Yui and K. Nakagawa, *Business History of Shipping* (Tokyo: University of Tokyo Press, 1985).

62. M. Matsukata, *The Adoption of the Gold Standard in Japan* (Tokyo: Government Press, 1899); N. Tamaki, 'Japan's Adoption of the Gold Standard and the London Money Market, 1881–1903', in Nish (ed.), *Britain and Japan*, vol. 1.
63. Treaty Series no. 33, 1894, 'Treaty of Commerce and Navigation between Great Britain and Japan', *BPP* [C.-7588].
64. T. Inoo, *Joyaku Kaisei Ron no Rekishiteki Tenkai* (Tokyo: Komine Shoten, 1976); T. Inoo (ed.), *Naichi Zakkyo Ron Shiryo Shusei* (6 vols, Tokyo: Hara Shobo, 1992).
65. 'British Trade Abroad: Yokohama', *Board of Trade Journal*, August 1904, p. 260.
66. Inoue Kaoru-ko Denki Hensan Iinkai, *Segai Inoue-ko Den*, vol. 5 (Tokyo: Inoue Kaoru-ko Denki Hensan Iinkai, 1968), p. 367.
67. It was Nawa Toichi who pointed out the significance of trade with Britain and the British Empire in Japan's prewar trade (T. Nawa, *Nihon Bosekigyo to Genmen Mondai Kenkyu* (Tokyo: Choryusha, 1937), pp. 467–70).
68. Gaimusho Tokubetsu Shiryobu (ed.), *Nihon ni okeru Gaikoku Shihon* (Tokyo: Kasumigaseki-kai, 1948), p. 43; T. Suzuki, *Japanese Government Loan Issues on the London Capital Market, 1870–1913* (London: Athlone, 1991), pp. 11, 198–201.
69. R. Wakatsuki, *Kofuan Kaikoroku* (Tokyo: Yomiuri Shinbunsha, 1950), pp. 146–7.
70. Gaimusho Tokubetsu Shiryobu (ed.), *Nihon ni okeru Gaikoku Shihon*, pp. 52–3; Suzuki, *Japanese Government Loan Issues*, pp. 200–1.
71. Gaimusho Tokubetsu Shiryobu (ed.), *Nihon ni okeru Gaikoku Shihon*, pp. 54–5; Suzuki, *Japanese Government Loan Issues*, pp. 202–3.
72. Gaimusho Tokubetsu Shiryobu (ed.), *Nihon ni okeru Gaikoku Shihon*, pp. 56–60; Allen and Donnithorne, *Western Enterprise in Far Eastern Economic Development*, pp. 232–6; M. Ito, *Nihon no Taigai Kinyu to Kinyu Seisaku* (Nagoya: Nagoya University Press, 1989), pp. 147–53; T. Kikkawa, *Nihon Denryokugyo no Hatten to Matsunaga Yasuzaemon* (Nagoya: Nagoya University Press, 1995), pp. 105–7. This does not mean that government loan issues lost their significance after 1931. In 1930 Japan's total indebtedness was estimated to be ¥2470 million, of which 77 per cent was government debt (Allen and Donnithorne, *Western Enterprise*, p. 264).
73. See P.J. Cain and A.G. Hopkins, *British Imperialism: Innovation and Expansion, 1688–1914* (London and New York: Longman, 1993), chs 5, 6.
74. Gaimusho Tokubetsu Shiryobu (ed.), *Nihon ni okeru Gaikoku Shihon*, ch. 3; essays by Udagawa, Wilkins, Nicholas, Trebilcock in T. Yuzawa and M. Udagawa (eds), *Foreign Business in Japan before World War II* (Tokyo: University of Tokyo Press, 1990); Allen and Donnithorne, *Western Enterprise*, pp. 229–32; R.P.T. Davenport-Hines and G. Jones, 'British Business in Japan since 1868' in Davenport-Hines and Jones (eds), *British Business in Asia since 1860* (Cambridge: Cambridge University Press, 1989), pp. 223–34.
75. Toyo Babcock was a joint venture between the two companies Babcock and Wilcox and Mitsui Bussan. According to a Japanese source, in 1906 Babcock and Wilcox started direct sales in Japan (M. Udagawa, 'Business Management and Foreign Affiliated Companies in Japan before World War II', in Yuzawa and Udagawa (eds), *Foreign Business in Japan*, p. 11.
76. See Christopher Madeley's chapter in this volume.

77. Gaimusho Tokubetsu Shiryobu (ed.), *Nihon ni okeru Gaikoku Shihon*, pp. 68–9.
78. See C. Hosoya, 'Britain and the United States in Japan's View of the International System, 1919–37' and I.H. Nish, 'Japan in Britain's View of the International System, 1919–37', both in I.H. Nish (ed.), *Anglo-Japanese Alienation, 1919–1952* (Cambridge: Cambridge University Press, 1982).
79. Z. Yan, *Zhongguo Mianfangzhi Shi Gao* (Beijing: Kexue Chubanshe, 1963), pp. 114–18, 130–3; E. Soejima, 'Nihon Bosekigyo to Chugoku Shijo', *Jinbun Gakuho*, 33, February 1972, pp. 103, 108ff.; R.M. Odell, *Cotton Goods in China* (USA Dept of Commerce, Special Agents Series no. 107, Washington, 1916), pp. 37, 43–6. For the Chinese cotton market see H.R. Burrill and R.F. Crist, *Report on Trade Conditions in China* (Washington: Government Printing Office, 1906).
80. Odell, *Cotton Goods in China*, p. 33.
81. A. Feuerwerker, 'Handicraft and Manufactured Cotton Textiles in China, 1871–1910', *Journal of Economic History*, 30, 2, June 1970, p. 372.
82. 'Yarns and Textiles: China', *Board of Trade Journal*, August 1905, p. 322.
83. Tomen Yonjunen Shi Hensan Iinkai, *Tomen Yonjunen Shi* (Osaka: Tomen Yonjunen Shi Hensan Iinkai, 1960), pp. 52, 54.
84. Y. Togai, *Mitsui Bussan Kaisha no Keieishiteki Kenkyu* (Tokyo: Toyo Keizai Shinposha, 1974), pp. 54–60; H. Matsumoto, *Mitsui Zaibatsu no Kenkyu* (Tokyo: Yoshikawa Kobunkan, 1979), pp. 466–7; K. Yamaguchi, 'Mitsui Bussan Kaisha', in K. Yamaguchi (ed.), *Nihon Sangyo Kinyu Shi Kenkyu: Boseki Kinyu Hen* (Tokyo: University of Tokyo Press, 1970), pp. 203–21; K. Suzuki, 'Mikomi Shobai ni tsuite no Oboegaki', *Mitsui Bunko Ronso* 15, 1981; Mitsui and Co., *The Hundred Year History of Mitsui and Co. Ltd.*, pp. 65–6.
85. Diplomatic and Consular Reports, Miscellaneous Series no. 629, 'Report on the Cotton Mills in China', p. 4, *BPP* 1905 [Cd 2237-10].
86. A.S. Pearse, *The Cotton Industry of Japan and China* (Manchester: International Federation of Master Cotton Spinners' and Manufacturers' Associations, 1929), p. 156; Yan, *Zhongguo Mianfangzhi Shi Gao*, pp. 186–7. For the development of the cotton industry in China, in addition to the above-mentioned book by Yan, see K. Chao, *The Development of Cotton Textile Production in China* (Cambridge MA: Harvard University Press, 1977), ch. 5; N. Takamura, *Kindai Nihon Mengyo to Chugoku* (Tokyo: University of Tokyo Press, 1982); H. Nishikawa, *Nihon Teikokushugi to Mengyo* (Kyoto: Mineruva Shobo, 1987), ch. 4; P. Duus, 'Zaikabo: Japanese Cotton Mills in China', in P. Duus, R.H. Myers and M. Peattie (eds), *The Japanese Informal Empire in China, 1870–1937* (Princeton NJ: Princeton University Press, 1989).
87. This description of Yangzi shipping is based on the following books: Nisshin Kisen Kabushiki Kaisha, *Nisshin Kisen Kabushiki Kaisha Sanjunen Shi oyobi Tsuiho* (Tokyo: Nisshin Kisen KK, 1941); NYK, *NYK Hyakunen Shi*, pp. 135–8; Osaka Shosen Mitsui Senpaku Kabushiki Kaisha, *Osaka Shosen Kabushiki Kaisha Hachijunen Shi* (Osaka: Osaka Shosen Mitsui Senpaku, 1966), pp. 25–6; Osaka Shosen, *Sogyo Hyakunen Shi*, pp. 84–5; Kokaze, *Teikokushugika no Nihon Kaiun*, pp. 270–86; K. Katayama, *Kindai Nihon Kaiun to Ajia* (Tokyo: Ochanomizu Shobo, 1996), chs 5, 6; Wray, *Mitsubishi and the NYK*, pp. 341–58, 384ff.; S. Sugiyama, 'A British Trading Firm in the Far East: John Swire and Sons, 1867–1914', in S. Yonekawa and H. Yoshihara (eds), *Business History of General Trading Companies* (Tokyo: University of Tokyo Press, 1987), pp. 179–86.
88. Nisshin Kisen Kabushiki Kaisha, *Sanjunen Shi*, pp. 34–47.
89. Ibid., p. 380. For the significance of government subsidies in the prewar devel-

opment of the Japanese shipping industry, see R. Miwa, 'Maritime Policy in Japan, 1868–1937', in T. Yui and J. Nakagawa (eds), *Business History of Shipping* (Tokyo: Tokyo University Press, 1985).

90. Kokaze, *Teikokushugika no Nihon Kaiun*, pp. 259–69; Katayama, *Kindai Nihon Kaiun to Ajia*, ch. 7; Osaka Shosen, *Sogyo Hyakunen Shi*, pp. 81–2; NYK, *NYK Hyakunen Shi*, pp. 139–40.
91. Imperial Shipping Committee, *British Shipping in the Orient* (London: Imperial Shipping Committee, 1939), ch. 13, para. 105.
92. For details see S. Sugiyama, 'Anglo-Japanese Trade Rivalry in the Refined Sugar Market in China', paper presented to the Anglo-Japanese History Project Workshop, Sunningdale, July 1996; S. Sugiyama, 'Marketing and Competition in China, 1895–1932: the Taikoo Sugar Refinery', in S. Sugiyama and L. Grove (eds), *Commercial Networks in Modern Asia* (Richmond: Curzon, 2001).
93. Seito Kenkyukai, *Togyo Binran* (Tokyo: Seito Kenkyukai, 1937), p. 167.
94. J.H. Dunning, 'Changes in the Level and Structure of International Production' in M. Casson, *The Growth of International Business* (London: Allen & Unwin, 1983), pp. 87–8.
95. For Hanyeping see M.B. Jansen, 'Yawata, Hanyehping, and the Twenty One Demands', *Pacific History Review*, 23, 1, 1954; A. Feuerwerker, 'China's Nineteenth Century Industrialisation: the Case of Hanyehping Coal and Iron Company Ltd.', in C.D. Cowan (ed.), *The Economic Development of China and Japan* (London: Allen & Unwin, 1964).
96. Yamazawa and Yamamoto, *Boeki to Kokusai Shushi*, pp. 56, 257. For Japanese investment in China see C.F. Remer, *Foreign Investments in China* (New York: Macmillan, 1933), ch. 17; W.G. Beasley, *Japanese Imperialism, 1894–1945* (Oxford: Clarendon Press, 1987), pp. 132–41. In Japanese H. Higuchi, *Nihon no Taishi Toshi Kenkyu* (Tokyo: Seikatsusha, 1939); Toa Kenkyujo Daiichi Chosa Iinkai (ed.), *Rekkoku no Taishi Toshi* (Tokyo: Toa Kenkyujo, 1941); Kokka Shihon Yushutsu Kenkyukai (ed.), *Nihon no Shihon Yushutsu* (Tokyo: Taga Shuppan, 1986). For Japanese investment in Manchuria F. Kaneko, *Kindai Nihon ni okeru Tai-Manshu Toshi no Kenkyu* (Tokyo: Kondo Shuppansha, 1991).
97. Remer, *Foreign Investments in China*, chs 6, 16, 17.
98. W.B. Cunningham, *Report on the Cotton Spinning and Weaving Industry in Japan, 1925–6* (London: HMSO, 1927), p. 74; Pearse, *Cotton Industry of Japan and China*, pp. 141–4. For criticism of these reports see F. Utley, *Lancashire and the Far East* (London: Allen & Unwin, 1931), p. 189ff.
99. For the trade negotiations between India and Japan, see Gaimusho (ed.), *Tsusho Joyaku to Tsusho Seisaku no Hensen* (Tokyo: Sekai Keizai Chosakai, 1951), pp. 900–24; O. Ishii, *Cotton Textile Diplomacy* (New York: Arno Press, 1981), ch. 3; Nishikawa, *Nihon Teikokushugi to Mengyo*, ch. 5; N. Kagotani, *Ajia Kokusai Tsusho Chitsujo to Kindai Nihon* (Nagoya: Nagoya University Press, 1999), ch. 6.
100. R. Vansittart to T.M. Snow, Foreign Office, 10 August 1933, 21 August 1933 (FO 410/95).
101. T.M. Snow to J. Simon, Tokyo, 13 May 1933 (FO 410/95).
102. For the Anglo-Japanese trade negotiations, see 'Documents used in Conversations with the Japanese Industrial Delegation' (Manchester Chamber of Commerce (hereafter MCC) Archives M8/5/18); 'Anglo-Japanese Textile Conference' (MCC Archives M8/5/22); O. Ishii, *Cotton Textile Diplomacy*, pp. 114–46; S. Sugiyama, 'The Expansion of Japan's Cotton Textile Exports into Southeast Asia', in S. Sugiyama and M.C. Guerrero (eds), *International Commercial Rivalry in South-*

east Asia in the Interwar Period (New Haven CT: Yale University, Southeast Asia Studies, 1994), pp. 54–60. See also the relevant diary entries of Raymond Streat, then Secretary of the Manchester Chamber of Commerce, in M. Dupree (ed.), *Lancashire and Whitehall: the Diary of Sir Raymond Streat*, vol. 1 (Manchester: Manchester University Press, 1987), pp. 294–304, 306–9.

103. 'Quotas: Memorandum on Present Policy of the Special Committee on Japanese Competition' (MCC Archives, M8/5/22).
104. Gaimusho (ed.), *Tsusho Joyaku to Tsusho Seisaku*, p. 979ff.
105. NYK, *NYK Hyakunen Shi*, pp. 116–22; Wray, 'NYK and the Commercial Diplomacy of the Far Eastern Freight Conference', p. 283.
106. Osaka Shosen KK, *Osaka Shosen KK Hachijunen Shi*, p. 63.
107. NYK, *NYK Hyakunen Shi*, pp. 218–19; Wray, 'NYK and the Commercial Diplomacy of the Far Eastern Freight Conference', p. 284. For the development of Japanese shipping, see K. Nakagawa, 'Japanese Shipping in the Nineteenth and Twentieth Centuries' p. 6ff., in Yui and Nakagawa (eds), *Business History of Shipping*.
108. *British Shipping in the Orient*, ch. 35.
109. Ibid., ch. 15, para. 126; ch. 19, para. 9.
110. Ibid., ch. 9, appendix VII; Osaka Shosen KK, *Hachijunen Shi*, p. 64.
111. *British Shipping in the Orient*, ch. 36, para. 326.
112. Ibid., chs 28, 29; Osaka Shosen KK, *Hachijunen Shi*, pp. 64–6.
113. Cargoes from New Zealand were not included in this agreement (*British Shipping in the Orient*, ch. 30; Osaka Shosen KK, *Sogyo Hyakunen Shi*, pp. 147–8, 271).
114. Osaka Shosen KK, *Hachijunen Shi*, p. 65.
115. *British Shipping in the Orient*, ch. 31, ch. 34, para. 313; I. Brown, 'The British Merchant Community in Singapore and Japanese Commercial Expansion in the 1930s', in Sugiyama and Guerrero (eds), *International Commercial Rivalry*, pp. 123–7. With the start of Sino-Japanese hostilities, shipping in other parts of East Asia, including Japan, grew in importance, and the Japanese share in the shipping of rubber had shrunk to 11 per cent by the end of 1937.
116. Calculated from Nihon Tokei Kyokai, *Nihon Choki Tokei Soran* (5 vols, Tokyo: Nihon Tokei Kyokai, 1988), vol. 3, pp. 69–76.
117. Board of Trade, *United Kingdom Trade*, annually.
118. I am indebted to Keiko Itoh for this information.
119. Davenport-Hines and Jones, 'British Business in Japan since 1868', pp. 232–3.
120. Ibid.
121. P. Newall, *Japan and the City of London* (London: Athlone, 1996), p. 107.
122. *Economist*, 2 August 1941, p. 143.
123. F. Warner, *Anglo-Japanese Financial Relations* (Oxford: Basil Blackwell, 1991), pp. 105–6.
124. Ibid., p. 104.
125. *Economist*, 7 June 1941.
126. Ibid., 2 August 1941.
127. Brown, *Britain and Japan*, p. 75.
128. H. Shimizu, *Anglo-Japanese Trade Rivalry in the Middle East in the Interwar Period* (London: Ithaca Press, 1986), p. 93.
129. Board of Trade, *Japan: Review of Commercial Conditions* (London: HMSO, April 1950), p. 12.
130. Davenport-Hines and Jones, 'British Business in Japan since 1868', pp. 229–31.

131. Board of Trade, *Japan: Review of Commercial Conditions*, p. 13.
132. Ibid., p. 274ff.; I.H. Nish, 'Japan in Britain's View of the International System, 1919–37', p. 53.
133. Mitsubishi Economic Research Bureau, *Japanese Trade and Industry: Present and Future* (London: Macmillan, 1936), pp. 503, 557.
134. W.L. Hichens, 'Anglo-Japanese Competition in the Shipping Trade', *International Affairs*, XVIII, 5, Sept.–Oct. 1939, p. 665.
135. Warner, *Anglo-Japanese Financial Relations*, p. 102.
136. Hosoya, 'Britain and the United States in Japan's View of the International System, 1919–37', pp. 19–20.
137. Ibid., p. 23.
138. J. Sharkey, 'Economic Diplomacy in Anglo-Japanese Relations, 1931–1941', in I. Nish and Y. Kibata (eds), *History of Anglo-Japanese Relations, 1600–2000*, vol. 2, *The Political–Diplomatic Dimension, 1931–2000* (London and Basingstoke: Macmillan – now Palgrave, 2000). In the same volume O. Ishii, 'Markets and Diplomacy: the Anglo-Japanese Rivalries over Cotton Goods Markets, 1930–36'.
139. Pearse, *The Cotton Industry of Japan and China*; 'The Truth about Japan' in *Birmingham Chamber of Commerce Report*, 36, 415, July 1937, p. 644.
140. Greater Manchester Centre for Japanese Studies, *Japan and the North West of England* (Manchester: Greater Manchester Centre for Japanese Studies, 1997), p. 22. Y. Tsurumi *Technology Transfer and Foreign Trade: the Case of Japan, 1950–1966* (New York: Arno Press, 1980), p. 127 gives a figure of £100 000.
141. D.A. Farnie, 'Marketing Strategies of Platt Bros.', *Textile History*, 24, 2, Autumn 1993, p. 155. I am grateful to Professor Farnie for drawing this to my attention.
142. A broader perspective on the British attitude to economic changes in Japan is discussed in P. Charrier, 'Paradigms of Development: British Perspectives on Social and Economic Change in Japan, 1900–1941', *Japan Forum*, 12, 2, 2000.
143. T.E. Gregory, 'Japanese Competition in World Markets', *International Affairs*, XII, 3, May–June 1934.
144. *Birmingham Chamber of Commerce Report* 36, 412, April 1937, pp. 414–15.
145. Ibid., 36, 419, November 1937, p. 918.
146. 'The National Economy of Japan' in ibid., 7, 421, January 1938; 'Japanese Commercial Policy' in ibid., 37, 428, August 1938.
147. W.L. Hichens, 'Anglo-Japanese Competition in the Shipping Trade', p. 678.
148. C. Hosoya, 'Britain and the US in Japan's View of the International System, 1919–37', p. 23.
149. A. Best, *Britain, Japan and Pearl Harbor: Avoiding War in East Asia, 1936–41* (London: Routledge/LSE, 1995), p. 194.
150. P. Lowe, 'Britain and the Opening of the War in Asia, 1937–41', in Nish (ed.), *Anglo-Japanese Alienation*, p. 113.
151. Quoted in A. Best, 'Sir Robert Craigie as Ambassador to Japan, 1937–41', in Nish (ed.), *Britain and Japan*, p. 247.
152. Quoted in P. Lowe, 'Britain and the Opening of the War in Asia, 1937–41', p. 106.
153. See, for example, the papers by Antony Best, John Sharkey and Osamu Ishii in Nish and Kibata (eds), *The Political–Diplomatic Dimension, 1931–2000*. See also the papers in Nish (ed.), *Anglo-Japanese Alienation* and M. Barnhart, *Japan Prepares for Total War: the Search for Economic Security, 1919–1941* (Ithaca NY: Cornell University Press, 1987).
154. C. Hosoya, 'Britain and the United States in Japan's View of the International

System, 1937–41', p. 73, and K. Usui, 'A Consideration of Anglo-Japanese Relations: Japanese Views of Britain, 1937–41', p. 84, also in Nish (ed.), *Anglo-Japanese Alienation.*

155. *Economist*, 14 June 1947, p. 932.
156. *Birmingham Chamber of Commerce Record*, 46, 536, August 1947, p. 546.
157. *London Chamber of Commerce Record* (1947), p. 61.
158. R. Buckley, *Occupation Diplomacy: Britain, the United States and Japan, 1945–52* (Cambridge: Cambridge University Press, 1982), pp. 130–2.
159. Board of Trade, *Japan: Review of Commercial Conditions* (London: HMSO, April 1950), p. 22.
160. Davenport-Hines and Jones, 'British Business in Japan', p. 238.
161. Attempts had been made in 1947 to organise a London syndicate to finance £6 million credit to cover Japan's imports, but this had been blocked by the authorities since the two countries were technically still at war (Newall, *Japan and the City of London*, p. 21).
162. B.R. Mitchell, *British Historical Statistics* (Cambridge: Cambridge University Press, 1988), p. 514; Nihon Tokei Kyokai, *Nihon Choki Tokei Soran*, vol. 3, p. 77ff., Table 10-5-b; Nihon Ginko Tokeikyoku, *Shiryo – Honpo Keizai Tokei*, pp. 250–5.
163. G. Daniels, 'Britain's View of Postwar Japan, 1945–9', in Nish (ed.), *Anglo-Japanese Alienation*, p. 274. See also *Economist*, 15 March 1947, p. 390; 21 June 1947, p. 998.
164. *London Chamber of Commerce Record* (1948).
165. Davenport-Hines and Jones, 'British Business in Japan', p. 234.
166. Nihon Ginko Tokeikyoku, *Honpo Keizai Tokei*, p. 258; Board of Trade, *Japan: Review of Commercial Conditions*, p. 30.
167. J.B. Cohen, *Japan's Economy in War and Reconstruction* (Minneapolis: University of Minnesota Press, 1949), p. 498.
168. For example, *Economist*, 13 November 1948, p. 806; 5 June 1948, p. 942; 31 July 1948, p. 200. See also *Bradford Chamber of Commerce Journal*, 28, 12, December 1948, pp. 38–9.
169. Mr E.A. Lingeman, reported in *London Chamber of Commerce Record* (1948), p. 63.
170. This issue is raised in John Weste's chapter in this volume. It has also been discussed at length in Noriko Yokoi, 'Searching for a Balance: Britain's Trade Policy Towards Japan, 1950–54' (unpublished University of London PhD thesis, 1998).
171. C. Thorne, 'Wartime British Planning for the Postwar Far East', in Nish (ed.), *Anglo-Japanese Alienation*, p. 213.
172. P. Lowe, 'Herbert Morrison, the Labour Government, and the Japanese Peace Treaty, 1951', in *Britain, the United States and Japan's Return to Normal, 1951–1972* (STICERD International Studies Discussion Paper IS/93/258: LSE, 1993), p. 5.
173. G. Daniels, 'Britain's View of Postwar Japan, 1945–9', p. 269.
174. P. Lowe, 'Sir Alvary Gascoigne in Japan, 1946–51', in Nish (ed.), *Britain and Japan: Biographical Portraits*, p. 282. Problems over supplying Hong Kong with affordable textiles are discussed in *Economist*, 21 December 1946, p. 1004.
175. G.C. Allen, 'Britain's Perception of Japan's Post-War Economic Prospects', *Proceedings of the British Association of Japanese Studies*, vol. 2, pt I, 1977, p. 156. Allen was in charge of the Economic and Industrial Planning Staff for Japan at the Foreign Office.
176. Ibid., p. 158.

177. Ibid., p. 159.
178. Economic policy towards Japan during the Occupation is discussed more fully in R. Buckley, *Occupation Diplomacy*, ch. 8.
179. G. Daniels, 'Britain's View of Postwar Japan', p. 273; *London Chamber of Commerce Record* (1950), p. 77.
180. Board of Trade, *Japan: Review of Commercial Conditions*, p. 5.
181. *Economist*, 8 January 1944, p. 33.
182. *Economist*, 13 November 1948, p. 807.
183. Ibid., 14 January 1950, p. 99. The *Economist*, of course, has been famous for its free market views, but it typifies comment on Lancashire that was later to become more widespread.
184. Ibid., 27 October 1951, p. 961. See also editions of 22 April 1950, p. 912; 20 May 1950, p. 1134.
185. P. Lowe, 'Sir Alvary Gascoigne in Japan, 1946–51', in Nish (ed.), *Britain and Japan: Biographical Portraits*, pp. 282, 285.
186. Board of Trade, *Japan: Review of Commercial Conditions*, p. 6.
187. Quoted in R. Buckley, 'British Diplomacy and the Allied Control of Japan, 1945–6', in *Proceedings of the British Association for Japanese Studies*, vol. 2, pt I, 1977, p. 170.
188. Quoted in A. Watanabe, 'From Bitter Enmity to Cold War Partnership: Japanese Views of the United Kingdom, 1945–52', in Nish (ed.), *Anglo-Japanese Alienation*, p. 250.
189. These percentages are lower than those given in G.C. Allen, *Japan as a Market and Source of Supply* (Oxford: Pergamon Press, 1967), p. 86, but have been used to give a consistent series over time.
190. Bureau of Statistics, Prime Minister's Office, *Statistical Yearbook of Japan*, vol. 18 (1967), pp. 310–1.
191. N. Yokoi, 'Searching for a Balance: Britain's Trade Policy towards Japan, 1950–54'.
192. *London Chamber of Commerce Record* (1954), p. 81; *Economist*, 6 February 1954, p. 408.
193. N. Yokoi, *Searching for a Balance*, pp. 139–60.
194. *Bradford Chamber of Commerce Journal*, 35, 5, May 1955, p. 19.
195. Quoted in *Economist*, 23 April 1955, p. 316.
196. R. Grey, 'The Anglo-Japanese Commercial Treaty of 1962: a British Perspective', in Nish (ed.), *Britain and Japan: Biographical Portraits*, vol. 2, p. 309; S. Hanaoka, 'Memories of the Anglo-Japanese Commercial Treaty: a Japanese Perspective', in ibid., p. 322.
197. R. Grey, 'The Anglo-Japanese Commercial Treaty of 1962', pp. 308–15.
198. H. Cortazzi, *Japan and Back* (Folkestone: Global Oriental, 1998), p. 100.
199. *Economist*, 8 March 1958, p. 28 (supplement).
200. G.C. Allen, *Japan as a Market and Source of Supply*, p. 103.
201. *Bradford Chamber of Commerce Journal*, 35, 8, August 1955, p. 17.
202. *Economist*, 10 November 1962, pp. 593–4.
203. The challenge of Japanese shipbuilding is well documented. See, for example, *Economist*, 4 March 1950, p. 284; 29 April 1950, p. 960; 20 March 1965, pp. 1293–5; 21 August 1965; 14 October 1967, pp. 195–9; 21 October 1967, pp. 302–5; 27 March 1971, pp. 71–2; 17 March 1973, pp. 56–7.
204. See, for example, *Birmingham Chamber of Commerce Journal*, 48, 557, May 1949, p. 403; 51, 600, December 1952, pp. 1193–4; 54, 632, August 1955, pp. 809–10.
205. For example, *London Chamber of Commerce Record* (1954), p. 81.

206. For example, *Bradford Chamber of Commerce Journal*, 39, 6, June 1959, pp. 29–31; 40, 2, December 1960, pp. 21–3.
207. *Economist*, 20 October 1956, p. 247.
208. Ibid., 31 May 1952, p. 597.
209. Ibid., 21 June 1952, p. 801.
210. *Birmingham Chamber of Commerce Journal*, 54, 632, August 1955, p. 810.
211. *Bradford Chamber of Commerce Journal*, 35, 8, August 1955, p. 11ff.
212. *Economist*, 20 August 1955, p. 608.
213. *Bradford Chamber of Commerce Journal*, 35, 3, March 1955, p. 21.
214. C. Braddick, 'Distant Friends: Britain and Japan in the Age of Globalization, 1958–1998', in Nish and Kibata (eds), *The Political–Diplomatic Dimension, 1931–2000*, fn.9.
215. *Economist*, 13 January 1962, p. 151. This example is also cited in T. Ozawa, *Japan's Technological Challenge to the West, 1950–74: Motivation and Accomplishment* (Cambridge MA: MIT Press, 1974), p. 76. See also H. Cortazzi, *Japan and Back*, p. 111.
216. Ibid.
217. The atomic energy issue is also discussed in *Economist*, 21 June 1958, pp. 1111–12; 14 February 1959, pp. 623–4; 28 February 1959, pp. 813–14.
218. T. Ozawa, *Japan's Technological Challenge to the West*, pp. 25–6.
219. Quoted in ibid., p. 25.
220. Ibid., p. 87.
221. *Economist*, 30 January 1965, p. 459. Cortazzi, however, has expressed the view that Lord Stokes had a condescending view of the Japanese car industry (*Japan and Back*, p. 113; 'A Personal View of Postwar Economic Relations', in T.G. Fraser and P.C. Lowe (eds), *Conflict and Amity in East Asia* (Basingstoke and London: Macmillan – now Palgrave, 1992), p. 170).
222. G.C. Allen, *Japan as a Market and Source of Supply*, p. 10.
223. H. Cortazzi, *Japan and Back*, p. 119ff.; *Economist*, 27 September 1969.
224. Davenport-Hines and Jones, 'British Business in Japan', p. 239.
225. Newall, *Japan and the City of London*, pp. 22–39.
226. Warner, *Anglo-Japanese Financial Relations*, p. 130.
227. Davenport-Hines and Jones, 'British Business in Japan', p. 256.
228. HMSO and Office for National Statistics, *Annual Abstract of Statistics* (London: HMSO, annually).
229. H. Cortazzi, *Japan and Back*, p. 140.
230. H. Cortazzi, 'A Personal View of Postwar Economic Relations', p. 179.
231. The British attitude towards Japan as an inspiration for institutional reform, particularly with respect to management and industrial relations issues, is discussed in some detail in Kevin McCormick's chapter in vol. 5 of this series ('Postwar Japan as a Model for British Reform', in G. Daniels and C. Tsuzuki (eds), *History of Anglo-Japanese Relations, 1600–2000*, vol. 5, *Cultural Relations* (Palgrave, forthcoming).
232. A. Berry, *Labour Relations in Japan* (Coventry: Coventry and District Engineering Employers' Association, 1979).
233. M. George and H. Levine, *Japanese Competition and the British Workplace* (London: CATS, Polytechnic of North London, 1984).
234. *Economist*, 5 June 1971, p. 75.
235. D. Wilson, 'Economic Links: Britain's Partner in the East', in Anglo-Japanese Eco-

nomic Institute, *Anglo-Japanese Collaboration: On to Global Partnership* (London: Anglo-Japanese Economic Institute, 1995), p. 34.

236. R.A. Belderbos, 'The Role of Investment in Europe in the Globalization Strategy of Japanese Electronics Firms', in F. Sachwald (ed.), *Japanese Firms in Europe* (Luxembourg: Harwood, 1995), pp. 122, 126; Newall, *Japan and the City of London*, p. 53. This contrasts with earlier complaints about unemployment induced by Japanese imports.
237. D. Wilson, 'Economic Links: Britain's Partner in the East', p. 35.
238. Cited in F. Sachwald, 'The Decisions of Japanese Firms to Produce in Europe', in Sachwald (ed.), *Japanese Firms in Europe*, p. 65.
239. See, for example, *Economist*, 3 March 1962, p. 787. See also Braddick, 'Distant Friends'.
240. *Economist*, 29 September 1973, p. 15.
241. This is described in M. Conte-Helm, *The Japanese and Europe: Economic and Cultural Encounters* (London: Athlone, 1996). See also the comments by K. Chiba in G. Bull (ed.), *Japan in Britain: the Changing Partnership* (London: Anglo-Japanese Economic Institute, 1989), p. 26.
242. L. Turner, 'Potential Collaboration in Science and Technology', in Anglo-Japanese Economic Institute, *Anglo-Japanese Collaboration*, pp. 26–31.
243. HMSO and Office for National Statistics, *Annual Abstract of Statistics* (London: HMSO, 1999), p. 311.
244. Warner, *Anglo-Japanese Financial Relations*, p. 194.
245. Newall, *Japan and the City of London*, pp. 32, 71.
246. British Overseas Trade Board, *Investment and Licensing in Japan* (London: BOTB, 1973), pp. 3, 5, 10, 14.
247. Ibid., pp. 15–16.
248. D. Wilson, 'Economic Links: Britain's Partner in the East', pp. 42–4.
249. Ibid., p. 40.
250. The significance of the language issue has been debated, with disagreement as to its significance. The Board of Trade, in advising on commercial conditions in Japan in 1950, assumed that few businessmen spoke Japanese, and effectively discouraged them from trying to learn it if they were making only a short trip. The London Chamber of Commerce in 1937 proudly announced that Lord Sempill had addressed a visiting Japanese economic mission in Japanese, and certainly such people were a rarity (*London Chamber of Commerce Annual Record*, 1937). See also H. Cortazzi, *Japan and Back*, p. 114.
251. Davenport-Hines and Jones, 'British Business in Japan', pp. 241–4.

2
British–Japanese Rivalry in Trading and Banking

Kanji Ishii

Introduction

It has been widely documented that after Japan opened up to the world in the middle of the nineteenth-century, the country's cotton industry developed rapidly. After the First World War it emerged as a strong challenger to Britain in world markets, and by 1933 the volume of Japanese cotton cloth exports exceeded that of the British. The international competitive power of the Japanese cotton industry was supported not only by technological innovations such as the automatic loom, the fall of wages and the exchange rate due to the Great Depression,[1] but also by the activity of the Japanese trading companies and foreign exchange banks.[2] In this chapter I would like to investigate what the Japanese trading companies and foreign exchange banks had learnt from their British counterparts after the opening up of the country, and how they competed with the British before the First World War.

Japanese trading companies were established from the 1870s onwards. In 1873 the Okuragumi Trading Co., with a capital of ¥150 000, was established by Okura Kihachiro, who had been an arms dealer. In 1876 the Mitsui Bussan Kaisha (hereafter Mitsui Bussan) was founded (with no capital) by Masuda Takashi and the Mitsui Family. In 1880, raw silk producers founded the Doshin Kaisha with a capital of ¥100 000. In 1881 Takada Shinzo, an importer of machines, founded the Takada Trading Co. In 1887 some cotton merchants in Osaka founded the Naigai Wata Kaisha with a capital of ¥500 000, and in 1892 some cotton-spinning companies founded the Nippon Menka Kaisha with a capital of ¥1 million. In 1893 Arai Ryoichiro and his friends established the Yokohama Kiito Gomei Kaisha with a capital of ¥500 000.[3]

Owing to the activities of these trading companies, the share of Japanese merchants in Japanese foreign trade increased from 13.4 per cent in 1880 to 38.1 per cent in 1900, and to an estimated 52.5 per cent in 1911.[4] Foremost among these was Mitsui Bussan, which accounted for 13.0 per cent of Japanese foreign trade in 1900 and 22.5 per cent in 1911.[5]

From 1900 to 1911 Mitsui Bussan accounted for two-thirds of the increased share of the Japanese trading companies in the country's foreign trade. This essay will concentrate on Mitsui Bussan as the country's leading trading company.

In 1880 the Yokohama Specie Bank (hereafter the Specie Bank) was founded, and soon began operating in the foreign exchange market, which had been dominated tithes to by the Oriental Bank Corporation, the Hongkong and Shanghai Banking Corporation and others. The share of the Specie Bank in the financing of Japanese foreign trade increased from 24.7 per cent in 1891 to 39.1 per cent in 1900, and to 45 per cent in 1911.[6] Therefore, the second part of this chapter will analyse the Specie Bank as the country's leading foreign exchange bank.

Mitsui Bussan

The combination of commission business with trade on the company's own account

Mitsui Bussan was established in 1876 by Masuda Takashi, who had been involved with the Senshu Kaisha in association with Inoue Kaoru, and by Minomura Rizaemon, head clerk of the Mitsui Family. The Mitsui Family invested no money in Mitsui Bussan, and Mitsui Takenosuke and Mitsui Yonosuke, who became the owners of Mitsui Bussan, were cut off from the Mitsui Family so that the family would not be affected by any possible losses incurred by Mitsui Bussan.[7] In 1892, Mitsui Bussan came under the direct control of the Mitsui Family. It became an unlimited partnership with a capital of ¥1 million in 1893, and a limited company with a capital of ¥20 million in 1909. Masuda Takashi, who became president of Mitsui Bussan, claimed in his autobiography that the company did not need any capital because it aimed to do business on commission.[8] This was not true. In reality, the affairs of the Mitsui Family at that time were so bad that no capital could be spared to invest in the new business.[9]

It was true that Mitsui Bussan aimed to do business on commission, a growing practice in international trade.[10] The articles of the company stated that the company would specialise in '*tonya*' or commission business, selling or buying on behalf of customers, although trade on the company's own account was allowed as long as it was profitable.[11] The commission business had existed in pre-modern Japan. In the Tokugawa era, wholesale merchants were divided into *tonya* (*toiya* in Kansai) and *nakagai*. *Tonya* sold merchandise on behalf of clients to *nakagai*, who sold on to the retail dealers. It should also be noted that *tonya* sometimes bought merchandise on their own account when they thought it would be profitable.[12]

After the collapse of the Tokugawa Government, Masuda, who had been a government cavalry commander, worked for Walsh, Hall & Co. in

Yokohama and gained experience of the newest style of foreign trade. It was natural for Masuda to adopt the principle of commission business for Mitsui Bussan. In a speech in 1904, he claimed that the company had held to this principle since its foundation in 1876.[13] He pointed out how business had changed. At first, Mitsui Bussan got commission on foreign sales or purchases of rice and coal for the government. Later, when they imported machines and raw cotton for Japanese cotton-spinning companies or exported raw silk ordered by American silk merchants, they sometimes made profits by buying goods at their own risk before getting the orders or by gathering orders before buying the goods. Thus the meaning of commission business had gradually changed. In 1913, it was openly admitted that the overselling and overbuying operations had become indispensable to the transactions relating to some articles.[14]

The combination of the commission business with trade on the company's own account was a key difference between Mitsui Bussan and the western merchants which enabled the former to overtake the latter. A Japanese businessman who had worked in the Yokohama branch of Jardine, Matheson and Co. between 1909 and 1926 testified that his firm could buy raw silk in the Yokohama market only after receiving orders from American weavers. They frequently lost out to Japanese trading companies, which could buy large amounts of raw silk on their own accounts without waiting for orders from the United States.[15] The staff of the Tokyo head office of Mitsui Bussan began to allow branch managers to overbuy or oversell merchandise within fixed limits after 1895. For example, the manager of the Yokohama branch, who was allowed in 1897 to overbuy up to 200 bales of raw silk, could buy up any raw silk he thought would be profitable. In 1899 the manager of the New York branch was also allowed to oversell up to 500 bales of raw silk.[16]

The efforts of the managers of Mitsui Bussan to lower the buying price led to purchases in the producing areas themselves. In 1904, the Bombay branch sent representatives to Nagpur to investigate the possibility of direct purchases, and in 1906 they began to buy up raw cotton directly in the producing areas. In 1914 Mitsui Bussan bought 55 per cent of the raw cotton exported to Japan directly from the cotton-producing areas, rising to 90 per cent in 1916.[17] The New York branch of Mitsui Bussan also began to buy raw cotton directly from Oklahoma in 1905. In 1911 the Southern Products Co., with a capital of US$100000, was established at Houston in Texas (moving to Dallas in 1912), and bought raw cotton as an agency of Mitsui Bussan. By 1916 most American raw cotton was being bought directly from the producing areas.[18]

Through such direct purchases, Mitsui Bussan pushed down the purchase price. Tsukada Kota, who graduated from the Tokyo Higher Commercial School (*Koto Shogyo Gakko*) in 1907 and went to the Bombay branch immediately after entering Mitsui Bussan, wrote that the direct purchases were made to prevent middlemen from raising the price and adulterating the cotton. According to Tsukada, Japanese cotton merchants went to any cotton-producing area in the world if the price was cheap and the quality was good, and consequently overtook the western cotton merchants, who bought raw cotton only from the local cotton merchants at the trading centres.[19]

The Bombay branch of Mitsui Bussan borrowed the ¥500000 necessary for direct purchase in the cotton-producing area from the Bombay branch of the Specie Bank.[20] As for the compradors who had been regarded as indispensable for transactions in the Chinese market, Mitsui Bussan replaced them by training its own Chinese-speaking staff. The branches in Shanghai, Tianjin, Taipei and Hong Kong all dismissed their compradors between 1899 and 1902.[21] Mitsui Bussan had to pay commission to compradors in the Chinese market who were not only employed by the foreign merchants, but also engaged in their own business. Thus by dismissing them Mitsui Bussan increased its competitiveness by reducing commissions.[22] The moves also led to expanded business opportunities for the firm. A report on the market for cotton cloth in Shanghai pointed out that the share of Japanese cloth increased both because of its cheapness compared with Manchester goods, and because of the ability of Japanese businessmen to speak Chinese. The report added that British merchants narrowed their circle of transactions by speaking only English, while the Japanese and German merchants expanded their opportunities by speaking Chinese.[23]

Attempts to reduce the rate of commission

The strong position of Mitsui Bussan was due not only to the combination of commission business with trade on its own account, but also to the firm's low commission rate.[24] At a meeting of branch managers in 1902, Masuda explained that the eclipse of western merchants in the East Asian market by Chinese and Japanese merchants was because the western merchants claimed 2.5 per cent commission, while the Chinese merchants, with their lower standard of living, claimed only one per cent.[25] Several branch managers stressed low commission rates as the key to success in the cotton markets.[26] It is not easy to confirm the rate of commission of Mitsui Bussan because it differed according to the commodity, and changed over time.[27] For example, in 1903 0.5 per cent was charged for goods associated with the railways, and 3 per cent was charged for Java raw sugar obtained from the sugar-refining companies in Osaka. It is interesting to note that the manager of the Osaka branch guaranteed that sales could be doubled if the rate of commission was halved. In the same year it was reported that the commission on coal was 2.5 per cent.

Matsumoto Hiroshi has pointed out that the commission rates for the sale of Miike coal after 1889 and for Kaishima coal in 1898 were 2.5 percent. Commission on cement sales paid by the Onoda Cement Co. to Mitsui

Bussan was reduced from 3.5 per cent in 1901 to 2.5 per cent in 1903. In 1892 1.5 per cent was charged on raw cotton bought for the Kanegafuchi Cotton Spinning Co. This was reduced to 1.25 per cent in 1901, and Mitsui Bussan also promised a rebate of 0.25 per cent or 0.5 per cent. Thus Mitsui Bussan received from Kanegafuchi commission of less than 0.5 per cent in 1903. Only 1 per cent was charged on sales of cotton yarn for the Kanegafuchi Cotton Spinning Co. and the Miike Cotton Spinning Co. In comparison, the 5 per cent charged on the sale of woollen cloth for the Goto Woollen Cloth Factory was exceptionally high due to the award by Mitsui Bussan of special finance amounting to ¥200 000. We can therefore conclude that although the general rate of commission claimed by the Japanese trading companies, as represented by Mitsui Bussan, was around 2.5 per cent, the same rate claimed by the western trading companies, in more competitive markets the Japanese firms lowered their rates to the one per cent charged by the Chinese merchants.

In 1904, however, it was reported that exports of sundry goods from Osaka and Kobe to China were controlled by Chinese merchants because their networks excluded Japanese merchants and their commission was lower than that of Japanese merchants. It was not easy for Japanese merchants to compete with the Chinese on commission rates alone. The decisive factor which allowed the Japanese merchants to overwhelm the Chinese was their superior organization. Ishida Reisuke, who worked in Mitsui Bussan from 1907 to 1941, stated that the Chinese merchants who could trade skilfully on their own account had been the strongest rivals of Mitsui Bussan, but that their weak point was lack of larger organizations.[28] The networks of Chinese merchants, which were only combinations of individuals based on territorial divisions or kinship ties, were gradually overwhelmed by the big trading organizations of Japanese merchants.

Effort and failure of the joint account

When Mitsui Bussan sought to lower its commission rates, how to adjust the commissions of buying offices and selling offices became a subject of internal discussion. Mitsui Bussan established branches and agencies all over the world. In 1890 they had 11 branches at home and four abroad (Shanghai, Hong Kong, Tianjin, London). By 1900 they had opened another nine offices at home and 11 abroad, and by 1910 they had a further two at home and 26 overseas.[29] The adjustment of commissions between offices became a serious problem for managers.

In 1898 a joint account system for the main goods such as raw cotton, cotton yarn, coal and soybeans was set up in order to avoid fruitless competition between branches of Mitsui Bussan. From 1899 this was extended to transactions in raw silk, cotton cloth, matches, exported rice, and fertilizer. The rules stated that the main office for each commodity controlled every transaction of both the buying and the selling offices.[30] It was assumed that only the selling office should claim commission. However, there was no provision preventing the buying office from claiming commission, and the buying office usually added commission to the price of the goods.[31] At a meeting of branch managers in 1904, one speaker proposed that the coal buying office should not be allowed to charge commission, but was opposed by Yamamoto Jotaro, manager of the Shanghai branch, who claimed that such a proposal undervalued the activities of the buying office. The meeting drafted a compromise, under which the profits gained by the selling office would be shared equally with the buying office.[32]

The above discussion reveals one of the secrets of the power of Mitsui Bussan, which was developing into a mammoth international trading company. The staff of the company, who concentrated their efforts on increasing the profits of their own branches, were indifferent to the total profits of the company as long as their individual contributions to those profits were correctly evaluated.[33]

What should also be noted is the opinion that the joint account system was difficult to apply to those fields in which trade on the branch's own account was combined with commission business, but was easy to apply to those fields with commission business alone. In a meeting in 1906, Fujino Kamenosuke, manager of the Osaka branch, argued that for transactions of cotton yarn, in which trade on the company's own account was indispensable, having a joint account for each transaction was nonsense. Endo Daisaburo, chief of the rice and fertilizer division, stated that it was questionable whether the buying office was informing the selling offices of the correct buying price. Isomura Toyotaro, chief of the business department, concluded that it was questionable whether the joint account system was in fact working. Yasukawa Yunosuke, manager of the Tianjin branch, insisted on the abolition of the system.[34] It is interesting that Yasukawa and Yamamoto, who were the most aggressive staff of Mitsui Bussan, called for the abolition of the system. It seems to me that the joint account system, which was intended to reduce commission, did not work well. This was because Mitsui Bussan's transactions were not pure commission business, but a combined operation of commission business with trade at the company's own risk, and the head office had to authorize branch managers to conduct such combined operations. As long as Mitsui Bussan was to challenge the western and Chinese merchants by means of such combined operations, the abolition of the joint account system was unavoidable. The revised 'Rules of Operation' of 1909 show that the joint account system was dropped except for transactions in raw silk.[35]

Recruitment from higher education institutions

Lastly, we shall look at how the staff of Mitsui Bussan was recruited. At first Mitsui Bussan had to depend on the abilities of foreigners who had experience in international trading. Until January 1883 Mitsui Bussan employed as an adviser Robert Walker Irwin, an American merchant, who had once been a partner of Walsh, Hall & Co., and who had established Edward

Fischer & Co. with Edward Fischer in 1873. Irwin's elder brother, Richard, was entrusted with the London agency of Mitsui Bussan, to which one Sasase Motoaki was sent to gain experience of international trade.[36]

At a meeting of branch managers in 1906, Yamamoto Jotaro, a director of Mitsui Bussan, proposed that more foreigners should be employed. Masuda replied that he had preferred to employ Japanese to foreigners since 1879, although other companies and government offices employed many foreigners. Yamamoto defended himself by stressing that foreigners should be hired as employees, while Masuda had in former times employed them as advisers.[37] Masuda's speech was a valuable testimony to his principle that the Japanese should conduct foreign trade on their own as much as possible.

Masuda was determined to employ Japanese who had received higher education. Mitsui Bussan employed many graduates of the Tokyo Higher Commercial School, established in 1875. Table 2.1 shows the educational background of the company's staff at the end of April 1919.[38] Tokyo Higher Commercial School graduates accounted for nearly half of all senior posts with a monthly salary of over ¥200. In December 1919, four out of five executive directors had graduated from the school. Although recruits from the imperial universities and private universities were gaining importance, they did not control the top management in 1919.[39]

For a trading company in its initial stage to depend on Japanese staff was a potentially risky policy. Although Mitsui Bussan had accumulated profits of ¥1.29 million by 1893, this profit had to be used to cover deficits resulting from the Matsukata deflation and the subsequent sudden rise of business.[40] These deficits, which could be seen as the price paid by the Japanese staff to acquire the necessary skills in international trade, were far higher because of Masuda's principle of depending on Japanese staff as much as possible. It was on these deficits, however, that the rapid development of Mitsui Bussan after the Sino-Japanese War was based.

The Yokohama Specie Bank

British bankers as advisors to the Japanese government

Before the Specie Bank was established in 1880, some of the British bankers who had come to Japan advised the Japanese government on its monetary and financial policy. Despite this, the Japanese government made all final decisions by itself. The most important problem was whether Japan should adopt the gold standard or the silver standard. At first the Japanese government opted for silver. John Robertson, the manager of the Yokohama branch of the Oriental Bank Corporation, and Thomas W. Kinder, who was invited to Japan as the chief of the Mint Bureau, advised that the Japanese government should adopt the silver standard because of Japan's location in Asia,

Table 2.1 Educational careers of Mitsui Bussan staff

Educational career		*Number*	*Number earning more than ¥200*
Imperial universities		276	(5)
of which	Tokyo	228	(5)
	Kyoto	37	(0)
	Kyushu	2	(0)
	Hokkaido	9	(0)
Commercial high school		834	(25)
of which	Tokyo	552	(25)
	Kobe	111	(0)
	Osaka	29	(0)
	Yamaguchi	56	(0)
	Nagasaki	52	(0)
	Otaru	34	(0)
Industrial high school		80	(4)
of which	Tokyo	65	(4)
	Others	15	(0)
Foreign language school		107	(2)
Private university, professional school		517	(8)
of which	Waseda	104	(0)
	Keio Gijuku	98	(3)
	Toa Dobunkan	66	(0)
	Takushoku	37	(0)
	Chuo	29	(2)
	Foreign	22	(1)
	Others	181	(4)
Commercial school		657	(7)
of which	Nagoya	87	(0)
	Kobe	58	(0)
	Osaka	14	(5)
	Others	495	(2)
Secondary school		126	(1)
Others		351	(8)
Total		2945	(62)

Source: Mitsui Bussan Kabushiki Gaisha, *Shitencho Kaigi Gijiroku*, 1919.

where the Mexican silver dollar was used in international trade. The Japanese government, however, changed its mind and decided to adopt the gold standard after Ito Hirobumi, who had been sent to the United States to investigate the monetary system there, suggested opting for the gold standard because the leading advanced countries were going to adopt it themselves. The government asked the opinion of William W. Cargil from the London head office of the Oriental Bank, but his warnings that the gold standard would be inconvenient for Japan were ignored.

Some Japanese scholars insist that this change of policy was a major failure.[41] I am inclined, however, to support the opinion that there had already been a tendency towards use of a gold standard in the development of the monetary system of the Tokugawa era.[42] This view contends that the Japanese monetary system at the end of the Tokugawa era was a de facto gold standard. The prohibition of silver coins and the issue of paper money in gold units by the new government further promoted this tendency. Though Ito Hirobumi himself thought of the gold standard as a completely new system, it was the most acceptable monetary system for the Japanese people. The problem was how to treat the Mexican dollars used in Asian international trade. The Japanese government approved unlimited circulation of the Mexican dollar at the ports for foreign trade.

This gold standard system could not be established immediately because the Japanese government had not withdrawn inconvertible paper money. Thus in 1872 national banks were set up in imitation of the American model. These were to replace the current note issue with convertible notes. To advise and instruct on the practicalities of modern banking, the government employed Alexander Allan Shand (1844–1930), the manager of the Yokohama branch of the Chartered Mercantile Bank of India, London and China, between 1872 and 1877. Why did they employ a British banker when they were introducing an American-style banking system?[43] Why did they select the young Shand instead of selecting an older, experienced banker?[44] Perhaps it is because the Japanese government wanted a banker who would instruct them in practical business rather than financial policy. Shand performed his duty earnestly, and consolidated the foundations of modern Japanese banking.

Senior officials of the Ministry of Finance did not consult Shand on the amendment of the National Bank Act in 1876, which permitted the national banks to issue inconvertible banknotes, because Shand's objections to such an amendment had been foreseen. Shand had criticized the move because of a fear of inflation, and advised the Japanese to establish a central bank which could issue convertible banknotes. Tokuno Ryosuke, a senior bureaucrat of the Ministry of Finance, claimed that Shand had not understood the thinking behind the amendment. As convertible notes could not circulate alongside inconvertible money, and as the value of the public bonds granted to the old feudal ruling class in place of stipends had to be maintained, the government could not avoid establishing national banks based on public bonds and with the right to issue inconvertible notes. The establishment of a central bank would have required the withdrawal of inconvertible notes and a reduction of expenditure on the old ruling class. It seems that Shand had failed to give due consideration to these circumstances.[45]

After returning to the United Kingdom in 1877, Shand obtained a position in the Alliance Bank, which was taken over by Parr's Bank in 1892, and was promoted to manager of the London branch of Parr's Bank in 1902, becoming director in 1909. There is a famous story that he cooperated with Takahashi Korekiyo in the issue of the Japanese government bonds during the Russo-Japanese War of 1904–05. Takahashi had studied English at Yokohama in 1867, working as a servant boy for Shand, who was then manager of the Yokohama branch of the Chartered Mercantile Bank. When Takahashi later visited Shand in London as a representative of the Japanese government, Shand welcomed Takahashi warmly, avoiding talk about their former relationship in Yokohama.[46]

As already mentioned, Shand insisted on the superiority of a British banking system characterized by specialization. In Britain in the 1870s, banks for internal finance and banks for foreign finances were clearly separated. When Shibusawa Eiichi, president of the Daiichi National Bank of Tokyo, applied for permission to the Ministry of Finance to open a European branch in 1874, and a Shanghai branch in 1875 and again in 1877, each application was rejected by the Ministry due to the opposition of Shand. Shand opposed the idea because he felt it was much too risky for the Daiichi National Bank, which had concentrated on domestic business, to expand its interests abroad.[47] Consequently the Pusan branch, the first foreign branch of the Daiichi National Bank, was only opened in 1878, after Shand had been dismissed by the Japanese government.

The Daiichi National Bank's branches in Korea were highly profitable. The financing of Korean–Japanese trade conducted in yen did not involve foreign exchange transactions.[48] This was also true for the Korean branches of the Eighteenth National Bank of Nagasaki. The foreign exchange business in Japan began with the establishment of the Yokohama Specie Bank in 1880. Until 1889, the Specie Bank engaged in authorized foreign exchange transactions solely using government funds, and only after that did it begin to rediscount foreign exchange bills at the Bank of Japan, becoming a real foreign exchange bank operating on its own account.[49]

Model of the Ordinance of the Yokohama Specie Bank

In 1887 the precise character of the Yokohama Specie Bank, which had been provisionally based on the National Banking Act, was clarified by the YSB Ordinance. The original draft of the Ordinance was submitted to Matsukata Masayoshi, the Minister of Finance, by Hara Rokuro, then President of the Specie Bank. The Ministry of Finance deleted a reference to authorized foreign exchange transactions and added an item stipulating that the Minister of Finance was empowered to appoint the vice-president of the Bank of Japan to the additional post of the president of the Specie Bank if he thought it necessary to do so. According to Matsukata's explanation at a meeting of the *Genroin* (Senate), the latter item was necessary to regulate the interests of these two banks. The president of the Specie Bank was to be elected from among the directors with the approval of the Minister of Finance, while those of the Bank of Japan and the Bank of Taiwan were to be nominated by the Minister of Finance.[50]

Japanese historians have argued that the Specie Bank Ordinance was modelled on the Ordinance for the Incorporation of the Hongkong and Shanghai Banking Company,[51] and that the former Ordinance became more liberal in character due to the influence of the latter. Taking into account Matsukata's report that the Ordinance of the Specie Bank was similar to those of the western chartered banks,[52] it seems certain that Hara and Matsukata did refer to the Ordinance of the Hongkong and Shanghai Bank. However, we should compare these Ordinances more carefully before accepting their similarities.

The British government regulated colonial banks either by Royal Charter or by the corporation ordinance of the colonial government. Although the Hongkong and Shanghai Bank was intended at first to be a corporation by Royal Charter, the British government opted for the latter form because the head office of the Hongkong and Shanghai Bank was located in Hong Kong Colony. This change did not mean that the Hongkong and Shanghai Bank was established freely based on the Company Act.[53] The Bank had sought to be exempted from the provision of double liability, which meant that shareholders were liable up to a limit of double the face value of their holdings. This was refused, and shareholders had to assume unlimited liability for issued banknotes.[54] Thus the Hongkong and Shanghai Bank was strictly regulated, because it was expected to act not only as a foreign exchange bank but also as the central bank of Hong Kong. By contrast, the Specie Bank was expected to be solely a foreign exchange bank without any central banking role. Thus the two ordinances were essentially different. There were, of course, some common points, such as the prohibition on investing in real estate stemming from their character as foreign exchange banks. The election of directors at meetings of shareholders rather than by government appointment was another similarity. This item in the Ordinance of the Specie Bank was, however, soon changed as it was apparently viewed as being too liberal. Afterwards all elected directors had to be approved by the Minister of Finance.[55]

Through these comparisons it is clear that the Specie Bank Ordinance was not based exclusively on that of the Hongkong and Shanghai Bank. Although the Japanese government had learned a great deal from the British financial system and its operation, there were other influences as well. The Japanese government took the concept of the national bank system from the United States, the organization of the central bank from Belgium, the credit association from Germany, and the industrial bank from France.

Recruitment of staff of the Specie Bank

The Specie Bank, which began foreign exchange business in October 1880, carried out business in the head office and inland branches without initially depending on foreign bankers. Table 2.2 shows the number of Japanese staff and foreign staff.

In 1886, the bank's half-yearly report stated that there were six foreigners out of a total of 49 staff members – two each in the branches or agencies in London, New York and Lyon. This roughly corresponds with the figures in the table. It seems likely that no foreigners were employed in Japan in the early years. According to the recollections of Takahashi Korekiyo, who became one of the managers of the head office of the Specie Bank in August 1895, about 80 people worked for the bank at that time. The president, Sonoda Kokichi, and the director, Soma Nagatane, occupied an upstairs room, while the managers Yamakawa Yuboku, Totsugi Heikichi, Kawashima Chunosuke and Takahashi himself worked together downstairs. Totsugi was in charge of foreign exchange and taught Takahashi the details of exchange rates, the selling and buying of bills of exchange, and the managing of relations with customers or foreign branches. From these recollections it is clear that such business at the Yokohama head office was conducted by Japanese staff. Takahashi also said that in the Specie Bank at that time graduates from the universities were not welcome, whereas graduates from commercial schools were most welcome.[56] It should be remembered, however, that apart from engineers, few graduates from the universities obtained jobs in large companies at this time. Interestingly, the predominance of graduates from commercial schools was similar to that at Mitsui Bussan.

According to Table 2.2, however, the number of foreigners in the bank increased dramatically in the twentieth century. This was due not only to the increase of offices abroad which employed compradors, but also to an increase in the number of compradors employed by the inland offices. During the economic crisis in 1907, it was reported that the Specie Bank suffered heavy losses due to bad loans to Chinese merchants, which had been guaranteed by compradors employed by the offices of the Specie Bank.[57] It was the Kobe branch that suffered the heaviest of these losses. Of course, we can assume that early on some foreign banker may have instructed the

Table 2.2 Number of staff at the Specie Bank, 1880–1919

Date (year end)	*1880*	*1886*	*1895*	*1899*	*1910*	*1919*
Japanese	36	55	117	212	541	719
Non-Japanese	0	8	18	26	145	348

Source: *History of the Yokohama Specie Bank* (1920).

staff of the Specie Bank in matters relating to the foreign exchange business.[58] Even so, it would not have taken the Japanese staff too long to acquire the necessary knowledge, because in the Tokugawa era Japanese people had been accustomed to remitting money by bills of exchange between the western silver region and the eastern gold region. They were used to fluctuations in the rate of exchange between silver- and gold-based currencies. Although the Tokugawa government had closed the country, Japanese merchants and financiers were well used to 'international' transactions and foreign exchange within Japan itself.

Funds of the Bank of Japan and the Chinese and Indian deposits

The next problem is how the Specie Bank raised the money for its foreign exchange business. As mentioned above, when the Specie Bank began exchange transactions on its own account in 1889, it used Bank of Japan funds at 2 per cent. The average rate of interest on private deposits in Japan was too high to allow the Specie Bank to compete with the foreign banks. This situation continued until the outbreak of the First World War. At a meeting of the oriental branch managers held in April 1908, general manager Yamakawa explained that because the bank held insufficient private deposits, it was obliged to borrow from the Bank of Japan and from the London and Lyon financial markets in order to meet its needs for foreign exchange and loans. Yamakawa stressed that the ratio of deposits to the net worth of the Specie Bank was very low in comparison with those of foreign banks.[59]

In 1907 the Specie Bank financed 42 per cent of the Japan's exports and 41 per cent of its imports, to the value of ¥386 million. Even when the foreign branches tried to circulate money efficiently by using the Specie Bank's own network to send money, at least ¥100 million was needed for the operation of the foreign exchange business. To meet the needs of the foreign exchange operations, which produced on average a profit of 5.5 per cent, the Specie Bank began to make use of fixed deposits on which 5.0 per cent was payable.[60] Although Japanese interest rates became sufficiently low for the Specie Bank to be able to use deposits for its foreign exchange business, it made little effort to attract deposits. The general manager Yamakawa explained that the bank sought to avoid competition for deposits with other Japanese banks, and proposed to collect deposits in China and India.[61]

While the value of the Specie Bank's deposits increased from ¥26 million in 1901 to ¥106 million in 1911, the deposits of its branches in China increased during the same period from ¥3 million to ¥22 million, and those in India from ¥2 million to ¥6 million.[62] The remarkable increase in deposits in China reflected the efforts of the branches to attract deposits in order to cover a shortage of funds, a shortage which resulted from the flight of silver funds in China to the London branch to avoid depreciation.[63] Table 2.3 shows the deposits of the foreign offices of the Specie Bank at the end of 1911.

Table 2.3 Deposits of the foreign offices of the Specie Bank, 1911 (¥ 000)

Office		*Deposits (A)*	*Fixed deposits (B)*	*B/A (%)*	*Foreigners (C)*	*C/A (%)*
Europe/America		37 580	3 401	9.0	1 837	4.9
of which	London	28 173	1 597	5.6	1 725	6.1
	New York	6 457	–	–	8	0.1
India (2)		6 444	5 115	79.4	6 220	96.5
of which	Bombay	6 135	4 881	79.6	5 948	96.9
China (13)		21 884	9 477	43.4	15 807	72.4
of which	Shanghai	7 353	3 277	44.6	5 393	73.3
	Tianjin	4 796	2 398	50.0	4 265	88.9
	Dairen	2 966	693	23.4	1 682	56.7
	Beijing	2 859	1 672	58.5	2 475	86.5
	Hankow	1 002	466	46.6	588	58.7
	Hong Kong	886	494	55.7	723	81.6
	Manchuria (7)	1 983	478	24.1	682	34.4
Total (20)		65 868	17 993	27.3	23 864	36.2

Source: Ministry of Finance, *Report on Banking*, no. 36.
Notes: Deposits = Sum of fixed deposits, current deposits, deposits at notice and special deposits. Figures in parentheses indicate number of offices.

It is obvious that most of the deposits in the offices in India and China were held by non-Japanese, while those in Europe and America were held by Japanese. Although there might have been some western depositors in China, it was reported that the main part of the fixed deposits at the Beijing and Tianjin branches were made by the Chinese mandarinate or the Chinese government.[64] At the meeting of the oriental branch managers, Suzuki Shimakichi, manager of the Shanghai branch, explained that the interest the bank offered was usually 0.5 per cent higher than the rates of the Hongkong and Shanghai Bank or the Chartered Bank of India, Australia and China (hereafter the Chartered Bank), and many Chinese customers came to their branch to make deposits.[65] Such a predominance of Chinese depositors at the Chinese offices of the Specie Bank was in sharp contrast to the case of the Hongkong and Shanghai Bank, whose depositors in China were mainly westerners. The total amount of deposits at the Chinese branches of the Hongkong and Shanghai Bank in 1913 was around £7 million, of which £5 million was held at the Shanghai branch. Considering that most of the depositors of the Shanghai branch were westerners, and that deposits at the Hongkong head office were estimated to be worth over £5 million,[66] we can guess that most of the deposits of the Hongkong and Shanghai Bank in China were made by western people. While the deposits of the Shanghai branch of the Hongkong and Shanghai Bank in 1913 were equivalent to ¥48 million, those of the Shanghai branch of the Specie Bank in 1913 were only ¥11 million.

As for the deposits of the Bombay branch of the Specie Bank, it was reported that the value of current deposits was around one million rupees, and of fixed deposits around nine million rupees. These sums had been deposited by wealthy Indians through money brokers at rates of 4.0 per cent to 4.5 per cent.[67] As shown in Table 2.3, almost all of the deposits of the Indian offices of the Specie Bank, including the Calcutta agency opened in October 1911, were made by Indians.

Thus in terms of deposits, the Specie Bank remained at a disadvantage compared to foreign banks, and had to continue to depend on funds supplied by the Bank of Japan. As for the internal circulation of funds for foreign exchange between the worldwide network of the offices, the author has written on this elsewhere.[68]

The worldwide network of offices and the depreciation of silver

How did the Specie Bank compete with other foreign banks? It opened branches or agencies all over the world and increased its number of clients by offering them worldwide services. In 1890 the bank had one branch at home (Kobe) and four overseas offices (New York, London, Lyon and San Francisco). By 1900 it had opened another two offices at home and six abroad, and by 1910 another one in Japan and a further ten overseas. It should be noted that the number of overseas offices increased in the eastern silver currency area. This means that the Specie Bank had to continue its struggle with the depreciation of silver even after Japan had adopted the gold standard in 1897.

The worldwide depreciation of silver after 1873 was also a difficult problem for the Hongkong and Shanghai Bank and the Chartered Bank. These banks tried to cut down the permanent transfer of funds between the gold- and silver-using countries and minimize the exchange position between these different areas. In the case of the Chartered Bank, the capital permanently employed in the silver-using countries was reduced from £550000 to £225000. Needless to say, the branches in the east had to depend for their working funds mainly on the deposits they collected from clients.[69] In the case of the Hongkong and Shanghai Bank, it did not have to worry about the depreciation of silver as seriously as the other banks because the capital of the bank was paid in Hong Kong in silver. It had to make efforts, however, to minimize the exchange position when transacting foreign exchange between silver- and gold-using countries. These efforts were dubbed the 'Even Keel Policy'.[70] It was pointed out that the London branch of the Hongkong and Shanghai Bank collected substantial deposits, which were mainly used for foreign exchange and investment business in London.[71] What covered the shortage of funds of the Asian branches was probably the net worth and the deposits of the Hong Kong head office.

After the sudden change of the price of silver in 1890 due to the enactment of the Silver Purchase Act in the United States, in 1891 the Specie Bank adopted the associated transaction system. This system minimized the exchange position by concentrating the accounts of exchange in the silver-using countries at the Yokohama head office, and accounts in the gold-using countries at the London branch. The system did not, however, work well, because it could not make the most of the Shanghai silver market.[72] Although it was abolished in 1897, the increase in exchange transactions in Asia created a serious silver depreciation problem for the Specie Bank. At meetings of the oriental branch managers held in April 1908 and in May 1909, the policy of exchange cover at the Shanghai branch was discussed. It was pointed out that when the Kobe branch bought silver bills and asked the Shanghai branch to cover them, the Shanghai branch could not always do this at a reasonable price. Aoki Tetsutaro, the manager of the Kobe branch, stated that the Hongkong and Shanghai Bank had special powers in the Shanghai financial market which the Specie Bank could not match, and argued that the Specie Bank should at least compete with the Chartered Bank and the International Bank.[73] From this we can see that the Specie Bank was liable to lose clients if it could not offer them at least the same rate of exchange as other exchange banks. As for the operations of other exchange banks, none of those present at the meeting had any concrete information. However, the bank's president, Takahashi, reported that the general manager of the Hongkong and Shanghai Bank was anxious about fluctuations in the value of silver. Takahashi believed that the Hong Kong head office concentrated its risks and did everything to minimize its exchange position, and proposed that the Specie Bank should concentrate its risks in the Shanghai branch.[74] From July 1909 a new policy of exchange cover between silver- and gold-using countries came into operation.[75] This policy reflected the Takahashi proposal, in that the Shanghai branch was responsible for covering exchange. The Shanghai branch investigated the Shanghai financial market, and reported that the foreign banks were selling silver bullion in Shanghai, Bombay and London.[76] After this report the Specie Bank began to sell and buy silver bullion more positively.

Rate of exchange and term of bills

In order to acquire new clients the Specie Bank had to offer more favourable terms than other banks. The main criteria were the rate of exchange and the term of bills. When Takahashi became one of the managers of the head office, the Specie Bank had few clients among importers. Takahashi therefore offered the Nippon (Nihon) Yusen Kaisha, the Mitsubishi Goshi Kaisha and the Standard Oil Co. more favourable terms than did other foreign banks, and succeeded in acquiring them as clients.[77] The concession he offered was to raise the rate of exchange by one-sixteenth of a penny per yen. Thus when the exchange rate for an import bill bought by the Hongkong and Shanghai Bank was 2s $2\frac{2}{16}$d per yen, the Specie Bank bought the import bill at 2s $2\frac{3}{16}$d per yen.[78] If an importer in Japan sent £10000 to London, he paid the Specie Bank only ¥91646, whereas he had to pay the Hongkong and Shanghai Bank ¥91866. The Specie Bank enabled the importer to save 0.24 per cent by comparison with the cost of the same transaction with the Hongkong and Shanghai Bank. For importers this must have been attractive.

As for the terms of bills of exchange, Kodama Kenji, the manager of the Bombay branch, reported one interesting fact at the meeting of the oriental branch managers in April 1909. He claimed the Bombay branch had been buying from exporters of raw cotton to Japan a large number of bills of exchange at 60 days. In February 1908, however, the term of the bills was suddenly shortened to 30 days and many clients moved to the branches of the Hongkong and Shanghai Bank or the Chartered Bank.[79] Fortunately the term of the bills was again extended to 60 days and all the former clients, with the exception of Mitsui Bussan, came back to the Specie Bank.[80] This shortening of the term of bills was part of the head office response to the economic crisis of 1907.[81] After the crisis of 1907, the Hongkong and Shanghai Bank, the Chartered Bank and the International Bank tried to maintain transactions with Mitsui Bussan by extending the terms of bills in conjunction with orders from the Kanegafuchi Cotton Spinning Co. from 60 days to 90 days. From November 1908 to March 1909, 42 per cent of the raw cotton exported by Mitsui Bussan was financed by these three foreign banks. In order to compete, the branch manager of the Specie Bank unsuccessfully asked head office for permission to buy the bills of exchange at 90 days.[82] Given that the share of the Specie Bank recovered to 85 per cent in 1911,[83] bills of exchange at 90 days may well not have been used for long by the foreign banks.

Though competing with the foreign banks, the Specie Bank sometimes cooperated with them when they could agree to do so. For example, the Specie Bank of Japan worked together with banks from the United Kingdom, France, Germany and Russia when these five countries raised a loan for the Republic of China in 1913. The Specie Bank joined the Eastern Exchange Banks' Association, which was headed by the Chartered Bank, and agreed to maintain the interest rate on eastern bills at around 6–7 per cent.[84] In July 1908 the eight foreign exchange banks in Japan, including the Specie Bank and the Hongkong and Shanghai Bank, agreed to shorten the term of export bills on Europe and the United States from six months to four months.[85] The same month seven foreign exchange banks in Japan, including the Specie Bank, decided to end the practice of delivering imported goods to clients before receiving payment.[86]

Apart from the Specie Bank, few Japanese banks developed a substantial foreign exchange business before the First World War. Although the Specie

Bank enjoyed remarkable growth, it could not challenge the Hongkong and Shanghai Bank or the Chartered Bank due to its shortage of private deposits. It should also be noted that the operations of the Specie Bank were in addition dependent on the London financial market.

Conclusion

It is apparent that the Japanese trading companies and exchange banks had caught up with those of the United Kingdom by the outbreak of the First World War. The Japanese trading companies and exchange banks, which had quickly mastered methods of modern trading and banking because of the traditions of the *tonya* merchants and moneychangers during the Tokugawa era, soon became independent of foreigners thanks to the recruitment of staff from the Tokyo Higher Commercial School and other institutions. Japanese trading companies such as Mitsui Bussan overtook their western competitors by combining commission business with trade on their own account, and by trying to minimize the commission rate. They also surpassed the Chinese merchants, whose trading habits were similar to their own, through their power of organization.

Only the Specie Bank developed in the field of foreign exchange business, dependent on cheap funds supplied by the Bank of Japan and money deposited by Chinese and Indians. Although the Specie Bank tried to compete with foreign banks such as the Hongkong and Shanghai Bank and the Chartered Bank, its shortage of funds made this difficult. However, the development of Japanese trading companies and foreign exchange banks before the First World War supported the growth of Japanese industries such as cotton and silk. In doing so they established one of the preconditions for the fierce competition between Japan and Britain in the world cotton market after the First World War.

Notes

1. C. Howe, *The Origins of Japanese Trade Supremacy* (London: Hurst, 1995).
2. In this respect the activities of the shipping and insurance companies are also important, but analysis of their activities is beyond the scope of this chapter.
3. There are many historical studies of Mitsui Bussan which will be referred to later in this chapter. For the prewar history of the Nippon Menka Kaisha, the only source is T. Ozawa (ed.), *Nippon Menka Kabushiki Kaisha Gojunenshi* (Osaka: Nichimen Jitsugyo, 1943). For the Naigai Wata Kaisha, which later became an integrated cotton company in China, see N. Takamura, 'Naigai Wata Kaisha', in K. Yamaguchi (ed.), *Nihon Sangyo Kinyushi Kenkyu, Boseki Kinyu Hen* (Tokyo: University of Tokyo Press, 1970). The history of the Okuragumi Trading Co., which went bankrupt in 1998, has not been studied, except for a brief piece in Okura

Zaibatsu Kenkyukai (ed.), *Okura Zaibatsu no Kenkyu* (Tokyo: Kondo Shuppansha, 1982). Recently Y. Sunagawa (*Okura Kihachiro no Gokainaru Shogai* (Tokyo: Soshisha, 1996)) proved false the story that Okuragumi sent tinned foods mixed with small stones to the Japanese army fighting the Sino-Japanese War. The history of the Takada Trading Co., which was a major importer of machines and warships, ranking alongside Mitsui Bussan and the Okuragumi Trading Co., and cooperating with these companies in exporting used Japanese weapons, has not been studied, probably because of its bankruptcy in 1925. For the same reason, there are no company histories of the Doshin Kaisha and Yokohama Kiito Gomei Kaisha, which rivalled Mitsui Bussan in the export of raw silk, but these companies are dealt with in K. Ishii, *Nihon Sanshigyoshi Bunseki* (Tokyo: University of Tokyo Press, 1972). Mitsui Bussan, the leading trading company in the transaction of raw cotton, cotton goods, machines, raw silk and many other commodities, was called a *sogo shosha* (general trading company). In the economic crisis of 1920, Suzuki Shoten in Kobe, Kuhara Shoji and Furukawa Shoji in Tokyo, Mogi Shoten and Abe Shoten in Yokohama, and Itochu Shoji in Osaka, all of which had expanded their businesses with a view to achieving *sogo shosha* status during the First World War, all suffered serious losses. Only Mitsubishi Shoji, which became independent of Mitsubishi Goshi Kaisha in 1918, continued to develop. The volume of business of Mitsubishi Shoji, however, was half that of Mitsui Bussan in the middle of the 1930s, and the profits of the former were only one sixth of those of the latter.

4. K. Ishii, 'Japanese Trade and the Yokohama Specie Bank', in O. Checkland, S. Nishimura and N. Tamaki (eds), *Pacific Banking 1859–1959: East meets West* (New York: St Martin's Press – now Palgrave, 1994), p. 2.
5. Y. Togai, *Mitsui Bussan Kaisha no Keieishiteki Kenkyu* (Tokyo: Toyo Keizai Shinposha, 1974).
6. Ishii, 'Japanese Trade and the Yokohama Specie Bank', p. 2.
7. Togai, *Mitsui Bussan Kaisha no Keieishiteki Kenkyu*, pp. 61–2. This author misunderstood the arrangement between Mitsui Bussan and the Mitsui Family. On this point, see Mitsui Hachiroemon Takamine Denki Hensan Iinkai (ed.), *Mitsui Hachiroemon Takamine Den* (Tokyo: Mitsui Bunko, 1988), p. 120.
8. M. Nagai (ed.), *Jijo Masuda Takashi Den* (Tokyo: M. Nagai, 1939, republished Tokyo: Chuo Koronsha, 1989), p. 119.
9. K. Ishii, *Kindai Nihon Kinyushi Josetsu* (Tokyo: University of Tokyo Press, 1999), ch. 2.
10. International trading companies which had engaged in business on their own account, taking advantage of differences between prices in distant countries, had to abandon such business after the 1870s, once the telegraph led to convergence in prices. Thus Jardine Matheson & Co. had to diversify after the 1870s. On these points, see K. Ishii, *Kindai Nihon to Igirisu Shihon* (Tokyo: University of Tokyo Press, 1984); M. Ishii, *Kindai Chugoku to Igirisu Shihon* (Tokyo: University of Tokyo Press, 1998).
11. K. Suzuki, 'Mikomi Shobai ni tsuite no Oboegaki', *Mitsui Bunko Ronso*, 15, 1981.
12. R. Hayashi, *Edo Tonya Nakama no Kenkyu* (Tokyo: Ochanomizu Shobo, 1976).
13. Mitsui Bussan Gomei Kaisha, *Shitencho Shimonkai Gijiroku*, 1904, p. 22.
14. K. Yamaguchi (ed.), *Kohon Mitsui Bussan Kabushiki Kaisha Hyakunenshi* (Tokyo: Nihon Keieishi Kenkyusho, 1978) (hereafter *Kohon Mitsui Bussan*), vol. 1, p. 308.
15. K. Ishii, *Joho Tsushin no Shakaishi* (Tokyo: Yuhikaku, 1994), pp. 88–9. The evidence was the recollection of Ishida Reisuke, who worked in Mitsui Bussan from 1907

to 1941, reproduced in Nihon Keieishi Kenkyusho (ed.), *Kaikoroku, Mitsui Bussan Kabushiki Kaisha* (Tokyo: Mitsui Bussan Kabushiki Kaisha, 1976); and a 1970 interview with Niwaya Harutaro, who worked in the Yokohama branch of Jardine Matheson & Co. from 1909 to 1926. Ishida's recollections compared the transactions of Mitsui Bussan with those of Mitsubishi Shoji and foreign trading companies, and echoes the reminiscences of Niwaya. Hashimoto Juro ('Kokusai Kotsu Rejimu no Keisei to Sozo sareta Sogo Shosha', *Historia* (Osaka Rekishi Gakkai) 158, 1998), criticizes the present author, but this criticism is based on a misunderstanding of the evidence. For the raw silk trade, see K. Hiraoka, *Sanshigyo Keizai no Kenkyu* (Kyoto: Yuhikaku, 1939), which makes it clear that the Japanese trading companies overtook their foreign rivals in 1912 by buying raw silk on their own accounts, while the others bought only after receiving orders from customers. It is true that Mitsubishi Shoji was comparatively careful in trading on its own account, as pointed out in Y. Nagasawa, *Mitsubishi Shoji Seiritsushi no Kenkyu* (Tokyo: Nihon Keizai Hyoronsha, 1990), but the firm suffered losses during the 1930s. See I. Hatade, *Nihon no Zaibatsu to Mitsubishi* (Tokyo: Rakuyu Shobo, 1978).

16. Suzuki, 'Mikomi Shobai ni tsuite no Oboegaki', pp. 23, 74. H. Yamazaki ('Nihon Shoshashi no Ronri', *Shakai Kagaku Kenkyu*, 39, 4, 1987) points out that the combination of the commission business with trade at the company's own risk was the decisive factor which enabled the Japanese trading companies to surpass foreign ones, and the formation of a control system for that risk was a key factor in their development as *sogo shosha*. The first of these two ideas was first presented by the author of this chapter at an international conference held in January 1986 (see S. Yonekawa and H. Yoshihara (eds), *Business History of General Trading Companies* (Tokyo: University of Tokyo Press, 1987), pp. 203–6).
17. The Nippon Menka Co. also opened a Bombay branch in 1907 and began to buy raw cotton directly from the producing areas. In 1911 the Gosho Co. opened a Bombay agency. After 1919 the Nippon Menka Co. was buying more cotton in the producing areas than any other Japanese trading company. See E. Kinoshita,'Nihon Shosha no Indo Menka Kaitsuke no Kiko' in K. Matsui (ed.), *Nichiin Mengyo Koshoshi* (Tokyo. Ajia Keizai Kenkyusho, 1960), pp. 182–3; N. Kagotani, 'Senzenki Nihonjin Shosha ni yoru Indo Menka no Okuchi Kaitsuke Katsudo', *Jinbun Gakuho* (Kyoto University) 82, 1999.
18. *Kohon Mitsui Bussan*, vol. 1, pp. 357–8. Nippon Menka Co. and Gosho Co. opened agencies in the cotton-producing areas of the United States in 1910 and 1912 respectively.
19. K. Tsukada, *Keirokushu* (Tokyo: Keizai Oraisha, 1953), pp. 185–6, 196–8. In the United States the British trading companies also bought raw cotton directly from the producing areas. See Yokohama Shokin Ginko, *Juyo Shohin no Kokusai Shijo* (Tokyo: Yokohama Shokin Ginko, 1931), p. 25.
20. Mitsui Bussan Gomeikaisha, *Shitencho Shimonkai Gijiroku*, 1907, p. 296.
21. *Kohon Mitsui Bussan*, vol. 1, p. 208.
22. Mitsui Bussan Gomeikaisha, *Shitencho Shimonkai Gijiroku*, 1902.
23. Shanghai Chuzai Shomu Shokikan, *Shanghai ni okeru Menpu Torihiki Jokyo* (Hiroshima: Hiroshima Kenritsu Shohin Chinretsusho, 1925), pp. 67–8.
24. Hashimoto, 'Kokusai Kotsu Rejimu no Keisei to Sozo sareta Sogo Shosha', p. 91. However, this work offers no original evidence.
25. Mitsui Bussan Gomeikaisha, *Shitencho Shimonkai Gijiroku*, 1902.
26. Mitsui Bussan Gomeikaisha, *Shitencho Shimonkai Gijiroku*, 1904, 1905.
27. Mitsui Bussan Gomeikaisha, *Shitencho Shimonkai Gijiroku*, 1903; H. Matsumoto,

Mitsui Zaibatsu no Kenkyu (Tokyo: Yoshikawa Kobunkan, 1979), p. 430ff. Matsumoto in fact misread the commission on cotton purchases for the Kanegafuchi Cotton Spinning Co. as 15 per cent instead of 1.5 per cent.

28. Noshomusho Shokokyoku, *Nisshin Boeki Jijo* (Tokyo: Noshomusho, 1904), p. 33; Nihon Keieishi Kenkyusho (ed.), *Kaikoroku, Mitsui Bussan Kabushikikaisha*, p. 129.
29. Togai, *Mitsui Bussan Kaisha no Keieishiteki Kenkyu*, p. 43.
30. *Kohon Mitsui Bussan*, vol. 1, pp. 209–11.
31. Mitsui Bussan Gomeikaisha, *Shitencho Shimonkai Gijiroku*, 1903, p. 205.
32. Ibid., 1904, pp. 81–102, 186.
33. H. Morikawa (*Zaibatsu no Keieishiteki Kenkyu* (Tokyo: Toyo Keizai Shinposha, 1980)) analyses the joint account system of Mitsui Bussan using the records of the branch managers' meetings. However, Morikawa understood the problem only in terms of the opposition between centralization and decentralization and did not seek to explain why the joint account system conflicted with the active performances of the branches. The real conflict existed between the joint account system for the reduction of commission based purely on commission business, and the active performance of branches combining commission business with trade at their own risk.
34. Mitsui Bussan Gomeikaisha, *Shitencho Shimonkai Gijiroku*, 1906, pp. 51–6.
35. *Kohon Mitsui Bussan*, vol. 1, p. 212. Though Morikawa argues that the joint account system was strengthened in the 1910s, this seems impossible because, as Suzuki makes clear, it was in this decade that the tendency for branches to trade on their own account became established.
36. Togai, *Mitsui Bussan Kaisha no Keieishiteki Kenkyu*, pp. 53–4.
37. Mitsui Bussan Gomeikaisha, *Shitencho Shimonkai Gijiroku*, 1906, p. 236.
38. Mitsui Bunko, *Mitsui Jigyoshi*, vol. 3-1 (Tokyo: Mitsui Bunko, 1980), p. 357. The number of graduates from higher commercial schools and others are different from those of Table 2.1. According to S. Yonekawa ('University Graduates in Japanese Enterprises Before The Second World War', *Business History*, XXVI, 1984), the company which employed the largest number of university (including higher commercial school) graduates was Mitsui Bussan, with 731 graduates.
39. *Kohon Mitsui Bussan*, vol. 1, p. 306. In 1900 among 341 salaried men at Mitsui Bussan, 66 were graduates of the Tokyo Higher Commercial School. In 1910 of 870 salaried men at Mitsui Bussan, 216 were graduates of the Tokyo Higher Commercial School. As a proportion of the total number of salaried men at Mitsui Bussan, graduates from the Higher Commercial School increased from 19.4 per cent in 1900 to 24.8 per cent in 1910, decreasing to 18.7 per cent in 1919.
40. M. Kasuya, 'Meiji Zenki no Mitsui Bussan', *Shakai Keizai Shigaku*, 61, 3, 1995.
41. K. Tatewaki, 'The Role of Foreign Banks in Japan during the Ansei Treaty Period 1859–1899', *Waseda Business & Economic Studies*, 28, 1992, p. 55.
42. R. Mikami, *Yen no Tanjo* (Tokyo: Toyo Keizai Shinposha, 1975), pp. 222–32.
43. Tatewaki, 'The Role of Foreign Banks in Japan', p. 58.
44. T. Tsuchiya, *Shand* (Tokyo: Toyo Keizai Shinposha, 1966), pp. 37–40.
45. K. Ishii, 'Gaikokujin no Keizai Koso', *Nihon Kindai Shiso Taikei 9, Keizai Koso* (Tokyo: Iwanami Shoten, 1988), pp. 504–6.
46. T. Uetsuka (ed.), *Takahashi Korekiyo Jiden* (Tokyo: Chikura Shobo, 1926, repr. Chuo Koronsha, 1976), vol. 1, pp. 30–3; vol. 2, p. 116.
47. Tsuchiya, *Shand*, pp. 108–14.

48. K. Murakami, 'Shokuminchi' in K. Oishi (ed.), *Nihon Sangyo Kakumei no Kenkyu* (Tokyo: University of Tokyo Press, 1975), vol. 2, pp. 276–94.
49. Ishii, 'Japanese Trade and the Yokohama Specie Bank', p. 8.
50. K. Furukawa, 'Yokohama Shokin Ginko Jorei no Seitei to Kawase Seisaku' in R. Shibuya (ed.), *Meijiki Nihon Tokushu Kinyu Ripposhi* (Tokyo: Waseda University Press, 1977), pp. 88–99.
51. F.H.H. King, *The History of the Hongkong and Shanghai Banking Corporation* (Cambridge: Cambridge University Press, 1987), vol. 1, pp. 625–33.
52. S. Hijikata, *Yokohama Shokin Ginko* (Tokyo: Kyoikusha, 1980), p. 92.
53. T. Matsuda, *Igirisu Shihon to Toyo* (Tokyo: Nihon Hyoronsha, 1950), pp. 163–4.
54. A.S.J. Baster, *The International Banks* (London: P.S. King & Son Ltd., 1935), pp. 170, 668–9.
55. Hijikata, *Yokohama Shokin Ginko*, p. 101.
56. Uetsuka (ed.), *Takahashi Korekiyo Jiden*, vol. 2, pp. 78–9, 89. According to Yonekawa (see note 38), the Specie Bank employed 197 university and higher commercial school graduates in 1914, while the Bank of Japan employed 189 and the Mitsui Bank employed 162.
57. *Yokohama Shokin Ginko Koho* (hereafter *Koho*) 3, 16 June 1908.
58. It should be noted that Koizumi Nobukichi, the first vice-president (1880–83) and manager of the head office of the Specie Bank (1890–94), Hara Rokuro, its fourth president (1883–90), Sonoda Kokichi, its fifth president (1890–97), Soma Nagatane, its sixth president (1897–1906), and Takahashi Korekiyo, its seventh president (1906–11), had all been abroad when they were young. Koizumi and Hara studied banking principles at King's College, London, as Professor Tamaki's contribution to this volume makes clear. N. Tamaki and O. Checkland ('Alexander Allan Shand, 1844–1930 – a Banker the Japanese Could Trust', in I. Nish (ed.), *Britain and Japan: Biographical Portraits*, vol. II (Folkestone: Japan Library, 1997)), suggest that Shand had introduced Koizumi, Sonoda, Soma and Nakamigawa Hikojiro to banking circles during his period of sick leave in London. This suggestion, however, cannot be supported, because when Koizumi and Nakamigawa arrived in London in December 1874, Shand had already returned to Japan, and neither Sonoda, who was staying in London as a diplomat, nor Soma, who was studying law in the United States, would have had any chance of meeting him.
59. Yokohama Shokin Ginko, *Toyo Shitencho Kaigiroku*, April 1908, pp. 14–18.
60. Ibid., pp. 21–4.
61. Ibid., p. 38.
62. T. Taira, 'Daiichiji Taisenzen no Kokusai Kinhon'iseika ni okeru Yokohama Shokin Ginko', *Kinyu Keizai*, 208, 1984, p. 70.
63. Ibid., pp. 72–3.
64. H. Kojima, *Nihon no Kinhon'isei Jidai 1897–1917* (Tokyo: Nihon Keizai Hyoronsha, 1981), pp. 131–45.
65. Yokohama Shokin Ginko, *Toyo Shitencho Kaigiroku*, May 1909, pp. 158–60. Although Nishimura Shizuya doubted the predominance of Chinese depositors in his paper 'Higashi Ajia Kokusai Ginkoshi' (*Kinyu Keizai Kenkyu*, 5, 1993), the situation of the Specie Bank was fundamentally different from those of the British banks such as the Hongkong and Shanghai Bank.
66. Nishimura, 'Higashi Ajia Kokusai Ginkoshi', p. 20; also his 'Kokusai Ginkoshi Kenkyu Josetsu 1870–1914', *Keiei Shirin*, 27, 3, 1990, p. 4.
67. *Koho*, 34, 1 October 1909.

68. Ishii, 'Japanese Trade and the Yokohama Specie Bank', pp. 9–17.
69. Ishii, *Kindai Nihon Kinyushi Josetsu*, ch. 1.
70. King, *History of the Hongkong and Shanghai Banking Corporation*, vol. 1.
71. Nishimura,'Higashi Ajia Kokusai Ginkoshi'; also his 'Chugoku ni okeru Kokusai Ginkogyo 1890–1914', *Keiei Shirin*, 32, 4, 1996.
72. Kojima, *Nihon no Kinhon'isei Jidai*, p. 143.
73. Yokohama Shokin Ginko, *Toyo Shitencho Kaigiroku*, May 1909, p. 171.
74. Ibid., pp. 200–1.
75. *Koho*, 27, 16 June 1909.
76. *Koho*, 28, 1 July 1909.
77. Uetsuka (ed.), *Takahashi Korekiyo Jiden*, vol. 2, pp. 79–84.
78. T. Saito,'Nisshin Senso Igo ni okeru Yokohama Shokin Ginko no Gaikoku Kawase Gyomu no Hatten to Shinyo', *Mita Shogaku Kenkyu*, 27, 6, p. 47.
79. *Koho*, 13, 6 November 1908.
80. *Koho*, 34, 1 October 1909.
81. Yokohama Shokin Ginko, *Toyo Shitencho Kaigiroku*, April 1908, p. 12.
82. K. Yamaguchi, 'Mitsui Bussan Kaisha', in K. Yamaguchi (ed.), *Nihon Sangyo Kinyushi Kenkyu, Boseki Kinyu Hen*, p. 171; *Koho*, 34, 1 October 1909.
83. Ishii, 'Japanese Trade and the Yokohama Specie Bank', p. 18.
84. Ibid., pp. 9–13.
85. *Koho*, 5, 16 July 1908.
86. *Koho*, 4, 1 July 1908. The exchange banks, however, could not always come to an agreement. For example, after the economic crisis of 1907, the Kobe branch of the Specie Bank decided to abolish the custom of guarantee by compradors and to use documentary bills in transactions with Chinese merchants, and proposed that other branches of the Specie Bank and other banks should carry out the same reform. However, no one agreed to this proposal. See *Koho*, 19, 16 February 1909; 37, 16 November 1909.

3

'Learn and Earn, Earn and Learn': British Influence and Fukuzawa Yukichi's Creation of the First Japanese Business Elite

Norio Tamaki

Keio graduates in business

In the late autumn of 1858 a 23-year-old man arrived in Edo and settled down in the Nakatsu clan house in Tsukiji, at the east end of the city. This man, Fukuzawa Yukichi, had been ordered by the senior clan officer to assume the headship of the domain school. This was the start of Fukuzawa's *Keio Gijuku* (Keio College), so named because it was started in the fourth year of the Keio era, in the midst of the Restoration turbulence. Keio College educated some 6300 men and produced some 500 graduates between the late 1850s and 1889. It was superseded by Keio University, founded in January 1890, which had produced 1047 graduates by 1910: 792 in economics, 132 in law, 68 in politics and 55 in arts.[1] These figures show clearly that the university was overwhelmingly economics-orientated.

Keio Gijuku Shusshin Meiryu Retsuden (*Directory of Distinguished Keio Graduates*), published in 1909, surveyed some 1600 graduates, including those of Keio College, and contained entries for 487 Keio men, of whom 277 had gone into business. The rival Imperial University produced 10351 graduates between 1876 and 1910, but only 13 per cent of the Law School graduates (roughly 200 each year) found jobs in the business world.[2] The private Keio University, lacking the official legitimacy of the Imperial University, was far ahead in producing business graduates. Table 3.1 shows that these 277 Keio graduates were concentrated in particular sectors. Thus these Keio graduates found employment in three main sectors: 89 in banking and finance (including insurance and securities), 64 in commerce, and 31 in transport (railway and shipping).

Of these three sectors, banking and finance, which embraced the largest number of Keio graduates, was of vital importance to the development of the modern Japanese economy, providing it with manpower. The most remarkable Keio achievements in this industry are epitomized by the fact that 49 of the 89 Keio men sat on the boards of directors of banks, insur-

Table 3.1 Business sectors entered by Keio graduates

Sector	*Number of graduates*
Commerce	64
Banking	62
Insurance	22
Textiles	21
Railways	16
Mining	16
Shipping	15
Zaibatsu (parent company)	10
Construction	7
Securities	5
Machine manufacturing	5
Printing	5

Source: Keio University, *Keio Gijuku Shusshin Meiryu Retsuden* (Tokyo: Keio University, 1909).

ance and securities companies, and 15 of them assumed presidency on their boards, including that of the Bank of Japan. Another, perhaps even more astonishing fact was that Keio graduates occupied senior posts in six of the top seven prestigious banks, that is to say, the Bank of Japan, Yokohama Specie Bank, Mitsui Bank, Mitsubishi Bank, Sumitomo Bank and Daiichi Bank. Although Keio men were not directly involved in the seventh, the Yasuda Bank (later Fuji Bank), many did enter the Toyokuni Bank, based in Tokyo, which eventually merged with the Yasuda Bank. Being actively engaged in banking business, Keio men, as Fukuzawa's disciples, formed an influential inner core in the finance industry and thus in the Japanese economy as a whole. On this particular point, no other private educational institution could rank with Keio in any way, including famous schools such as *Meiji Horitsu Gakko* (founded 1880, later Meiji University) and *Tokyo Senmon Gakko* (founded 1882, later Waseda University), though they increased their numbers of graduates.[3] *Tokyo Shogyo Gakko* (later Hitotsubashi University) and its predecessor were also sending out graduates into the business world, particularly from the 1880s onward,[4] but the number of graduates was far smaller than that of Keio.[5] The present chapter tries to shed light on Fukuzawa's college and its graduates, and to establish the extent of any British influence in the process whereby the first generation of Japanese businessmen was born.

There is no doubt that Fukuzawa Yukichi was a champion of Japanese enlightenment, and this aspect of Fukuzawa has been researched extensively,[6] but in a sense also overworked. One other aspect of Fukuzawa, his role as an entrepreneur, has been somewhat neglected, except for his activities in the publishing business.[7] This neglect is partly due to Fukuzawa's own remarks in his autobiography, namely that 'I put under my control what publishers have hitherto done. I employed them only to distribute books and gave them commissions. It was a great revolution. This was the only business I was engaged in.'[8] Perhaps more importantly, scholars working on Fukuzawa have been deceived by his image as a diligent teacher and prolific writer into looking at only one aspect of his career. The 'Sage of Mita', as his *Japan Times* obituary called him,[9] has perhaps distracted researchers away from the theme of Fukuzawa as business entrepreneur. The present chapter will demonstrate how deeply Fukuzawa was involved in creating the first generation of the Japanese business elite, and show that British influences played some part in this.

Fukuzawa in London (April–June 1862) and the creation of *Keio Gijuku* (1868)

Fukuzawa was born into a lower-class samurai family of the Nakatsu clan, an area now part of Oita Prefecture. Orphaned at the age of one and a half, he was raised in poverty, a circumstance from which he learnt much. The feudal atmosphere in Nakatsu was anathema to him,[10] and fortune for him came in 1854 when, at the age of 19, he grasped an opportunity to go to Nagasaki, never really to return to Nakatsu again. The following year he was admitted to the *Tekijuku*, a school for Dutch studies in Osaka, run by the leading scholar Ogata Koan (1810–63). Fukuzawa thrived at the *Tekijuku* and he became the head of students in 1857. As a result of this service at Ogata's school Fukuzawa was offered the headship of the Nakatsu domain school in Edo.

Settling down in Edo, Fukuzawa was shrewd enough to realize that his second language should be English rather than Dutch. He rigorously disciplined himself to learn English, and his hard work was rewarded by his being three times offered a position in foreign missions: to America in 1860, to Europe in 1862 and again to America in 1867. He was the only Japanese to make three overseas journeys before the Restoration. It was during this period that Fukuzawa was re-employed as an English translator by the Bakufu administration in Edo. Of the three missions, the year spent in Europe was most enlightening for Fukuzawa, and he benefited tremendously in particular from his stay in London.

Arriving in London shortly before the 1862 Exhibition opened, Fukuzawa and his fellow translators were most likely entertained by a Dr Robert Chambers (1802–71) of the Edinburgh publishers W. & R. Chambers, which also had a bookshop in Paternoster Row near St Paul's Cathedral.[11] Bookshops in Paternoster Row, including Chambers' and Trubner's, proved a treasure trove for Fukuzawa, who was able to build a library of books in English unprecedented for any Japanese. Although Fukuzawa did not leave any list of books bought in Paternoster Row, it is possible to try and reconstruct such a list, with prices, through an examination of two sources, namely Fukuzawa's own later writings and the 1862 issue of the *English Catalogue of Books*. Table 3.2 suggests the contents of such a reconstructed list.

The English library Fukuzawa built in London, together with his personal experiences in the West, became the source for the first major description of the West in Japanese, his *Seiyo Jijo* (*Conditions in the West*), published in two volumes 1866–67. *Seiyo Jijo* was a tremendous success, with over 150000 copies of the first volume alone being sold.[12] It naturally earned Fukuzawa fame and fortune, sufficient to enable him to become independent of the Nakatsu clan and to take over the Nakatsu domain school. In the spring of 1868, in the midst of the Restoration turbulence, he abandoned the Nakatsu domain house and set up his own school.

Table 3.2 Possible list of books bought by Fukuzawa in London

W. Blackstone (ed. Hargreaves), *Commentaries on the Laws of England* (1844)	£3 15s
H.T. Buckle, *History of Civilization in England* (2 vols, 1861)	£1 17s
J.H. Burton, *Political and Social Economy*	2s 6d
W. & R. Chambers, *Chambers' Encyclopaedia* (5 vols [A to L], 1860/62)	£2 5s
W. & R. Chambers, *Moral Class-books, Advanced Reading Lessons*	1s 6d
W. & R. Chambers, *Information for the People* (2 vols, 1857/58)	16s
W. & R. Chambers, *Political Economy for Use in School and for Private Instruction*	no price
W. Ellis, *Outlines of Social Economy* (1860)	1s 6d
Encyclopaedia Britannica (8th edn, 21 vols & Index, 1853/61)	£25 12s
F.P.G. Guizot, *History of the Origin of Representative Government in Europe* (1852)	3s 6d
F.P.G. Guizot, *History of Civilization in Europe* (3 vols, 1856)	10s 6d
J.R. McCulloch, *The Principles of Political Economy* (1849)	15s
J.R. McCulloch, *A Dictionary, Geographical, Statistical, and Historical, of Various Countries, Places and Principal Natural Objects in the World* (1854)	£3 3s
J.R. McCulloch, *A Dictionary, Practical, Theoretical, and Historical of Commerce and Commercial Navigation* (new edition, 1860)	£2 10s
W.H. Medhurst, *An English and Japanese and Japanese and English Vocabulary* (1830)	10s
W.H. Medhurst, *English and Chinese Dictionary* (2 vols)	£5
F. Wayland, *Elements of Political Economy* (new edition, 1859)	2s
F. Wayland, *Elements of Moral Science* (1860)	3s 5d

Note: Fukuzawa said he bought a copy of Wayland's *Elements of Political Economy* during his second journey to the USA in 1867, and that one of his colleagues obtained a copy of the other Wayland book in Edo in 1868. It is thus unlikely that Fukuzawa had seen these books in London. See *FYZ*, vol. 1, p. 48; vol. 4, p. 477. Professor Craig has also argued that the J.H. Burton book can be ruled out, identifying Burton as the author of Chambers' *Political Economy*. See A. Craig, 'John Hill Burton and Fukuzawa Yukichi', *Kindai Nihon Kenkyu* 1, 1984.

As Fukuzawa declared in his account of the origins of *Keio Gijuku*, his intention was to set up an institution modelled on the western public school. *Gijuku* identified the institution as a school, and *Keio* was taken from the Japanese era name (1865–68).[13]

There is no doubt that the college was based on King's College Junior School in London, which Fukuzawa mentions in his diary and refers to in *Seiyo Jijo*.[14] At its new site the college's curriculum emerged in its modern form thanks to the collection of English textbooks Fukuzawa had bought during his second voyage to America.[15] As Baba Tatsui (1850–88), one of Fukuzawa's brightest students, noted in his autobiography, he 'went to Shinsenza where Mr. Fukuzawa removed his school, . . . saw at once the great progress which the study of the English language had made . . . learned, for the first time in his life, the laws of currency, supply and demand'.[16]

In 1870, Fukuzawa formulated the Keio curriculum in which western subjects should be studied. According to this, the student should ideally start learning the alphabet and the primer at the age of ten. He should then go on to geography, arithmetic, physics, history and moral philosophy. At the final stage, the student was to study economics and law, with Fukuzawa apparently placing greater emphasis on the first of these two:

> This subject explains the daily necessities of human life. It explains how to produce, exchange and distribute products. It explains how to augment necessities by enhancing knowledge and regulation. It can be applied on a large scale to the revenue and expenditure of the state, and on a small scale to the household. It is the branch of learning that explains that those who adhere to natural laws become richer and that those who fail to do so become poorer. Those who do not know the science do not know the reason even if they do become richer, and do not know the reason why they become poorer. This leads to a wealthy man easily becoming poor and makes it difficult for a poor man to have wealth. Without a knowledge of economics, therefore, the millionaire is no better than the poor man who possesses no property.[17]

What should be stressed here, however, is the fact that Fukuzawa did not see economics as the ultimate aim and final target of study, as he argued in a letter to his favourite nephew, Nakamigawa Hikojiro (1854–1901):

> My opinion is that a scholar of these days should not be absorbed only in reading books. Being absorbed in reading books makes him as guilty as if he gave himself up to wine and women. Only a talented man is able to do business while reading books and read books while doing business. Learn and earn, earn and learn, then you could obtain the status both of the scholar and of the rich man, and then for the first time you could change the minds of the people of Japan.[18]

For Fukuzawa there was an absolute interaction between economics and business in the real world. His students had every reason to follow the motto 'learn and earn, earn and learn', with which Keio graduates went into business from the early Meiji period.

Maruzen and Maruya Bank – trade and banking

The astonishing sales of successive books by Fukuzawa led him to launch a publishing business in 1868. This eventually grew into the Keio College Press, from which his paper *Jiji Shinpo* was launched in 1882.[19] Fukuzawa's interest in books, however, went beyond Keio, when in November 1868 he suggested that Hayashi Yuteki (1837–1901), a Keio graduate and head of a syphilis hospital in Yokohama, should set up a shop for western books and goods there.[20] Responding to the suggestion, Hayashi announced on 1 January 1869 the foundation of Maruya Shosha (Maruya Trading Co.), a title soon changed to Maruzen.

The prospectus, prepared by Fukuzawa, advised that Japan and her people should promote foreign trade on their own account in order to improve welfare and bring about prosperity.[21] What was significant in the foundation of Maruzen was the fact that the company was formed according to the joint stock principle. The prospectus provided for the partners of Maruzen to be constituted of two categories, that is to say active partners and sleeping partners. The regulations attached to the prospectus stipulated that the active partners would be responsible for the daily management of the company, whereas sleeping partners, not engaged in the day-to-day business, would have to subscribe larger sums than the active partners. Sleeping partners would be allowed to transfer shares to a third party at any time, while active partners could only do so with the consent of their colleagues.[22] This division of labour and difference in share transferability between the two categories of partner give a co-partnership flavour to the company, but Maruzen was essentially a joint stock company with limited liability, the first of its kind in modern Japan. Share transferability was a basic requirement for joint stock company limited liability.

Where did this idea come from? Fukuzawa certainly wrote about *shonin kaisha*, or merchant companies, in the first volume of *Seiyo Jijo*, which was undoubtedly the first Japanese account of a western joint stock company. This account might have led to the setting up of the Hyogo Shosha (Hyogo Trading Company) by the Bakufu with the backing of a large number of opulent merchants, primarily in Osaka.[23] However, the Hyogo Shosha was not sufficiently well-known to be able to provide Maruzen with a model. It is possible that the idea may have come from Wayland's *Elements of Political Economy*, but Wayland never touches upon co-partnership.[24] The only book available in Japan at that time that dealt with the concept was

McCulloch's *Dictionary, Practical, Theoretical, and Historical, of Commerce and Commercial Navigation*. According to this:

> In a private copartnery, no partner, without the consent of the company, can transfer his share to another person, or introduce a new member into the company. Each member, however, may, upon proper warning, withdraw from the copartnery, and demand payment from them of his share of the common stock. In a joint stock company, on the contrary, no member can demand payment of his share from the company; but each member may, without their consent, transfer his share to another person, and thereby introduce a new member.[25]

Maruzen's company form was undoubtedly based on a skilful translation of McCulloch, which at the time could be done only by someone like Fukuzawa. Hayashi must have read *Seiyo Jijo*, but did not understand McCulloch. The only scholar capable of understanding these difficult western ideas was Fukuzawa himself.

One might wonder why Fukuzawa and his Maruzen colleagues needed a joint stock company with limited liability, because at that stage there was no legal framework in which limited liability was either required or particularly useful. Fukuzawa must have felt that 'united we stand, divided we fall', as the Maruzen prospectus states.[26] In addition, as he knew from McCulloch, 'Whenever the capital required to carry on any undertaking exceeds what may be furnished by an individual, it is indispensable, in order to the prosecution of the undertaking [*sic*], that an association should be formed.'[27] Maruzen opened a branch at Nihonbashi, in the very centre of Tokyo, in February 1870. This was followed by branches in Osaka in January 1871, Kyoto in August 1872 and Nagoya in August 1874. For the first two years Maruzen bought in western books and other goods from westerners in Yokohama. The only trade name which can be identified is Hartley & Co., British book and drug merchants.[28] Direct imports of western books commenced in 1872, when Maruzen first contacted Roman & Co. in San Francisco. Then in 1874 British contact was started through Wayland and Short, Short & Co. of Cannon Street in London.[29] Although the contacts with British agents came after those with the Americans, the British connection proved to be crucial in the early Meiji business for Maruzen.

Maruzen supplied goods other than books, but it was increasingly known as *the* western bookseller in Japan, and as such soon became a great provider of western knowledge through the book trade. Keio College was no doubt one of the biggest customers, but in spite of the close relationship there remains no record about books Maruzen supplied to Keio. One rare record found among the Maruzen archives is a book list, dated 12 March 1878, for the newly founded but short-lived *Mitsubishi Shogyo Gakko* (Mitsubishi

Table 3.3 Fukuzawa's Maruzen accounts

	Investment (¥)	*Advances* (¥)	*Savings*
Jan. 1873	3336	900	553
Oct. 1873	3753	1900	533
Jan. 1874	2200	1900	553
Jan. 1875	3420	2400	618
Jan. 1876	17702	–	–
Jan. 1877	17702	1250	–
Jan. 1878	17702	2200	1090
Jan. 1879	17702	3400	3530
Jan. 1880	6339	–	3200

School of Commerce).[30] The school ordered 29 titles, of which four are known. These were McCulloch's *Dictionary of Commerce and Commercial Navigation*; H.D. McLeod, *The Theory and Practice of Banking*;[31] L. Levi, *International Commercial Law*; and E.A. Andrews, *Latin–English Lexicon*. In April that year the school ordered W.S. Jevons's *Money and the Mechanism of Exchange*. By this time Maruzen could offer a catalogue of western books. The only surviving copy of this catalogue, dated October 1883, was entitled *A Select List of General Works comprising English, French and German Imported and Published Works and Stationery, Z.P. Maruya & Co.*, which lists some 1200 books.

From the outset, Maruzen borrowed ideas and also money from Fukuzawa. According to Fukuzawa's personal accounts, as shown in Table 3.3, Maruzen owed him large sums.[32]

The investment was Fukuzawa's shareholding in Maruzen stock. Advances were made mainly to the clothing department. Fukuzawa placed his savings in an account in Sairyusha, set up in December 1871 as the financial wing of Maruzen. Besides these large sums, Fukuzawa lent Hayashi and his fellow directors ¥3000 in 1874 and 1875.[33] There can be no doubt that Fukuzawa was the largest personal lender to Maruzen. He thus had to be very cautious, particularly in a situation where high inflation might act to depreciate the value of his advances. In 1877 he complained:

> On account of the mood (caused by the Satsuma Rebellion), business is dull. The rate of gold coin is said to be one to a hundred. If it continues to rise and the dollar becomes dearer, it will be dangerous. Someone argues that the government is prepared to see the rises. If so, we will have to accept it. Maruya won't suffer because its portfolio is rich in goods and scarce in money, but Sairyusha must face losses through its securities. As I have told you yesterday, I do not like to see any more my lending to Maruya repaid in paper.[34]

The creeping inflation of the early Meiji era took its toll from 1877 as a result of war expenditure. Fukuzawa was no exception and the value of his advances to Maruzen depreciated heavily. For the first time since the success of *Seiyo Jijo*, Fukuzawa faced financial difficulties.

Fukuzawa's anxiety was echoed by those at Maruzen. In September 1879 the Maruya Bank was founded in Nihonbashi, Tokyo. In the prospectus, the bank was to offer savings banking with a capital of 500 shares to a value of ¥50 000. Of the total stock, the Hayashi family was responsible for ¥20 000 and the rest was to be allotted to their friends.[35] Fukuzawa subscribed ¥10 000, and there were many Keio men among the 48 other shareholders, whose aggregate holdings amounted to ¥8700.[36] The establishment of the bank was immediately reflected in Fukuzawa's accounts. His investments in Maruzen decreased from ¥17 702 to ¥6339 in January 1880, and from then on advances to Maruzen entirely disappeared.[37] Fukuzawa's claims were shouldered by Maruzen's newly founded financial wing, the Maruya Bank.[38] It was in looking at the process of building a bank, that Fukuzawa was inspired by the idea of launching a banking project on a national scale.

The Yokohama Specie Bank and *Boeki Shokai* – banking and trade

Observing the hyperinflation that followed the Satsuma Rebellion, Fukuzawa in 1878 published *Tsukaron (On Currency)*, in which he raised the vital question of how much paper currency should be permitted to circulate. Though he did not specify precisely what policies the government should follow, Fukuzawa warned the Finance Minister, Okuma Shigenobu, that:

> The rise of the Mexican dollar must be due to an American affair, but an advance to this extent is unprecedented. If this situation is echoed in the provinces, it will be a disaster. In the meantime demand for Mexican dollars does not seem to be strong. The people who buy them these days are those who take the opportunity to gain speculative earnings. My proposal, though it is rather a sour one, is that you inject ¥1 million worth of Mexican dollars into the market in order to stabilise the situation.[39]

Fukuzawa sought the counsel of Maruzen men, and he asked Hayashi for his thoughts on the causes of the rise of the dollar.[40] Having made the suggestion of selling Mexican dollars on the open market, however, Fukuzawa's thoughts turned towards the idea of a specie bank. From the beginning it was in his mind that Maruzen men would found such a bank. It is therefore safe to conclude that the Maruya and Specie Banks were founded alongside each other.

The Specie Bank project finally materialized in August 1879. As Fukuzawa proposed to Finance Minister Okuma:

> It is good to see that the value of the Mexican dollar at Yokohama continues to be stabilised since the uproar last spring, but it will rise again in as far as the fundamental cause is not eliminated. . . . Discussions I have had with several of my friends on the matter have produced an idea laid down on the enclosed paper. Please look at it carefully. If the proposed scheme is left to speculators, the government would only be helping them to accumulate their own profits. I think I know the people who can be trusted. . . . If you are interested in the matter, we should consult further and I would introduce the people to you.[41]

Okuma responded positively, and negotiations proceeded well during the summer. In September Fukuzawa recommended his nephew Nakamigawa and Koizumi Nobukichi (1849–94) as suitable candidates to set up the bank.[42] Both were Keio graduates in whom Fukuzawa had total confidence. He had sent them to Britain in 1874, entrusting them to the care of Baba Tatsui, then in London.[43] The two men had studied under the supervision of Leone Levi (1821–88). The Italian-born Levi had arrived in Liverpool as an apprentice of a merchant house, and had then become naturalized and led an active life in business. When a chair in Principles and Practice of Commerce and Commercial Law was created at King's College, London, Levi was appointed the first professor. His magnum opus, *A History of British Commerce and of the Economic Progress of the British Nation, 1763–1870*, appeared in 1870. The merchant-turned-professor Levi was extremely kind to the Japanese students. He later wrote to Hara Rokuro (1842–1933), later president of the Yokohama Specie Bank:

> Your visit has been most gratifying and we do preserve a most agreeable recollection of the pleasant intercourse and interesting studies we have had together. . . . It will be for you to shape the future destinies of your country and to keep her on the path of solid advancement. . . . Our friends Koyzumi, Nacomagna and Kusaka are well. The two former will speedily close their studies.[44]

We may ask what these young men learnt from Professor Levi. Koizumi Shinzo (1888–1966), the only son of Koizumi Nobukichi and later president of Keio University, recalled:

> My father, who went to London with Mr. Nakamigawa in 1876 [*sic*], was put under the supervision of Mr. Leone Levi and was taught privately at

> his office. Looking at his notebooks on law, economics, public finance, insurance, warehouse, foreign trade etc., I think that Mr. Nakamigawa was taught in the same way.[45]

From this evidence it seems almost certain that Levi used as their textbook his *International Commercial Law*, published in 1863 in two volumes, the book which the Mitsubishi School of Commerce later bought from Maruzen in 1878. The book covered a wide range of topics including agency, banking, bankruptcy, bills of exchange, book-keeping, cheques, copyright, corporations, courts and joint stock companies. Levi's tutorials must have been most useful in enabling Koizumi and Nakamigawa to acquire knowledge essential for their future business careers. During their London stay they had the opportunity of meeting Inoue Kaoru (1836–1915), as the influential statesman was then travelling in Europe. It was Inoue who later introduced Koizumi to the Finance Ministry and Nakamigawa to the *Kobusho* (Ministry of Works) and the Foreign Ministry. It was in these capacities that Koizumi and Nakamigawa worked to enable Fukuzawa to communicate with Okuma.

After receiving Okuma's consent regarding the selection of the would-be management of the Specie Bank, within a month Fukuzawa had nominated an ex-Maruzen director, Nakamura Michita (1836–1921) as the man to head the bank:

> The matter which we discussed when we last met has since been updated for me by Koizumi, and I think you are about to move it forward. I think that I should at this stage mention one person, Nakamura Michita. He used to be an accountancy officer in the Toyohashi domain. He is highly appreciated in that locality and has set up a bank in Toyohashi. I have known him for a long time and he is a very reliable man. If we are to embark upon this enterprising scheme at all, we need experienced men as well as intellectuals. As I believe that Nakamura is a man who could be trusted with the scheme, I have already leaked a small part of it to him, and he says he has his own ideas – but please be sure that he will never talk to anybody. The next crucial step is to invite subscriptions from the public. As far as these are concerned, Nakamura has a wide network covering Goshu, Osaka and so on, which is very useful. If your consent might be obtained, he would proceed with the business. Though at this stage the bank scheme cannot be disclosed, Nakamura will be able to sound out his circles in places such as Goshu, Osaka and Niigata. I had thought to let you know this through Koizumi, but I decided that it would be better for you to see Nakamura so I wrote first to you. When Nakamura comes up here, please permit him to meet you at your earliest conveniences. He will himself tell you all the details. He has his own ideas on the Mexican dollar. Please let him have an hour.[46]

Fukuzawa chose not to disclose that Nakamura was a Maruzen man, as well as one of the promoters and larger shareholders in the emerging Maruya Bank. He probably suspected that such a disclosure would arouse Okuma's suspicions that the projected bank would be an offshoot of the Maruya Bank and Maruzen.

Within three weeks it was reported that Nakamura, with the aid of Hayashi of Maruzen, could expect to secure a sum up to ¥2 million.[47] On this basis Nakamura and Koizumi worked together to draft a prospectus of the Specie Bank in Yokohama. On 11 December 1879, Finance Minister Okuma announced to the *Dajokan* meeting that the Yokohama Specie Bank was to deal in specie and issue notes backed by bonds convertible into gold.[48] He claimed that huge amounts of gold and silver coins, worth a possible ¥100 million, were being hoarded. The Specie Bank would seek to create a free market for such coins and encourage holders to deposit them with the bank.[49] This in some sense is a restatement of Gresham's Law that 'bad money', i.e. paper money, 'drives out good', that is specie. Fukuzawa may well have known this law from MacLeod's *Elements of Political Economy* (1858).

As a pump-priming exercise the government was to invest ¥1 million in specie out of the bank's total stock of ¥3 million, to attract specie currently being hoarded. This was precisely the method and the sum Fukuzawa had suggested to Okuma in March 1878, making the Yokohama Specie Bank very clearly Fukuzawa's brainchild. The bank opened its doors on 28 February 1880, with Nakamura as president and Koizumi as vice-president. Before the opening, Nakamura, Koizumi and their fellow promoters had been busy inviting subscriptions. Apart from the government's subscription, they were successful in attracting 91 shareholders subscribing to 4415 shares to a value of ¥88 300. By July 1880, the number of proprietors had increased to 282, with a total of 30 000 shares and paid-up capital of ¥1 906 580.[50] The leading shareholders of the bank are listed in Table 3.4. Osaka subscribers such as Godai, Hirose and Konoike were invited to join by Namakura, and their Tokyo counterparts such as Shibusawa, Masuda and Minomura by Koizumi. Iwasaki subscribed through Nishiwaki Teijiro, a Keio graduate. Both Fukuzawa's and Hayashi's holdings included those of their families. Fukuzawa's brainchild had grown into a nationwide institution.

Closely observing the early days of the Yokohama Specie Bank, Fukuzawa sounded out Okuma and Iwasaki Yataro (1834–85) of Mitsubishi about setting up a trading company to export silk with financial support from the Specie Bank. Fukuzawa was known to Iwasaki, because his company employed many Keio graduates. They agreed to take the project forward, and in July 1880 the simply entitled *Yugensekinin Boekishokai* (Trading Company Ltd.) was launched at Nihonbashi, near Maruzen. Hayashi Yuteki of Maruzen assumed the presidency and Asabuki Eiji (1849–1918), a Keio graduate who had entered Mitsubishi a year earlier, became the manager. Of

Table 3.4 Leading shareholders of Yokohama Specie Bank

	February 1880 *Shares (¥ paid in)*	*July 1880* *Shares (¥ paid in)*
Hayashi Yuteki	340 (4000)	770 (50 200)
Horikoshi Kakujiro (Tokyo wool merchant)	–	630 (63 000)
Yasuda Zenjiro (Yasuda Bank)	–	450 (29 000)
Iwasaki Yataro (Mitsubishi)	100 (2000)	300 (18 000)
Fukuzawa Yukichi	100 (2000)	200 (12 000)
Godai Tomoatsu (Osaka Chamber of Commerce)	100 (2000)	100 (6 000)
Hirose Saihei (Sumitomo)	100 (2000)	100 (6 000)
Hara Rokuro (Daihyaku Bank)	20 (400)	70 (5 600)
Okura Kihachiro (Okuragumi)	–	90 (5 400)
Minomura Risuke (Mitsui)	50 (1000)	50 (5 000)
Konoike Zen'emon (Konoike)	50 (1000)	50 (3 000)
Shibusawa Eiichi (Daiichi Bank)	50 (1000)	50 (3 000)
Masuda Takashi (Mitsui)	50 (1000)	50 (3 000)

Note: Figures in parentheses show value in *yen*.

the total capital of ¥200 000, Iwasaki took on ¥80 000, and the rest was put up by Fukuzawa and his colleagues.[51] According to the prospectus, the company was to seek 'export orders of silk, tea, silkworm-egg cards, minerals, metals, copper, china, lacquer ware and any other products', import orders from both the government and the private sector, and was to provide all 'facilities for domestic and foreign trade'.[52] The company soon came to specialize in the silk trade and immediately appointed agents in London, New York and Vladivostok.

Both the Yokohama Specie Bank and the Trading Company were launched successfully, but all did not go as smoothly as Fukuzawa and Okuma had expected. This was partly due to the political turbulence of 1881 (the so-called *juyonnen no seihen*), when Okuma was ousted from the government, and partly due to inexperience. Even so, the Yokohama Specie Bank did well. In 1884, when the Oriental Bank, which had hitherto carried out business in London for the Japanese government, went into liquidation, the Specie Bank elevated its London agency to branch status. The London office of the bank, which had previously been accommodated in the Japanese Legation, moved out to an independent existence at 84 Bishopsgate. The London branch was to become indispensable for the modernization of the Japanese economy, as well as for the smooth working of the bank's overall business. By the turn of the century the Yokohama Specie Bank had become one of the biggest banks in Japan, with a capital of ¥18 million. This compared with an aggregate ¥14 million for the five big city banks (Mitsui, Mitsubishi,

Yasuda, Sumitomo and Daiichi). The success of the Yokohama Specie Bank may well have exceeded the expectations of its creator, Fukuzawa.

The Sanyo Railway Company and the Mitsui Bank

In the aftermath of the political turbulence in the autumn of 1881, in which Okuma was ousted from power by the Satsuma–Choshu faction, Keio men were also expelled from the government, as Fukuzawa was seen as Okuma's friend. Nakamigawa Hikojiro was no exception, and he joined Fukuzawa in editing and publishing *Jiji Shinpo*. His ability proved indispensable for Fukuzawa in the newspaper business, but in January 1887 Nakamigawa was offered the presidency of the newly proposed Sanyo Railway Company. This offer was made through Shoda Heigoro (1847–1922), a Keio graduate and manager at Mitsubishi. Shoda had been sounded out by Makino Nobuaki (1861–1949), then secretary (*shokikan*) for Hyogo Prefecture, about Mitsubishi's giving financial help and suggesting possible candidates for the presidency. Mitsubishi decided to join the railway scheme, and by the end of 1886 was looking for a capable manager for the job. Shoda's invitation delighted and even excited Nakamigawa. It was to be the first non-government railway project under the 1887 Decree on Private Railways (*Shisetsu Tetsudo Jorei*), and the first genuine large-scale railway of its kind in Western Japan. Nakamigawa promised to consult Fukuzawa, however, before accepting.[53] However important Nakamigawa was to him on the *Jiji Shinpo*, Fukuzawa had to accept that his favourite nephew was being offered an exciting prospect in the modern transport sector. In a letter to Motoyama Hikoichi (1853–1932), a manager of the Fujitagumi, builder and big investor in the Sanyo Railway, and ex-editor of *Jiji Shinpo*, Fukuzawa wrote: 'Regarding the railway project, Mr. Shoda personally talked to Hikojiro a little while ago. I have considered it over and over again. As it looks very interesting, I effectively told him that he should accept it.'[54] Fukuzawa also showed his interest in the scheme by becoming a shareholder.[55]

The prospectus of the Sanyo Railway Company, prepared in December 1886, was signed by 15 promoters including Shoda, Hara Rokuro (by now president of the Yokohama Specie Bank), Fujita Densaburo (1841–1912), head of the Fujitagumi based in Osaka, and Kuki Takayoshi (1837–91), an ex-lord of Sanda clan in Hyogo and one of Fukuzawa's close friends.[56] There was some difference of opinion between the two big investors, Mitsubishi and Fujita, regarding nominees for the presidency. At the final stage of the promoters' meeting a second nominee was still being proposed, but Nakamigawa's nomination was successful because of his command of English, a skill which was thought to be essential by the promoters for forthcoming negotiations with British suppliers.[57] To begin with, Nakamigawa was elected as the promoters' representative. He embarked upon preparations energetically, taking upon himself the duty of negotiating with the government over the planning of routes and the drafting of the company's regulations.[58]

The first railway line in Japan had been pioneered by the British in 1869,[59] and in the late 1880s was being extended as far as Kobe. It was therefore natural that the Sanyo Railway should follow British practice. As Fukuzawa wrote to his son, Sutejiro (1865–1926), who was studying civil engineering at the Massachusetts Institute of Technology, this reliance upon British methods might make it difficult for those such as himself, who had 'learnt the American method of management'.[60] To follow British practice, Nakamigawa had to read W.M. Acworth's *Railways of England* (1889) while supervising construction.[61]

Before construction started, Nakamigawa wrote in May 1887 to Inoue Masaru (1843–1910), head of the Railway Agency:

> We understand that the Sanyo Railway Company will not only have to adhere to all the building methods used in the construction of the national railways under your supervision, but is also expected to depend on the British for engineers and rolling stock. With regard to this matter, the company wishes to use Malcolm Brunker & Co. in London, and we would be grateful if you could provide us with and introduction to them.[62]

Malcolm Brunker & Co. was a British supplier of railway building materials and rolling stock, employed since 1870 by the Japanese government.[63] In a separate letter on the same day Nakamigawa reported to Minister Inoue:

> Our intention has been to invite a suitable British engineer to join our company as advisory engineer. As we knew that Mr. C.A.W. Pownall, the chief engineer in your Agency, was going to Britain on leave, we asked him to find such a person. Fortunately with his kind help, the selection of an advisory engineer has been settled.[64]

Pownall was a civil engineer specializing in bridge construction who was employed by the *Kobusho*.[65]

Once the London agent was decided, Nakamigawa was ready to dispatch orders to Malcolm Brunker & Co. through one A.S. Aldrich (1840–1908). Aldrich had been in the service of the railway department of the Works Ministry till 1885, and was now back in Britain.[66] The orders included £37 000 worth of rails; nine locomotive engines; 50 coaches and ten wagons to the value of £39 000; two sets of turntables for £250; other rolling stock to the value of £4500; and £750 worth of building materials.[67] The makers of the locomotives, coaches and wagons were Dubs & Co. in Glasgow and the Vulcan Foundry.[68]

In January 1888 the Sanyo Railway Company was finally authorized and given the go-ahead by the government, and at the inaugural general meeting of shareholders, held on 27 April 1888, Nakamigawa assumed the presidency. The capital stock of Sanyo was to be ¥13 million (¥100 per share), and of this 260000 shares were acquired by 1862 subscribers. Mitsubishi took 25490 shares in the name of Iwasaki Hisaya (1865–1955), Yataro's son and a Keio graduate. Fukuzawa subscribed to 200 shares in the name of his son, Sutejiro.[69] Once construction of the railway started, Nakamigawa himself, accompanied by a British advisory engineer,[70] visited building sites, examining progress and making points he felt to be necessary. Back in the office he prepared railway service regulations and timetables, and even made decisions regarding uniforms for drivers, conductors and station officers. One of his most important tasks was the conducting of negotiations with the Yokohama Specie Bank.[71] Thanks to his diligence, the project made remarkable progress. The first stage between Hyogo and Akashi, of just under 11 miles, was opened in November 1888, and the line further extended to Himeji by the end of the year. Eventually, on 1 September 1889, the Sanyo line was connected at Kobe to the Tokaido line of the national railway, which had been completed only two months before.[72]

Shortly before the connection of the two lines, in June 1889, Fukuzawa Sutejiro was employed by the Sanyo Railway on Nakamigawa's recommendation.[73] Apart from Sutejiro, Nakamigawa recruited at least ten Keio graduates for Sanyo.[74] Unfortunately, Nakamigawa resigned from the presidency in October 1891. As the company grew so did disagreements between Nakamigawa and his fellow directors. Nakamigawa was perhaps too energetic, and probably too demanding, for the rest of the directors. When he was offered the job of de facto top manager of the House of Mitsui, he did not hesitate to make the move.[75]

In the face of the rising Mitsubishi, the time-honoured merchant house of Mitsui was underperforming. Mitsui barely weathered the turbulent years of the Restoration period, but in 1876 set up trading and banking wings, Mitsui Bussan (Mitsui Trading Co.) and Mitsui Bank. However, its management was slow to modernize, and together with the economic fluctuations of the 1880s, this led to a crisis in the spring of 1890.[76] The question even reached the cabinet agenda.[77] Failing to find a capable man who would be able to cope with the difficulties within the company, Mitsui consulted their adviser, Inoue Kaoru, who recommended Nakamigawa for the job.[78] As with the Sanyo Railway, Nakamigawa immediately wrote to Fukuzawa. The latter replied:

> The matter of Mitsui is very delicate indeed. When I met Takahashi the other day and asked in a casual manner about the progress of reform, he did not explain in detail at all, as it seems still to be confidential. But in reality it does not appear to be difficult. What can Takahashi do in

> cleaning this large cathedral? He is no more than a clerk. Even someone like Koizumi is not up to the job. My only worry is that Shibusawa and Masuda might have problems with your appointment, but this would be coped with by Inoue anyway. Otherwise, it is only the senior and junior staff in the house that matter, and it will be easy enough for you to treat them so that they will co-operate with you. The secret is sincerity and kindness. With regard to business, you could do everything with the Mitsui reputation. . . . On the other hand, they are unreasonably afraid of the government, and as a result accept a range of government business. This has, I guess, led to a lack of prosperity on their part. As long as you don't make mistakes in this respect the job will be very pleasant for you. Anyway, you should make up your mind to accept the offer. Sanyo is not worth your worrying about.[79]

The Takahashi referred to was Takahashi Yoshio (1861–1937), a Keio graduate, who had formerly worked for Fukuzawa in *Jiji Shinpo* and recently moved to Mitsui. Shibusawa Eiichi (1841–1931), one of the most energetic business promoters in Meiji Japan, was an adviser to the Mitsui business, while Masuda Takashi (1848–1938) was the head of Mitsui Bussan. These latter two were senior businessmen, and both were hostile to Nakamigawa.

Nakamigawa joined the Mitsui businesses first as a director of Mitsui Bank in August 1891. During his first six months he encountered fierce resistance from Mitsui's senior managers, particularly when, on Fukuzawa's advice, he tried to curtail governmental business. In order to push on with his reforms, Nakamigawa asked Inoue to intervene. This resulted in his becoming vice-president of the bank, and de facto chief executive.[80] This marked the beginning of the so-called Nakamigawa era in the history of Mitsui Bank.[81] Having succeeded in cutting unprofitable government business, Nakamigawa then tackled the bank's bad debts, including an unsecured ¥1 million loan to Higashi Honganji, a prestigious temple in Kyoto; advances to the failed 33rd National Bank of Tokyo worth more than ¥700000; ¥100000 lent to Shibaura Seisakusho (later Toshiba) and ¥360000 to an officer at the Yokohama Specie Bank. He recovered the temple loan and wrote off the rest by October 1894.[82] Within three years or so Nakamigawa had succeeded in re-establishing the Mitsui Bank upon sound principles.

In the meantime, with the help of Inoue, the whole business structure was modernized. In October 1893 the Family Board of the House of Mitsui was formed as the supreme decision-making organization, with Nakamigawa participating as an observer. In September 1896 the Board of Directors for Mitsui Companies was set up to oversee the business under the Family Board, and Nakamigawa was, of course, one of its members. In fact the Board of Directors replaced the Family Board as the top layer of management. In July 1900 when the *Mitsui Kaken*, or the Mitsui Constitution, was issued, the Board of Directors for Mitsui Companies was reorganized as the Board of

Table 3.5 Post-Mitsui business positions of Keio graduates recruited by Nakamigawa Hikojiro for Mitsui Bank

Asabuki Eiji	Kanegafuchi Spinning (Kanebo)
Tsuda Koji (1852–1938)	Tokyo Trust Co.
Hatano Shogoro (1854–1929)	Oji Paper Making (Oji)
Murakami Sadamu (1857–1957)	Kyodo Fire Insurance
Hiraga Satoshi (1859–1931)	Fujimoto Bill Brokers
Hibi Osuke (1860–1931)	Mitsukoshi
Yoda Seki (1860–1940)	Tojin Warehouse
Suzuki Umeshiro (1862–1940)	Oji
Yanagi Sotaro (1862–1938)	Daiichi Fire & Marine Insurance
Fujiwara Raita (1863–1938)	Dai Nihon Sugar Refining
Hayashi Ken (1863–?)	Oji
Wada Toyoji (1861–1924)	Fuji Spinning
Ono Tomojiro (1864–1921)	Hokkaido Coal & Shipping
Noguchi Torajiro (1866–?)	Silk merchant
Koide Osamu (1865–?)	Tokyo Trust Co.
Nishimatsu Takashi (1865–1937)	Shibaura Manufacturing
Izawa Ryoritsu (1867–1927)	Dai Nihon Sugar Refining
Muto Sanji (1867–1934)	Kanebo
Ikeda Nariakira (1867–1950)	Bank of Japan
Fujiwara Ginjiro (1869–1960)	Oji

Source: Nihon Keieishi Kenkyujo (ed.), *Nakamigawa Hikojiro Denki Shiryo.*, pp. 299–304.

Directors for Mitsui Business. Nakamigawa's membership of the new board was purely nominal, because he had been ill since the autumn of 1899, and died in October 1901.[83]

In serving Mitsui's business Nakamigawa was vigorous in recruiting Keio graduates for Mitsui Bank, as he had previously done at the Sanyo Railway Company. At least 20 men were chosen, most of whom occupied positions on the boards of directors in various companies after their careers at Mitsui. Their destinations are shown in Table 3.5. The Keio graduates who worked for Mitsui Bank thus dispersed to serve the modern development of the Japanese economy. Fukuzawa's favourite nephew, Nakamigawa, certainly did more than either of them expected.

Conclusion: British influence and Fukuzawa's lessons for the first generation of businessmen in Japan

With Nakamigawa's struggles with the old men of Mitsui in mind, Fukuzawa expressed his beliefs on the necessary qualification for a businessman in his *Jitsugyoron* (*Genuine Businessmen* or *On Business*), published in 1893. According to this, a businessman had to broaden his knowledge so that he could take any opportunity, either domestic or global, of making profits. To accomplish this he had to have suitable education and read the daily papers carefully. A businessman was required to abide strictly by laws and also by his words. To practise the latter, he had to endeavour to improve his character.[84] It might appear that Fukuzawa had in mind some mixture of Confucianism and western gentlemanly codes, but when his arguments moved from the character of the businessman to business itself, he became more straightforward.

Did Fukuzawa regard anyone as an ideal businessman for modern Japan? He picked up Iwasaki Yataro (1835–85), a close friend,[85] and argued for the secret of his success:

> If business in the world of civilisation is to advance, you must depend upon gentlemen who have had education. This is quite clear in theory. Let me show an example to prove it. One person who has founded a huge enterprise in the business world in modern Japan and won unprecedented fame throughout the country is the late Mr. Iwasaki Yataro, president of the Mitsubishi Company. His nature was to be bold and resolute, and yet accurate in deciding matters, leaving nothing untouched. It is not incidental that in cooperation with his younger brother he laid a basis for this tremendous business house. In particular no one else can claim to have employed so many scholarly gentlemen and to have appreciated their personalities.[86]

Naturally Fukuzawa had asked Iwasaki why he found scholarly gentlemen, in other words college graduates, indispensable for his business. Iwasaki's reply to the question was reproduced in *Jitsugyoron*:

> When I projected a steamship company, I started the business by employing ordinary young people. However, although such people are tame and obedient enough to do casual things, they from time to time make errors in important matters, and even worse make simple mistakes. This is because they do not have education, and thus do not know how to distinguish the invaluable from the unvalued. I then changed my mind and employed the educated, but found a problem. They are snobbish and difficult. At the shop they behave as if the customers are their enemies. To see this is intolerable. However, if you change your viewpoint, their character can be seen as beautiful and honest. Furthermore, having some knowledge in their brains, they are not frightened by anything. One had no choice but to employ the educated, who can cope with difficult negotiations and correspondence. Both ordinary youth and the educated have merits and demerits, but it is hard to turn the ordinary into the educated and easier to polish up the educated so that they can fit into business. That is why I nowadays employ exclusively the educated.[87]

As Fukuzawa noted, Mitsubishi had already recruited many graduates from Keio College. The cohort from Keio, sensible and well educated, was typified by Shoda Heigoro. From the fact that Keio students were from the outset overwhelmingly lower-class samurai and their sons and brothers, it can safely be argued that this profile was reflected in the young men Keio dispatched to the business world, at least until the mid-1880s. Fukuzawa thus played a remarkable role in placing Japan upon a modern footing. His disciples successfully emerged as the first generation of the Japanese business elite, relying on diligence and talents which had been largely muzzled under the ancient regime.

What then did Keio College and Fukuzawa give these former humble samurai? Keio's curriculum, composed of English and a wide range of new sciences and economics and law, taught through English books, aroused the students' interests and drew them into a modern age in which business was essential in creating wealth. Becoming rich, which had been almost impossible under the ancient regime and had been regarded as immoral in Confucian rubric, was, astonishingly, the very purpose of Fukuzawa's College, reflected in his motto 'learn and earn, earn and learn'.[88] This encouragement of the interaction between learning and earning owed a considerable amount to British influence, and finally emancipated the energy which had been latent in Japan's youth for centuries, thereby contributing to the emergence of the modern businessman in Japan.

Notes

1. Keio University, *Keio Gijuku Hyakunenshi* (Tokyo: Keio Tsushin, 1958/64).
2. Tokyo Daigaku, *Tokyo Daigaku Hyakunenshi* (Tokyo: University of Tokyo Press, vol. 2, 1984–87), p. 172; H. Morikawa, 'Naibu Shoshingata Keieisha Kigyo no Ichi Kosatsu', *Keio Business Forum*, 1998, p. 8.
3. I. Amano, *Kyusei Senmon Gakko Ron* (Tokyo: Tamagawa Daigaku Shuppanbu, 1993), p. 148.
4. S. Yonekawa, 'University Graduates in Japanese Enterprises before the Second World War', *Business History*, XXVI (1984), pp. 203–4.
5. Josuikai Gakuenshi Kanko Iinkai, *Shogyo Kyoiku no Akebono* (Tokyo: Josuikai, 1990/91), vol. 2, pp. 479–506.
6. The pioneering work in this field is C. Blacker, *The Japanese Enlightenment* (Cambridge: Cambridge University Press, 1964).
7. For Fukuzawa as a publisher, see M. Nagao, *Fukuzawaya Yukichi no Kenkyu* (Tokyo: Shibunkaku Shuppan, 1988).
8. *Fukuzawa Yukichi Zenshu* (hereafter *FYZ*) (Tokyo: Iwanami Shoten), vol. 7, p. 224.
9. *Japan Times*, 5 February 1901.
10. His *Kyu Hanjo* (Conditions in the Old Clan) vividly expounds how controlled clan life was for the lower-class samurai. See *FYZ*, vol. 7, pp. 261–80. The work is translated by Carmen Blacker in *Monumenta Nipponica*, 9, 1953, pp. 304–29.

11. Chambers was one of the judges at the International Exhibition of 1862. He also received an honorary LLD from the University of St Andrews. See W. Chambers, *Memoir of William and Robert Chambers* (Edinburgh: W. & R. Chambers, 1879), pp. 307, 325. Fukuzawa had noted in his diary 'W. & R. Chambers, 47 Paternoster Row, London'. See *FYZ*, vol. 19, p. 68.
12. *FYZ*, vol. 1, p. 26.
13. *FYZ*, vol. 19, p. 368.
14. *FYZ*, vol. 1, pp. 302–4; vol. 19, p. 139.
15. Fukuzawa's purchases can be reconstructed from two sources: K. Kaneko 'Hangaku Yokendo Zosho Mokuroku ni tsuite', *Fukuzawa Yukichi Nenkan*, 1981, and the *New York Times*, 26 June 1867.
16. T. Baba, *Baba Tatsui Zenshu* (Tokyo: Iwanami Shoten, 1988), vol. 3, pp. 153–4. For Baba, see H. Ballhatchet, 'Baba Tatsui and Victorian Britain: a Case Study of an Early Meiji Intellectual', *Kindai Nihon Kenkyu*, 1994.
17. *FYZ*, vol. 19, p. 379.
18. *FYZ*, vol. 17, pp. 150–1.
19. M. Nagao, *Fukuzawaya Yukichi no Kenkyu*, part II, has the whole story.
20. Maruzen, *Maruzen Hyakunen Shi* (Tokyo: Maruzen, 1980/81), vol. 1, p. 32; Y. Suzuki, *Nenpyo ni Yomu Maruzen no Rekishi* (Tokyo: privately printed by Maruzen, n.d.).
21. K. Kimura, *Maruzen Gaishi* (Tokyo: Maruzen, 1969), pp. 77–99, does not say that Fukuzawa wrote the prospectus, but neither does he deny that the idea definitely came from him.
22. Maruzen, *Maruzen Hyakunen Shi (Shiryohen)*, pp. 4–5.
23. N. Tamaki, *Japanese Banking* (Cambridge: Cambridge University Press, 1995), p. 16.
24. See the section 'Of Stocks' in F. Wayland, *Elements of Political Economy*, 1859, book 3, ch. 2.
25. J.R. McCulloch, *A Dictionary, Practical, Theoretical, and Historical of Commerce and Commercial Navigation* (London: Longman, Green, Longman & Roberts, 1860), p. 386.
26. Maruzen, *Maruzen Hyakunen Shi*, vol. 1, p. 46.
27. McCulloch, *Dictionary of Commerce and Commercial Navigation*, p. 386.
28. Suzuki, *Nenpyo ni Yomu Maruzen no Rekishi*; Yokohama Kaiko Shiryokan, *Zusetsu Yokohama Gaikokujin Kyoryuchi* (Yokohama: Yurindo, 1998), p. 85.
29. Suzuki, *Nenpyo ni Yomu Maruzen no Rekishi*; Maruzen, *Maruzen Hyakunen Shi*, vol. 1, p. 52.
30. Maruzen, *Maruzen Hyakunen Shi*, vol. 1, pp. 152–4.
31. This could be *Elements of Banking*.
32. *FYZ*, vol. 21, pp. 7–25.
33. Ibid., vol. 21, pp. 8–9.
34. Ibid., vol. 17, p. 207. The letter is probably dated 28 August 1877.
35. Maruzen, *Maruzen Hyakunen Shi*, vol. 1, pp. 140–4.
36. Ibid., vol. 1, pp. 148–50.
37. *FYZ*, vol. 21, pp. 20–3.
38. The Sairyusha continued to operate.
39. Ibid., vol. 17, p. 231.
40. Ibid., pp. 232–3.
41. Ibid., pp. 328–9.
42. Ibid., pp. 341–2.

43. Ibid., pp. 175–6.
44. K. Hara, *Hara Rokuro-o Den* (Tokyo: Hara Kunizo, 1937), vol. 1, pp. 232–4. Kusaka Yoshio (1851–1923) later became an official in the Ministry of Finance.
45. Nihon Keieishi Kenkyujo, *Nakamigawa Hikojiro Denki Shiryo* (Tokyo: Toyo Keizai Shinposha, 1969), p. 51.
46. *FYZ*, vol. 17, pp. 345–6.
47. Ibid., p. 357.
48. Okurasho, *Meiji Zaisei Shi* (Tokyo: Meiji Zaiseishi Hakkojo, 1925/28), vol. 13, pp. 811–12.
49. Ibid., p. 813.
50. Yokohama Shokin Ginko, *Yokohama Shokin Ginko Shiryo* (Tokyo: Nihon Keizai Hyoronsha, 1976), vol. 1, pp. 21–8, 35–55.
51. R. Onishi, *Asabuki Eiji Den* (Tokyo: Tosho Shuppansha, 1990), pp. 80–4; Iwasakike Denki Kankokai, *Iwasakike Denki* (Tokyo: University of Tokyo Press, 1979–80), vol. 2, pp. 334–5.
52. Ibid., vol. 2, pp. 334–5.
53. Nihon Keieishi Kenkyujo, *Nakamigawa Hikojiro Denki Shiryo*, p. 188.
54. *FYZ*, vol. 18, p. 86.
55. Ibid., p. 84.
56. Tetsudosho, *Nihon Tetsudo Shi* (Tokyo: Tetsudosho, 1921), pp. 820–7.
57. Nihon Keieishi Kenkyujo, *Nakamigawa Hikojiro Denki Shiryo*, p. 197.
58. Ibid., pp. 134, 155–8; Tetsudosho, *Nihon Tetsudo Shi*, pp. 827–9.
59. R.H. Brunton, *Building Japan 1868–1876* (Folkestone: Japan Library, 1991), ch. 9.
60. *FYZ*, vol. 18, p. 106.
61. Nihon Keieishi Kenkyujo, *Nakamigawa Hikojiro Denki Shiryo*, p. 167.
62. Ibid., p. 156.
63. N. Yamada, *Oyatoi Gaikokujin – Kotsu* (Tokyo: Kajima Kenkyujo Shuppankai, 1968), pp. 48–9.
64. Nihon Keieishi Kenkyujo, *Nakamigawa Hikojiro Denki Shiryo*, p. 156.
65. Yamada, *Oyatoi Gaikokujin – Kotsu*, p. 48.
66. Ibid., pp. 143, 168–9; UNESCO, *Shiryo Oyatoi Gaikokujin* (Tokyo: Shogakkan, 1975), p. 243.
67. Nihon Keieishi Kenkyujo, *Nakamigawa Hikojiro Denki Shiryo*, pp. 156–7.
68. Tetsudosho, *Nihon Tetsudo Shi*, p. 829.
69. Nihon Keieishi Kenkyujo, *Nakamigawa Hikojiro Denki Shiryo*, pp. 160, 170–4.
70. His name is recorded only in Japanese as Belcher. See ibid., p. 166.
71. Nakamigawa left a notebook in which he recorded his activities between July 1889 and May 1890. See ibid., pp. 166–70.
72. Tetsudosho, *Nihon Tetsudo Shi*, pp. 828–9.
73. *FYZ*, vol. 18, pp. 304–5.
74. Nihon Keieishi Kenkyujo, *Nakamigawa Hikojiro Denki Shiryo*, p. 182.
75. Ibid., p. 185; Tetsudosho, *Nihon Tetsudo Shi*, pp. 844–5.
76. Mitsui Bunko, *Mitsui Jigyo Shi* (Tokyo: Mitsui Bunko, 1980–94), vol. 2, pp. 435–46.
77. Nihon Keieishi Kenkyujo, *Nakamigawa Hikojiro Denki Shiryo*, p. 227.
78. Mitsui Bunko, *Mitsui Jigyo Shi*, vol. 2, p. 486.
79. *FYZ*, vol. 18, pp. 481–2.
80. Mitsui Bunko, *Mitsui Jigyo Shi*, vol. 2, pp. 468–9.
81. Ibid., p. 563; Mitsui Ginko, *Mitsui Ginko Hachijunen Shi* (Tokyo: Mitsui Ginko, 1957), p. 120.

82. Mitsui Ginko, *Mitsui Ginko Hachijunen Shi*, pp. 121–2; see also Nihon Keieishi Kenkyujo, *Nakamigawa Hikojiro Denki Shiryo*, pp. 233, 259–60, 265–9.
83. Mitsui Bunko, *Mitsui Jigyo Shi*, vol. 2, pp. 538–41, 598–604, 651–8, 661–4.
84. *FYZ*, vol. 6, pp. 191–2.
85. For their friendship, see a letter from December 1876 in *FYZ*, vol. 17, p. 198.
86. *FYZ*, vol. 6, p. 155.
87. Ibid., pp. 155–6.
88. Ibid., vol. 17, pp. 150–1.

4

A Munition-Steel Company and Anglo-Japanese Relations Before and After the First World War: the Corporate Governance of the Japan Steel Works and its British Shareholders*

Bunji Nagura

Introduction

It is possible to observe a great change in Anglo-Japanese relations between the turn of the century and the 1930s, from the 'honeymoon' of the Anglo-Japanese Alliance in 1902 to the 'alienation' of the Washington Naval Conference in 1921–22, and then 'hostility' after the Manchurian Incident in 1931.[1] At the end of the nineteenth century, Britain was already a mature economy, while Japan was just beginning to industrialize, importing modern systems, products and technology from Britain and other advanced western countries. While Japan grew rapidly during the First World War, though, Britain, the former great power, had begun to experience relative decline.

British capital had been invested throughout the world before the First World War, including in Japan. Britain's direct investment in Japan, however, was not substantial as a percentage of Britain's total overseas holdings, partly because 'British capital exports to Asia often took the form of portfolio investment', and partly because the Japanese government had excluded foreign capital, especially direct investment, from the beginning of the Meiji era.[2] Although the amount of foreign capital invested in Japan was relatively small, its role in Japanese industry was still important, especially after the Japanese government changed its policy on foreign investment from exclusion to acceptance around 1900, mainly because of the adoption of the gold standard in 1897 and the revision of the Commercial Code in 1899. In manufacturing, foreign companies made inroads into Japan 'either by themselves or by way of joint ventures or capital affilia-

* I would like to thank Mr Clive Trebilcock for his comments on my draft chapter.

tions'. Most were the leading multinationals of the time (British firms before the First World War, mainly American after the war), and many were involved in heavy industry – for example, heavy and electrical engineering. They made a large and lasting contribution to the modernization of Japanese industry and business.[3] Japan wanted technology transfer from western countries through foreign affiliates, but without ceding any control over Japanese business.[4] The concern in this chapter is to analyse how this might have been possible.

This question is considered here by examining the history of the KK Nihon Seikosho (Japan Steel Works, hereafter JSW), a big munition-steel company and joint venture between Britain and Japan before the Second World War. In particular, the aim is to analyse the involvement of the three investors in the JSW, namely, the Hokkaido Tanko Kisen Company (Hokkaido Colliery and Steamship Co., Sir W.G. Armstrong, Whitworth & Co. Ltd. and Vickers, Sons & Maxim, Ltd.[5] It is also essential for our analysis to clarify the role of the Imperial Japanese Navy (IJN), which actively supported the foundation of the Japan Steel Works (JSW). This chapter focuses on the way in which the British shareholders participated in the top management of the JSW and the way in which the Japanese side attempted to prevent the British from actively participating while still acquiring technology from them. Hence the subtitle of this chapter is 'The Corporate Governance of the JSW and the British Shareholders'.[6] No previous study has attempted to examine this topic, but through using primary manuscript sources in Britain it is possible to reveal a number of examples of the involvement of the British shareholders.[7] Accordingly, it is to be hoped that this chapter will make a contribution towards enhancing our historical understanding of the nature of foreign investments by British multinationals on the one hand, and of the involvement of foreign capital in Japan before the Second World War on the other.[8]

The formation of the Japan Steel Works[9]

The JSW was established at Muroran in Hokkaido in 1907 against the background of the Anglo-Japanese Alliance. The initiative came from Hokutan, the IJN, and the British munitions companies, Armstrongs in particular. The original idea had come from Inoue Kakugoro, the managing director of Hokutan.[10] As Hokutan had acquired surplus funds by selling a railway to the government during the railway nationalization of 1906, Inoue sought to fulfil his long-held ambition of investing in the iron industry.

However, the original plan changed in the early summer of 1906, when Vice-Admiral Saito Makoto, the Navy Minister, introduced Inoue to Vice-Admiral (later Baron) Yamanouchi Masuji, Governor of the Kure Naval Base and Arsenal (naval dockyard) in Hiroshima prefecture, and one of the navy's leading authorities on armament technologies. Yamanouchi advised Inoue to found a works making high-grade steel for big guns, and introduced him to E.L.D. Boyle, the resident officer of Armstrongs in Tokyo. Boyle duly contacted Armstrongs in Britain, which led to a series of discussions in both countries.

In November 1906, Armstrongs approved the project to set up a 'Steel and Ordnance Works in Japan', and instructed Boyle to settle the details.[11] The Japanese government also invited Vickers to join the project, and this offer was accepted at the beginning of 1907.[12] The fact that the invitations were issued by the government rather than by Hokutan was to become an issue later on when the British firms sought so-called 'retrenchment compensation' and attempted to sell their JSW shares to the Japanese government. They claimed they had merely accepted an explicit invitation from the government. However, British scholars have often overemphasized this point.[13] While the British companies would not have gone to any country without the security of an invitation or similar assurance, they certainly had every intention of investing in Japan. They saw this as an arrangement that could prove mutually beneficial.

By the turn of the century, Armstrongs and Vickers, the two largest British munitions companies, had already achieved a measure of vertical integration from steelworks through to shipyards and armaments factories, and had also begun to invest abroad, in countries such as Spain, Italy, Austria-Hungary and Russia.[14] They cooperated in investing abroad while at the same time competing with each other to sell their products. They were both willing to accept the invitation from the IJN because in the aftermath of the Russo-Japanese War they were anxious to invest in Japan instead of relying on the export of warships and armaments.

Needless to say, the Russo-Japanese War had been fought against the background of the Anglo-Japanese Alliance, and almost all the main warships of the IJN that took part in the fighting had been supplied by the British companies, Armstrongs in particular.[15] During and after the war the IJN encouraged its own arsenals and private dockyards to build capital ships and cruisers. The Yokosuka and Kure Arsenals built several capital ships and cruisers such as the *Satsuma* and the *Aki*. The Kure Arsenal also had its own steel works and began to make guns by using its own steel. The *Tsukuba*, the first domestically-built 10000-ton armoured cruiser, completed in January 1907, was equipped with four 12-inch guns made by Kure Arsenal. Until the Russo-Japanese War almost all large naval guns had been imported, especially from Britain. Still, however, the delay in making naval guns of sufficient quality in Japan hindered the construction of home-built capital ships in the navy's armament expansion programme. This is the reason why the IJN, and especially Yamanouchi, urged Hokutan to establish a munition-steelworks and then persuaded the two British munitions companies to invest in Japan.

Inoue was not entirely satisfied with the idea of establishing a munition-steelworks in cooperation with the British companies. He had another plan for a company to construct an Ironworks with a small furnace which would manufacture pig iron from the iron sand in Hokkaido. This was the Wanishi Ironworks, launched in 1909 (see Figure 4.1). Wanishi in fact ceased operations soon after its founding, but was revived in 1913, after Inoue's departure from Hokutan, this time to produce pig iron from iron ore.

In March 1907, representatives of Hokutan, Armstrongs and Vickers met at the official residence of the Navy Minister in Tokyo to agree a draft contract. The meeting was attended by Japanese government officials, and by J.H.B. Noble (a director of Armstrongs) on behalf of the two British companies. The company to be established, the JSW, was to be a private company with strong backing from the Japanese government. The official agreement was signed in London in July 1907. Its main points were as follows:[16]

(a) The works would be founded at Muroran in Hokkaido.[17]
(b) The objectives of the company would be: the manufacture and sale of arms, ammunition, machinery, vessels, steel materials and steel products for supply to the Imperial Japanese Army and Navy.
(c) The capital of the Company would be fixed at ¥10 m at its foundation. (This was later increased to ¥15 m in 1909. In both cases, Hokutan invested 50 per cent of the total amount of capital, with Vickers and Armstrongs contributing 25 per cent each.)
(d) There were to be a maximum of nine directors and three auditors. Half of the directors were to be nominated by Hokutan, and the other half by the British companies. One director was to be nominated by mutual consent. This so-called 'neutral director' was a characteristic feature of the JSW. It is also noteworthy that every British director had the right to name someone as his 'proxy' according to the addendum to the agreement, which will be considered more fully later.

The British companies were bound by a Supplementary Agreement to give the JSW all such information and advice as might be required to construct the new works and to carry out its business. On the other hand, the British companies received in return the preferential right to manufacture or supply to the JSW all such machinery, appliances and other resources that it might require for the purpose of completing or maintaining the works, and where such goods could not be obtained from its own works or from other producers in Japan.

The Supplementary Agreement stipulated that the orders and contracts received by the JSW, which it could not fulfil from its own works, should be handed over to the British companies at 'a discount or commission at a rate of 2.5 per cent on the contract price or a discount or commission at such rate as may be arranged where the British companies consider that the circumstances justify a higher rate'. What these provisions meant in practice will be examined in the next section. Another important item in the

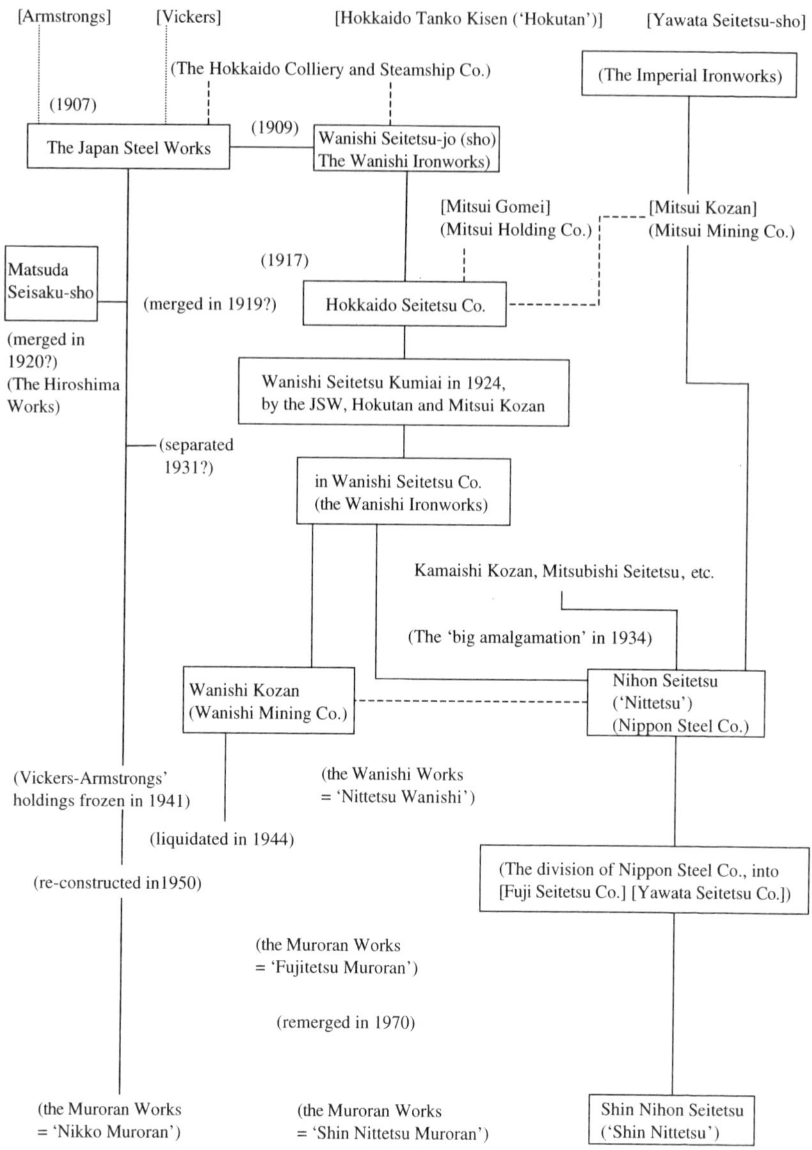

Note: Dotted lines indicate investments or holdings.

Figure 4.1 Lineage of the Japan Steel Works (with reference to the Wanishi Ironworks and Nippon Steel Corp.)

agreement was that Hokutan and the British companies were bound not to sell or transfer their respective shares except by mutual consent. This will also be considered further.

The top management of the JSW and the participation of the British directors before the First World War

The purpose of this section is to show how the JSW's British shareholders committed themselves to the top management in the early years of the company before the First World War.

The period of 'sole control' by Inoue

It is often said that Inoue Kakugoro, the managing director of Hokutan and the first chairman of the JSW, had 'sole control' of both firms. However, it cannot be said that the British shareholders had nothing to do with the top management of the JSW, because they had invested a great deal of money and provided technical support. Little has been written about the precise nature of the British involvement. This is in part due to a lack of sources. However, careful analysis of a number of primary sources in Britain leads to the following conclusions.[18] Although approximately half of the positions of director and auditor in the JSW had been occupied by Britons acting for Armstrongs or Vickers, these members could rarely attend the board meetings of the JSW, because they were directors of Armstrongs or Vickers living in Britain. However, each of them had the right to nominate someone as his 'Proxy' as laid down in the addendum to the original agreement. Proxies were able not only to attend the board meetings of the JSW, but also to exercise equal rights to those of the directors and auditors. In fact, proxies usually attended JSW board meetings, became members of some committees of the board, and even made important proposals to the board. Moreover, E.L.D. Boyle, the proxy for Armstrongs' director Andrew Noble, was elected as the neutral director in August 1908, succeeding Kondo Sukemune, Yamanouchi's younger brother-in-law, who had been the first man to hold the post (see Figure 4.2).

Most of the proxies were British businessmen living in Japan,[19] some of them resident officers of Armstrongs or Jardine Matheson & Co. (agent for Armstrongs in Japan at that time), in Tokyo. One was a Japanese, Count Hirosawa Kinjiro, a member of the House of Peers, who acted as proxy for A.T. Dawson, a director nominated by Vickers. Hirosawa seems to have played an important role not only as Dawson's proxy but also as an active communicator between the British directors, auditors and proxies and their Japanese counterparts.[20]

Proxies often communicated with the directors and auditors in Britain by cable, telegram or letter. Meetings of the British directors of the JSW were occasionally held in Britain, where various differences of opinion between

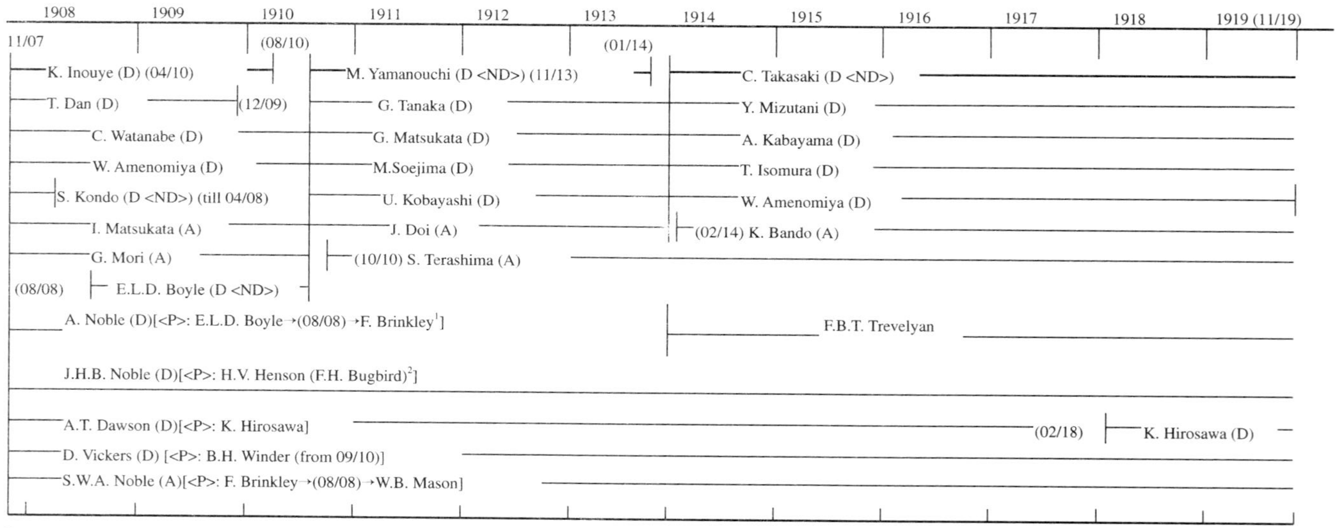

Sources: *Minutes Of The Meetings Of Directors And Auditors Of The Nihon Seiko-Sho* [VA-287, 288]. *Nihon Seiko-sho Shashi Shiryo* (*A History and Documents of the JSW*), the JSW, 1968. *Nihon Seiko-sho, Eigyo Hokoku-sho (Annual Reports of the JSW)*. See the details (attendances at the Board Meeting, etc.), in B. Nagura, *Heiki-Tekko Kaisha no Nichiei Kankeishi: Nihon Seiko-sho to Eikokugawa Kabunushi, 1907–52 (A Munition-Steel Company and the Relation between Britain and Japan: A Historical Study of the Japan Steel Works and the British Shareholders, 1907–52)*. Tokyo: Nihon Keizai Hyoronsha Ltd., 1998, pp. 52–5, 94–5, 153, etc.

Notes: (D); Director (The bold lines indicate the Chairman or the President on the Board), <ND>; Neutral Director, (A); Auditor, <P> Proxy.

1. Deceased in October 1912.
2. A Proxy of J.H.B. Noble in the absence of H.V. Henson during his stay in Britain

Figure 4.2 Directors, auditors and their proxies of the JSW, 1907–1919

Armstrongs and Vickers were ironed out. The results of these consultations were then transmitted to the proxies in Japan. At first, though, the power held by Inoue made it difficult for the proxies to participate in the management of the JSW in any meaningful way, and they were unable to convey the opinions of the British shareholders with sufficient weight.

In November 1908, the British companies decided to send to Japan J.H.B. Noble (representing Armstrongs) and Douglas Vickers, both of whom were directors of the JSW, to consult directly with the JSW board.[21] Both arrived in Japan in February 1909. After his visit, Vickers complained that 'all the arrangements and contracts in Japan had been made by Mr. Inowye [*sic*] who not only consulted nobody in these matters but also even resented discussion of, or comment on, what he did. He said, Tanko [Hokutan] left everything to him, and why not Seikosho too?'[22]

Noble and Vickers attended three JSW board meetings during their stay in Japan, and made several important proposals. The most significant related to the formation of a new Managing Committee of the board.[23] This comprised Boyle and Hirosawa, together with Inoue and Watanabe Chifuru (representing Hokutan). British directors and their proxies could become members of executive committees of the JSW, but only for a short period.

The setting up of the Managing Committee failed to prevent further friction between Inoue and the British, so Admiral Yamanouchi, technical adviser to the JSW since its foundation, found himself expected to play a more active role on the board and to mediate between both sides. As a result of further deliberations, the Managing Committee was soon abolished and the post of general manager – to supervise the head office and the Muroran Works – was created in January 1910. Kondo Sukemune, the first general manager, was de facto Yamanouchi's representative, and was able to attend JSW board meetings.

The British directors and their proxies played an important role in the raising of funds for the JSW. The board of the JSW drew up a plan to increase the capital from ¥10 million to ¥15 million, and to issue debentures worth £1 million (approximately ¥10 million) in Britain. A special committee was set up for this purpose, comprising H.V. Henson (proxy for Noble) (see Figure 4.1), Hirosawa and Inoue.

Although the increase in the capital of the JSW was approved by the ordinary general meeting of the shareholders in March 1909, Hokutan could not pay its part in the second fund by the end of March 1910 because of financial difficulties. Inoue consequently resigned as the managing director of Hokutan and the chairman of the JSW in April 1910.[24]

The British shareholders subsequently offered emergency financial support to the JSW, but also demanded the concession of a 'permanent majority' on the board and rigid conditions for the proposed debenture issue in Britain.[25] These demands, especially the first, angered Yamanouchi, and were probably unacceptable to the Japanese side.[26] In the end, the British modified their stance and tried to cooperate with Yamanouchi.[27] Yamanouchi subsequently accepted the position of Chairman of the JSW in June 1910, taking up the post formally from August, after his retirement from the IJN. To the surprise of the British, this brought about the resignation of Boyle as neutral director, which meant that the influence of the British shareholders in the top management of the JSW was correspondingly reduced.[28]

The 'Yamanouchi Regime' and the British shareholders

The next issue is the extent to which the British directors were involved in the top management of the JSW under the 'Yamanouchi Regime' from 1910 to 1913. During this period, Hokutan began to come under the increasing influence of Mitsui *Zaibatsu*, Japan's largest corporation. In January 1913 it was restructured under the auspices of Mitsui.

After Inoue's resignation, Yamanouchi was expected to mediate between the Japanese directors from Hokutan and the British directors and proxies. In August 1910 he was elected neutral director and chairman of the board by mutual consent of Hokutan and the British (see Table 4.1), and with strong support of the IJN. Yamanouchi was thus in a position to play an important role in a number of ways during the difficult period when plants were being built and beginning to operate. It must be admitted, however, that he was not particularly successful in his efforts to mediate between the British and Japanese sides.

Yamanouchi was not given any formal information about the proposed debenture issue, although a representative of Hokutan was negotiating with Armstrongs and Vickers in London in August 1910. In September, the plan was eventually changed to an issue of ¥10 million worth of debentures in Japan under the leadership of Hokutan.[29] Another disagreement at the time concerned the depreciation of the fixed assets of the JSW. The British insisted that there should be a certain rate of depreciation once the plants were in operation, but the Japanese opposed it on the grounds that the plants were not fully operative. Yamanouchi tried unsuccessfully to reach a compromise on this issue at a lengthy board meeting in July 1912.[30] A further important problem, unresolved since the founding of the JSW, was the range and size of commission to be paid to the JSW by Armstrongs and Vickers in return for receiving ordnance orders from the Japanese government. The JSW also wanted to be nominated as sole agent for the British firms.

It was agreed in November 1910, after Vickers received the order for the battle cruiser *Kongo*, that Armstrongs and Vickers should pay 2.5 per cent commission to the JSW, although the order was obtained officially through Mitsui Bussan, the largest trading company in Japan.[31] Afterwards it became customary for Vickers and Armstrongs to pay to the JSW 2.5 per cent commission, or sometimes more depending on the circumstances, in return for Japanese government orders, even if these were not received through the JSW.[32] The serious rivalry between Vickers and Armstrongs helped the JSW to be successful in taking advantage of its position. On one occasion, the Japanese directors of the JSW told Vickers that if they would not agree commission or sole agent terms, then various orders from the IJN would be given to Armstrongs.[33] At the same time, the Japanese side sought to avoid an open breach between the two British companies on the board of the JSW. On occasion, Yamanouchi warned the British not to conflict on the board,[34] but to little avail.

The JSW's Muroran works were reorganized at the end of 1912. F.B.T. Trevelyan, a gunnery expert from Armstrong's Elswick, had pointed out in a report to the British directors a series of shortcomings at Muroran.[35] After lengthy discussions between the British directors, Trevelyan and Yamanouchi, reforms were introduced.[36] After the restructuring of Hokutan in January 1913, the JSW came under the influence of Mitsui. Yamanouchi, irritated by the selfish stance of both Mitsui and the British companies, threatened to resign as chairman in August 1913. He carried out this threat in November, before he had completed his mediation between Hokutan and the British.[37]

The growth of the JSW and the 'retreat' of the British directors during the First World War

Our next concern is to consider how the JSW grew and acquired technology, and examine the partial withdrawal from the JSW board of the British shareholders during the First World War. The Japanese economy prospered during the war, and the JSW grew accordingly, particularly during the second half of the conflict. Its profits and dividends were high, thanks partly to the high rate of depreciation of its equipment (see Table 4.1). Naturally, this was also satisfactory for the British shareholders.[38]

The JSW had already acquired technology from the British companies before the First World War. Not only had Japanese employees of the JSW been sent to the British companies for training,[39] but also many engineers and assistants from the British companies had also been sent to the Muroran Works (see Table 4.2). Specialists in fields such as steel smelting, forging and gun manufacturing had been sent to Muroran every year at the request of the JSW board.[40] Almost all had completed their contracts and returned home before the onset of war, but Muroran was still able to produce large guns and munitions, though some specific techniques in metallurgy and forging continued to cause problems.[41] It is therefore possible to argue that the necessary technology for armament manufacturing had already been acquired, enabling the JSW to accept many lucrative orders from Japan's navy and army during the war.

Table 4.1 Profits and dividends of the JSW, 1911–31

	The JSW				*Returns from the JSW (£)*	
	Profits (¥ 000)	*% of capital*	*Dividends (¥ 000)*	*% of capital*	*Vickers*	*Armstrongs*
1911	–105	–0.7	0	0	0	0
1912	–336	–2.2	0	0	0	0
1913	405	2.7	0	0	0	0
1914	264	1.8	150	1.0	3808	3808
1915	474	3.2	375	2.5	9788	9788
1916	1850	12.3	975	6.5	25957	25957
1917	2574	17.2	1875	11.7	50415	50415
1918	4050	27.0	2250	15.0	61926	61926
1919	3027	22.0	1750	12.7	51782	51782
1920	2856	9.5	2700	9.0	44482	44482
1921	2045	6.8	1500	5.0	19748	19748
1922	4023	13.4	3000	10.0	37026	37026
1923	3026	10.1	2250	7.5	27664	27664
1924	2692	9.0	2100	7.0	21659	21659
1925	917	3.1	750	2.8	7277	7277
1926	158	0.5	0	0	0	0
1927	219	0.7	0	0	0	0
					Vickers-Armstrongs	
1928	1076	3.9	825	3.0	18139	
1929	1229	4.1	900	3.0	19884	
1930	1051	3.5	750	2.5	17640	
1931	–239	–0.8	0	0	0	

Sources: Nihon Seikosho, 'Eigyo Hokoku-sho'; 'Histories of Japanese Investments' [VA-1239] p. 15.
Note: 11 months in the case of 1919 and 1928.

In the meantime, the two British companies were totally preoccupied by the war. Although Armstrongs and Vickers gained large profits by supplying armaments to the Royal Navy and the British Army, they were forced to evacuate their head offices from London, and it was impossible to hold regular meetings of shareholders. Under these circumstances, they were forced to reduce their role in the JSW, both in terms of technical assistance and in terms of their participation in top management.

It can also be claimed that the British companies in part retreated because they had already transferred technology to the JSW and during the war received high dividends from the company. However, it must be stressed that it was never the intention of the British companies to downplay their role in the JSW. They were compelled to do so by the difficulties posed by the war. This is clearly shown in the case of F.B.T. Trevelyan, the senior

Table 4.2 British technicians in the JSW, 1911–17

Name	*Company*	*Type of job*	*Arrival date in Japan*	*Departure date from Japan*
G. Blyth	Vickers	assistant engineer of steel smelting	June, 1911	Oct., 1912
S. Pearson	Vickers	steel smelter	June, 1911	Oct., 1912
J. Eason	Vickers	steel smelter	June, 1911	Oct., 1912
J. Foster	Vickers	steel smelter	June, 1911	Oct., 1912
B. Wild Smith	Vickers	steel smelter	June, 1911	Oct., 1912
M.W. Baldock	Armstrongs	designer	July, 1911	Feb., 1914
E. Yong	Armstrongs	engineer of forging	Oct., 1911	Jan., 1912
G.W. Taylor	Armstrongs	forger	Oct., 1911	Feb., 1914
G.A. Atkinson	Armstrongs	mechanical engineer	May, 1912	Feb., 1914
W. Longstaff	Armstrongs	assistant mechanical engineer	May, 1912	Feb., 1915
E. Freiling	Armstrongs	assistant mechanical engineer	May, 1912	Feb., 1915
A.A.C. Bell	Armstrongs	assistant mechanical engineer	May, 1912	Feb., 1914
J. Jackson	Armstrongs	assistant engineer of steel smelting	Aug., 1913	June, 1914
F. Wilson	Vickers	assistant mechanical engineer	Aug., 1913	May, 1915
F. Stirland	Vickers	assistant mechanical engineer	Aug., 1913	May, 1915
C. Gibbs	Vickers	assistant mechanical engineer	Aug., 1913	May, 1915
J W. Brown	Armstrongs	assistant mechanical engineer	Aug., 1913	May, 1915
W.C Pawl	Armstrongs	assistant mechanical engineer	Aug., 1913	May, 1915
J.T. Geggie	Armstrongs	assistant mechanical engineer	June, 1914	Feb., 1916
J.J. Wilson	Armstrongs	checker	June, 1914	Feb., 1916
J.S. Greaner	Armstrongs	checker	June, 1914	Feb., 1916
D.J. Atherton	Armstrongs	checker	June, 1914	Feb., 1916
A.W.R. Ward	Armstrongs	checker	June, 1914	Feb., 1916
J. Stobbs	Armstrongs	checker	June, 1914	Feb., 1916
H.H. Ashdown	Armstrongs	engineer of steel smelting	July, 1914	April, 1917
E.L. Robertson	Armstrongs	engineer of steel smelting	July, 1914	June, 1915

Sources: *Nihon Seiko-sho Shashi Shiryo*, pp. 182–3. Some mistakes have been corrected (for details see Nagura, *Heiki Tekko Kaisha no Nichiei Kankei Shi*, p. 145).
Note: In addition, there was F.B.T. Trevelyan, a higher engineer (a gunnery expert), from Armstrongs (Elswick Works), who stayed in Japan May 1912–Feb. 1914.

engineer mentioned previously. He was elected resident director in Japan on behalf of Armstrongs in January 1914[42] (see Figure 4.2), and his contract to assist the JSW as a gunnery expert was renewed for two more years in February of that year. In March, he returned to Britain for a short leave, but was unable to return to his post in Japan because Armstrongs needed his expertise at home.[43]

While the Japanese directors of the JSW positively welcomed British technical advice, they did not always welcome the British participation in top management. The directors from Mitsui, in full control of Hokutan from January 1913, appear to have deliberately sought to exclude the British from participation in the top management of the JSW. In November 1913, Dr (later Baron) Dan Takuma, a director of the JSW 1907–09, and chairman of Hokutan, who in 1914 became the top director of Mitsui, proposed that the British proxies should no longer attend meetings of the board of the JSW. Indeed, none of the proxies, except for Hirosawa, as representative of Vickers and also an official of the JSW's Tokyo branch,[44] were present at JSW board meetings from January 1914.[45]

It should be stressed that Admiral Mizutani Yoshihiko (a rear admiral of the engineers) played an important role in establishing good relations between the British shareholders and the Japanese directors. Mizutani was a manager of the Muroran Works from January 1913, and managing director of the JSW from January 1914, after the resignation of Yamanouchi. While it goes without saying that the IJN supported Mizutani, we should also note that Mizutani felt extremely friendly toward the British directors, especially J.H.B. Noble from Armstrongs.[46] The probable reason for this was that Mizutani had graduated not only from the Naval Engineering School in Japan but also from Greenwich Naval College. His position on the JSW board was somewhat complicated because he was representing Hokutan.[47]

Mizutani asked the British shareholders, and especially Armstrongs, to send a highly skilled engineer to the JSW, and to nominate a 'resident director' in Japan to replace Trevelyan. Despite their enthusiasm for the idea, the British companies were unable to comply during the war.[48] Thus the British could not fully commit themselves to the management of the JSW, and, in conjunction with the reduced role of the proxies, it is clear that the war witnessed a significant change in the relationship between the two sides.

The 'alienation' of the British shareholders

It has already been shown how the British companies partly withdrew from the board of the JSW during the First World War. Another important change in the relationship which occurred just after the war was the result of the merger between the Wanishi Ironworks and the JSW. This put the British shareholders in a minority position in the JSW. From then on, the British companies were torn between resuming full participation in the board and withdrawing from Japan altogether.

The merger with the Wanishi Ironworks

In 1919, the JSW merged with the Wanishi Ironworks (formally Hokkaido Seitetsu Kaisha – Hokkaido Iron Manufacturing Company), which had been founded in 1917 jointly by Hokutan, Mitsui Gomei (the holding company heading the Mitsui *Zaibatsu*) and Mitsui Kozan (Mitsui Mining) (see Figure 4.1).

As a result of this merger, the capital of the JSW was increased from ¥15 million to ¥30 million. The holdings were distributed as follows:

Hokutan	¥15 million
Mitsui Gomei	¥3.75 million
Mitsui Kozan	¥3.75 million
Vickers	¥3.75 million
Armstrongs	¥3.75 million

The overall share of the British companies was thus halved to 25 per cent. As Hokutan had already been under the total control of Mitsui since 1913, the distribution of the capital suggests that JSW, too, was controlled by Mitsui.[49] It was commonly accepted that this merger was brought about with the objective of constructing an integrated enterprise, combining the Wanishi Ironworks, which produced pig iron, with the Muroran Works (the JSW), which produced high-grade steel. However, the Wanishi Works was to produce pig iron for ordinary steel for civilian consumption, while the Muroran Works was to produce special steel for munitions. One can therefore speculate that the real intention of the merger may have lain elsewhere, namely that the Japanese directors of the JSW, especially those from Mitsui, were attempting to free themselves from the British shareholders.[50] In a later document written around 1930 Vickers claimed that the

> reasons for taking over the Wanishi Ironworks and combining pig iron manufacture with the production of high grade steel and armaments are not quite clear, except that it was done on the recommendation of the Japanese directors, of whom the Mitsui Company were well represented. At the time Vickers and Armstrongs accepted their recommendation it seems that each company viewed the venture with doubtful success [*sic*].[51]

The Wanishi merger was first proposed to the British shareholders 'when the Great War was at its zenith'.[52] Even after end of the war, the British companies had little time to consider the problem carefully. Despite their doubts about the purpose of the merger, they approved it unwillingly, relying on the advice of their 'Japanese colleagues'.[53] In fact, the Wanishi merger turned the JSW into a company with three plants with divergent characters: Muroran, with the Hiroshima Works,[54] produced munitions from special steel (and was 'the munition works for the IJN'), while the Wanishi Iron-works produced pig iron for common steel. While the Japanese interests may have been satisfied by the merger, the British companies came to distrust the Japanese directors, particularly those from Mitsui. The Wanishi merger was thus a turning point in the relationship between the JSW and its British shareholders.

Changes on the board of the JSW at the request of the IJN and the British shareholders

After the First World War, and especially following the Washington Naval Conference in 1921–22 and the expiry of the Anglo-Japanese Alliance, the JSW faced severe difficulties as it entered the era of disarmament and the long Depression. The JSW tried to reorganize, and both the British shareholders and the Japanese navy made efforts to regain their influence on the JSW board during this process. This led to complex interactions between Mitsui, the navy and the British companies. As far as the JSW board was concerned, two important events took place in 1925. One was the election of Rear Admiral Yutani Kenzo as resident director in Japan on behalf of Vickers. The other was the return of Admiral Mizutani as managing director, with the strong backing of the IJN.

Since Yutani had already been appointed as Vickers' agent in Japan in 1923 after retiring from the IJN,[55] he had already represented Vickers in the case of the so-called 'retrenchment compensation' after the Washington Naval Conference. To boost his standing within the JSW, Vickers persuaded the JSW board to accept him as resident director in June 1925.[56] He thus fulfilled the same functions as had Count Hirosawa, who had left in December 1920 on being appointed Japan's ambassador to Spain. Admiral Yutani played an important role in all subsequent developments at the JSW, and, as will be shown later, made full use of his connections with the IJN.

What is noteworthy here is the extraordinary lack of communication after the First World War between the board of the JSW and the British companies, in particular with Vickers. When Vickers sought Admiral Yutani's appointment as a director, they believed that there would be no room for him on the board because a director from Mitsui had already taken Hirosawa's place. The cause of this misunderstanding was that Vickers was following the old articles of association of the JSW before the Wanishi merger, which allowed for a maximum of nine directors, whereas the new articles allowed for 14.[57]

There were three reasons for this lack of communication. The war was in itself sufficient, but the distrust arising from the Wanishi merger was also important. A further reason was a shift affecting the British shareholders. Although Armstrongs declined more rapidly after the war than did Vickers, the JSW office in Britain was in Newcastle-upon-Tyne, where the head office and main works of Armstrongs were located, and the 'English Secretary' of the JSW had been an Armstrongs appointment ever since the establishment of the JSW. Accordingly, the JSW board was in much closer contact with Armstrongs than it was with Vickers.

With the election of Admiral Yutani, the IJN sought to secure the return of Admiral Mizutani as managing director. Mitsui had displayed little interest in reorganizing the JSW, and was reluctant to open new markets, relying on the retrenchment compensation that followed from the Washington Naval Conference. Under these circumstances Mizutani, who had resigned as managing director in October 1921, continued to present various restructuring plans in his capacity as adviser to the JSW.[58] The IJN forced Mitsui to agree to Mizutani's return as managing director in October 1925, half-threatening to withhold orders from the firm if Mitsui failed to go along with the proposal.[59]

The British shareholders and Yutani welcomed Mizutani's return, because of his friendly stance towards the British and his active role in the board since 1914.[60] They also supported his reconstruction plans for the JSW. Many elements of Mizutani's plans were realized, but the most important and drastic reorganization measure was not undertaken. This was the plan for opening new markets, especially those related to civilian consumption, including the construction of sheet-steel manufacturing facilities at the Wanishi Ironworks. The JSW board declined to pursue this proposal owing to Mitsui's unwillingness to commit investment during the long Depression.[61]

The 'retrenchment compensation' and British attempts to sell their shares in the JSW

The Washington Naval Conference brought about a slump in naval orders, and threatened the entire basis of the JSW as a munition works for the IJN. Under these circumstances, armaments manufacturers pressed the Japanese government for monetary compensation for their capital investment in shipyards and factories. The whole issue of this 'retrenchment compensation' took a tortuous course before being finally solved between 1923 and 1926.[62] The Retrenchment Compensation Bill was considered by the Japanese government in the latter half of 1923. At this time, Armstrongs and Vickers sent separate representatives to Japan to try and sell their holdings in the JSW. These representatives were Trevelyan, still at the time a JSW director and the Far Eastern representative of Armstrongs, and B.H. Winder, the 'Asiatic' Supervisor of Vickers.[63] In a petition presented to the Japanese government in July 1923, Trevelyan claimed that the measures agreed at the Washington Conference meant it would be 'impossible for the Japanese Admiralty to supply the Seikosho in future with sufficient orders to enable the Works to be operated on a paying basis'. Given that the Muroran plant was entirely geared towards military orders, the British shareholders of the JSW sought some return on the capital they had invested.[64]

After it was rumoured that the JSW would receive approximately ¥10 million in compensation, the British companies suggested that the Japanese government should buy their holdings out instead.[65] From then on, the two firms cooperated closely on these issues. In particular, Vickers, through Yutani, tried hard to persuade the government to purchase their holdings in the JSW.[66] The reason why the British shareholders took this action seems to have been that after the First World War their role had changed from that of a positive investor and technical supporter to that of some kind of 'rentier'. As it became more and more difficult to get dividends from Japan (see Table 4.1), the need to sell the holdings became more urgent. As B.H. Winder informed the Japanese naval attaché in London in March 1925, the British companies no longer felt the need to remain shareholders of the JSW.[67]

In March 1926, the modified Retrenchment Compensation Bill passed the Diet. It authorized the payment of Government 5 per cent bonds to the country's 13 armament manufacturers. ¥9 807 475, nearly 50 per cent of the total, was allocated to the JSW. The payment to the JSW was, however, unique, in that the government assumed nominal ownership of 'all buildings, plant and equipment used solely for the production of Armaments' in return for bonds worth ¥7.7 million. Because the buildings and the like had been mortgaged to the bank, the JSW was forced to exchange the bonds for the sum of ¥7.621 m.[68]

This solution was incomprehensible to the British, because they would have preferred to sell their shares in the JSW. The lack of communication between the British and Japanese sides, and the British distrust of Mitsui, added to the difficulties. This was despite active attempts on the part of Yutani to act as an intermediary between the British and the IJN. In fact, when Vickers submitted a petition regarding 'retrenchment compensation' to the Navy Ministry in Japan, Yutani drafted the formal document and acted as an intermediary between V.C. Vickers (a director of Vickers) and the Navy Minister.[69]

In January 1928 Vickers merged with Armstrongs. The new company, Vickers-Armstrongs Limited (hereafter V-A),[70] took over the JSW shares of the two firms. After the compensation settlement, and in particular after the ending of the merger with the Wanishi Ironworks in 1931, V-A and Yutani tried vigorously to extricate the British company from the JSW. Unfortunately, this period lies beyond the scope of this chapter.[71]

The ending of the merger with Wanishi

The final section of this chapter will consider the ending of the merger with the Wanishi Ironworks in 1931, because this was probably the last chance for the British shareholders to resume genuine participation in the activities of the board of the JSW. The demerger has usually been considered only as a domestic issue, normally in terms of the rationalization of either the JSW or Wanishi, or as an episode in moves towards the large-scale amalgamation of iron and steel companies in Japan, which eventually led to the founding of the Nippon Steel Company in 1934 (see Figure 4.2).[72] Careful consideration of the documents, however, reveals important new facts.[73] It was Admiral Yutani who originally proposed the separation from Wanishi. Yutani had strong doubts about the merger ever since he had first been involved with Vickers.[74] In early 1929, he asked the Japanese directors of the JSW whether the original object of the merger had actually been achieved. In November 1929, he strongly advised V-A to try to end the merger. He added that the IJN had similar doubts about it, given that the original object of the JSW was to produce high-grade steel and armaments.[75]

The board of V-A discussed Yutani's proposal and officially asked the board of the JSW to terminate the merger in March 1930.[76] The original V-A plan (hereafter 'Plan A') was that V-A would purchase the complete holdings of Mitsui Kozan and Mitsui Gomei in the JSW, at a cost of ¥7.5 million. Then the shareholders of the JSW would be:

Hokutan	¥15 million
V-A	¥15 million
Total	¥30 million

The JSW would then transfer ¥19 million to a new company, to be known as 'Wanishi Seitetsu', in exchange for ¥15 million in cash and ¥4 million in Wanishi Seitetsu shares. ¥15 million would then be returned to V-A and Hokutan in equal proportions – ¥7.5 million each – to cancel out the equivalent value of shares. This would leave the JSW with ¥15 million split equally between V-A and Hokutan (see Table 4.3 'Plan A'). Mitsui Gomei and Mitsui Kozan would each purchase shares worth ¥3.75 million in Wanishi Seitetsu, with Hokutan taking shares to the value of ¥7.5 million. The capital of Wanishi Seitetsu would then be as shown in Table 4.3 ('Plan A').

This plan came to nothing. In November 1930, after lengthy discussions, Japanese directors (presumably those representing Mitsui) put forward a counterproposal (Plan G).[77] This envisaged the transfer of half of the V-A shares in the JSW to Wanishi Seitetsu (see Table 4.3). In January 1931 V-A replied that although they had hoped to end all participation in Wanishi Seitetsu, they would accept Plan G in order not to embarrass the board of the JSW.[78] In September 1931 Wanishi Seitetsu was formed with a capital of ¥19 m. The following December saw a reduction in its capital, with two shares being consolidated to form one new share. The respective capital and the shareholders of the two companies (the JSW and Wanishi Seitetsu) were then as shown in Table 4.3 ('Plan G'). Shares in Wanishi Seitetsu to the value of ¥15 million were thus allotted in the same ratio as had been the case with

Table 4.3 Plans for the separation of the Wanishi Ironworks

New companies / Shareholders	'Plan A' (proposed by V-A)		'Plan G' (counterproposal by the JSW)	
	JSW (¥)	Wanishi Seitetsu (¥)	JSW (¥)	Wanishi Seitetsu (¥)
Hokutan	7500000	7500000	7500000	7500000
V-A	7500000		3750000	3750000
Mitsui Gomei		3750000	1875000	1875000
Mitsui Kozan		3750000	1875000	1875000
The JSW		4000000		4000000
Total	15000000	19000000	15000000	19000000

Sources: Documents in VA-685 and VA-1239.
Note: V-A = Vickers-Armstrongs Ltd.

the original shareholders of the JSW, and the remaining ¥4 million was taken up by the JSW itself. V-A and the other JSW shareholders therefore found themselves in the same position they had been in before the ending of the merger.[79]

The essential objective of Vickers-Armstrongs' Plan A was to revert to the original situation prior to the merger with Wanishi. This was understandable given the company's doubts about the merger and poor performance of Wanishi. However, as the original British shareholders had themselves merged into one company, Plan A would have left V-A holding 50 per cent of the shares in the JSW. This was clearly unacceptable to Mitsui, which would have lost its controlling interest in the JSW. The essential point of Plan G was that half of the capital invested in the JSW by each shareholder would be transferred to Wanishi Seitetsu, in addition to the capital invested by the JSW itself. In fact, Plan G was not so different from the Wanishi Seitetsu Kumiai (Wanishi Iron and Steel Union), a partnership formed in 1924 between Hokutan, the JSW, and Mitsui Kozan.[80]

We may ask why V-A compromised with and approved Plan G. It is likely that V-A no longer had any intention of returning to full participation in the board of the JSW, but, as a rentier, wanted to see the JSW recover by ending the merger with Wanishi. From information supplied by Yutani, V-A was convinced that the link should be severed before the imminent 'big amalgamation of iron and steel companies' took place.[81]

Conclusions

I would like to emphasize four points at the end of this chapter. The first is the fact that, in the early years of the JSW, British shareholders committed themselves to the top management of the new company, although the Japanese directors had overall control of the board. British directors communicated their opinions to the board via their proxies. Furthermore, E.L.D. Boyle, the British proxy at the beginning, acted as neutral director for a period, and Count Hirosawa, a Japanese proxy for A.T. Dawson from Vickers, played a significant additional role as an active communicator between the British and the Japanese parties.

However, collaboration was not always good despite the background of the Anglo-Japanese Alliance. Admiral Yamanouchi tried to mediate between the two sides, but in vain. Significantly, the British directors at home participated in the top management of the subsidiaries abroad via proxies. It is not clear whether Armstrongs or Vickers applied such methods to their subsidiaries in any other countries, or whether other British multinationals did so, but this would be a point worthy of further investigation.[82]

The second major point is that the First World War marked a watershed in relations between the JSW (by then the biggest munitions company in Japan) and Vickers and Armstrongs. The JSW grew rapidly due to technology transfer from the British companies, while challenges posed by the war forced the latter to reduce their role in Japan. In other words, in this industry the British multinationals were already beginning to lose their influence in the joint venture in Japan. In contrast, many foreign-affiliated companies in other manufacturing industries such as petroleum, electrical engineering and automobiles grew after the First World War, and did not encounter restrictive or exclusive policies until the first half of the 1930s.[83] The difference lies in the fact that the armaments industry had already achieved a large measure of technology transfer before the First World War.

The third is that the merger of the Wanishi Ironworks put the British in a minority position on the board of the JSW, and generated a great deal of mistrust. Cooperation became even more difficult after the Washington Conference. In these circumstances, the British shareholders were torn between trying to return to the top management of the JSW on the one hand, or withdrawing altogether on the other. The severance of the link with Wanishi was the final chance for the British shareholders to regain their former position, but their efforts were in vain.

A final point worth emphasizing is that technocrats from the IJN played important roles on the JSW board. Yamanouchi, Mizutani and Yutani were the most notable of these, but there were many other directors and auditors from the IJN from the time of the JSW's establishment through to the 1930s. These men were active on both the technology transfer side and the corporate governance side. They not only served as technical specialists, but also acted as intermediaries with the British shareholders. Yutani is the most noteworthy in the latter category, though he was not strictly a technocrat. To what extent IJN technocrats played an active role in any other foreign-affiliated companies is a question worthy of further investigation.

Notes

1. I.H. Nish, *The Anglo-Japanese Alliance: the Diplomacy of Two Island Empires, 1894–1907* (London: Athlone Press, 1966); also *Alliance in Decline: a Study in Anglo-Japanese Relations 1908–23* (London: Athlone Press, 1972).
2. R.P.T. Davenport-Hines and G. Jones, 'British Business in Asia since 1860', 'British Business in Japan since 1868', both in Davenport-Hines and Jones (eds), *British Business in Asia since 1860* (Cambridge: Cambridge University Press, 1989).
3. Y. Horie, *Gaishi Yunyu no Kaiko to Tenbo* (Tokyo: Yuhikaku, 1950); M. Udagawa, 'Business Management and Foreign-Affiliated Companies in Japan Before World War II', in T. Yuzawa and M. Udagawa (eds), *Foreign Business in Japan before World War II* (Tokyo: University of Tokyo Press, 1990).
4. Davenport-Hines and Jones, 'British Business in Japan', p. 219. The term 'technology transfer' is used here in a broad sense as the 'spread of a specific technology from one enterprise or industry in advanced countries to the other in developing countries'.
5. For ease of reference these three companies will be referred to hereafter as Hokutan, Armstrongs and Vickers respectively.
6. The term 'corporate governance' is used here to mean 'the relation between not only shareholders but also various stakeholders including the IJN (or the Japanese government) and top managers (management)'.
7. British companies and their investments in Japan are discussed in R.P.T. Davenport-Hines, 'Vickers as a Multinational before 1945', in G. Jones (ed.), *British Multinationals: Origins, Management and Performance* (Cambridge: Cambridge University Press, 1986), and C. Trebilcock, 'British Multinationals in Japan, 1900–41: Vickers, Armstrong, Nobel, and the Defence Sector', in Yuzawa and Udagawa (eds), *Foreign Business in Japan before World War II*. Neither article, however, pays much attention to how the British shareholders were involved in the board of the JSW. In terms of the primary sources used for this study, the Vickers Archives (hereafter VA) at Cambridge University Library, and various documents relating to Armstrongs (including the Armstrongs papers and Rendel papers) at the Tyne and Wear Archives Service, Newcastle-upon-Tyne (hereafter TWAS), were particularly valuable.
8. For a full account of this topic see my recent book in Japanese, *Heiki Tekko Kaisha no Nichiei Kankei Shi: Nihon Seikosho to Eikokugawa Kabunushi, 1907–52* (Tokyo: Nihon Keizai Hyoronsha, 1998), on which this chapter is based.
9. Except where otherwise cited, the historical survey of the JSW is based on JSW, *Nihon Seikosho Shashi Shiryo*, vol. 1 (Tokyo: JSW, 1968).
10. Hokutan was established by the state in 1889 to manage its coal mines and the railways in Hokkaido. At first, its largest shareholder was the Imperial Household Agency with 8 per cent of the issued capital. Later, Hokutan diversified into other areas, including shipping, forestry and coke manufacturing. Amenomiya Keijiro, the boss of the so-called 'Koshu *Zaibatsu*' (a family business group from Koshu district, now Yamanashi prefecture), became the second largest shareholder and invited his old and intimate friend, Inoue Kakugoro, to join the board of Hokutan in 1893. Inoue, who was a political leader of the Seiyukai (one of the largest parties in Japan at that time), became Managing Director in 1899, and headed the top management of Hokutan. After 1906 Hokutan had neither a chairman nor a president, and Inoue thus had 'sole control' over its board. For details, see Nagura, *Heiki Tekko Kaisha no Nichiei Kankei Shi*, p. 17.

11. TWAS-130/1267, Sir W.G. Armstrong Whitworth & Co. Limited, Minute Book No. 2, 30 November 1906.
12. VA-1363, Vickers Sons & Maxim Limited, Minute Book, No. 5 (1901–1907), 28 February 1907; see also VA-L16, & R313, B.H. Winder, 'Nihon Seiko Sho (The Japan Steel Works Ltd.)', and VA-57 & 1239, 'K.K. Nihon Seikosho (Japan Steel Works)', 31 December 1934.
13. See, for example, J.D. Scott, *Vickers: a History* (London: George Weidenfeld & Nicolson, 1962), p. 85; Davenport-Hines, 'Vickers as a Multinational before 1945', p. 52; Trebilcock, 'British Multinationals in Japan', p. 90.
14. Scott, *Vickers: a History*, pp. 83–8; C. Trebilcock, *The Vickers Brothers: Armaments and Enterprise, 1854–1914* (London: Europa Publications, 1977), pp. 93–6, 122–5, 133–4; Davenport-Hines, 'Vickers as a Multinational before 1945', pp. 46–8; K. Warren, *Armstrong of Elswick: Growth in Engineering and Armaments to the Merger with Vickers* (London: Macmillan – now Palgrave, 1989), pp. 69–85, 122–7.
15. The Russo-Japanese War marked a turning point in naval construction policy. The Royal Navy built the *Dreadnought*, the all big gun battleship, just after the war. Although the Alliance was revised in August 1905, Anglo-Japanese relations became closer so far as both navies and the munitions industries were concerned. For details, see K. Kobayashi, 'Nichiro Sengo no Nichiei Domei no Gunjiteki Ichi', in *Nihonshi Kenkyu*, 293, January 1987; K. Kobayashi, 'Nichiei Domei Ron', in K. Iguchi (ed.), *Nisshin Nichiro Senso* (Tokyo: Yoshikawa Kobunkan, 1994). For the relationship between the IJN and Armstrongs and Vickers, which had already become very close before the Russo-Japanese War, see M. Conte-Helm, *Japan and the North East of England: From 1862 to the Present Day* (London: Athlone Press, 1989), pp. 20–51; M. Conte-Helm, 'Armstrong's, Vickers and Japan', in I. Nish (ed.), *Britain and Japan: Biographical Portraits* (Folkestone: Japan Society Publications, 1994); O. Checkland, *Britain's Encounter with Meiji Japan, 1868–1912* (London: Macmillan – now Palgrave, 1989), pp. 60–4, 153–6, 188–90; K. Kobayashi, 'Nichiei Kankei ni okeru Nichiro Senso no Gunjishiteki Ichi', *Nihonshi Kenkyu*, 305, January 1988; Kobayashi, 'Nichiei Domei Ron', pp. 105–8; T. Onozuka, 'Igirisu Minkan Zosen Kigyo ni totte no Nihon Kaigun', *Yokohama Shiritsu Daigaku Ronso (Shakai Kagaku Keiretsu)*, 46, 2–3, March 1995.
16. JSW, *Nihon Seikosho Shashi Shiryo*, vol. 1, pp. 51–75.
17. Muroran was chosen because Hokutan had many mines, lands and equipment in the neighbourhood and the IJN also had land where the so-called 'fifth arsenal' was to be constructed.
18. Especially, VA-R287, R288, Minutes of the Meeting of Directors and Auditors of the Nihon Seiko-Sho (Minutes of the Meeting of the Board of Directors of the Nihon Seiko-Sho), part of which are at Muroran Works of the JSW; and VA-G267, R287, R288, Minutes of the Meeting of the English directors of the Japan Steel Works (Minutes of the Meeting of the English Shareholders' Committee of the Japan Steel Works). For details see Nagura, *Heiki Tekko Kaisha no Nichiei Kankei Shi*, ch. 2, and p. 373.
19. One of them was the well-known Captain Frank Brinkley, proprietor and chief editor of the *Japan Mail*, one of the three biggest English newspapers in Japan at that time.
20. Count Hirosawa, Baron Mori Goro (member of the House of Peers, auditor of the JSW 1907–10); Count Soejima Michimasa (chamberlain to the Crown Prince, director of the JSW 1910–14); and Tanaka Ginnosuke (grandson of Tanaka

Heihachi, a famous silk merchant, director of companies including Tanaka Kogyo and Hokutan, and director of the JSW 1910–14) had all been at college in Cambridge between 1890 and 1896. Hirosawa, Soejima and Tanaka had also studied at the Leys School, the first British Wesleyan public school at Cambridge. They had become intimate friends, and may well have communicated in English with the British directors, auditors and proxies of the JSW. The board of the JSW appears to have included a strong 'Cambridge connection'. See N. Koyama, 'Japanese Students in Cambridge during the Meiji Era', in R. Bowring (ed.), *Fifty Years of Japanese at Cambridge: 1948–98* (Cambridge: Faculty of Oriental Studies, University of Cambridge, 1998); N. Koyama, *Hatenko Meiji Ryugakusei Retsuden: Daiei Teikoku ni mananda Nihonjin* (Tokyo, Kodansha, 1999), pp. 175–83; S. Tanaka, 'Eikoku Kenburijji, Riizu Sukuuru e no Meiji-Taisho-ki Nihonjin Ryugakusei' pt 1, *Aoba Gakuen Tanki Daigaku Kiyo*, 23, 1998.

21. VA-G267, R287, R288, Minutes of the Meeting of the English directors of the Japan Steel Works, 9 October, 13 November 1908.
22. TWAS-31/7773, Notes on the Muroran Works By Mr. Douglas Vickers.
23. Muroran Works, Minutes of the Meeting of Directors and Auditors of the Nihon Seiko-Sho, 5th, 15th and 22nd February 1909.
24. VA-R288, Minutes of the Emergency Meeting of the Board of Directors and Auditors of the Nihon Seiko-sho, 18th April 1910; Muroran Works of the JSW, Minutes of the 53rd Meeting of Directors and Auditors of the Nihon Seiko-sho, 28th April 1910.
25. See several documents in TWAS-31/7770–7807, Letters and Papers concerning the Seikosho Company: October 1908–December 1912; particularly TWAS-31/7776, 7777, 34 telegrams in April 1910.
26. TWAS-31/7776–22, 24, Translation of telegram [from H.V. Henson in Tokyo to the English Secretary of the JSW], 28–29 April 1910; Muroran Works of the JSW, Minutes of the 53rd Meeting of Directors and Auditors of Nihon Seiko-sho, 28 April 1910; JSW, *Nihon Seikosho Shashi Shiryo*, vol. 1, p. 154; M. Yamanouchi, *Kaikoroku* (private publication, 1914), pp. 217, 221.
27. TWAS-130/1268, Sir W.G. Armstrong Whitworth & Co. Limited, Minute Book, No. 3, 16 June 1910.
28. VA-R287, Boyle's letter to the directors and auditors of the JSW on 22 June 1910 (Minutes of the 60th Meeting of Directors and Auditors of Nihon Seiko-Sho, 27 June 1910). For details see Nagura, *Heiki Tekko Kaisha no Nichiei Kankei Shi*, pp. 77–87.
29. TWAS-130/1268, Sir W.G. Armstrong Whitworth & Co. Limited, Minute Book, No. 3, 1 September, 19 and 20 October 1911; VA-G267, R287, R288, Seikosho Debentures, and Minutes of a Meeting [of the English directors of the Japan Steel Works], 24 August, 20 and 28 September 1910 (Watanabe Senjiro, managing director of Mitsui Bussan, represented Hokutan at the meetings on 20 and 28 September); VA-R287, R288, Minutes of the 66th Meeting of Directors of the Nihon Seiko-Sho, 17 September 1910. For details Nagura, *Heiki Tekko Kaisha no Nichiei Kankei Shi*, pp. 100–2.
30. VA-R287, Minutes of the 95th Meeting of Board of Directors of the Nihon Seiko-Sho, 8 July 1912. See ibid., pp. 103–7.
31. VA-1006A, Albert Vickers (Chairman of Vickers) to G. Matsukata (Director of the JSW), 7 November 1910; VA-1009, V. Caillard (Director of Vickers) to G. Matsukata, 8 November 1910; VA-G267, R287, Minutes of meeting of the JSW, 8 November 1910; VA-G267, R287, Minutes of a Meeting (of the English Directors

of the JSW), 8 and 24 November 1910. The *Kongo* was the last warship which the IJN ordered abroad before the Second World War. As is well known, the order involved bribery on the part of IJN officials, and this became part of the 'Siemens–Vickers scandal,' which was brought to light in January 1914. Although there is no room to explain the details, it should be noted that the '*Kongo* commission' was thus increased from the original 2.5 per cent to 7.5 per cent (including the additional 2.5 per cent demanded by Mitsui). See Nagura, *Heiki Tekko Kaisha no Nichiei Kankei Shi*, pp. 108–13.

32. For details see ibid., pp. 108–19. In 1917 the JSW signed a sole agent contract with Armstrongs and Vickers, but this was soon broken, and was replaced by another in 1919 (ibid., pp. 159–60).
33. VA-1009, Douglas Vickers to Basil H. Winder, 15 February 1912.
34. VA-R287, 'The 104th Minutes of the Meeting of the Board of Directors of the Nihon Seiko-Sho', 14 April 1913; Yamanouchi, *Kaikoroku*, p. 235.
35. The JSW had requested a gunnery expert to advise on the manufacturing of big guns at the Muroran Works. Accordingly, Trevelyan had been sent with G.A. Atkinson (a mechanical engineer) and three assistant mechanical engineers from Elswick. They arrived in Japan in May 1912 (TWAS-130/1268, 'Sir W.G. Armstrong Whitworth & Co. Limited, Minute Book, No. 3', 14 December 1911, 25 April 1912; VA-G267, R287, 288, 'Minutes of the Meeting of the English Directors [of the JSW]', 25 October, 29 November 1911, and 5 February 1912. See also Table 4.3; Conte-Helm, *Japan and the North East of England*, p. 103, Conte-Helm, 'Armstrong's, Vickers and Japan', p. 100. For the report see TWAS-31/7806, F.B.(T.) Trevelyan, 'Report on the condition of the K.K.N. Seikosho'. This report is undated, but it is understood that it was submitted to the British directors of the JSW on 21 November 1912 (TWAS-31/7801, Trevelyan to J.H.B. Noble, 29 December 1912).
36. TWAS 31/7802, Yamanouchi to Trevelyan, 27 December 1912; TWAS-31/7801, 7804, Trevelyan to J.H.B. Noble, 29–30 December 1912; TWAS-31/7803, H.V. Henson to J.H.B. Noble, 29, 31 December 1912; TWAS-31/7805, Yamanouchi to J.H.B. Noble, 31 December 1912. For details see Nagura, *Heiki Tekko Kaisha no Nichiei Kankei Shi*, pp. 120–5.
37. Ibid., pp. 127–9.
38. TWAS-130/1287, Sir W.G. Armstrong Whitworth & Co. Ltd., Finance Committee, 11 October 1916, et al.
39. Nagura, *Heiki Tekko Kaisha no Nichiei Kankei Shi*, p. 144, JSW, *Nihon Seikosho Shashi Shiryo*, vol. 1, pp. 128–9, 182. In addition, during the early years (1907–11) JSW workers learned about techniques for making steel and guns from engineers and assistant engineers from the Kure Arsenal. For details, see ibid., pp. 110–11, 130.
40. VA-G267, R287, 288, Minutes of the Meeting of the English Directors (of the JSW), 24 November 1910, 10 May, 7 June, 8 August, 25 October, 29 November 1911, 5 February 1912, 6 February, 4 April, 26 May, and 23 July 1913; TWAS-130/1268, Minute Book, no. 3, 25 May and 14 December 1911. See also Conte-Helm, *Japan and the North East of England*, pp. 102–3; Conte-Helm, 'Armstrong's, Vickers and Japan', pp. 99–100.
41. See Nagura, *Heiki Tekko Kaisha no Nichiei Kankei Shi*, pp. 143–9.
42. TWAS-130/1268, Sir W.G. Armstrong Whitworth & Co. Ltd., Minute Book, no. 3, 16 October 1913. The need for a resident director in Japan was considered by Armstrongs in early 1913 (TWAS-130/1268, Minute Book, no. 3, 20 February 1913).

43. See Nagura, *Heiki Tekko Kaisha no Nichiei Kankei Shi*, pp. 144–8.
44. Muroran Works of the JSW, Letters to and from Mr John B. Noble 1914–1915; J.H.B. Noble to Y. Mizutani, 28 November 1914, and Mizutani to Noble, 30 January 1915.
45. See Nagura, *Heiki Tekko Kaisha no Nichiei Kankei Shi*, pp. 154–5, 160–1.
46. As Mizutani told Noble, 'You are the only one to whom I can disclose my innermost feelings', Muroran Works of the JSW, Letters to and from Mr John B. Noble 1914–1915, Y. Mizutani to J.H.B. Noble, 15 July 1915.
47. Muroran Works of the JSW, Letters to and from Mr John B. Noble 1914–1915, Y. Mizutani to J.H.B. Noble, 25 March 1915.
48. See Nagura, *Heiki Tekko Kaisha no Nichiei Kankei Shi*, pp. 153–5.
49. Some documents in the Vickers Archives state that Mitsui took over Hokutan in 1917 VA-1239, K.K. Nihon Seikosho (Japan Steel Works), p. 2, et seq. This is a result of confusing the fact that Hokutan was restructured by Mitsui in 1913 with the formation of Hokkaido Seitetsu by the three Mitsui companies in 1917.
50. B. Nagura, *Nihon Tekkogyo Shi no Kenkyu* (Tokyo: Kondo Shuppansha Ltd., 1984), pp. 417–18.
51. VA-57/23, and -914, Wanishi Ironworks Limited, p. 2; VA-685, Wanishi Ironworks.
52. VA-L16, G.G. Sim (Deputy Chairman of V-A) to the board of directors of the JSW, 31 March 1930.
53. VA-L15, -L55, H. Harrison (the JSW, 'English Secretary') to A. Kabayama (a managing director of the JSW), 7 February 1919.
54. The Hiroshima Works, which had been established as the Matsuda Seisakusho in 1917, was a plant in which the JSW had already considerable interests. It was acquired by the JSW in 1920 (see Figure 4.1). The company's capital was ¥1 500 000. Located near the Kure Arsenal, the Hiroshima Works manufactured munitions and machinery.
55. VA-685, 'Assistant Resident Representative in Japan of Vickers Ltd.', Agreement between Rear Admiral Kenzo Yutani, late of the IJN, and Messrs. Vickers Limited, 23 August 1923. Among Yutani's posts in the navy had been naval attaché at the Japanese Embassy in Britain, officer of the General Staff, and a member of the teaching staff of the Naval Academy and the Torpedo College. See JSW, *Nihon Seikosho Shashi Shiryo*, vol. 1, p. 378.
56. VA-L16 & -L55, K. Yutani to Vickers, 5 September 1924; VA-L16 & R284, Asiatic Supervision (B.H. Winder) to the Chairman (of Vickers), 'Japan Steel Works', 1 October 1924; VA-1368, Vickers Limited, Minute Book of Board Meeting No. 10 (1924–29), 19 December 1924; VA-L55 & -R284, DV (Douglas Vickers) to Count Kabayama, 30 December 1924, and the Chairman of Vickers to the Chairman of the JSW, dated the same day. For details on these and other materials, see Nagura, *Heiki Tekko Kaisha no Nichiei Kankei Shi*, pp. 238–42, 245–6.
57. VA-L16 & R284, 'Extract from Articles of association of the JSW' attached to 'The Japan Steel Works' (Asiatic Supervision to the Chairman, 1 October 1924).
58. Various documents in Y. Mizutani, 'Kaisha Shorai no Keiei Hoshin' [kept at the Head Office of the JSW].
59. Muto (an official of the Head Office of the IJN), 'Nihon Seikosho Kanbu Ido no Keii', 8 October 1925 [also held at the Head Office of the JSW].
60. VA-L55, K. Yutani to Major Winder, 3 May and 12 June 1925; VA-L55, R313, Asiatic Supervision (BHW) to the Chairman, 7 July and 21 October 1925. It is suggestive that Winder said 'When the war was nearly over, the Mitsui interests

conceived the idea of the Seikosho taking over the Wanishi Iron Works, which was opposed by Admiral Midzutani [*sic*]. This led to his dismissal.'

61. For details see Nagura, *Heiki Tekko Kaisha no Nichiei Kankei Shi*, pp. 247–58.
62. Ibid., ch. 6.
63. VA-R284, DV to Harrison, 'Seiko-sho', 1 May 1923.
64. VA-R284, F.B.T. Trevelyan to Admiral Takarabe, the Minister of Marine, 'K.K.N. Seikosho', 6 July 1923. This document is also held at the Kobunshokan (Public Record Office of Japan) as 'Kobun Betsuroku (2A-1 *betsu* 240).
65. VA-R284, H. Harrison to Douglas Vickers, 2 July 1923, and DV to B.H. Winder, 11 July 1923.
66. VA-L16 & L55, K. Yutani to Vickers, 5 September 1924; VA-L16 & L55, Asiatic Supervision, B.H. Winder, to Capt. T. Toyoda, IJN, 4th March 1925, and others. According to some VA documents, 'By March 1925, Armstrongs had joined Vickers in their endeavour to sell their shares in the JSW'. See VA-57/18, Nihon Seiko Sho (Japan Steel Works), p. 4; VA-1239, K.K. Nihon Seikosho (Japan Steel Works), p. 4, et seq.
67. VA-L16 & L55, Asiatic Supervision, B.H.W. to Capt. T. Toyoda, IJN, 4 March 1925.
68. VA-57/18, Nihon Seiko Sho (Japan Steel Works), pp. 3–5; VA-1239, K.K. Nihon Seikosho (Japan Steel Works), pp. 3–5.
69. VA-L55 & R313, V.C. Vickers to the Minister of Marine (in Japan), 23 March 1926; VA-L55, Rough idea – [illegible] –: Proposal to the Minister of Marine – an analysis of the handwriting shows the author of this document to be Yutani; VA-L55, Vincent Vickers, 'Diary of Visit to Japan'.
70. Vickers became a kind of holding company controlling Vickers-Armstrongs and other interests.
71. For details see Nagura, *Heiki Tekko Kaisha no Nichiei Kankei Shi*, ch. 8 and supplement.
72. Nagura, *Nihon Tekkogyo Shi no Kenkyu*, p. 422.
73. For details see ibid., ch. 5.
74. According to Yutani, 'It [the Wanishi merger] was a great blunder, –, it seems strange to the writer why the English Shareholders agreed to such a foolish amalgamation', VA-L55 & -R313, K. Yutani to Major B.H. Winder, 'Re: Nihon Seiko Sho (N.S.S.)', 26 September 1925.
75. VA-R338, K. Yutani to V-A, 26 November 1929.
76. VA-R338, Kabushiki Kaisha Nihon Seiko Sho: Proposed Separation of Wanishi Iron Works from NSS (For the English directors of NSS), 21 January 1930; VA-L16 & R338, Nihon Seiko Sho: Notes of Meeting held at Vickers House, on 26 March 1930, to consider a report dated 21 January 1930, regarding proposed separations of Wanishi Ironworks; VA-L16, G.G. Sim (Deputy Chairman of V-A) to the board of directors of the JSW, 31 March 1930.
77. VA-L16, K. Yutani to Antony Vickers (Director of the JSW, on behalf of V-A), 1 and 4 July 1930; VA-L17, A. Kabayama to Antony Vickers, 11 August 1930; Antony Vickers to L.G. Abel ('English Secretary' of the JSW), 25 September 1930; VA-L16 & R338, L.G. Abel to Mark Webster Jenkinson (Director of V-A), 8 October 1930; VA-L16, J.R.Y. (Secretary of V-A) to the Chairman and Directors of the JSW, 6 January 1931.
78. VA-1223, V-A, Minute Book of Board Committee Meetings No. 2 (1928–1931), 15 January 1931.
79. VA-57/18, Nihon Seikosho (Japan Steel Works), pp. 7–9; VA-57/23, The Wanishi Ironworks Limited, pp. 3–6.

80. Nagura, *Nihon Tekkogyo Shi no Kenkyu*, p. 419.
81. VA-L16, To Colonel J. Neilson (an auditor of the JSW, on behalf of V-A), 9 December 1930 (anon., possibly Antony Vickers or L.G. Abel); VA-1223, Minute Book of Board Committee Meetings No. 2 (1928–1931)', 20 August 1931.
82. In the case of Armstrongs in Italy, see Warren, *Armstrong of Elswick*, pp. 69–85. For Vickers in general see Davenport-Hines, 'Vickers as a Multinational Before 1945'; for Vickers in Italy see L. Segreto, 'More Trouble than Profit: Vickers' Investments in Italy 1906–39', *Business History*, 27(3) (November 1985); and in Russia, E.R. Goldstein, 'Vickers Limited and the Tsarist Regime', *Slavonic and East European Review*, 58(4) (October 1980). Further investigation is also required to ascertain whether or not the investments in Japan by Armstrongs and Vickers were profitable. For this we would need to consider the total returns from Japan including 'the restoration or the return of properties in Japan by V-A after World War II', which have not been examined before. See details in Nagura, *Heiki Tekko Kaisha no Nichiei Kankei Shi*, ch. 9.
83. Udagawa, 'Business Management and Foreign-Affiliated Companies in Japan Before World War II'.

5

Japanese Government Loan Issues on the London Capital Market During the Interwar Period*

Toshio Suzuki

Introduction

The City established its pre-eminent position in international finance after the Franco-Prussian War (1870–71), and many countries, including British dominions and colonies, raised necessary funds there. For the Japanese government it was imperative from the time of its first foreign loan issue in 1870 to build up close financial relations with the City.[1] From the outset banks with Far Eastern and Japanese connections, such as the Oriental Banking Corporation, the Hong Kong & Shanghai Banking Corporation and the Yokohama Specie Bank, tended to be involved in the Japanese government's financial operations in London. However, these banks were not experts in international financial operations, and played only a limited role in accessing international capital markets. It was merchant banks such as Baring Brothers & Co. that, under the leadership of the London market, quietly paved the way for Japanese government loan issues during the Russo-Japanese War. The banks floated these loans simultaneously in London and New York.

The Japanese government was obliged to pay closer attention to diplomatic considerations when it launched a loan issue in France, where, unlike in the Anglo-American markets, the government had always regarded foreign loans as a diplomatic tool. However, the London capital market was

* The author would like to express sincere thanks to Edwin Green (Midland Bank), M.J. Orbell (ING Barings), Henry Gillet (Bank of England), Sarah Millard (Bank of England), F. Maccoll (National Westminster Bank) and Jun-ichi Terai (Japanese Ministry of Finance) for their kind assistance and permission to consult relevant records at their archives. The author is also much obliged to Ito Masanao (University of Tokyo), Ishii Kanji (Tokyo Keizai University), Kasuya Makoto (University of Tokyo), and Kishida Makoto (Keio University), who kindly helped secure access to the Juichi Tsushima Papers held at the Japanese Ministry of Finance Archives.

less important for the Japanese government after 1905. The London and Paris markets no longer depended upon each other, and the Japanese government could now access Paris directly, rather than through the London banks. This competitive market structure enabled the Japanese government to arrange its loan issues on more favourable terms.

The rise of the Paris capital market following the Russo-Japanese War produced a flurry of activity among financiers concerned with Japanese loans. The international capital market became relatively decentralized, although the markets were not really separate and there remained potential for cooperation in simultaneous loan issues (see Figure 5.1). With its improved standing abroad and direct access to the world's principal capital markets, the Japanese government was in a position to obtain loans on highly favourable terms. Nevertheless, from 1914 until the disastrous 1923 earthquake there was no need for any loans, mainly because Japan enjoyed large trade surpluses during and after the First World War.[2]

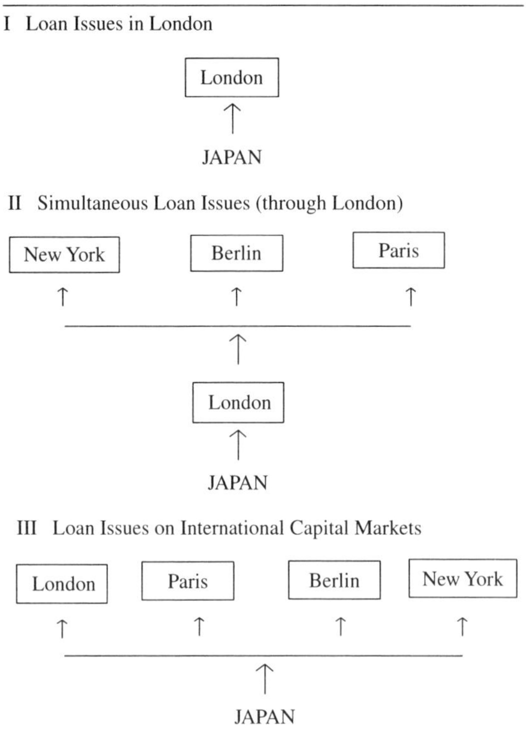

Figure 5.1 Linkages of loan issue markets

The London capital market during the 1920s

Government regulations for overseas investment

The City had always pursued its financial interests on the principle of 'laissez-faire'. Before the First World War, there was no government control over foreign loan issues on the London capital market, except 'in circumstance of political importance to the Empire'.[3] Even in 1922, the Earl of Crawford, referring to a government loan to Greece, admitted in Parliament that 'there is no Government control over capital issues and it is the policy of the Government not to intervene between foreign Governments and potential lenders in this market'.[4] Effectively, the involvement of the Treasury and the Bank of England in foreign loan issue negotiations in the prewar period was minimal.

After the outbreak of the First World War the British government gradually changed its policy, and began to introduce official regulation of foreign investment. Mori Kengo, the Japanese Government Financial Commissioner, later commented on the disappearance of the prewar 'free market', and was surprised to find the London capital market under the strict control of the Treasury and the Bank of England.[5] Capital controls were introduced from January 1915. The Treasury stated 'they feel it imperative in the national interest, that fresh issues of capital shall be approved by the Treasury before they are made'. This applied only to foreign loans; capital issues for domestic purposes and for the Empire were permitted as before.[6] In December 1917 the British government imposed an embargo on capital exports, prohibiting not only loan issues but also security transactions. No resident of the UK could subscribe to any foreign loan issue or purchase any assets other than merchandise outside Britain without written permission from the Treasury.[7] Atkin's analysis of overseas loan embargoes on the London capital market between 1918 and 1931 makes it clear that even after the First World War the free market for foreign loan issues was not fully restored (Table 5.1).[8] The Japanese government raised two loans in 1924 and 1930. These were floated during the relatively free period for foreign loans, after the lifting of restrictions in January 1924. Foreign government issues, worth £26 million in 1923, soon rose to £40 million in 1924 (Table 5.2).

The Treasury often consulted the Bank of England on whether a proposed loan issue could be allowed, and to prevent excessive foreign loans often cooperated in manipulating the capital market.[9] As R.M. Kindersley, director of Lazards, claimed, 'everybody who wants to make a foreign loan would naturally discuss, let us say, with the Bank of England, what should be done, whether it is a suitable time, or whether it is not desired'.[10] Before 1914 it had not been unusual for merchant banks to consult the Foreign Secretary regarding projected loan issues, particularly those involving countries where

Table 5.1 Embargo on loan issues in Britain

Period	*Controlling agent*	*Extent*
1918–Nov. 1919	Capital Issues Committee	Most overseas issues
1920	Bank of England	Overseas government issues & foreign company loans
1921–Feb. 1924	Bank of England	Short- and medium-term foreign government and company loans
Feb. 1924–Nov. 1924		Free
Nov. 1924–June 1925	Bank of England	Foreign government loans
June 1925–Nov. 1925	Bank of England	Colonial and foreign government loans
Nov. 1925–mid-1929		Free
Mid-1929–May 1930	Bank of England	Foreign government and foreign company loans
May 1930–Sept. 1930		Free
Sept. 1930–1931	Bank of England	Foreign loans extending to most issues in 1931

Source: J.M. Atkin, 'British Overseas Investment, 1918–1931', unpublished PhD thesis, University of London, 1968, p. 28.

the diplomatic situation was extremely delicate.[11] This practice was confirmed during the interwar period. Controls on loan issues were based not on law but on informal or unofficial negotiations with the Treasury and the Bank of England. This was termed 'moral suasion',[12] although Montagu Norman, the Governor of the Bank of England, depicted it as Niemeyer's 'unwritten law'. Norman was of the firm opinion that only applications for reconstruction purposes deserved his consideration. He would often tighten the level of control by raising the Bank Rate or concluding a secret agreement with stockbrokers that they would not make any loan issues during a specific period.[13]

Excessive lending and the British economy

Around the turn of the twentieth century a number of authors endeavoured to calculate the exact extent of British overseas investment and to suggest that such large capital exports were behind a marked decline in British domestic investment.[14] In the interwar period statistical data prepared by Kindersley[15] and the *Midland Bank Monthly Review* made the same case, and there was a general feeling that too much capital was being invested abroad.[16] Montagu Norman complained about 'too many loans being issued in London. They must exceed savings and may upset exchanges.'[17] The final

Table 5.2 New overseas loan issues, 1923–1931 (by type of borrower)

Year	Empire						Foreign						Total (£000)	Midland Bank estimate	Foreign government securities in
	Government		Municipal		Company		Government		Municipal		Company				
	(£000)	No. of issues	(£000)	No. of issues	(£000)	No. of issues	(£000)	No. of issues	(£000)	No. of issues	(£000)	No. of issues		Total (£000)	the United States (£000)
1923	64 406	16	4788	10	18 430	72	26 461	7	–	–	18 491	30	137 376	136 176	62 700
1924	50 080	10	6085	9	16 014	66	40 619	6	2412	1	9 350	20	124 560	134 223	188 000
1925	30 648	10	2625	11	27 262	142	–	–	1350	1	14 970	30	77 055	87 708	168 700
1926	31 866	8	1222	4	20 227	81	23 817	8	6235	2	18 361	36	101 723	112 404	138 800
1927	55 697	13	5135	7	38 851	77	11 027	6	7186	6	30 546	34	148 422	138 671	200 600
1928	40 222	11	7304	9	15 344	61	15 937	8	4331	4	22 204	34	105 342	143 384	180 400
1929	26 366	5	3859	3	30 881	70	3 650	2	472	1	22 469	35	81 697	94 347	52 200
1930	49 080	11	3031	44	9 207	28	21 330	3		–	14 387	21	97 035	108 803	144 800
1931	30 571	5	–	–	7 983	26	1 740	1	–	–	5 658	11	45 952	46 078	

Sources: D.E. Moggridge, *British Monetary Policy 1924–31* (London: Cambridge University Press, 1972), p. 204; I. Mintz, *Deterioration in the Quality of Foreign Bonds Issued in the United States* (New York, 1951, repr. 1979), p. 19.

report of the Committee on the Currency and Bank of England Note Issues also expressed such fears, warning against 'excessive lending' and lending 'more than we can afford'.[18]

In October 1925 a report by the Committee of Civil Research provided a thought-provoking view of the influence of British foreign loans on the domestic economy.[19] The report, regarded by Niemeyer as 'an essential preliminary' to the subject, defined two factors as setting the limit of lending capacity of the contemporary British economy: firstly, current savings or the balance of savings after meeting home capital requirements; secondly, surpluses in the balance of payments. The report estimated the surplus available for lending abroad at £100–120 million, and concluded that 'the resumption of overseas lending on anything like the prewar scale is impossible'.[20]

The bias for colonial loan issues

In 1924 J.M. Keynes described the pattern of British overseas investment as a legacy 'from a time when we had a surplus of savings which we could invest much more profitably abroad than at home and when the demand for our exports was highly elastic'. He identified the Colonial Stock Act as unduly encouraging capital exports and creating a bias against new domestic investment.[21] The Colonial Stock Act could effectively work to divert more British capital into the dominions and colonies. The first Colonial Stock Act of 1877 enabled holders of colonial government stocks to pay a lower stamp duty of 2s 6d/£100 (0.125 per cent) when they transferred inscribed stocks.[22] Colonial governments were also able to compound a transfer duty by payment of a lump sum of 7s 6d/£100. By this all future transfer of the stocks would be exempt from duty. By contrast, foreign government stocks had to pay 2 per cent stamp duty (40s/£100) at market issue. The second Colonial Stock Act of 1892 allowed by deed the transfer of colonial government stocks registered under the 1877 Act, while the third, passed in 1900, added to the colonial government stocks registered under the previous two acts trustee securities stipulated by the Trustee Act of 1893.[23]

These acts gave considerable impetus to colonial government loan issues on the London market. According to Kindersley, colonial government securities worth £944 million accounted for 67.4 per cent of all capital invested abroad owned by UK residents at the end of 1928, compared with foreign government securities worth £324 million (23.1 per cent).[24] Keynes estimated that the average interest differential between colonial and foreign government loans gave colonial issues a 0.5 per cent market advantage.[25] It was evident that the London capital market showed a firm preference for the colonies where funds were most needed to promote economic development.[26]

The gold standard and foreign loan issues in Britain

The illusion of the gold standard

Keynes levelled scathing criticisms at the 'unbelievable rashness of high finance in the City', which recklessly pursued the restoration of the gold standard.[27] At the time there was a widespread illusion, especially among many city financiers, that a return to gold would revive Britain's prewar pre-eminence in international finance, and, as the economist and Treasury official R.G. Hawtrey admitted, 'it is emphatically a British interest that the Pre-war system should be restored'.[28]

City financiers were dissatisfied with the long-imposed embargo because it deprived them of lucrative business opportunities. They desired its removal and the reopening of the London capital market for foreign loan issues.[29] Eric Hambro, director of Hambros, warned that if the London market 'remained closed indefinitely for a very long period' the foreign loan business 'would be completely atrophied'.[30] Montagu Norman himself admitted that the continuation of the embargo would seriously damage the 'prestige (as well as the profits) of the London market', and regarded the embargo as inconsistent with the free trade principle.[31] In order to resume foreign loan business the City considered restoration of the gold standard essential.[32]

The First Interim Report of 1918 of the Committee on Currency and Foreign Exchanges after the War (the Cunliffe Committee) insisted on the early restoration of gold, claiming that 'it is imperative that they [the conditions necessary to the maintenance of an effective gold standard] should be restored without delay'.[33] The gold standard could also avert undue credit expansion and a drain of gold abroad. In addition, the Committee on the Currency and Bank of England Note Issues (presided over by Austin Chamberlain and Lord Bradbury) pointed out the need to 'restore and maintain the gold standard at the Pre-war parity'.[34] The report claimed that restoration of the gold standard would bring about credit restriction and falling prices in the British economy.[35] As for foreign loan issues in London, the Committee was of the firm opinion that

> unless a free gold market [under the gold standard] is restored, the danger of such overlending on foreign account in the near future will be considerable and a situation may easily develop in which the pressure on our foreign exchanges, resulting from overlending to foreign countries, will necessitate a restriction of general credit.[36]

In addition, the Committee of Civil Research considered maintenance of the embargo impractical, and wondered whether it would be desirable to introduce new regulation of foreign loan issues by 'a statutory authority'. In the end, it concluded that all restrictions on loan issues abroad should be abolished. Instead, 'the general financial policy embodied in the gold standard' should be introduced into the economy. It mentioned that under the gold standard 'the constitution of the investment market itself provides some safeguard' in order to avoid the tendency towards overlending.[37]

On these recommendations, Winston Churchill announced Britain's return to the gold standard at the prewar parity in his budget speech on 28 April 1925. At the same time, all official controls on loan issues abroad were lifted. In November 1925 Churchill declared that

> from this time forward [until July 1929] no objection will be raised on general grounds by the responsible financial authorities to the issue of Dominion, Colonial and foreign loans on the London market. What has been known as the embargo will now be removed. The old and full freedom of the market will be restored.[38]

Many believed that the return to gold would restore stability and confidence in the postwar international economy. Stable exchange rates meant smoother international transactions. In fact, the representative of the Federation of British Industries admitted that 'no country with a unstable currency will be permitted to obtain any loan in the British market'.[39] For borrowing countries foreign exchange stability was equally important. As will be seen later, Inoue Junnosuke firmly believed that Japan's restoration of the gold standard was a necessary prerequisite for the 1930 loan issue.[40]

Foreign loans and exports

Before the First World War many borrowing countries had spent most of their loans purchasing British goods and services. Britain's prewar prosperity in the export trade was viewed largely as a direct consequence of trade facilities given in the form of loans, and the view still prevailed that the granting of loans abroad could stimulate British exports.[41] Restoration of the gold standard and the lifting of the embargo on loan issues thus appeared imperative for the British economy. Bankers such as Felix Schuster, Chairman of the Union Bank of London, and Kindersley testified before parliamentary committees that foreign loans could foster British exports.[42]

Over time it became apparent that the granting of credit in London could neither encourage British exports to the pre-1914 extent nor lead directly to any improvement in Britain's trade balance. R.G. Glendy of the Federation of British Industries remarked 'it is no longer safe to assume that an export of capital funds will result in an export of goods' and proposed a reconsideration of the 'old Pre-war laissez-faire attitude'.[43] At the Treasury Frederick Phillips frankly admitted 'the idea that we can encourage our export trade by passing only such foreign issues as will be largely spent on initial purchases in this country seems rather farfetched', while R.V.N. Hopkins, the Permanent Secretary, wrote that the old view was 'now pretty generally abandoned', and declared that 'we shall not get the maximum possible improvement in British trade unless the business of making foreign issues here is consciously managed with a view to securing as large orders as possible for British goods'.[44] This is why Montagu Norman was so keen to restrict foreign lending to reconstruction loans only. It was obvious that reconstruction work could spur demand for various kinds of manufactured goods from Britain. At the end of the 1920s, however, the Bank of England understood there was a 'lack of coordination' between foreign loan issues and opportunities for British exports.[45]

Effect on home investment

While a high interest rate policy might effectively curb possible overlending abroad, it could also discourage home investment, and Niemeyer was fully aware of this dilemma.[46] Most of Britain's staple industries, such as coal, iron and steel, textiles, machinery, ships and railway equipment, were based on the raw materials and products of the nineteenth-century industrial revolution, and depended on exports to a far greater extent than was the case in other industrial nations. Yet the percentage of exports to total output in these industries fell sharply during the interwar period, as export competitiveness declined.[47] There was an urgent need for innovation in the 'old industries' and the building up of the 'new industries' by securing 'an automatic first claim on national savings' for the capital requirements of industry at home.[48]

The rise and decline of international financial centres and the decline of London

The structural change in international trade, and the immense increase in America's exports to Britain during and following the First World War, resulting in depreciation of the pound, paved the way for the rise of the New York capital market.[49]

In the interwar period British financial authorities sought to divert even dominion and colonial loan issues to New York. In 1925 Montagu Norman told the Chancellor that if 'the amounts which are required cannot be raised in London, the New York market is undoubtedly able to provide funds for those borrowers on reasonable terms'.[50] The London capital market was unable to meet the demand for funds from abroad because of fears that overlending would have negative repercussions on the balance of payments and exchange rates. This negative attitude towards foreign loan business ultimately brought about London's decline in international finance, and accelerated the rise of New York.

The writer Hartley Withers warned of New York's likely challenge after the war, arguing:

> America will have been enormously enriched by the war, which we shall certainly have not. America will have been opening up channels of international trade and international finance, and so New York will have been gaining at the expense of London. It is certain that when the war is over America's dependence upon London for credits against the shipments of goods to and from her shores will have been very lessened.[51]

Ernest Harvey, Deputy-governor of the Bank of England, was pessimistic regarding London's future position, recognizing that London's earlier leadership was now passing elsewhere.[52]

William Adams Brown, Jr, explained London's decline during the inter-war period as stemming from the existence of 'a divided responsibility for international trade and finance' between London and New York, which prevented the gold standard from working smoothly.[53]

Stamp duty

During the 1920s, foreign governments seeking to float loans on the London market were at a disadvantage. Stamp duty of 0.5 per cent, introduced by the 1891 Finance Act, was raised to 2 per cent in 1920. No comparable levy was payable in New York, hence the London Chamber of Commerce urged the government to abolish the stamp duty on foreign loans.[54] For the Foreign Office, the duty was one of the 'obstacles in the way of placing foreign loans in this country'.[55] Lord Revelstoke, head of Barings, complained that the '2 per cent duty is now the cause of diverting from London nearly all first class foreign loan business [to New York] and fear has been generally expressed that London may have to content itself with second class foreign investments'.[56] The great London merchant banks such as N.M. Rothschilds, Morgan Grenfell, Schroders and Barings, felt that

> the stamp duty of 2 per cent at present levied in Great Britain on Bonds 'to bearer' debars many prospective borrowers from coming, as they otherwise would, to the London market, acts consequently as a check to our foreign trade, and tends to jeopardise the good will which British merchants have acquired.[57]

On the other hand, the British financial authorities at that time did not regard New York as a 'serious competitor with London' in the foreign loan business. They felt it necessary to remedy 'over-lendings abroad', and to reduce the strain on Britain's balance of payments.[58] R.H. Brand, managing director of Lazard Brothers, underestimated the position of the New York capital market, saying that 'New York would sell back the whole, or nearly the whole, of an issue to London'.[59]

The rise of New York

From the Boer War London and New York cooperated on loan issues,[60] but with the rapid rise of the New York capital market, this close cooperation was gradually dissolved, and London faced fierce competition from New York. During the 1920s London failed to attract first-rate issues for European and South American governments. Nevertheless in 1924, the Japanese Government Financial Commissioner saw the New York capital market in a different light: he felt that American investors were more anxious to invest in domestic industry and that the New York capital market was less important for foreign investment than London.[61] As will be seen, the Japanese government was able that year to float a loan in London more cheaply than could have been done in New York.

Table 5.2 shows that between 1920 and 1930 the value of foreign government issues in America invariably surpassed those in Britain. The lower interest rates on loan issues would seem to have been the main attraction: between 1922 and 1929, governments were able to borrow more cheaply in New York than in London. However, not all governments were able to enjoy low interest rates in New York. Those with low credit ratings had to pay a premium on the interest reflecting quotation prices on the market, or a high rate of loan issue commission to compensate financiers for their lesser creditworthiness. London's established familiarity with such governments, as well as their sometimes greater popularity among investors, sometimes resulted in lower costs of loan issues.[62] Otto H. Kahn, partner of Kuhn Loeb Co. in New York, attributed London's supreme position in international finance to 'a market for all kinds of securities of all kinds of countries',[63] and even during the interwar period there was ample room for banks in London to submit competitive issue terms to borrowing countries. The foreign governments which issued loans on both the London and the New York capital markets from 1920 to 1929 are shown in Table 5.3. It is clear that not all the countries were able to place loans on more favourable terms in New York than in London.

Competition in New York

Before the First World War, the American investment bank Kuhn Loeb had been able to compete fully with its Anglo-American counterpart J.P. Morgan for most of the loan issue business in New York. Jacob H. Schiff, senior partner at Kuhn Loeb, had played a major role in placing a series of Japanese government loans in New York during the Russo-Japanese War (1904–5). However, as a German-born Jew, Schiff was unwilling to become involved in financing the war on behalf of the United States and Britain. After the end of the war, Morgan's reputation was enhanced through its energetic wartime activities, and it became the leading investment bank in the New York capital

Table 5.3 Foreign government simultaneous loan issues in London and New York, 1920–1929

Year	*Country*	*London Interest Rate*	*Yield*	*New York Interest Rate*	*Yield*
1922	Chile	7.5	7.895	7.0	7.254
	Czechoslovakia	8.0	8.290	8.0	8.290
	Brazil	7.5	7.732	7.2	7.400
	Peru	7.5	7.895	8.0	8.000
1923	Austria	6.0	7.500	7.0	7.778
	Finland	6.0	6.061	6.0	6.667
1924	Japan	6.0	6.857	6.5	7.027
	Czechoslovakia	8.0	8.290	8.0	8.290
	Hungary	7.5	8.523	7.5	8.562
	Germany	7.0	7.609	7.0	7.609
	Greece	7.0	7.955	7.0	7.955
1926	Chile	6.0	6.383	6.0	6.431
	Belgium	7.0	7.447	7.0	7.447
	Bulgaria	7.0	7.609	7.0	7.609
1928	Greece	6.0	6.667	6.2	6.828
	Chile	6.0	6.283	6.0	6.410
	Peru	6.0	6.593	6.0	6.593
1929	Roumania	7.0	7.955	7.0	7.955
	Chile	6.0	6.349	6.0	6.417

Sources: *Stock Exchange Official Intelligence, 1921–1930*; C. Lewis, *America's Stake in International Investments* (Washington DC, 1938), pp. 632–6.

market. By contrast, Kuhn Loeb concentrated on railway securities and maintained conservative business attitudes. Otto H. Kahn took over the management from Schiff, but Kuhn Loeb lost its previous dominance.[64]

Decline of Paris

Before 1914 France was regarded as one of the greatest lending countries, and was particularly significant for the Japanese government. With the outbreak of war, however, the Paris capital market was closed to foreign governments to focus investment on French government bonds and to discourage capital export. The French government itself had to issue a number of war loans in Britain and America. An act passed in May 1916 officially prohibited new foreign loan issues and sales in France, unless authorized by the Minister of Finance. A steep income tax on foreign securities was also introduced. Transfer and stamp duties, and the annual income from foreign securities, were set at 25 per cent, compared with 18 per cent for domestic securities.

Following Poincaré's successful stabilization policy between 1926 and 1928, France returned to the business of foreign loan issues. This was encouraged partly by the reduction of income tax on foreign securities from 25 per cent to 18 per cent. However, the Paris capital market was unable to recover its prewar position, in terms of either number or value of foreign loans.[65] As Mori frankly admitted, Paris had attained its zenith of foreign investment just on the eve of the First World War.[66]

Japanese government loan issues during the interwar period – the 6 per cent loan of 1924

The policy of dependence on foreign loans

In January 1924 the British authorities lifted most restrictions on new overseas loan issues, and even before this many Japanese bankers visited leading City banks. According to a general manager at the Midland Bank, T. Tomita from the Hypothec Bank of Japan (*Kangyo Ginko*) collected information on the British banking system, G. Odachi of Mitsui Bank visited to pay his respects, and Y. Harada and J. Saito, of the Yasuda Bank, asked the Midland Bank for an opportunity to study its banking organization.[67]

In this context Inoue Junnosuke, Minister of Finance in the Yamamoto cabinet, sought a foreign loan for reconstruction following the Great Kanto Earthquake of 1923. However, the poor result of the 6 per cent loan issue negotiations was to teach Inoue a valuable lesson regarding dependence on foreign loans, and he subsequently held very pessimistic views regarding Japan's external finances. The marked decline in the prices of Japanese government bonds in London and New York which ensued, reflecting Japan's low creditworthiness among foreign investors, put Japan on the verge of a financial crisis resulting from a shortage of specie held abroad, and a rapid fall in the foreign deposits of the Yokohama Specie Bank.[68] This led Inoue to fear that Japan could secure further foreign loans only on very unfavourable terms:

> . . . we could only borrow on very onerous terms, and this makes me feel that a loan issue abroad by this country is a virtual impossibility at the present time. Here I may well be met by the objection that Japan succeeded in putting the Hydro-Electric Company's bonds on the New York market in 1924 and 1925. Yes, she did, but I do not think that she could do it on the London market today. If we were to turn to New York we may find conditions there somewhat different now from those in London, and it might be just possible to do something in that quarter.[69]

Pre-negotiations

Following the disastrous Kanto earthquake on 1 September 1923, Inoue immediately decided to issue a new foreign loan for reconstruction work. He also needed to obtain approximately ¥35 million for the forthcoming conversion of the first and second $4\frac{1}{2}$ per cent loans floated in March and July 1905, which were due to mature in January 1924. Mori, the Japanese Government Financial Commissioner, was ordered to arrange a loan issue abroad, and on 8 October Mori left for London via Seattle and Montreal, together with his secretary, Tsushima Juichi, and an officer from the Japanese Finance Ministry.

Although Takahashi Korekiyo, Financial Commissioner during the Russo-Japanese War, had established close personal relations with Jacob Schiff of Kuhn Loeb, and strongly advised Mori through Tsushima to offer Kuhn Loeb the intended issue in New York, the size of the issue led Mori to seek a newer and stronger investment bank than Kuhn Loeb to handle operations in New York.[70] Even so, Kahn, one of Kuhn Loeb's partners, came to London to meet the banks concerned with Japanese government financial operations, and to discuss possible cooperation by American banks in the forthcoming Japanese issues. He proposed that the group of banks involved in Japanese finances in the past should be reconstituted, but the London banks replied that no 'formal constitution of "the group" [had] ever existed'.[71]

Inoue had formed a close liaison with J.P. Morgan, especially with its partner T.W. Lamont. Both had been members of the new China Loan Consortium, and Inoue was also well aware of J.P. Morgan's growing financial influence following the First World War. Mori, too, had known Lamont since the Paris Peace Conference of 1919, and both he and Inoue wanted Morgan's to head the loan issue operations in New York. However, before starting actual negotiations, Mori had to deal with the delicate issue of the entangled interests of the two banks, something recognized by Lamont himself:

> However, as to the handling of any loan we have told Tatsumi [director of the Yokohama Specie Bank] frankly that it appeared to us there were only 2 courses for him to adopt. First to go to Kuhn, Loeb & Co. and state to them that because of the relations existing during the loan operation of the Russian War 20 years ago they desire them now to undertake the projected operation; or second as a complete alternative to go to them and say that because of the national crisis confronting their country; because of the grave necessity they felt themselves under for securing co-operation throughout the entire American investment public; because too of the importance for careful co-operation between New York and London markets they had determined to invite us to make the lead in the projected operation and expected their friends Kuhn, Loeb & Co. to tell them this course was the wise one.[72]

Kahn finally agreed on 24 January 1924 that J.P. Morgan's would head the issue in New York, but that his company would participate on an equal footing.[73]

The loan issue negotiations

The British business community evidently considered reconstruction work following the earthquake as a great business opportunity.[74] In November 1923 Mori arrived in London, having two months earlier informed the Westminster Bank of his mission. John Rae, general manager of the Westminster Bank, believed that the Japanese government had quickly to restore its economic position, in order to facilitate borrowing in London. He advised that as much information as possible should be supplied to the British press, and that Japan's improving economic outlook would probably improve the quotation prices of existing Japanese government bonds on the London Stock Exchange.[75]

From the outset Mori was thinking of a simultaneous loan issue in London and New York.[76] He still regarded London, at the time the world's largest financial centre, as the main loan issue market, and Takahashi had established a network of financiers to handle loans in London. The Westminster Bank, the Hongkong & Shanghai Banking Corporation, the Yokohama Specie Bank and the stockbroker Panmure Gordon had placed a number of Japanese government loans on the London capital market, and could be relied upon for support on this occasion.

It was usual for a financial commissioner to collect market information and communicate informally with concerned financiers and civil servants.[77] Following discussions with representatives of the Westminster Bank and the Hongkong and Shanghai Banking Corporation, as well as with Niemeyer at the Treasury, Mori realized that conditions on the London capital market were unfavourable to a Japanese loan.[78] Firstly, as shown in Figure 5.2, since the earthquake the quotation prices of existing Japanese government bonds had fallen and stayed low. Quotes of Japanese issues were 'to be lowered all round'.[79] Expectations that Japan needed a new loan for reconstruction had a calamitous effect on all Japanese government bonds. Secondly, after the end of the war there was a general shortage of capital. In London there was an immense demand for funds not only for Britain and the colonies but also for the reconstruction of European countries, especially Germany. With Paris losing its international significance and the New York capital market not yet matured for investment abroad, London showed a 'tight market'. Thirdly, as already noted, the London capital market was no longer 'a free market', being under strict Treasury and Bank of England control.

To implement the intended issue smoothly, the British government considered the possibility of relying upon the Trade Facilities Act.[80] This would mean the British government could guarantee the payment of the loan on a basis of *c*.5 per cent interest, with Japan having to spend the loan proceeds in the British market.[81] L.W. Evans, the Postmaster General, even suggested that the government make a direct loan of £10 million to Japan

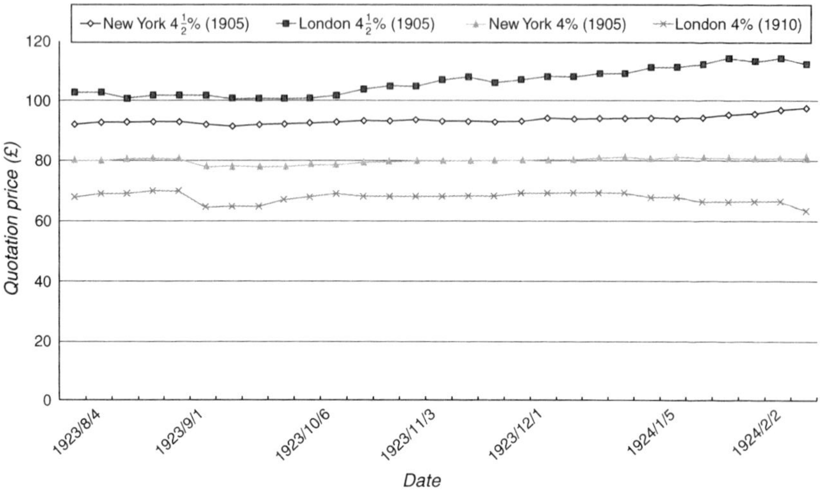

Sources: *The Economist*, *Commercial and Financial Chronicle*, both weekly.

Figure 5.2 Quotation prices of Japanese government bonds, 1923–24

on condition that Japan purchase materials in Britain.[82] Eric Hambro also proposed loans of £5 million to Japanese banks and companies for reconstruction works.[83] British industries could expect orders for reconstruction materials from Japan, and the increased exports would narrow Britain's enormous trade deficits. However, Prime Minister Stanley Baldwin suddenly dissolved Parliament, and following the general election in December 1923, the Conservative government lost its parliamentary majority, making Mori afraid that political instability would cause immense damage to the forthcoming negotiations with the London banks.

Prior to negotiations, Mori had to decide the parameters of his intended loan issue. There were three possible options: a conversion loan of ¥350–360 million (*c*.£35 million) for the 4½ per cent loans; a reconstruction loan for ¥200–300 million; or a composite (conversion and reconstruction) loan of ¥600 million.[84] At the beginning of November 1923 a budget for the earthquake reconstruction had yet to be finalized. Inoue in Japan thought about issuing a conversion loan first and a reconstruction loan later, but Mori believed that if the loans were floated separately, British investors anticipating a more favourable reconstruction loan would hesitate to subscribe to the conversion loan. This likelihood of a fiasco led Mori to think more in terms of a composite loan.

On 4 November Mori had an interview with Montagu Norman and explained his idea of a £36 million conversion loan for reconstruction.[85] The two agreed that separate loans would be undesirable. When Mori and

Tsushima returned later in the month, Norman advised that the Japanese government should issue a composite loan, but that negotiations should wait until political stability had been restored in Britain. He suggested that the choice of London banks for the forthcoming issue should be left entirely to his advisor, Addis, and that it would be wise to invite American banks to participate in the issue. The following day Allan Cameron, partner in Panmure Gordon, went to Norman to report on the progress of the loan issue negotiations.[86]

At the end of November the Japanese government decided to allocate ¥1.5 billion (£150 million) for reconstruction, and Mori proposed that the Japanese government issue a composite loan for ¥600 million (£30 million in London and $150 million in New York).[87] Negotiation commenced on these lines. On 6 December the London banks proposed a composite loan of £30 million over 40 years at 6 per cent. Security should be the same as for the 1905 loan, and negotiations for both issues would be centred in London.[88] Mori considered a 6 per cent interest rate too high,[89] and counterproposed a 4.5 per cent loan of £36 million for either reconstruction or conversion, to be progressively redeemed by the operation of sinking funds without any specific security. However, given that the yield of existing Japanese government bonds on the New York Stock Exchange was above 6 per cent, the London banks felt it would be impossible to issue a loan at 4.5 per cent. They refused to float an unsecured loan, and the converted $4\frac{1}{2}$ per cent loans had been firmly secured with the revenue from the tobacco monopolies.[90] On hearing of the difficulties, Inoue suggested it might be advisable to issue a conversion loan in London and a separate reconstruction loan in New York, making it likely that Mori would be instructed to concentrate on New York.[91] With his intimate relations with J.P. Morgan, Inoue attached considerable importance to the New York capital market for the forthcoming reconstruction loan, and he criticized the attitude of the London bankers and financiers who firmly insisted on 'London first and New York after' during the ongoing negotiations. Neither Inoue nor the Japanese Ministry Finance in Tokyo agreed to Mori's plan for a composite loan.[92] Nevertheless Mori thought it would not be feasible to arrange a loan in New York alone, as London was still the world's largest financial centre, and managed to persuade Inoue to issue a composite loan in London and New York simultaneously.[93]

The political chaos in Britain following the defeat of the Conservative government had an 'overshadowing effect on new offerings of capital'[94] in London, which made it impossible to float the loan immediately in London. On 29 December Mori left for New York to negotiate an issue there,[95] but the London loan issue banks had already officially decided to take up a composite loan issue for the Japanese government, and strongly recommended it to Mori.[96] Japan also experienced a change of cabinet at this time. Yamamoto resigned as Prime Minister on 31 December, and was replaced the next day by Kiyoura Keigo. Shoda Kazue replaced Inoue as Finance Minister, and the negotiations between Mori and the Finance Ministry entered a new phase. At first Shoda paid more attention to a reconstruction loan issue, but eventually agreed to Mori's plans for a composite loan.[97]

Formation of the extended loan issue consortium in London and relations with New York

The £30 million issue seemed too large for the existing consortium to place on the market, so Rae and Addis felt it necessary to expand the group. Four reputable merchant banks were invited: Barings, N.M. Rothschilds, Schroders, and Morgan Grenfell.[98] These four were called the 'New Group', to differentiate them from the 'Old Group' of four (including Panmure Gordon). Barings and N.M. Rothschilds had played a key role behind the scenes in extending the Japanese government loan issue market from London to New York and the European continent during and following the Russo-Japanese War. Schroders had issued the Japanese government 9 per cent loan of 1870. These three merchant banks had already been, to a certain extent, involved in Japanese government financial operations on the London capital market, although there was 'pressure from Lord Revelstoke [for them] to be included'.[99] Morgan Grenfell's participation in the issue hinged on its ability to help communication between the London loan issue banks and J.P. Morgan in New York.[100] Mori was very proud of his success in organizing such a large syndicate, including the leading merchant and investment banks in both London and New York.[101]

Although Lord Norman advised Mori to invite American banks to participate in the London banks' issue – that is, under London's leadership, Mori seemed to think that the formation of an international Anglo-American syndicate, in which British and American banks cooperated on an equal footing, would be more 'helpful'.[102] This ambitious concept went beyond a simultaneous issue on the Anglo-American markets. However, the London loan issue banks were unanimously opposed to the idea and decided there should be separate syndicates. J.P. Morgan shared this view.[103] The loan issue markets for Japanese government financial operations thus became separated.

The London banks aimed to arrange simultaneous issues in London and New York, but emphasized the introduction of a 'safe-guarding provision', which would permit either group to abandon its particular issue under unavoidable circumstances.[104] They were also of the firm opinion that if the Japanese government dollar bonds were convertible into sterling this would discourage subscriptions in London, so sterling bonds should not be offered in America, nor dollar bonds in London.[105] In the end, it was decided that bonds issued in America and Holland should be payable at the option of the holders in London in sterling at a rate of $4.8665 to the pound, but bonds issued in London should be payable in sterling only. It seems that before the First World War subscriptions in America had been regarded as 'somewhat fictitious, and based to a great extent on the desire for a hastily snatched premium'.[106]

The loan issue terms and performance

The London loan issue banks told Mori that they were unable to take up the proposed loan at 4.5 per cent. The interest rate of a new loan was usually fixed according to the yield on loans issued by the same issuing body, and in January 1924 yields of Japanese government 4 per cent bonds quoted on the London Stock Exchange were above 6 per cent. The London banks felt it would be impossible to issue any type of Japanese government loans at a lesser rate, and suggested that the yield at issue should be at least 7 per cent including redemption. The *Financial Times* commented that 'British investors would probably subscribe to a new Japanese loan offered upon anything like a $6\frac{1}{2}$–$6\frac{3}{4}$%'.[107] Actually the London banks calculated the yield of a 6 per cent loan for 30 years at 87.5 per cent of the issue price as 7.006 per cent.[108] Under these circumstances, Mori had to agree to 6 per cent for London and to 6.5 per cent for New York, which, given New York quotation prices, seemed somewhat high.

Mori also attempted to raise the proposed issue price from 87.5 per cent to 88.5 per cent, but the London banks refused. The issue price in New York was fixed at 92.5 per cent. Different borrowing periods were also decided: 30 years for London and 35 years for New York. The wide discrepancies between the London and New York capital markets meant that issues were carried out on completely different terms.

Initially the Japanese government aimed to obtain a composite loan of ¥600 million, half in London and half in New York. The ¥300 million ($150 million) issue was easily accepted by the American banks, but the London banks refused to take on the full £30 million because of the unfavourable market conditions in London. At their first meeting on 24 January the London consortium requested that the Japanese government should guarantee conversion of bonds to a value of about £10 million. They also requested the purchase of new bonds to a value of up to £3–4 million in the open market. At a second meeting the banks insisted on reducing the issue from £30 million to £25 million. In addition, they insisted that the Japanese government guarantee the conversion of bonds to a value of £12 million in the subscriptions taking place in London.[109] The Japanese government had also to agree that the Bank of Japan would privately purchase the issued bonds within 6–12 months of the loan issue if the price declined on the market.[110] It is clear from these negotiations that only £13 million of the £25 million was actually to be placed on the London capital market. To compensate for the £5 million reduction, Mori raised the possibility of issuing the loan in Canada as well through the American loan issue banks, but J.P. Morgan informed him that its Canadian sub-group had definitely withdrawn from the proposed business.[111] The American banks did decide to organize subscriptions in the Netherlands, although the London loan issue banks objected to this on the ground that it might divert investors from London-held subscriptions.[112]

The matured bonds of the earlier $4\frac{1}{2}$ per cent loans had been secured with the revenue from the tobacco monopolies, and the London banks considered special security for the new loan as a sine qua non, essential for attracting investors. They were afraid they would be unable to find 'new money (subscriptions in cash)' for more than £13 million.[113] Mori was keen to achieve the issue without special security, and insisted that it was the firm determination of the Japanese government to avoid providing security for foreign loan issues, because the 'increasing national credit and standing have enabled Japan to float several loans without security' and the 'existing security is a blot unwarranted and unjustified in view of the present position of Japan'.[114] In the negotiations with Mori, J.P. Morgan had agreed to include a negative security clause, as applied to Belgian and French government loan issues. Mori suggested a similar clause for the London issue, to which the banks agreed.[115]

The contract stipulated that 4.5 per cent of the issue be paid to the London banks as commission. Special refunds reduced the real level of commission to around 4 per cent. Although no statement has survived, the 4 per cent is likely to have been broken down to give 1.5 per cent each to the London issuing banks and to the underwriters and 0.25 per cent to Panmure Gordon. 0.25 per cent would go to both brokerage and expenses, with the remaining 0.25 per cent divided equally among the banks. The Japanese government also had to bear the cost of the 2 per cent stamp duty.[116]

Under Ramsay MacDonald's new Labour government the political situation in Britain stabilized. The London banks told Mori that it was imperative that the loan be floated after 12 February, as the embargo on loan issues was to be lifted.[117] Another important factor to be taken into consideration was that the Dawes Commission, organized at the end of 1923, was now preparing for German reparation loan issues, so the Japanese issue negotiations had to be concluded quickly.[118]

The Japanese government regarded the proposed loan terms as unacceptable, as Mori had originally planned a 6 per cent loan for £30 million at an issue price of 92 per cent, payable over 40 years,[119] but with the deadline approaching, Mori had to decide whether to conclude or break off negotiations. On 9 February Mori asked Shoda for permission to accept the terms.[120] Despite Aoki Tokuzo's strong objections at the Japanese Finance Ministry, Shoda agreed, taking full responsibility for the decision.[121] He saw it as imperative to secure funds for earthquake reconstruction as soon as possible. It was decided that the subscriptions would start from 13 February in London and from 14 February in New York. The issuing banks' archival records give little detailed information on the underwriting in London. All

Table 5.4 Subscriptions to the 1924 loan issue

	Amount (£)	*Number*
Cash total	43 127 200	28 587
Westminster Bank	23 000 000	20 000
Conversion total	15 250 000	3957

Source: WBA, File 2469. Figures include the £12 million conversions under control of the Japanese government.

we know from the Japanese side is that 'the preliminary work of securing underwriting to the London syndicate was progressing well'.[122]

On 13 February London subscriptions started at 9 a.m. They closed at noon. Within three hours the London banks had received a large number of applications, and the issue was heavily oversubscribed, as shown in Table 5.4. Despite the lack of security, there was heavy demand for the issue as the terms, especially the yield of nearly 7 per cent at issue, were extremely attractive to investors. However, *The Times* commented that 'lower terms would have imperilled the success of the loan', and reminded its readers that the previous week, a £2 million Western Australian government 5 per cent loan had been floated at 98 per cent, but only 58 per cent of the issue had been taken up by the public.[123] At issue the yield on this loan was only 5.102 per cent (see Table 5.3).

Nevertheless in Japan the loan generated doubts. Inoue depicted it as a 'national dishonour',[124] while the British Embassy reported expressions of 'great disappointment' in the Japanese press. It was felt that Japan had been treated like a third-rate power. The Foreign Office considered that

> this criticism is not surprising. It is difficult for an outsider to understand why the loan should have been offered in terms so favourable to the purchasers [subscribers]. Possibly, better terms could not have been obtained on the American market, where foreign loans are less popular with the public; and the Japanese did not wish to see too great a discrepancy between the terms of the two markets.[125]

Indeed, it is fair to say that the terms offered by the American banks were even less favourable to the Japanese government than those offered in London. On the other hand, the *Financial Times* commented sympathetically that 'it is [Japan's] misfortune that through a strange working of Providence she has been compelled to borrow money on terms which would have been ridiculed before the great earthquake'.[126]

Deeply aware of the urgent need for reconstruction funds, Mori and Shoda were prepared to accept scathing criticism from various quarters in Japan.

Shoda even prepared a 'vindication' for the public,[127] while Mori later confessed that the negotiations over the loan were the most difficult in his life.[128] After retiring from the Finance Ministry, Mori told university students at a public lecture that they 'should never obtain the position of a Japanese Government Financial Commissioner, however difficult it is to find a job'.[129] With most Japanese at that time uninformed of the real situation in foreign capital markets, it was only the interest rate on the loan that attracted their attention.[130]

The Japanese government 5.5 per cent loan of 1930

During the 1920s financial commissioners and Bank of Japan representatives in London met regularly with Montagu Norman.[131] Their aim was to collect financial information and build up close personal relations. Mori and Tsushima also had many informal interviews with eminent city bankers such as Addis and Rae, who invariably got involved in Japanese government loan issue negotiations.[132] Towards the 1930s, however, Japan's policies in Manchuria threatened the long-standing harmonious relations between the two countries, and as early as 1926 hindered the progress of negotiations over a City of Tokyo 5.5 per cent loan issue.[133] In 1932 the Manchukuo government hoped to raise a ¥30 million (*c.*£3 million) loan through the Yokohama Specie Bank, but the British Foreign Office and Addis agreed that the British government was unable to give its support to the British banks involved.[134] The US government proposed to refuse financial facilities to Japan, and the question of whether the British government was 'prepared to co-operate in placing an embargo on British loans [to Japan]' caused heated arguments in Parliament.[135] During the 1930s circumstances were worsened by the Great Depression, but despite this unfavourable, even hostile, situation, Tsushima was obliged in 1930 to attempt to float another loan on the London market.

The immediate cause was the 4 per cent loan of 1905 raised by Takahashi Korekiyo in London, New York, Paris and Germany. Of the original £25 million only £1.56 million had been redeemed between 1912 and 1930, with £23.44 million still outstanding. The Japanese government had either to repay this amount, or to issue a new or conversion loan. Many Japanese banks held large shares in this loan.[136] As Finance Minister, Inoue was of the firm opinion that Japan's return to the gold standard was an essential prerequisite for future foreign loans.[137] In 1929 Montagu Norman noted in his diary that Tsushima had returned to Japan to arrange the stabilisation of credit needed to return Japan to the gold standard.[138]

Tentative plans for a loan issue

In the autumn of 1929, Rae visited Montagu Norman and explained his tentative plan for the forthcoming Japanese government £25 million loan issue.[139] Norman's attitude to foreign loan issues at the time was lukewarm. With the bank rate at 6.5 per cent since September of that year, he felt it was 'not wise to press just now'.[140] Tsushima himself submitted a provisional plan to the Japanese Finance Ministry. He suggested either a conversion loan or a composite loan to be issued in London and the US by those involved in the 1924 loan, and in France by M.M. Rothschilds. The suggested amount for a conversion loan would be £25–28 million, depending on the rate of interest, or £36–40 million for a composite loan. In both cases New York would be the largest contributor. The loan, which would be issued after Japan returned to the gold standard, would bear a rate of interest lower than that on the 1924 issue, and would be taken out over 30 years.[141]

During the 1924 loan issue, the Japanese government had relied overwhelmingly upon J.P. Morgan, but Tsushima saw London as the main market, and believed 'London first and New York after'.[142] In order to communicate closely with J.P. Morgan in New York and M.M. Rothschilds in Paris, Tsushima considered inviting two London merchant banks, Morgan Grenfell and N.M. Rothschilds, to join the impending issue operations in London. The Paris capital market attracted Tsushima's attention at the outset. Although he was aware of the important role of Paris, the much higher rate of stamp duty in France discouraged Japanese financial operations there. Tsushima thought that unless the stamp duty was lowered, any issue in Paris had to be abandoned.[143] On 20 March 1930, however, Tanaka Tetsusaburo, the Bank of Japan representative dispatched to London, visited Émile Moreau, Governor of the Bank of France, and obtained unofficial authorization to negotiate the Japanese loan issue in France.[144] On 28 April 1930 the Banque Franco-Japonaise informed Tsushima of the reduction of the stamp duty on foreign securities from 2 per cent to 1 per cent – 'une loi fixant d'importants dégrèvements d'ordre fiscal'. Yet it seemed too late for Tsushima to change his mind.[145]

Diplomatic matters, too, seriously influenced the progress of any loan issue negotiations. At the London Naval Disarmament Conference in 1930, Addis, after a 22-year interval, met Wakatsuki Reijiro, who had served as Japanese Government Financial Commissioner from 1907 to 1908. At a joint lunch with Tsushima at the Savoy Hotel, they did not talk about the ongoing loan negotiations.[146] Diplomatic circumstances were sufficiently delicate that the Japanese government was afraid that the planned loan in London and New York might affect the progress of the Naval Disarmament Conference. Wakatsuki and Takarabe Takeshi, the plenipotentiaries at the conference, therefore demanded that the Japanese government should not officially begin the loan negotiations until the conference was over.[147] They were concerned at the right possessed by the US State Department since March 1922 to object to a loan issue in the light of 'possible national interests'. Although there had been no such objection to the 1924 issue, Tsushima was obliged to wait until the conclusion of the conference in April 1930.[148]

Negotiations leading to the issue

Japanese government bonds enjoyed a good reputation among investors in London. As one observer wrote, the 'experience of this country by European investors is of a most satisfactory nature'.[149] The bank rate peaked at 6.5 per cent in September 1929, then steadily dropped, reaching 2.5 per cent on 14 May 1930. Low interest rates seemed likely to favour Japan's financial operations. Finance Minister Inoue announced a policy of restoring the gold standard in Japan, and the quotation prices of Japanese government bonds in both London and New York improved. However, bad news from Japan, such as the suspension of the Tokyo Stock Exchange on 11 April 1930, or the financially awkward position of the Tokyo Electric Light Co. Ltd., could still trouble investors.[150]

On 7 April 1930 Lamont suggested that Tsushima should start the actual negotiations. He advised that the Japanese issue should precede the German government reparation loan, which would be probably floated in June 1930.[151] A week later Tsushima and Rae discussed issue terms in London. They concluded that a London issue would be possible in mid-May. However, as the French government was opposed to any foreign issues in France before the flotation of a German reparation loan, the issue would proceed in London and New York alone. Tsushima insisted on a 5 per cent loan, but Rae considered 5.5 per cent more appropriate. He also thought it favourable to depend upon the same bank groupings used in 1924. Tsushima suggested that the Japanese government could offer the 4 per cent conversion bonds under its control for £4.5–4.6 million.[152] After discussion with the other banks involved, Rae submitted the following specific terms: a 5.5 per cent loan at more than 90 per cent issue price, with a simple yield of 6.11 per cent; a negative security clause as in 1924; a sinking fund clause; the issue and the conversion bonds to be divided equally between London and New York. Tsushima believed that the issue price would be calculated from the yield of 1924 Japanese government $6\frac{1}{2}$ per cent bonds on the New York Stock Exchange; their quotation price on 5 April 1930 was 104 (simple yield 6.25 per cent). The price of 1924 Japanese government 6 per cent bonds in London was approximately 102 (simple yield 5.88 per cent).[153] He also understood that as the issue was to take place in London and New York simultaneously, the terms must be almost the same.

From 23 April Tsushima started official negotiations with the banks, and after consulting with Montagu Norman, the London banks finally agreed terms on 24 April.[154] The size of the issue (including the conversion), which would be made in New York on 12 May, and in Britain on 13 May, would be £12.5 million in Britain and $71 million (£14.58 million) in the US. The interest rate would be 5.5 per cent, giving a simple yield of 6.11 per cent, and 6.43 per cent to subscribers. The redemption period would be 35 years, with a right to redeem the loan to commence ten years from the date of issue. The sinking fund would commence after ten years and run for 30 years, while pound/dollar bonds were to be payable at the option of the holder in pounds/dollars at the fixed exchange rate of £1 = $4.865. Significantly, there was no security clause, not even a negative one. The Japanese government agreed to guarantee the conversion for £2.5 million (Britain) and £3.8 million (US) in 1905 Japanese government 4 per cent bonds. The loan issue bank groups in London were the 'Old Group' (Westminster Bank, Hongkong and Shanghai Banking Corporation, Yokohama Specie Bank) and the 'New Group' (Barings, Morgan Grenfell, N.M. Rothschilds, Schroders). They would together receive 1.75 per cent commission, with underwriters receiving 1.5 per cent, and 0.25 per cent each to Panmure Gordon, and for expenses and brokerage, giving a total of 4 per cent commission.

The currency option clause was the most controversial. The 1924 loan contract had stipulated that the dollar bonds be payable at the option of the holder in sterling at a fixed exchange rate. This time the London banks insisted that the sterling bonds should also be payable in dollars at a fixed exchange rate, a reflection of the existence of an increased number of British investors who availed themselves of investment facilities in New York.[155] With increased international transactions in dollars and the relative decline of London's role in international finance, London banks paid more heed to the 'market for the bonds in both centres', and although Tsushima expressed strong objections to this, the London banks considered the clause as 'in the best interests of the proposed issue'.[156] In line with a general reluctance to furnish security when borrowing money, Tsushima persistently objected to the negative security clause proposed by the London banks, and it was duly dropped.[157] In Tokyo Inoue approved the 5.5 per cent interest rate but still believed the issue price should have been raised from 90 to 92. Yet the London banks were only able to 'offer the tentative figure of 90 in the hope that it might be possible to float the loan at this figure'.[158]

The Japanese government had required £26.5 million, but the London banks were not prepared to accept an issue in excess of £12.5 million, forcing Tsushima to rely on New York for the remainder. Although at the start of negotiations the American banks foresaw difficulties in issuing in excess of $62.5 million (£12.8 million), they finally agreed to $71 million (£14.5 million).[159] On 11 March Rae had visited Montagu Norman and explained his tentative plan for the Japanese conversion loan issue, emphasizing that the Japanese government and banks held around one-third of the converted bonds, and the loan proceeds would be used for conversion purposes only. Montagu Norman had suggested a possible floatation in June, with the issue divided between London and New York, and if possible including Paris and the Netherlands. He had hoped to limit the London issue to £5 million.[160]

Performance

The issues in both London and New York were considerably oversubscribed, and in London the subscription list had closed by 10.30 on the opening day.[161] Investors judged that 'the atmosphere is favourable and there is talk of a premium on the bonds'.[162] The *Financial Times* reported that 'the credit status of Japan is extremely high, and the bonds . . . are an exceptionally attractive investment'.[163] In Japan, however, the terms were subject to scathing criticism. A British diplomat in Tokyo informed the Foreign Office that

> prior to the floatation there was very little in the Japanese press about this conversion loan, and the Japanese authorities seem to have deliberately kept silent. When the terms were announced, several newspapers described the loan as the second national disgrace, the first disgrace having been the loans which Japan contracted in 1924 after the earthquake, at $6\frac{1}{2}$% interest. This was a great blow to Japanese pride, and it is argued that to have to pay $5\frac{1}{2}$% now is almost as disgraceful.[164]

Many Japanese, ignorant of conditions in foreign capital markets, complained about the 5.5 per cent interest rate, although most of the terms were almost identical to those of the German reparation loan of June 1930.

Little information has survived on the profitability of loan issues in general, but it is possible to obtain some figures on the underwriting, application, allotment and profits for this particular issue. For example, the Westminster Bank's profits from the issue amounted to £51 759, or 2.84 per cent of its net annual profits for 1930.[165] By 9 May the underwriting of the issue for £10 million was successfully completed by a syndicate of eight institutions at a commission of 1.5 per cent, with Panmure Gordon taking the lion's share. The application of £2.5 million was guaranteed by the Japanese government. Applications and allotment by financial institution are shown in Table 5.5. It is apparent that the Westminster Bank was by far

Table 5.5 Applications in cash by financial institutions for 1930 loan issue

Banks	*Number*	*Amount (£)*	*Allocation (£)*
Westminster Bank	5 906	12 804 900	2 011 410
Hongkong & Shanghai	1 045	2 218 200	485 500
Yokohama Specie Bank	935	2 045 600	463 300
Baring Brothers & Co.	986	3 372 200	532 100
Morgan, Grenfell Co.	538	3 831 200	563 700
N.M. Rothschild & Sons	807	4 300 300	619 300
J.H. Schroder & Co.	1 032	2 231 400	416 000
Total	11 248	30 803 800	5 091 310

Table 5.6 Profits by financial institution from 1930 loan issue

Loan issue bank	*Underwriting (£) (1.5%)*	*Syndicate (£) (1.75%)*	*Total (£)*
Westminster Bank	11250	40509	51759
Yokohama Specie Bank	7506	40509	48009
Hongkong & Shanghai	10500	40509	51009
N.M. Rothschild & Sons Co.	7500	24305	31805
Baring Brothers & Co.	7500	24305	31805
J.H. Schroder & Co.	7500	24305	31805
Morgan Grenfell & Co.	7500	24305	31805
Panmure Gordon & Co.			184500

the largest applicant, and received by far the largest allocation. Out of a total of £12.5 million, around £7.4 million went for conversion, and just under £5.1 million for cash. The profits accruing to the financial institutions concerned are shown in Table 5.6.

Conclusion

Until the First World War British manufacturing industries were highly competitive in international markets, and from the late nineteenth century British exporters of staple goods occupied overwhelming shares of the Japanese market. During the interwar period these industries came to lose their former dominance of world trade. In 1910 Japan exported to Britain around one-quarter of the value of her imports from Britain, but in 1930 the equivalent figure was two-thirds. By 1935 the value of Japanese exports to Britain exceeded the value of imports from Britain by nearly 50 per cent.[166] By the 1920s the Lancashire cotton industry, Britain's major exporter, was losing out to competitors from the United States, Japan and India, and there were heated conflicts between British and Japanese producers exporting to the Indian market. In 1930 one member of Parliament complained that 'Lancashire's trade with India had been greatly affected, and was now being largely transferred to Japan'.[167]

The interests of the City were different, and the financial sector was still favourable to Japan. Japan's financial operations in London were regarded as a great business opportunity,[168] although some merchant bankers maintained a risk-averse attitude towards Japanese investment.[169] A fundamental change in British government policy had taken place, and the harmonious relations between Lancashire and the government of the pre-First World War years no longer existed. The City had established much closer ties with Westminster and Whitehall. As one expert noted in the 1930s, 'Lancashire is less important than it used to be. More of the electorates are in the South of England.'[170]

In the broader context of Anglo-Japanese economic relations, Japan's financial activities in London during the interwar period remained of crucial importance, as the Japanese government still needed to raise considerable sums abroad. However, the Japanese government loans of that period became less significant from the general viewpoint of the London capital market. Reaching their zenith during the Russo-Japanese War, Japanese loans were unable to sustain a long heyday, something predicted by Lord Rothschild as early as 1906.[171] Financiers and investors in the London market came to pay much more serious attention to the financing of European reconstruction, while the Japanese government began to consider the possibility of cultivating the New York capital market.

Notes

1. For background see F. Warner, *Anglo-Japanese Financial Relations: Golden Tide* (Oxford: Basil Blackwell, 1991); P. Newall, *Japan and the City of London* (London: Athlone, 1996).
2. See T. Suzuki, *Japanese Government Loan Issues on the London Capital Market 1870–1913* (London: Athlone, 1994), ch. 7.
3. D.C.M. Platt, *Finance, Trade, and Politics in British Foreign Policy 1815–1914* (Oxford: Clarendon Press, 1968), p. 23.
4. *Parliamentary Debates (Lords)*, 5th series, vol. xlix (1922), pp. 279–80.
5. K. Mori, 'Gaisai Tenmatsu Kanso Dan (1)', *Zaimu Tsuho*, 1, 9 (Tokyo, 10 September 1924), pp. 442–6. Mori also noted the effect of the Trade Facility Act, whose role was to encourage Empire trade (*Financial Times*, 9 October 1923).
6. E.V. Morgan, *Studies in British Financial Policy, 1914–25* (London: Macmillan, 1952), p. 263.
7. *London City & Midland Bank Limited Monthly Review*, January 1918, p. 2.
8. J.M. Atkin, 'British Overseas Investment, 1918–1931', unpublished PhD thesis (University of London, 1968), p. 28.
9. H. Clay, *Lord Norman* (London: Macmillan, 1957), pp. 144–5.
10. Minutes of Evidence taken before the Committee on Finance and Industry, vol. 1 (1931), Q. 1584.
11. Suzuki, *Japanese Government Loan Issues*, p. 89; D.E. Moggridge, 'British Controls on Long-term Capital Movements, 1924–1931', in D.N. McCloskey (ed.), *Essays on a Mature Economy: Britain after 1840* (Princeton NJ: Princeton University Press, 1971), p. 117.
12. D.E. Moggridge, *British Monetary Policy 1924–31* (London: Cambridge University Press, 1972), p. 199.
13. Niemeyer was the Controller of Finance at the Treasury. See Bank of England Archives (hereafter cited as BEA), G85/56, Treasury Committee Minutes, 25 January 1925. In his diary Norman commented 'Foreign loans, except for reconstruction will jeopardise our liquidity and bring rise in Bank Rate' (BEA,

ADM34/13, Norman Diary, 16 May 1924). Also R.S. Sayers, *The Bank of England 1891–1944*, 3 vols (Cambridge: Cambridge University Press, 1976), vol. 1, p. 148.

14. [A. Crammond], 'British Investment Abroad', *Quarterly Review*, ccvii, 412, 1907; G. Paish, 'Great Britain's Capital Investments in Other Lands', *Journal of Royal Statistical Society*, lxxii, 1909; G. Paish, 'Great Britain's Capital Investments in Individual Colonial and Foreign Countries', *Journal of Royal Statistical Society*, lxxiv, 1911; 'A Stockbroker' and 'The Depreciation of British Home Investment', *Economic Journal*, June 1912.
15. 'A New Study of British Foreign Investments', *Economic Journal*, xxxix, March 1929, pp. 8–24.
16. BEA, G8/55, Treasury Committee Minutes, 9 April 1924.
17. BEA, ADM34/14, Norman Diary, 12 February 1925. Norman also wrote in his diary that foreign loans 'depress the exchange and cause comment at Westminster' (ADM34/13, 3 April 1924). For factors influencing sterling/dollar exchange rates, see N.H. Dimsdale, 'British Money Policy and the Exchange Rate 1920–1928', *Oxford Economic Papers*, new series supplement, 33, 1981, pp. 306–13.
18. Para 34–36, British Parliamentary Papers (hereafter BPP), 1924–25, xi [Cmd 2393].
19. PRO, CAB 58/9 (1925). See also Moggridge, *British Monetary Policy*, pp. 209–11.
20. PRO, T176/17, O.E. Niemeyer, 21 July 1925; PRO, CAB 58/9; BEA, G1/386, Paras 9, 15, 19, 20.
21. D.E. Moggridge (ed.), *The Collected Writings of John Maynard Keynes*, vol. xix (London: Macmillan – now Palgrave, 1981), pp. 280–1, 284.
22. The rate was doubled in the 1920s.
23. A.S. Baster, 'A Note on the Colonial Stock Acts and Dominion Borrowing', *Economic History*, ii, January 1933, pp. 602–3; Atkin, 'British Overseas Investment', p. 20.
24. R.M. Kinderseley, 'British Foreign Investments in 1928', *Economic Journal*, xl, June 1930, p. 180.
25. Minutes of Evidence taken before the Committee on National Debt and Taxation , vol. 2 (1927) Q. 4002.
26. S.R. Cooke and E.H. Davenport, *Imperial Finance* (London: Pelican Press, 1929), p. 201.
27. Keynes, *Collected Writings*, vol. ix, p. 240.
28. Churchill College, Cambridge University, R.G. Hawtrey Papers, 1/26, R.G. Hawtrey, 'Gold Standard', 2 February 1923. See also F.C. Costigliola, 'Anglo-American Financial Rivalry in the 1920s', *Journal of Economic History*, xxxvii, 1977, pp. 917–18; P. Williamson, 'Financiers, the Gold Standard and British Politics, 1925–1931', in J. Turner (ed.), *Businessmen and Politics: Studies of Business Activities in British Politics, 1900–1945* (London: Heinemann, 1985), p. 106.
29. T.E. Gregory, 'Foreign Investments and British Public Opinion' in *Foreign Investments* (Lectures on the Harris Foundation) (Chicago: University of Chicago Press, 1928), pp. 98–9.
30. PRO, T167/17, Otto Niemeyer, 21 July 1925.
31. PRO, T175/4, the Chancellor of the Exchequer, 16 June [no year]; Clay, *Lord Norman*, p. 220. Frederick Phillips also recognized that the embargo meant 'a more definite change from the traditional British policy' (PRO, T175/17, Part I).

32. The famous Genoa Resolution of 1922 had urged the nations of the world to return the gold standard (P.J. Grigg, *Prejudice and Judgement* (London: Cape, 1948), pp. 181–2.
33. BPP, 1918, vii [Cd 9182], para. 15.
34. BPP, 1924–25, xi [Cmd 2393], para. 11.
35. Ibid., para. 14.
36. Ibid., para. 36.
37. PRO, CAB58/9, paras 21, 27, 30, 32.
38. BEA, G1/349, Extract Speech by Mr Churchill. See also Parliamentary Debates (Commons), 5th series, vol. 183 (1924–25), p. 53. For the return to gold see Moggridge, *British Monetary Policy*, chs 3, 4; R.W.D. Boyce, *British Capitalism at the Crossroads 1919–1932* (Cambridge: Cambridge University Press, 1987), chs 2, 3.
39. PRO, T160/111/F4319/21, F.V. Willey, 24 November 1925; *Financial Times*, 10 January 1925. Also G. Cassel, *The Downfall of the Gold Standard* (Oxford: Clarendon Press, 1936), pp. 42–3; Hawtrey Papers, 1/25, R.G. Hawtrey, 'Industry and Overseas Investment', 22 June 1923.
40. Inoue Junnosuke Ronso Hensankai (ed.), *Inoue Junnosuke Den* (Tokyo: Inoue Junnosuke Ronso Hensankai, 1935), p. 606.
41. PRO, CAB58/9, paras 2, 4.
42. For Schuster, see Minutes of Evidence taken before the Committee on National Debt and Taxation, vol. 1 (1927), Q. 114; for Kindersley, see Minutes of Evidence taken before the Committee on Finance and Industry, vol. 1 (1931), Q. 1326.
43. Ibid., QQ. 3149 and 3155.
44. PRO, T160/740/F13296/02/1, Frederick Phillips, 24 July 1937; T160/533/F13296/2, R.V.N. Hopkins, 9 November 1933.
45. BEA, G8/58, Treasury Committee Minutes, 27 March 1929.
46. PRO, CAB58/9, para. 35; PRO, T176/17, Norman to Niemeyer, 11 May 1925; BEA, G8/55, Treasury Committee Minutes, 21 May 1924. For Niemeyer's earlier opinion about a high money rate policy, see S. Howson, *Domestic Monetary Management in Britain 1919–38* (Cambridge: Cambridge University Press, 1975), p. 36.
47. D.H. Aldcroft, *The Inter-war Economy: Britain, 1919–1939* (London: Batsford, 1970), pp. 121 (table 21), 241–56; D.H. Aldcroft and H.W. Richardson, *The British Economy 1870–1939* (London: Macmillan, 1969), pp. 219–38; A.E. Kahn, *Great Britain in the World Economy* (New York: Columbia University Press, 1946, repr. 1968), pp. 65–70; N.K. Buxton and D.H. Aldcroft (eds), *British Industry between the Wars* (London: Scolar Press, 1979), pp. 12–13; R.P.T. Davenport-Hines, *Dudley Docker* (Cambridge: Cambridge, University Press, 1984), p. 195.
48. PRO, CAB58/9, para.43. Industrialists and manufacturers frequently attributed the erosion of their foreign competitiveness to the shortage of investments at home. They insinuated that financial institutions in the City, especially merchant banks, were strongly biased in favour of international business, and in contrast were loath to give long-term credits to home industries. See B.W.E. Alford, *Depression and Recovery? British Economic Growth 1918–1939* (London: Macmillan, 1972), pp. 40–4.
49. Minutes of Evidence taken before the Committee on Currency and Bank of England Note Issues, G. Paish, 10 July 1924 (A.C. Pigou Papers, Marshall Library, Cambridge University, no ref. number).
50. PRO, T176/17, Norman to Chancellor of the Exchequer, 9 June 1925.

51. Hartley Withers, *War-time Financial Problems* (London: Murray, 1919), pp. 25–7. During the 1920s the *Financial Times* often carried articles entitled 'Can the Dollar Oust the Pound?'. These emphasized that the basis of international finance lay in the willingness of investors to devote their capital to the use of foreign countries (*Financial Times*, 16 May 1924).
52. Minutes of Evidence taken before the Committee on Finance and Industry, vol. 2, Q. 7515. Significantly during the First World War, Jacob H. Schiff had been rather pessimistic about New York's future position as an international financial centre (Japanese National Diet Library, Takahashi Korekiyo Papers, letters, 110–17, Schiff to Takahashi, 24 March 1915).
53. W.A. Brown, Jr, *The International Gold Standard Reinterpreted 1914–1934*, vol. 1 (New York: NBER, 1940), pp. x–xi, xiii, 29, 158 and 523. Brown's thesis is echoed in C.P. Kindleberger, *The World in Depression 1929–1939* (Berkeley CA: University of California Press, 1986), p. 299. For a critical view of Brown see M. Palyi, *The Twilight of Gold 1914–1936: Myth and Realities* (Chicago: Henry Regnery, 1972), pp. 114–15.
54. PRO, T160/470/F10549/1, 21 July 1928; Atkin, 'British Overseas Investment', pp. 49–50.
55. PRO, T160/394/F11324/F10792, Foreign Office Notes on British Industry and the Fiscal and Banking Policy of this Country, 28 January 1929.
56. PRO, T160/470/F10549/2, Memorandum on the Stamp Duty of 2% on Bearer Bonds and its Effect on the Issuing of Foreign Loans in London, 26 March 1928.
57. Ibid., 24 June 1929.
58. PRO, T160/470/F10549/2, Mr Phillip's Note (to Sir Richard Hopkins), no date; D. Williams, 'Montagu Norman and Banking Policy in the Nineteen Twenties', *Yorkshire Bulletin of Economic and Social Research*, July 1959, p. 42.
59. Churchill College, Cambridge University, R.G. Hawtrey Papers, 1/47, Brand to Hawtrey, 5 March 1931.
60. K. Burk, *Morgan Grenfell 1838–1988* (Oxford: Oxford University Press, 1989), p. 112.
61. Japanese Ministry of Finance Archives (hereafter JMFA), Kazue Shoda Papers, 28–14.
62. PRO, T160/470/F10549/1, Memorandum on 2% Stamp Duty on Bearer Bonds by John W.W. Hopkins, no date.
63. O.H. Kahn, *Reflections of a Financier* (London: Hodder & Stoughton, 1921), p. 258.
64. V.P. Carosso, *Investment Banking in America* (Cambridge MA: Harvard University Press, 1970), pp. 255–7.
65. M.G. Meyer, *Paris as a Financial Centre* (London: King, 1936), p. 140, ch. vi. See also G. Ramon, *Histoire de la Banque de France* (Paris: n.p., 1929), pp. 443–4; A. Sauvy, *Histoire Economique de la France entre les Deux Guerres* (Paris: Fayard, 1965), pp. 83–99; B. Eichengreen, *Elusive Stability* (Cambridge: Cambridge University Press, 1990), ch. 7.
66. K. Mori, 'Gaisai Tenmatsu Kanso Dan (1)', *Zaimu Tsuho*, vols 1–9, p. 440; 'Kokusai Kinyu', reprinted in Kinyu Keizai Kenkyujo (ed.), *Kinyu Kenkyukai Koenshu*, vol. 1 (Tokyo: Kinyu Keizai Kenkyujo, 1973), pp. 343–4.
67. HSBC Group Archives, Midland Bank Archives, 30/337, Reference Book (Mr Buchanan), 23 January 1922, 7 July 1922, 10 April 1923.
68. PRO, FO371/10964/F778/78/23, R. Boulter to Foreign Office, 29 January 1925.

Tokyo Ginko (Bank of Tokyo), *Shokin Kawase Shikin no Shiteki Hatten* (Historical Development of Specie Exchange Funds), vol. 3 (Tokyo, no date), pp. 27–9.

69. J. Inoue, *Problems of the Japanese Exchange 1914–1926* (London: Macmillan, 1931), p. 163. Inoue had initially disapproved any foreign loan issue (PRO, FO371/10312, Eliot to Foreign Office, 18 February 1924).
70. J. Tsushima, *Hoto Zuiso* 12 (Tokyo: Hoto Kankokai, 1964), p. 175.
71. Royal Bank of Scotland Group Archives, Westminster Bank Archives (hereafter WBA), File 2469, 17 October 1923.
72. Baring Brothers & Co. Archives (hereafter BBA), 200390, J.P. Morgan to Morgan Grenfell, 1 January 1924. This is also confirmed from J.P. Morgan & Co., Japanese Loan Negotiations, f. 1 in JMFA, Tsushima Juichi Papers. Morgan's initially thought Mori would pursue the first option.
73. Tsushima, *Hoto Zuiso* 9 (Tokyo: Hoto Kankokai, 1962), pp. 152–6; JMFA, Tsushima Juichi Papers, Mori to Shoda, 19 January 1924.
74. PRO, FO371/9235/F3438, Eliot to Foreign Office, 30 November 1923.
75. WBA, File 2469 and JMFA, Juichi Tsushima Papers, 26 September 1923.
76. Tsushima, *Hoto Zuiso*, vol. 12, p. 175.
77. For the loan issue negotiations see Mori, 'Gaisai Tenmatsu Kanso Dan (1)', pp. 436–77, 520–40; K. Mori, 'Gaisai Tenmatsu Kanso Dan (2)', *Zaimu Tsuho*, vols 1–10 (Tokyo, 25 September 1924), pp. 520–40; K. Mori, 'Saikin no Gaisai Seiritsu no Tenmatsu', *Ginko Tsushin Roku*, 76, 463, August 1924, pp. 132–7; Tsushima, *Hoto Zuiso*, vol. 12, pp. 179–202.
78. JMFA, Tsushima Juichi Papers, Mori to Katsu Masanori (Japanese Government Financial Commissioner in New York), 10 December 1923.
79. *Financial Times*, 4 September 1923.
80. JMFA, Tsushima Papers, Mori to Minister of Finance, 22 November 1923.
81. PRO, T160/172/F6626, Foreign Office to Palairet, 17 September 1923.
82. PRO, T160/172/F6626, H.E. Fass, no date.
83. JMFA, Tsushima Papers, Mori to Minister of Finance, 22 November 1923.
84. JMFA, Tsushima Papers, Inoue to Mori, 8 December 1923.
85. BEA, ADM34/12, Norman Diary, 4 November 1923.
86. BEA, ADM34/12, Norman Diary, 29 November 1923, 30 November 1923; JMFA, Tsushima Papers, Mori to Katsu, 10 December 1923.
87. JMFA, Tsushima Papers, Mori to Katsu, 26 November 1923; Mori to Inoue, 23 November 1923; Minutes of a Meeting on 6 December 1923. Also WBA, File 2469; Okurasho, *Meiji-Taisho Zaiseishi*, vol. 12 (Tokyo, 1937), p. 358.
88. BBA, 200390, Minutes, 6 December 1923.
89. JMFA, Juichi Tsushima Papers, Inoue to Mori, 11 December 1923. Inoue wrote that an interest rate above 5% would not be acceptable in Japan.
90. WBA, File 2469, Rae to Mori, 14 December 1923; JMFA, Tsushima Papers, Memorandum of Conversation between Mori and Addis, 12 December 1923.
91. JMFA, Tsushima Papers, Inoue to Mori, 7 December 1923.
92. Ibid., Inoue to Mori, 11 December 1923; BBA, 200390, Cameron to Lord Revelstoke, Thursday morning, no date; T. Sagami, 'Higeki no Zaimukan – Mori Kengo Hiroku', 2, *Finance*, 8, 4, 1972, p. 38.
93. JMFA, Tsushima Papers, Mori to Inoue, 27 December 1923. On 17 December Inoue had officially ordered Mori to issue a conversion loan in Britain only and a reconstruction one in America simultaneously or in the future (Ibid., Inoue to Mori, 17 December 1923).

94. *Financial Times*, 5 December 1923.
95. Tatsumi Konojo, director of the Yokohama Specie Bank, had explained the proposed issue in New York to Benjamin Strong, Governor of the Federal Reserve Bank of New York (JMFA, Tsushima Papers, Masahiko Wada to Mori, 28 December 1923).
96. WBA, File 2469 and JMFA, Tsushima Papers, Rae to Mori, 28 December 1923.
97. JMFA, Tsushima Papers, Mori to Shoda, 7 January 1924; Sagami, 'Higeki no Zaimukan – Mori Kengo Hiroku (3)', *Finance*, 8, 5, 1972, p. 44.
98. WBA, File 2469, Minute no. 1, 24 January 1924.
99. D. Kynaston, *The City of London*, vol. 3 (London: Chatto & Windus, 1999), p. 92.
100. BBA, 200390, J.P. Morgan & Co. to Morgan Grenfell & Co., 19 January 1924.
101. JMFA, Shoda Papers, 28–12.
102. WBA, File 2469, Comparison between Group and Mori, 31 January 1924.
103. BBA, 200390, J.P. Morgan & Co. to Morgan Grenfell & Co., 28 January 1924.
104. WBA, File 2469, Minute no. 2, 31 January 1924.
105. Ibid., Minute no. 6, 7 February 1924.
106. *Anglo-Japanese Gazette*, November 1905, p. 108. Mori also regarded London as the main loan issue market. Many Japanese government bonds issued in New York were repurchased by British investors (Mori, 'Gaisai Tenmatsu Kanso Dan (1)', *Zaimu Tsuho*, 1, 9, p. 458).
107. *Financial Times*, 6 September 1923.
108. WBA, File 2469, Minute no. 4, 5 February 1924. The yield of the American loan issue (a $6\frac{1}{2}$ per cent loan for 35 years at $92\frac{1}{2}$% of the issue price) was calculated at 7.1042 per cent.
109. WBA, File 2469, Minute no. 2, 31 January 1924; JMFA, Tsushima Papers, Copy of Cable, J.P. Morgan & Co. to Morgan Grenfell & Co., 25 January 1924; JMFA, Shoda Papers, 28–27, Contract §7.
110. BEA, ADM34/13, Norman Diary, 8 February 1924; JMFA, Tsushima Papers, Nakane Sadahiko to Bank of Japan, 8 February 1924.
111. WBA, File 2469, Minute no. 5, 6 February 1924, Minute no. 6, 7 February 1924.
112. Ibid., Minute no. 3, 4 February 1924.
113. Ibid., Minute no. 2, 31 January 1924.
114. Ibid., Second Meeting of Sub-committee, 30 January 1924.
115. Ibid., Minute no. 7, 11 February 1924; BBA, 200390, J.P. Morgan & Co. to Morgan Grenfell & Co., 25 January 1924.
116. WBA, File 2469, Minute no. 1, 24 January 1924.
117. Ibid., Minute no. 1, 24 January 1924; BEA, G3/180, Montagu Norman to Chairman of Bankers' Clearing House, 14 January 1924.
118. Mori, 'Gaisai Tenmatsu Kanso Dan (2)', pp. 526–8.
119. JMFA, Shoda Papers, 28–28, 29.
120. JMFA, Tsushima Papers, Mori to Shoda, 9 February 1924.
121. Sagami, 'Higeki no Zaimukan – Mori Kengo Hiroku (3)', p. 55; JMFA, Tsushima Papers, Shoda to Mori, 10 February 1924; Tsushima, *Hoto Zuiso* 12, pp. 218–20.
122. JMFA, Tsushima Papers, J.P. Morgan & Co., Japanese Loan Negotiations (1924), f. 16.
123. *The Times*, 14 February 1924; Ibid., 'Trade and Engineering', 16 February 1924; *Financial Times*, 6 February 1924.
124. J. Inoue, *Kinkaikin* (Tokyo: Senshinsha, 1929), p. 51.

125. PRO, FO371/10306, Palairet to Foreign Office, 14 February 1924.
126. *Financial Times*, 14 February 1924.
127. JMFA, Shoda Papers, 28–14.
128. Mori, 'Gaisai Tenmatsu Kanso Dan (2)', p. 529.
129. Mori, 'Kokusai Kinyu', vol. 1, p. 294.
130. 'Zaimukan Mori Kengo Shi no Gyoseki o Shinobite', *Zaisei*, November 1948, p. 40.
131. BEA, ADM34/9–19, Montagu Norman Diary [1920–30], passim.
132. School of Oriental & African Studies Library (hereafter SOAS), Ms. 14, Box 4 (41–43) and Box 5 (46–48), C.S. Addis Papers, Diary.
133. WBA, 2469, City of Tokyo $5\frac{1}{2}$% Loan of 1926, Rae, 11 February 1926.
134. HSBC Group Archives, Hongkong Bank Archives, SHG 322.3, Wellesley to Addis, 28 November 1932.
135. PRO, FO 371/16247/F2596/1568/23, Parliamentary Questions (N. MacLean), 10 March 1932.
136. Most was held by the Bank of Japan or the Yokohama Specie Bank, but other institutions, such as Tokyo Marine Insurance and Mitsui and other banks, were also large holders. For details see MFA, Tsushima Papers, 'Dainikai Yoburi Eika Kosai Karikae Sonota ni kansuru Ken', 18 September 1929.
137. Inoue Junnosuke Ronso Hensan Kai (ed.), *Inoue Junnosuke Den*, p. 606. This view is confirmed in Okurasho, *Showa Zaisei Shi*, 6 (Tokyo: Toyo Keizai Shinposha, 1954), pp. 119–21.
138. BEA, ADM 34/18, Norman Diary, 30 May 1929; G8/58, Treasury Committee Minutes, 5 June 1929.
139. BEA, ADM 34/18, Norman Diary, 14, 18 November 1929.
140. Ibid., 31 October 1929.
141. Full details of the proposals are in JMFA, Tsushima Papers, 'Dainikai Yoburi Eika Kosai Karikae Sonota ni kansuru Ken', 18 September 1929.
142. WBA, 2469, City of Tokyo $5\frac{1}{2}$% Loan of 1926, Kengo Mori to Allan Cameron, 15 April 1925.
143. JMFA, Tsushima Papers, 'Showa Gonen Rokugatsu Gobuhan Ri Beika Kosai Kisai Hokokusho'.
144. Ibid., Tanaka Tetsusaburo to Tsushima Juichi, 20 March 1930. The Chargé d'Affaires of the Japanese Embassy in Paris also mentioned a favourable attitude in the financial press towards Japan's loan issue operation (Japanese Ministry of Foreign Affairs Archives (hereafter JMFAA), E-1-5-0-J1, Honpo Naigaisai Kankei Zakken, Kawai Hiroyuki to Shidehara Kijuro, 17 May 1930).
145. In order to carry out a loan issue in Paris the Japanese government had also to settle serious problems with French investors over City of Tokyo bonds, as Edouard de Rothschild, head of M.M. de Rothschild Frères, suggested (JMFAA, E-1-5-0-J1, No. 17, Kuriyama Shigeru to Shidehara Kijuro, 22 January 1931). One French investor resorted to litigation to get the City of Tokyo to pay the interest on its franc bonds of 1912 in an equivalent value of gold (JMFAA, E-1-5-0-J1, No. 175, Shidehara Kijuro to Ishii Kikujiro, 22 June 1926).
146. SOAS Library, PP.MS, Addis Papers, 14-Box 48, Diary (10 January 1930).
147. JMFAA, E-1-5-0-J1, No. 158, Plenipotentiaries to Shidehara Kijuro, 21 February 1930.
148. It was believed that at the conference there would be no 'bargain' in exchange for Japan's loan issue (J. Tsushima, 'Kin no Kaikin to Saikinshi', in Y. Ando (ed.), *Showa Keizai Shi e no Shogen*, 1 (Tokyo: Mainichi Shinbunsha, 1965), p. 69).

149. A.E. Davies, *Foreign Investments* (London: A.W. Shaw, 1928), p. 211.
150. JMFA, Tsushima Papers, Governor of the Bank of Japan, 12 April 1930; Ibid., Memorandum for Minister Inoue, 5 May 1930. On the Tokyo Electric Light Co. see also Bodleian Library, Oxford University, R.H. Brand Papers, 49/1, Brand to Kindersley, 14 February 1923.
151. JMFA, Tsushima Papers, Lamont to Kashiwagi, 7 April 1930.
152. Ibid., 'Showa Gonen Rokugatsu Gobuhan Ri Beika Kosai Kisai Hokokusho'.
153. *Commercial & Financial Chronicle*, 5 April 1930; *Investors' Monthly Manual*, April 1930.
154. BBA, 200391, Memorandum, 24 April 1930. The terms summarized in the text are extracted from Okurasho, *Gaisai Kankei Shiryo* 1 (Tokyo: Okurasho, 1937), pp. 433–40 (for Britain), pp. 475–94, 511–16 (for America); WBA, 2469, 'Imperial Japanese Government 5½% Conversion Loan of 1930', *Japanese Finance*, 23 April 1930; JMFA, Tsushima Papers, 'Showa Gonen Rokugatsu Gobuhan Ri Beika Kosai Kisai Hokokusho'. For the conversion, see Okurasho, *Showa Zaisei Shi*, vol. 6, pp. 139–42.
155. PRO, T160/470/F10549/1, Memorandum on 2% Stamp Duty on Bear Bonds by J.W.W. Hopkins.
156. WBA, 2469, Imperial Japanese Government 5½% Conversion Loan of 1930, Japanese Finance; JMFA, Tsushima Papers, Rae to Tsushima, 24 and 29 April 1930; ibid., Tsushima to Rae, 25 April 1930, On Some Objections to a Clause Authorising Payment of Interest and Repayment of Principal to be Optional in Sterling or Dollars.
157. JMFA, Tsushima Papers, [presented to J.P. Morgan & Co.] Refunding the Negative Pledge Clause, 23 April 1930; Ibid., Tsushima to Kawase, 26 April 1930.
158. WBA, 2469, Imperial Japanese Government 5½% Conversion Loan of 1930, Japanese Finance, esp. Minute 3, 1 May 1930; JMFA, Tsushima Papers, Memorandum of Interview with Mr. J. Tsushima, 1 May 1930.
159. JMFA, Tsushima Papers, Memorandum of Interview with Mr. J. Tsushima, 1 May 1930; ibid., 'Showa Gonen Rokugatsu Gobuhan Ri Beika Kosai Kisai Hokokusho'.
160. BEA, ADM 34/19, Norman Diary, 11 March 1930; ibid., G1/349, Japanese Government 4% Sterling Loan 1905.
161. *Financial Times*, 14 May 1930.
162. BBA, 200497, A.G.C. Villiers to A.C. Tod, 9 May 1930.
163. *Financial Times*, 13 May 1930.
164. PRO, FO371/14752/F3297/206/23, J. Tilley to A. Henderson, 19 May 1930.
165. T.E. Gregory, *The Westminster Bank through a Century*, vol. 2 (London: Westminster Bank Ltd., 1936), p. 326. The following details come from WBA, 2469, Imperial Japanese Government 5½% Conversion Loan of 1930.
166. Statistical Department (Bank of Japan), *Meiji Iko Honpo Shuyo Keizai Tokei* (Tokyo: Bank of Japan, 1966), pp. 294, 296.
167. *Parliamentary Debates (Commons)*, 5th series, vol. 234 (1929–30), p. 1064 (S.F. Perry). See also John Sharkey's chapter in this volume.
168. For instance, Lazards desired to get involved in the Japanese government loan business of 1924, saying 'we were always ready to join' (Bodleian Library, R.H. Brand Papers, File 57/1, Lazard Brothers & Co. to Gerard D'Abo, 28 January 1924).
169. For example, BBA, 20039, Memorandum of Conversation between Kengo Mori and Lord Revelstoke, 4 November 1926.

170. Comment by Professor Henry Clay in B. Ellinger, 'British Foreign Policy in Relation to the Lancashire Cotton Industry', *International Affairs*, 16, 1937, p. 261. See also P.J. Cain and A.G. Hopkins, *British Imperialism: Crisis and Deconstruction 1914–1990* (London: Longman, 1993), p. 261.
171. Quoted in Suzuki, *Japanese Government Loan Issues*, p. 142.

6

A Case Study of Anglo-Japanese Cooperation in the Motor Vehicle Industry: Ishikawajima, Wolseley, Isuzu and Rootes

Christopher Madeley

Introduction

Japan is today the world's second-largest producer of motor vehicles after the United States. In 1997, 10.97 million units were produced in Japan, and Japan's total domestic output of motor vehicles accounted for about 20 per cent of world production.[1] Attention has thus focused on the changing relationship between the world's two principal motor vehicle industries from the prewar period, when motor vehicles assembled by North American manufacturers in Japan dominated the Japanese domestic market, to the postwar period, during which Japanese motor vehicles made significant inroads into the North American market and Japanese manufacturers began production in North America.[2] The Japanese motor vehicle industry has also come to play a significant role in Britain, however. Four Japanese manufacturers had production facilities in Britain in 1997: Nissan, IBC (an Isuzu–General Motors joint venture), Honda and Toyota. These facilities produced 5 094 000 vehicles in 1997, almost one-third of UK total output, though General Motors subsequently took control of IBC. Approximately three-quarters of those vehicles were exported, and exports of vehicles made by Japanese companies in Britain accounted for more than one-third of Britain's total vehicle exports in 1997.[3] Indeed, motor vehicles are now Britain's single largest export item to Japan.[4]

Despite the importance of Japanese motor vehicle manufacturers for the UK motor industry, and despite the fact that the contribution of British educationalists, industrialists and people in other fields to the development of Japan's education system, industry and infrastructure, particularly during the Meiji Period, is amply documented,[5] little attention seems to have been paid to links between the UK and Japanese motor vehicle industries, in particular those links through which British companies contributed to the development of the Japanese motor vehicle industry. In this chapter I shall examine one such set of links between two British companies, Wolseley

Motors Limited and Rootes Motors Limited, and two Japanese companies, the Ishikawajima Shipbuilding and Engineering Company Limited and Isuzu Motors Limited. The origin of Isuzu Motors, and of the associated Hino Motors Limited,[6] may be traced back to an agreement of 6 November 1918, under which the Ishikawajima company obtained the rights to manufacture and sell cars and trucks of Wolseley design from Wolseley Motors. Ishikawajima's motor vehicle manufacturing division eventually became Isuzu Motors, and the Isuzu company renewed its links with the British motor vehicle industry on 13 February 1953, when it entered into a technical assistance agreement with Rootes Motors to build Hillman cars and vans, and to sell all types of vehicles manufactured by Rootes in Japan. Similar agreements were formed between Nissan and Austin in December 1952, Hino and Renault in March 1953, and Shin Mitsubishi Juko and Willis Overland in September 1953, but a consideration of these lies outside the scope of the present discussion. Isuzu is unique in that it is the only Japanese motor vehicle manufacturing company to have entered into two agreements with different British motor vehicle manufacturers at important stages in its history, namely at the company's foundation, and at the stage of modernization following the Second World War, when Japanese companies sought to close the technological gap which had developed between them and western companies as a result of Japan's isolation and focus on military production during the Second World War. Ishikawajima, the forerunner of Isuzu, was also the first Japanese company to have entered into a formal agreement with an overseas company to manufacture motor vehicles in Japan, contrary to the claim made by Cusumano that Nissan was the first company to form such a link.[7] In addition, the licensing agreement between Wolseley and Ishikawajima seems to have been one of the earliest examples of a British motor vehicle manufacturer licensing its technology abroad, though the agreement is not among those discussed by Maxcy.[8]

English-language accounts of the agreements between Wolseley and Ishikawajima, and Isuzu and Rootes, are frequently at variance with the accounts contained in histories published by the two Japanese companies which participated in these agreements. Baldwin states that Wolseley vehicles were made under licence by Ishikawajima from 1919 to 1929, and were sold under the trade name 'Sumida' from 1923.[9] According to the Ishikawajima company history, however, the licensing agreement ran from 1918 to 1927, and the trade name 'Sumida' was only adopted after the cancellation of the agreement in 1927, the first 'Sumida' vehicle being produced in 1928.[10] Ruiz states that Isuzu dates back to the 1916 merger between the Tokyo Ishikawajima Shipbuilding and Engineering Company and the Tokyo Gas and Electric Industry Company Limited.[11] Ishikawajima company history states that the merger between the Jidosha Kogyo Kabushiki Kaisha (Car Industry Company Limited), a descendant of Ishikawajima's motor vehicle manufacturing division, and the vehicle division of Tokyo Gas and

Electric Industry Company Limited took place in April 1937.[12] According to Chang, top managers of the Tokyo Ishikawajima Shipyard decided in 1923 that it was unwise to continue producing motor vehicles in Japan.[13] However, the Isuzu company history states that despite the destruction of motor vehicle production facilities and stocks of completed vehicles by the Great Kanto Earthquake on 1 September 1923, it was decided at a meeting held on 4 September to continue vehicle production.[14] Chang also states that the Ishikawajima Motor Works became an independent business in 1919,[15] while according to Ishikawajima company history this separation occurred in May 1929.[16] Wilkins, on the basis of an interview with Benjamin Kopf, former head of Ford's operations in prewar Japan, states 'Isuzu, which built army trucks, had a royalty agreement with British Leyland, while another Japanese firm had an arrangement with the British Wolseley, related to the latter's trucks.'[17] In fact Isuzu built passenger cars and goods vans under licence from Rootes, while it was Ishikawajima which under licence from Wolseley built trucks which qualified for subsidy under the Japanese government's Military Vehicle Subsidy Law, and Wolseley which was finally absorbed by British Leyland. Rhys states that 'the only firms in existence prior to the mid-1930s were Hino, which was established in 1917, and Nissan, which can trace its origins back to 1912 . . . Isuzu entered the CV (commercial vehicle) industry in 1937.'[18] Davenport-Hines and Jones mention the agreement between Nissan and Austin in their discussion of Britain's contribution to Japan's postwar recovery and development, but no mention is made of the parallel agreement between Isuzu and Rootes in the same period.[19] Though Bloomfield states that the development of the Japanese car industry 'was heavily dependent on imported technology', he does not mention the licensing agreement between Wolseley and Ishikawajima.[20] Similarly, the agreement is ignored by Allen and Donnithorne, who ascribe the pioneering role in the development of the Japanese motor vehicle industry to Ford and General Motors.[21] The only satisfactory, albeit brief, English-language account of Isuzu's early history, and of its links with Wolseley and Rootes, is contained in Shimokawa's book,[22] while Genther contains details of the background to the formation of the agreement between Isuzu and Rootes.[23]

One reason which may account for confusion in English-language accounts is the fact that though these links are amply documented in Ishikawajima and Isuzu company histories, they receive little or no attention in Wolseley and Rootes company histories. There is no mention of the licensing agreement between Wolseley and Ishikawajima in Nixon's study, despite the author's remark that

> in compiling this narrative, the labour has been eased considerably by the remarkable care with which all the early Wolseley records have been kept by the Company. Catalogues from the first ones issued, details of

> early design, particulars of dates and other matters, so essential for historical accuracy, have all been available, and so research work has been reduced to a minimum.[24]

Discussions of the agreement with Isuzu in Rootes histories are so brief that they may be quoted here in full. Robson states that 'Rootes was also trying to expand overseas. In 1953, an agreement had been concluded with Isuzu of Japan for that company to build the Hillman Minx under licence. In 1960, that agreement was extended, and it continued until the end of 1964, by which time 60000 cars had been produced.'[25] Bullock states that

> in 1953 a visit to the Ryton-on-Dunsmore factory by His Imperial Highness Prince Akihito, the Crown Prince of Japan, was arranged to announce plans for Rootes Group products to be assembled over there by the Isuzu Motor Company, one of the country's largest truck manufacturers. The negotiations had been conducted by Joe Chaldecott, who spent some months in the Far East doing the groundwork. The visit had to be cancelled at the last minute when the Crown Prince went down with a fever, but the deal went ahead and it was agreed that the cars and trucks would be merchandized throughout the Japanese islands by Yamato, a company owned jointly by the Isuzu Motor Company and Rootes. This tie-up did much to increase the export of all Rootes products in the Far East.[26]

Yet another reason may be the apparent absence of any records of correspondence relating to these links in Foreign Office and other governmental archives.

In the absence of comprehensive or reliable English-language accounts of the licensing agreements between Ishikawajima Shipbuilding and Engineering and Wolseley Motors, and between Isuzu Motors and Rootes Motors, the present account relies principally on the published company histories of Ishikawajima and Isuzu.[27] However, in addition to this, relevant material has come to light both in the Wolseley archives and, to a limited extent, in the Rootes Archives.[28] I have also been fortunate enough to gain access to the unpublished diary kept by Albert James Penniall during his posting from Wolseley to Ishikawajima in Tokyo to help establish car production between 1920 and 1922, which, though principally concerned with his impressions and experience of life in Japan, does contain information concerning the progress and problems of technology transfer in the motor vehicle industry at that time.[29] It is hoped that this combination of British and Japanese published and unpublished sources will form the basis of a balanced study. The value of case studies in business history is a matter of controversy. While Coleman questions the value of commissioned company histories,[30] Gourvish believes that 'good case studies are a critical part of business history, an indispensable aid to the academic analysis of business activity and the formulation of theory to explain economic behaviour'.[31] Criticism of case studies focuses on the lack of comparability due to the fact that such studies have not been produced on the basis of a common research design. Both Jeremy and Yuzawa and Udagawa have examined the transfer of technology between Britain and Japan, and propose guidelines for the study of technology transfer.[32] In this latter volume, Udagawa proposes a set of questions under three topics on which I shall attempt to focus in this study.

The first topic area relates to Japan as a host country of foreign capital operations, the second examines the business activities of overseas companies in Japan, and the third is concerned with the impact on Japanese companies of foreign companies operating in Japan. Under the first topic Udagawa proposes that the researcher should examine the attitude of foreign governments and companies towards the Japanese market, the influence of Japanese government policies on foreign companies in Japan, and the reaction of Japanese entrepreneurs to the expansion of foreign companies. The second deals with how and why foreign companies entered the Japanese market, and their problems and successes in Japan. The third relates to the influence of foreign companies on Japan's industrialization, the transfer of foreign business methods and technology to Japanese companies, the efforts made by Japanese companies to adopt foreign practices, and the help given by foreign companies in this.[33]

Wolseley and Ishikawajima: 1918–1927

Plowden's 1971 study examines the evolving relationship between motorists, the motor vehicle manufacturers, and politicians in Britain. Though it seems that the British government did not have any positive policy concerning the exportation of motor vehicles after the First World War, two of its policies may have mitigated against car exports. One was the imposition during the First World War of import duties known as McKenna Duties. These had the effect of giving British motor vehicle manufacturers a protected home market, and thus less need or incentive to develop export markets. The other was the adoption of the horsepower tax, under which cars were taxed more heavily as their power output increased. This was said to make British motor manufacturers focus on the design of small to medium-sized cars, providing them with little incentive to produce high horsepower vehicles which might have been suitable for export markets, though the influence of the horsepower tax on vehicle design is a matter of controversy.[34] While Nixon states that after the First World War 'the Wolseley Company was swift to see the possibilities of considerable developments in overseas trade',[35] he makes no mention of how Wolseley regarded the

Japanese market. British businessmen wishing to trade in or with Japan during the 1920s and 1930s could, however, refer to a series of reports on commercial, industrial, economic and financial conditions in that country emanating from Her Majesty's Stationery Office. The 1923 report states, 'Motor Cars – The situation is slightly better, but Japan will not become a really important market for motor cars until a radical improvement has been made in the roads and traffic is more efficiently controlled.... The Americans enjoy over 75 per cent of the business and are very firmly established.'[36] According to the 1926 report, 'Japan is a difficult market to cultivate for British cars. The cost of high grade vehicles makes business very hard to obtain in a land where price is the outstanding consideration.... The hold upon this market obtained by American manufacturers at a time when British makers were unable to compete is a factor to be combated.'[37] It therefore seemed difficult for a British company like Wolseley to enter the Japanese car market after the First World War. A similar message was conveyed to the Birmingham Chamber of Commerce, of which Wolseley was a member, at a business conference held on 5 January 1922, during the visit of the Japanese Industrial Mission led by Baron Dan Takuma, following a visit to the Wolseley works and other Birmingham manufacturers. A speech devoted in part to the prospects for motor vehicles in Japan was delivered by Mr C. Kadono, vice-president of Okura & Co., who stated:

> I do not think that Motor Car industry can be very promising in Japan [*sic*]. The demand will not be very big, and I rather think the assembling work instead may pay better ... Motor Lorries may have a greater future in Japan then passenger cars [*sic*]. It might be worth your attention for an assembling works for motor lorries.[38]

It is possible that this speech was one influence on the subsequent course of the agreement between Wolseley and Ishikawajima.

Nor were Japanese government policies at that time favourable to passenger car production.[39] From after the Russo-Japanese War the Japanese Army had begun to examine the potential military applications of motor vehicles, importing trucks from France, England and Germany to study, and building its own experimental vehicles. In 1912 a Military Motor Vehicle Evaluation Committee (*Gunyo Jidosha Shinsa Iinkai*) was established by the Army, which recommended that, rather than manufacturing and maintaining its own fleet of trucks, the Army should follow the European model of offering subsidies for vehicles built to a certain specification, with the provision that these could be requisitioned in time of war. This led to the passage in 1918 of the Military Vehicle Subsidy Law (*Gunyo Jidosha Hogoho*), which, while not penalizing the construction of passenger cars, offered financial incentives for both the manufacturers and purchasers of trucks built to the required specification.[40] This law was to have a powerful influence on the development of Ishikawajima's motor vehicle manufacturing division.

In response to knowledge or experience of the increasing manufacture and use of cars overseas, and the small but growing number of foreign cars imported and used in Japan, Japanese manufacturers sought to enter the motor vehicle field. The first Japanese car manufacturers were individuals or small companies which lay outside the established business, industrial and financial circles of Japan at that time, and which produced only limited numbers of cars, though Hashimoto Masujiro's company Kaishinsha, founded in April 1911, was the producer of DAT cars, and the forerunner of the Nissan of today.[41] It was only during the First World War that companies already established in other fields of industry began to show an interest in entering the field of motor vehicle production. Ishikawajima Shipbuilding and Engineering was one such company. The Ishikawajima shipyard had been established in 1853 by the Bakufu, with a view to the construction of western-style ships, the first of which, the *Asahimaru*, was completed the following year.[42] Thereafter the company entered a number of engineering and manufacturing fields, constructing the *Tsuunmaru*, the first steamship built by a private Japanese shipbuilder, in 1877, the first Japanese steel bridge in 1883, mining machinery in 1885, and in 1892 Japan's first high-speed steam engine for electricity generation, Pelton wheels for Kyoto's hydroelectric power station, railway carriages and air compressors. Subsequently the company manufactured electric pumps from 1895, Japan's first domestically-produced large capacity electricity generators in 1896, cranes in 1898, Japan's first large-sized submersible in 1901, light railway locomotives in 1902, gas holders in 1907 and electricity pylons in 1909. In 1911 the company was responsible for the fabrication and erection of the steel work for Tokyo Central Station (now Tokyo Station). Diversity in the products of the Japanese shipbuilding industry is accounted for in Fukasaku's study of Mitsubishi Nagasaki Shipyard thus:

> The most characteristic feature of the industry was that, compared to an early industrializing country like Britain, where the shipbuilding industry grew in a context of well-developed machinery- and material-supplying industries, the industry in Japan developed without them. This meant that the shipbuilding industry had to assume the role of the supplier for itself. Consequently, the industry was also a machinery industry. It made not only engines and other machinery needed for ships, but also machinery for other industries, such as mining and electrical power generation. . . . In the case of Mitsubishi, specialized producers of electrical machinery, internal combustion engines (including aircraft) and optical instruments branched out from its shipbuilding enterprise. The shipbuilding industry was, therefore, a diversified and complex industry, which fostered other machinery industries.[43]

The positive impact of the First World War on the Japanese economy, in particular the growth in demand for ships and shipping, led to Ishikawajima making substantial profits during the war years. However, it was realized that once the war ended these favourable business conditions would cease, thus the company sought to invest some of its profits in entering a new field. The growth of land transport, and particularly the use of cars, was predicted, and so the decision was made that Japan should enter the car manufacturing industry. Despite its accumulated experience in various manufacturing and engineering fields, Ishikawajima did not feel ready to go it alone in this venture, and decided to seek an overseas partner. At the same time the company purchased a Fiat car from the Japan Car Company (*Nihon Jidosha*) in 1916, and set about the production of a similar vehicle by the process of reverse engineering. This proved more difficult than expected, and it took more than one year to get Ishikawajima's vehicle to the stage where it would run.

To select a suitable overseas partner was difficult for Ishikawajima for a number of reasons. Firstly, the motor vehicle industry was a newly-established one, and it would have been difficult to make an informed choice between the many competing technologies and approaches available at that time. Secondly, though truck and other military vehicle production continued during the First World War, passenger vehicle development and construction was curtailed in Europe, thus it was difficult to see the latest designs which potential partners might offer. Thirdly there was the problem of distance from the established centres of motor vehicle production in the United States and Europe. The latter seems to have particularly influenced Ishikawajima's choice of partner. Ishikawajima company history states that only the Italian Fiat company and the British Wolseley company were represented in Tokyo at the time it began to seek out a foreign partner during the First World War. Ishikawajima thus approached both companies about a licensing agreement and, as Wolseley offered the cheaper terms, it was Wolseley that Ishikawajima selected as its partner.

Wolseley was a pioneering company of the British motor vehicle industry.[44] Frederick York Wolseley founded the Wolseley Sheep-Shearing Machine Company Limited in Sydney, Australia, in 1887, and when the company subsequently transferred its manufacturing operations to Britain, Herbert Austin, an engineer who had cooperated with the company in improving its sheep-shearing machinery, was invited to take the post of manager. Austin became interested in the newly-developing motor vehicle industry in Europe, and using Wolseley's production facilities, built several experimental vehicles, culminating in a car which won a prize in the Automobile Club of Great Britain and Ireland's Thousand Miles Trial in 1900. This success established the reputation of Wolseley cars, and won orders for motor vehicles beyond the capacity of the sheep-shearing machinery company. Austin was in contact with Sir Hiram Maxim of Vickers Sons and

Maxim Limited, and the latter company took over Wolseley's car manufacturing operations, establishing the Wolseley Tool and Motor Car Company Limited in 1901. Though Austin left shortly thereafter to establish his own independent motor vehicle manufacturing company, Wolseley grew under the aegis of Vickers to become one of Britain's most prolific manufacturers of motor vehicles before the First World War. In 1914 it changed its name to Wolseley Motors Limited. According to Saul Wolseley produced approximately 3000 vehicles in 1913, the largest output of any manufacturer listed, and employed 4000 workers.[45] It was presumably through Vickers that Ishikawajima was able to approach Wolseley. Vickers did business with Japan in the field of shipbuilding, in which Ishikawajima was already engaged, as well as having an interest in the Japan Steelworks in Muroran.[46] Ishikawajima company history states that negotiations were handled by a Mr Matsuo, a former Japanese Imperial Navy lieutenant who had taken on an agency for Vickers. Under the terms of the agreement signed on 6 November 1918, Ishikawajima obtained the rights to produce three types of vehicles of Wolseley design, the A9 type car, the E3 type light car and the CP type $1\frac{1}{2}$ ton truck, as well as exclusive sales rights for East Asia. In return for these rights Ishikawajima was to pay Wolseley the sum of £80 000 in annual instalments of £8000 over a period of ten years.

It is evident that the role of Wolseley was largely limited to that of a licencer. It was the performance of Ishikawajima that determined the success or otherwise of the motor vehicle manufacturing venture involving the two companies. In the absence of any records of Wolseley's motives in entering the Japanese market, it must be assumed that these were principally financial. The licensing agreement with Ishikawajima was to provide Wolseley with a steady source of income over a ten-year period irrespective of the number of products manufactured under the agreement by Ishikawajima, and Ishikawajima also made purchases of vehicles and components from Wolseley, as will be seen below. Wolseley's strategy to enter the Japanese market was to form a licensing agreement with an established local manufacturer of a range of engineering products. However, as noted above, it seems that the initiative was taken by Ishikawajima, which sought to establish itself as a motor vehicle manufacturer by finding an overseas partner, rather than Wolseley's seeking to enter the Japanese market, though a licensing agreement with Ishikawajima did not contradict Wolseley's policy of overseas expansion following the First World War. Wolseley's entry into the Japanese market was facilitated by its position as a subsidiary of Vickers, and Vickers' established reputation in Japan is likely to have been a further incentive for Ishikawajima to select Wolseley as its partner in this licensing agreement.

The difficulty which Wolseley and Ishikawajima encountered in the Japanese market was that mentioned in the HMSO reports quoted above, namely the problem of competing with American-made cars. The fact that

Photograph 6.1 Unpacking of CPD packs

Wolseley had similar problems in its home and other overseas markets suggests that this was a result of Wolseley's designs and production methods as much as Ishikawajima's inability to manufacture Wolseley cars in a cost-effective way. According to Isuzu company history, the cost of production of one Wolseley A9 type car was over Y10000, while an American-made Buick or Hudson could be purchased for around Y6–7000. Even when the Wolseley car was offered at below cost price the company failed to find buyers, and the vehicles remained unsold. Ishikawajima's response to this problem was to change from the production of cars to the production of trucks which would qualify for subsidies under the 1918 Military Vehicle Subsidy Law. Though Ishikawajima had purchased the rights to manufacture and sell the Wolseley CP type truck, it was not until car manufacture had failed to prove profitable that it turned its attention to the manufacture of this vehicle. Despite the damage caused to production facilities and work in progress by the 1923 Kanto earthquake, the company was able to manufacture two Wolseley CP type trucks, one of which is preserved by Isuzu today.[47] These trucks successfully completed the subsidy law qualifying trials in March 1924. Thereafter Ishikawajima was able to receive a subsidy for each truck produced, and approximately 580 Wolseley CP type $1\frac{1}{2}$ ton trucks, CG type 1 ton trucks, and buses were manufactured and sold up to 1928.

Photograph 6.2 Installing an engine on the overhead line

Photograph 6.3 Final adjustment shop

This is contrary to Cusumano's claim that 'the military subsidies failed to stimulate domestic production except for a few experimental vehicles'.[48]

The manufacture of these vehicles provided a source of income for Ishikawajima's vehicle manufacturing division, and enabled Ishikawajima to establish as a motor vehicle manufacturer specializing in the production of commercial vehicles, as do Isuzu and Hino today. Indeed, according to one contemporary account, 'the Ishikawajima Automobile Company owns the patent right of building Wolseley cars, and this has proved such a profitable business that the company has been reluctant to go in for any other kind of manufacturing'.[49] Wolseley had less to gain from Ishikawajima's business success, however. Ishikawajima failed to pay Wolseley the annual royalties of £8000 spread over a period of ten years as set out in the initial agreement. Though a royalty payment of £7184 8s was received from Dr Matsuo via the Bank of Taiwan in November 1918, subsequent annual payments never came close to the agreed figure of £8000, falling as low as £1500 in 1924. No payments were recorded after 1926. Despite this, Wolseley continued to pay Dr Matsuo commission in connection with the agreement with Ishikawajima, a figure of around £300 per year.[50] Ishikawajima tried to negotiate a reduction in the £8000 annual payment in 1922, and in 1927 was successful in cancelling the licensing agreement, a year before the final royalty payment was due. The failure of Ishikawajima to pay Wolseley the royalties could only have added to the problems that Wolseley was facing at home. Wolseley was declared bankrupt in 1926, and purchased by William Morris in 1927, to be incorporated into his vehicle manufacturing group.

Let us now consider the impact of foreign companies on Japanese companies as revealed in this case study. It is difficult to assess the broader role played by the licensing agreement between Wolseley and Ishikawajima. Clearly the licensing agreement facilitated Ishikawajima's entry into the motor vehicle manufacturing industry for, as noted above, it was difficult for Ishikawajima to manufacture a Fiat car by reverse engineering, notwithstanding Ishikawajima's accumulated experience in producing a wide range of engineering products. Once established in the motor vehicle industry, the Ishikawajima motor vehicle manufacturing division and the companies which evolved from it stayed in production, forming the basis of both Isuzu and Hino, two of Japan's commercial vehicle manufacturers of today. The Ishikawajima motor vehicle manufacturing division was also involved in a number of mergers with other vehicle manufacturing companies, and in this way designs and manufacturing practices which had been learnt from Wolseley may well have been diffused to other companies. However, other Japanese motor vehicle manufacturing firms such as Daihatsu or Mazda were established without cooperation with foreign firms, so such cooperation was not the only way to enter the motor manufacturing field.[51]

As Ishikawajima signed a licensing agreement with Wolseley, and paid royalties to use the latter's designs, this agreement contained provisions for the direct transfer to Ishikawajima of Wolseley's production facilities, technology, business management methods and know how. Fukasaku identifies a number of strategies employed in technology imports both at national level in Japan and at the level of the Mitsubishi Nagasaki shipyard. These include the purchase of manufacturing and sales licences, overseas missions, employment of foreigners, imports of machinery and materials, and journals, books and professional societies.[52] All but the last of these strategies were employed by Ishikawajima in the context of the licensing agreement with Wolseley. We should note that Ishikawajima's use of licensing agreements to acquire overseas technology was not limited to motor vehicles. An advertisement of 1923 states,

> The Ishikawajima Shipbuilding and Engineering Co. Ltd. Tokyo (*Tokyo Ishikawajima Zosenjo*). Established 1876. Manufacturing Licensees of Woodeson's Patent Water Tube Boilers, Clarke Chapman and Co.'s Patent Pumps, Wolseley's Motor Cars, Zoelly's Marine Steam Turbines, and Mitchell's Luffing Crane. Shipbuilders, Engineers, Boiler-Makers, Bridge-Builders, Crane Makers, Designers and Contractors for Structural Steel Work.[53]

The agreement between Wolseley and Ishikawajima provided for Ishikawajima staff to visit the Wolseley factory and learn production techniques firsthand. Isuzu company history states that a group of six staff left Japan at the end of 1918, returning about a year later. Ishikawajima staff did not limit themselves to visiting Wolseley on this first overseas mission, however. The journey was arranged to take them via the United States, where they visited the factories of Ford and other companies in Detroit. They also returned to Japan via the United States, and on the return journey purchased machine tools according to advice which Wolseley had given them to establish a motor vehicle production plant in Japan, which would have a capacity of between 50 and 100 vehicles per year. A second overseas mission took place in 1922, when a Mr Murakami of Ishikawajima was sent to Wolseley both to seek to negotiate a reduction in the annual royalty payment of £8000, and to obtain plans for the CP type $1\frac{1}{2}$ ton truck which Ishikawajima now planned to manufacture. The final recorded visit of Ishikawajima personnel to Wolseley was in 1927, when Managing Director Shibusawa Masao was able to obtain annulment of the licensing agreement while on a trip to Europe. By this time, Wolseley had in any case gone bankrupt, and been taken over by Morris, so the company with which the licensing agreement had originally been drawn up was no longer in existence.

One member of Wolseley staff was sent to Japan to help Ishikawajima establish car production. Albert James Penniall, a motor engineer, arrived in Tokyo on 9 August 1920, and left on 11 July 1922.[54] During his stay in Japan he oversaw completion of the first Wolseley car to be built under licence by Ishikawajima. Penniall's portrayal of his colleagues and working conditions at Ishikawajima is far removed from the stereotype of hard work and efficiency which surrounds Japanese industry today. In his diary for 10 October 1920 he notes, 'As regards the works, it looks as if it will take 12 months or more to get out one car, as things go very slow out east, tomorrow will do style of thing.' On 18 November 1920, 'I have done more work this week than I have done ever since I left Adderley Park.[55] I have actually designed some tools. This is one continual restful holiday out here.' Similarly on 3 February 1921, 'Things are about the same at the works, no one seems to put themselves out, everyone sits about smoking all day. Workmen all smoke whilst at work.' Nevertheless, Penniall was able to write on 31 December 1921, 'We are making good progress at the works, on the 26th December we took our first car made in Japan on a satisfactory road test.'

As noted above, Ishikawajima imported machine tools from the United States following advice given by Wolseley to equip its motor vehicle production plant. Ishikawajima purchased patterns from Wolseley to use in the manufacture of the A9 type car. Ishikawajima also imported vehicle chassis from Wolseley, and it seems that these were fitted with a body built by Ishikawajima, rather than Ishikawajima being responsible for the construction of the whole vehicle. Wolseley production records list 24 E3 type 10 h.p. Colonial Models, chassis only, with ebonite cells, delivered to Ishikawajima during 1920 and 1921 at a cost of £430 each. Similarly 21 A9 type 15 h.p. Colonial Type, chassis only, with ebonite cells, were delivered to Ishikawajima in 1921 at a cost of £650 each, giving a grand total of 45 chassis of both types.[56] Isuzu company history states that about 50 cars which could not be sold were destroyed in the Kanto earthquake of September 1923. This figure roughly corresponds with the total number of chassis imported by Ishikawajima, suggesting that these cars were built up on chassis supplied by Wolseley. In addition, the account of the problems faced by Ishikawajima in manufacturing the first cars focuses on the difficulty of producing a satisfactory finish to the bodywork, and states that the high level of hand finishing required was a factor which increased the production cost of the vehicles. However, photographs in the Penniall Collection show the machining of engine castings, and the assembly and testing of motor car engines, so it seems that Ishikawajima also undertook engine manufacture in Japan. In addition to the import of machinery and materials, Fukasaku states,

> Also, it was the policy of the yard to purchase the first one or two products for which a licence agreement was made rather than manufacturing them. . . . This became a strictly observed pattern of procedure for all machinery purchased under licence. Thus, machines were imported not only for use but also to study how they were made so that eventually the yard itself could make them.[57]

Though there is no record of whether Ishikawajima followed this practice for the A9 type cars which it manufactured and sold under licence from Wolseley, Isuzu company history states that Ishikawajima imported and sold E3 type compact cars, and when Ishikawajima turned its attention to the production of the CP type 1½ ton truck it imported two trucks, one of which was dismantled and used as a model for the production of Ishikawajima's own vehicles, while the other was loaned on trial to a Tokyo bus company. When the first dismantled truck was destroyed in the Kanto earthquake, the second truck was returned from the bus company and dismantled in its turn to serve as a model for production.

Our third concern relates to the efforts made by Japanese companies to introduce and anchor overseas business practices in their own business management, and the assistance offered by their foreign counterparts in this attempt. The various strategies employed by Ishikawajima in its licensing agreement with Wolseley have been noted above, and it is evident that, despite Wolseley's failure to receive the agreed royalty payments from Ishikawajima, the company continued to cooperate with Ishikawajima. This was particularly evident with regard to the shift from the production of cars to the production of trucks which enabled Ishikawajima to receive government subsidies, and to establish itself as a commercial vehicle manufacturer. Ishikawajima moved from a position where it had great difficulty in reverse engineering a car in 1916, through the production of car bodies, and perhaps also engines, which could be fitted to chassis supplied by Wolseley in 1921 with the help of a British engineer, to the stage in 1924 at which it could manufacture complete trucks without any guidance by British personnel. After the annulment of the licensing agreement with Wolseley in 1927, Ishikawajima staff were able to use their accumulated know-how not only to continue manufacture, but to improve upon the designs which they had purchased from Wolseley. The Wolseley CP type truck was followed by a Sumida CL type vehicle, equipped with a CL type engine, which was based on the CP type engine, but delivered more power. In May 1929 the motor vehicle manufacturing division of Ishikawajima became a separate company named Ishikawajima Car Works Company Limited (*Ishikawajima Jidosha Seisakujo KK*). In March 1933 this company merged with the DAT Car Manufacturing Company Limited (*DAT Jidosha Seizo KK*), becoming the Car Industry Company Limited (*Jidosha Kogyo KK*). Subsequently in April 1937 this company in turn merged with the Tokyo Gas and Electric Industry Company's vehicle section (*Tokyo Gasu Denki Kogyo KK*), becoming the Tokyo Car Industry Company Limited (*Tokyo Jidosha Kogyo KK*). In April 1941 this company was renamed the Diesel Car Industry Company Limited (*Diesel Jidosha Kogyo KK*), and finally in July 1949 this firm took its present name of Isuzu Motors Limited. Hino Heavy Industries, the forerunner of Hino Motors Limited, became a separate company in 1942. Thus it may be seen that the designs and manufacturing techniques acquired by Ishikawajima from Wolseley were the starting point of a period of development in which the company took on board influences from other manufacturers, culminating in the Isuzu and Hino of today.

Rootes and Isuzu: 1953–1964

While Wolseley was one of Britain's pioneering motor vehicle manufacturers, Rootes Motors Limited found its origin in motor vehicle sales and service.[58] William Rootes owned a cycle shop in Hawkhurst in Kent, which developed into a garage. His two sons, William Edward Rootes and Reginald Claud Rootes, became involved in the motor trade after the First World War, and established Rootes Limited in Maidstone, a successful garage company which expanded into London and then Birmingham. In 1925 the Rootes brothers took over a prestigious London coachbuilder, Thrupp and Maberly, and in 1926 moved into new offices in Devonshire House in Piccadilly. At the end of the 1920s the Rootes brothers gained control of two Coventry-based car manufacturing companies, Hillman and Humber. The Rootes brothers then set about the rationalization of existing Hillman and Humber products and production facilities, and the introduction of new products, while continuing to expand the range of companies under their control. In 1934 Rootes acquired the Karrier commercial vehicle company, in 1935 the car manufacturers Sunbeam and Talbot, in 1937 British Light Steel Pressings, in 1951 Tilling Stevens, manufacturers of commercial vehicles, and in 1955–56 the car manufacturer Singer. The Hillman Minx, launched in 1931, was one of Rootes' most successful and enduring passenger cars. The name was still being used in 1961, and it was a postwar version of the Hillman Minx which Isuzu were to manufacture under licence. Rootes Motors Limited was also a successful exporter, particularly in the postwar period.

Unlike in the period following the First World War, the promotion of exports was a priority for the British government after the Second World War. The country had exhausted its overseas reserves and borrowed a large amount of money, particularly US dollars, to finance the war. In order to build up its foreign reserves again and pay off these debts, Britain needed to export substantially. The British government was now aware of the export-revenue-earning potential of the motor vehicle industry, and in an April 1945 report entitled 'Post War Resettlement of the Motor Industry' set out a series of recommendations for the future development of the industry which the government believed would help the industry to achieve greater exports. These centred on the achievement of economies of scale by a reduction in the range of models manufactured by individual companies, or a reduction in the number of companies, or cooperation between companies to mass produce a vehicle suitable for export. The report also highlighted the concern that the majority of Britain's prewar car exports had been to the British Empire under favourable trading terms which might not continue in the future. In addition, the report noted that Britain's prewar car exports had principally been of small cars, and that trade in large cars was dominated by the United States and Canada. It was recognized that one cause of this was the horsepower tax in Britain, which favoured the development of small cars for the home market, and thus gave manufacturers little incentive to produce large vehicles which might have been suitable for export. Ironically, it was because British manufacturers produced small cars that Japanese manufacturers were advised to seek them out as potential partners. The government therefore wanted British motor vehicle manufacturing companies to mass produce large cars for export, and to seek out new markets beyond their traditional Empire markets.[59] At the annual dinner of the Society of Motor Manufacturers and Traders held in November 1945 Sir Stafford Cripps, President of the Board of Trade, told motor manufacturers that henceforth at least 50 per cent of production must be exported.[60] The government was able to use the threat of non-allocation of sheet steel, which was then in short supply, against companies which failed to satisfy their export quota. According to Plowden, this target was subsequently increased to 60 per cent, and then to 75 per cent, though actual export figures remained around 60 per cent.[61]

Isuzu company history states that Rootes had a strong desire to enter the Japanese market, and in April 1952 attracted attention by announcing plans to assemble and sell cars in Japan without going into partnership with any Japanese firm. Udagawa notes that 'European manufacturers were much more aggressive in going into the Japanese market at that time than their American counterparts.'[62] According to Genther, 'by April, six companies had conducted market research studies of the Japanese market: Rootes, Renault, Standard, Opel, Fiat, and Chrysler. The Rootes Group led the movement and had already applied to the Foreign Capital Council for approval to set up a knock-down factory and had established a subsidiary in Japan, the Rootes company.'[63] This plan was opposed by the Japanese government, so Rootes was obliged to seek a Japanese partner. In response

> they next tried to develop an agreement with Ikegai Motors by which Rootes would set up a subsidiary, Rootes Motors Japan, to import parts for 1500 cars a year. Ikegai would then produce the knock-down cars that Rootes would sell. All investments would be made by Rootes, and all profits would be returned to England. MITI also rejected this plan. Ultimately, Rootes entered into an agreement with a major producer, Isuzu, to make its Hillman car in Japan under the terms set by MITI.[64]

Thus, unlike the licensing agreement between Wolseley and Ishikawajima, in which it was the Japanese firm which took the initiative in seeking out an overseas partner in order to enter the motor vehicle manufacturing industry, in the case of Rootes and Isuzu, it was the British firm which took the initiative in seeking out a Japanese partner in order to gain access to the Japanese market. Though there is no indication of whether the initial agreement with a British firm, Wolseley, was a factor in Isuzu's acceptance of a second British partner, Rootes, Isuzu's staff in the 1950s were at least aware of the former agreement with Wolseley, and seem to have been well-disposed towards Britain as a result. According to *The Autocar*, 'particularly courteous and helpful to me were the staff at the Isuzu Motor Company, who make the Hillman Minx. This firm claims the longest historical background in Japanese car production – 40 years. In 1918 one predecessor company, Ishikawajima, obtained a licence to manufacture Wolseley private cars for sale in Japan and the Orient, and four years later Wolseley trucks and buses, this agreement lasting until 1927.'[65] Rootes' entry into the Japanese market was consistent with the company's strategy of expanding exports in order to satisfy British government demands, and according to Robson 'the government target of 70% exports was regularly beaten until the early 1950s, when a change of government policy released more cars for the home market. Even so, Rootes pushed up its exports from 40000 to around 70000 cars a year during the 1950s.'[66] Even without British government policy, Rootes might have sought to enter the Japanese market. As Bullock states, 'Rootes were always looking for fresh markets and for ways of overcoming import restrictions and increasing their market penetration.'[67]

Let us now consider the second issue raised by Udagawa, namely the influence on foreign companies' business expansion into Japan and business operations of Japanese government policies on tariffs, industries, and foreign capital. In the case of the agreement between Wolseley and Ishikawajima Japanese government policy caused a change from the manufacture of passenger cars to that of commercial vehicles, a change whose influence is still visible today as both Isuzu and Hino specialize in the manufacture of commercial vehicles, though the influence of Japanese government policy on this occasion did not make itself felt until after the agreement between Wolseley and Ishikawajima had been sealed. In the case of the agreement between Rootes and Isuzu it was the influence of Japanese government policy that brought the agreement itself into being for, as noted above, Japanese government policy in the early 1950s did not allow Rootes to manufacture cars by themselves in Japan. The development of Japanese government policy concerning the Japanese motor vehicle industry and overseas vehicle manufacturers during this period is charted by Genther.[68] The agreement between Rootes and Isuzu was a result of MITI's 'Basic Policy for the Introduction of Foreign Investment into Japan's Passenger Car Industry' of June 1952.

> MITI stated in June that it would allow foreign firms to enter the market only through technical tie-ups with existing chassis makers. . . . MITI announced four additional provisions that it wished to see included in the technology contracts. First, small European cars were more suitable than large American cars. Second, MITI supported the use of foreign currency allocated for the import of cars for the import of parts instead. It could, however, allocate only enough currency to build 1200 cars per company. Third, the Japanese company should try to obtain the right to sell the knock-down cars in Southeast Asia. And fourth, if parts were initially imported, they should eventually be made completely in Japan.[69]

On 3 October 1952 MITI published its 'Policy Relating to the Treatment of Technical Tieups and Assembly Contracts in the Passenger Car Industry'. The major provisions of this policy were as follows:

> 1. Foreign capital for sales operations is not permitted in Japan. 2. Foreign capital for production, if it contributes to the development of the domestic industry, will be approved. 3. The remittance of royalties and patent

> fees will be guaranteed for foreign producers. 4. Within five years of the initiation of the technology contract, at least 90 per cent of parts must be produced domestically (the parts were listed in accordance with their importance). 5. Manufacturing rights for foreign cars must be transferred to domestic companies. 6. The importation of raw materials not produced in Japan will be permitted.[70]

It was under these conditions that the agreement between Isuzu and Rootes was drawn up, and MITI subsequently intervened to hasten the process of domesticization.

> By 1955, MITI believed that the parts domesticisation process was proceeding too slowly, especially in the case of Hino and Isuzu, which were more inefficient and not as technologically experienced as Nissan. MITI suspected that Renault and Rootes were purposefully causing delays in approving Japanese-made parts in order to increase brand loyalty, hoping to someday enter the Japanese market independently.[71]

MITI thus threatened to reduce foreign currency allocation for knock-down production if domesticization was proceeding too slowly, increasing it if domesticization was ahead of schedule, as well as establishing a schedule for the completion of domesticization, which Isuzu, along with Hino and Shin-Mitsubishi, agreed to meet.

> Eventually, MITI agreed to extensions of the contracts for two years for Hino and Isuzu, and five years for Shin-Mitsubishi, with three conditions: the foreign partner allow export of the KD (knock down) car, the Japanese company be allowed to buy the manufacturing rights to avoid patent royalties, and the Japanese company must be making a durable and exportable car at the end of the extension period. Total production of these cars was 165 630.[72]

Japanese business managers in the motor vehicle industry reacted to the desire for business expansion on the part of foreign companies by entering into licensing agreements with them under the terms laid down by MITI, and, as noted at the beginning of this chapter, four such agreements were made at this time. There were also a number of other agreements which did not receive approval. 'The seven abandoned contracts were Fuji Jidosha Kogyo/Chrysler, Prince Jidosha Kogyo/Morris Motors, Kyosan Seisakusho/Simca, Tokyo Jidosha/Standard-Triumph, Daihatsu Kogyo/Studebaker, Komatsu Seisakusho/Volkswagen-Benz, and Mitsubishi Nihon Jukogyo/Kaiser.'[73]

The terms of the agreement between Isuzu and Rootes signed on 13 February 1953 were as follows:[74]

Photograph 6.4 Yamato Motor Company Limited, Tokyo

(1) Isuzu would receive the sole rights to import into Japan all types of vehicles manufactured by Rootes Motors Limited.
(2) Isuzu would acquire the rights to manufacture the Hillman Minx passenger car and Commer delivery van, beginning with assembly of imported components, and moving to domestic production, to which end Rootes would provide assistance in terms of blueprints, documents, technical guidance, etc.
(3) Isuzu would pay £25 per car in royalties, though the first 2000 cars would be exempt from any royalty payment. In addition, Isuzu would pay Rootes approximately £50 000 as a one-off payment.
(4) Rootes would not remit this sum of £50 000 to Britain, but use it to form a sales company in Japan, along with a similar but slightly larger sum put up by Isuzu, and this company would conduct the sales and servicing of all Rootes products in Japan, including those manufactured under licence by Isuzu. Any profits made by this sales company would not be remitted to Britain.
(5) Once the first five years of the licensing agreement had elapsed, it could be terminated by giving one year's notice. Otherwise the agreement would be valid for 25 years.

Photograph 6.5 Sueyoshi Factory

Let us now consider the business activities of foreign companies in Japan in relation to Rootes and Isuzu. The first question is what motives such companies had in entering the Japanese market, and what strategies and operations they adopted to do so. As noted above, Rootes' principal motive in entering the Japanese market was to increase its export sales, a strategy which was in line with both company and British government policy. Though initially Rootes had sought to establish its own independent manufacturing facility in Japan for the assembly of completely knocked-down cars despatched from Britain, the strategy which Rootes was obliged by the Japanese government to adopt to enter the Japanese market was to form an agreement with an already established local manufacturer of motor vehicles. This manufacturer would initially assemble certain Rootes products imported in completely knocked-down form as well as acting as agents for other products in the Rootes range. It may be noted that Rootes had successfully established a number of factories in other overseas markets. 'Many of the Hillmans, Humbers and Sunbeam-Talbots exported at this time were shipped in CKD (completely knocked down) form, final assembly taking place in the modern factories Rootes had established in Australia, New Zealand and South Africa.'[75] It is worthy of note that, unlike the agreement between Wolseley and Ishikawajima, the agreement between Rootes and

Isuzu made provision for not only the manufacture but also the sales of the motor vehicles made under licence, and it is possible that this was something learnt from the failure to sell cars manufactured under the licensing agreement between Wolseley and Ishikawajima. However, the other Japanese companies which entered into licensing agreements with overseas firms in the early 1950s also made specific provisions for the sales of their products. Permission for the licensing agreement between Isuzu and Rootes to proceed was granted on 6 March 1953, and on 3 April the sales company was established with the name Yamato Jidosha. Its president was Sannomiya Goro, the then president of Isuzu, and its managing director Laurence Phillips of Rootes.

Unlike the agreement between Wolseley and Ishikawajima, the agreement between Rootes and Isuzu seems not to have encountered any insurmountable difficulties, though there were temporary setbacks. In June 1958 *The Autocar* stated, 'When I visited the Isuzu factories in mid-April, an economic situation was affecting all manufacturers, and Minx production was down to about three-fifths of capacity.' Nonetheless, the reporter was full of praise for what he saw.

> The body assembly plant now in use was opened only in March of this year, and is completely up-to-date on European lines – a very impressive sight. Considerably more individual attention is given to detail than in most mass-production lines, particular care being taken, for instance, with the preparation of body panels before they reach the paint shop. . . . At the Tsurumi engine factory, where I was escorted by Mr Aramaki himself, I was impressed by the very high standard of manufacture, assembly and testing. Minx engines are produced to the same standards as six-cylinder diesels of high power output.[76]

The arrangements made for sales and after-sales service for the products of the agreement have been outlined above. Bullock notes that 'this tie up did much to increase the export of all Rootes products in the Far East',[77] while Robson states that 60000 cars were produced under the agreement.[78] We have little information regarding our other concern, namely what business results foreign companies achieved in Japan, and how these results affected their business activities at home and in other countries. However, in the absence of evidence to the contrary, it must be assumed that Isuzu was able to pay Rootes the agreed royalties, and that these payments contributed to Rootes' income while the licensing agreement remained in force.

Finally, we need to consider the impact of foreign companies on Japanese companies. First of all, we need to think about what role such companies' business activities may have played in Japan's industrialization and the development of business management. Unlike the agreement between Wolseley and Ishikawajima, which was essentially a private agreement, the agreement between Rootes and Isuzu was one of four similar agreements framed in response to a government policy with clearly defined goals.

> The Japanese automobile industry, which could not replace equipment and modernize technology during World War II and directly afterwards, was far behind the technological level of American and European counterparts. It was estimated that Japan was twenty or thirty years behind Western countries in the production of passenger cars.[79]

As a result of the licensing agreements, however, all four Japanese companies succeeded in the domestic production of licensed automobiles within the period of contract, and established a technological base for subsequent expansion. It must be remembered, however, that Toyota was able to develop without entering into a licensing agreement with a foreign firm at this stage.

In May 1958 *The Autocar*'s reporter concluded:

> First, the Japanese cannot yet produce cars cheaply enough to compete on equal terms with European manufacturers. Secondly, they do not expect to become competitive for at least three years. Thirdly, there is ample evidence of original thought behind their designs, despite the fact that road conditions and universal speed restrictions in Japan make intense demands only on the strength of a chassis and the suppleness of its suspension system. Fourthly, materials and workmanship now appear to be fully up to European standards for parallel products. . . . Although Japan's overall industrial capacity has doubled since the late war, and although she has the means and ability wherewith to build good cars in large numbers (at present she lies eighth in world production figures) she has still many problems to solve. But increased exports are so essential to her trading balance that we must keep a weather eye firmly and appreciatively on the Far East during the coming years.[80]

The strategies employed to transfer Rootes' production facilities, technology, business management methods, and know-how to Isuzu were similar to those employed by Wolseley and Ishikawajima. The purchase of manufacturing and sales licences has already been discussed above, though it may be noted here that, contrary to the wishes of MITI, the licensing agreement between Rootes and Isuzu initially forbade the export of vehicles manufactured under licence by Isuzu. A number of Isuzu staff visited Rootes and related production facilities in the UK, and in 1956 Isuzu staff visited the Pressed Steel Company, which manufactured Hillman bodies. Isuzu company president Sannomiya also visited Rootes in the UK, as did a Mr Takada of Yamato Jidosha, who received training in Coventry, returning to Japan to teach the servicing of Rootes products. A number of British staff, including Laurence Phillips, were employed by Isuzu and Yamato Jidosha. Derek Benson and Kurt Becker were directors of Yamato Jidosha, while Eric Hut was one of the company's auditors. In addition, two British engineers arrived in Japan on 28 September 1953 to give guidance in assembly of the first completely knocked-down Rootes products, which began to arrive in Yokohama on 2 September, though Isuzu company history does not record their names. Between January and April 1954 a Mr Jeffrey and a Mr Hands were seconded by Rootes from the Pressed Steel Company to give assistance with the assembly of vehicle bodies in Japan, and it is possible that there were other staff, from both Isuzu and Rootes, taking part in visits not mentioned above.[81] Isuzu company history states that the layout of the Omori factory in Tokyo where Rootes products were to be assembled and subsequently manufactured was completely planned by Rootes, and Rootes technology was transferred to Isuzu by the importation of completely knocked-down vehicles, which were assembled in Japan, though domestically manufactured tyres, inner tubes, and batteries were employed from the very beginning. Progressively Isuzu and its suppliers took over the manufacture of the vehicle components, until the whole vehicle was manufactured in Japan, though domestically manufactured components had to be submitted to Rootes for inspection and approval before they could be fitted to the vehicles. The first car made completely of Japanese components came off the production line on 28 October 1957, just over four years after assembly of the first completely knocked-down product made almost entirely of imported components.

It is evident that Isuzu was successful in introducing and anchoring the technology and techniques purchased from Rootes into its own business. As in the case of Ishikawajima, Isuzu was able to employ what it had learnt from Rootes as a starting point for the development of its own products. The *Bellel* passenger car was put on sale in October 1961. The *Bellel* was the first car offered in Japan with a diesel engine, thus combining Isuzu's know-how in diesel engine manufacture with what it had learnt from Rootes concerning the manufacture of passenger cars. This was followed by the *Bellett* car in 1963, and a number of other models thereafter. The licensing agreement between Isuzu and Rootes came to an end in 1964. In 1993 Isuzu announced that it would withdraw from passenger car production, to focus once again on commercial and recreational vehicles.

Summary and conclusion

This chapter has examined cooperation between British and Japanese motor vehicle manufacturers in which British manufacturers contributed to the development of the Japanese motor vehicle industry, an aspect of the changing relationship between the British and Japanese motor vehicle industries which seems hitherto to have received little attention. The links between

Wolseley and Ishikawajima, and between Rootes and Isuzu, were selected as the focus of this chapter not only because the Wolseley–Ishikawajima link was the first one established between a Japanese and an overseas company with the purpose of fostering the production of motor vehicles in Japan. It is also the only occasion on which a Japanese company has cooperated twice with British companies in the motor vehicle manufacturing field, Ishikawajima's motor manufacturing section being the forerunner of both Isuzu and Hino, which cooperated with Rootes and Renault respectively. The case study suggests both similarities in and differences between the agreements between Wolseley and Ishikawajima, Rootes and Isuzu. Both agreements were influenced by Japanese government policy, but only the latter by British government policy. Both agreements were successful for the Japanese partner, but only the second was profitable for the British partner. However, it was the first agreement which was to have a lasting influence on both Isuzu and Hino, setting these companies on the road to specialization as manufacturers of commercial vehicles. Both agreements employed similar strategies to achieve technology transfer, namely the provision of plans and blueprints, the purchase of components, the training of Japanese staff in Britain, and the secondment of British staff to Japan. However, while the first agreement was initiated by the Japanese partner to gain access to motor vehicle technology, it was the British partner which sought out the second agreement to gain access to the Japanese market.

By 1972 one writer could state that 'probably the most remarkable feature of the world motor industry in the 1960s was the huge expansion of Japan into a major vehicle producer'.[82] Though it is difficult to quantify the contribution of British firms such as Wolseley and Rootes to the development of the Japanese motor vehicle industry, the licensing agreements in the periods following the two world wars had a significant impact on the development of this industry. Today Japanese motor vehicle manufacturing plants in Britain act as models for British and other motor vehicle manufacturers. Yet Britain was the first country to formally transfer motor vehicle product and production technology to Japan just after the First World War, and even in the 1950s British car manufacturers still had something to teach Japan in the fields of motor vehicle design and manufacture. British designs, production techniques and vehicles made under licence by Japanese companies found markets in Japan during both the 1920s and the 1950s, even though by the latter decade British high-technology products failed to find Japanese buyers on a large scale.[83]

Notes

1. Japan Automobile Manufacturers Association, Inc. Public Relations Department, *1998 – the Motor Industry of Japan* (Tokyo: Japan Automobile Manufacturers Association, Inc, 1998), p. 4.
2. For example, C.S. Chang, *The Japanese Auto Industry and the US Market* (New York: Praeger, 1981); H. Mutoh, 'The Automotive Industry', in R. Komiya, M. Okuno and K. Suzumura (eds), *Industrial Policy of Japan* (Tokyo: Academic Press, 1988); M. Wilkins, 'The Contributions of Foreign Enterprises to Japanese Economic Development', in T. Yuzawa and M. Udagawa (eds), *Foreign Business in Japan before World War II* (Tokyo: University of Tokyo Press, 1990); M. Udagawa, 'The Prewar Japanese Automobile Industry and American Manufacturers', in K. Nakagawa and H. Morikawa (eds), *Japanese Yearbook of Business History*, 2, 1985; T. Abo, 'Japanese Motor Vehicle Technologies Abroad in the 1980s', in D. Jeremy (ed.), *The Transfer of International Technology: Europe, Japan and the USA in the Twentieth Century* (Aldershot: Edward Elgar, 1992).
3. The Society of Motor Manufacturers and Traders Limited, *The UK New Car Market: Review of 1997 and Outlook to 1999* (London: Society of Motor Manufacturers and Traders Limited, 1998), pp. 22–3.
4. For further information see the chapter by Marie Conte-Helm in this volume.
5. For example, O. Checkland, *Britain's Encounter with Meiji Japan, 1868–1912* (London: Macmillan – now Palgrave, 1989); N. Pedlar, *The Imported Pioneers: Westerners who Helped Build Modern Japan* (Folkestone: Japan Library, 1990); H.J. Jones, *Live Machines: Hired Foreigners and Meiji Japan* (Tenterden, Kent: Paul Norbury Publications, 1980); H. Cortazzi and G. Daniels (eds), *Britain and Japan 1859–1991: Themes and Personalities* (London: Routledge, 1991); I. Nish (ed.), *Britain and Japan: Biographical Portraits* (Folkestone: Japan Library, 1994); I. Nish (ed.), *Britain and Japan: Biographical Portraits Volume II* (Folkestone: Japan Library, 1997).
6. Hino Heavy Industries, subsequently Hino Motors, separated from Diesel Heavy Industries, Isuzu's forerunner, in 1942. Isuzu currently supplies Honda, Nissan and Nissan Diesel, in turn receiving items from Honda and Nissan. Hino, however, is currently affiliated to Toyota (*This is Isuzu: Data Book 1997* (Isuzu Motors Limited, Public Relations Department, 1997), p. 25; K. Shimokawa, *The Japanese Automobile Industry: a Business History* (London: Athlone, 1994), p. 134).
7. 'Nissan was also the first Japanese company to introduce automobile product and production technology directly from the United States and Europe' (M.A. Cusumano, *The Japanese Automobile Industry: Technology and Management at Nissan and Toyota* (Cambridge, MA: Harvard University Press, 1985), p. xviii).
8. G. Maxcy, *The Multinational Motor Industry* (London: Croom Helm, 1981).
9. N. Baldwin, *The Wolseley* (Princes Risborough: Shire Publications, 1995), p. 19.
10. Ishikawajima Jukogyo Kabushiki Kaisha Shashi Hensan Iinkai, *Ishikawajima Jukogyo Kabushiki Kaisha 108 Nenshi* (Tokyo: Ishikawajima Harima Jukogyo KK, 1961), p. 394.
11. M. Ruiz, *The Complete History of the Japanese Car: 1907 to the Present* (Sparkford: Haynes, 1986), p. 130.
12. *Ishikawajima Jukogyo Kabushiki Kaisha 108 Nenshi*, p. 402.
13. Chang, *The Japanese Auto Industry and the US Market*, p. 12.
14. Isuzu Jidosha Kabushiki Kaisha, *Isuzu Jidoshareki* (Tokyo: Isuzu Jidosha KK, 1957), p. 28.
15. Chang, *The Japanese Auto Industry and the US Market*, p. 13.

16. *Ishikawajima Jukogyo Kabushiki Kaisha 108 Nenshi*, p. 399.
17. M. Wilkins, 'The Contributions of Foreign Enterprises to Japanese Economic Development' in Yuzawa and Udagawa, *Foreign Business in Japan before World War II*, p. 52, note 28.
18. D.G. Rhys, *The Motor Industry: an Economic Survey* (London: Butterworths, 1972), p. 191.
19. R.P.T. Davenport-Hines and G. Jones, 'British business in Japan since 1868', in R.P.T. Davenport-Hines and G. Jones (eds), *British Business in Asia since 1860* (Cambridge: Cambridge University Press, 1989), pp. 235–6.
20. G. Bloomfield, *The World Automotive Industry* (Newton Abbot: David & Charles, 1978), p. 227.
21. G.C. Allen and A.G. Donnithorne, *Western Enterprise in Far Eastern Economic Development: China and Japan* (London: George Allen & Unwin, 1954), p. 230.
22. Shimokawa, *The Japanese Automobile Industry*, pp. 130–2.
23. P.A. Genther, *A History of Japan's Government–Business Relationship: the Passenger Car Industry* (Ann Arbor MI: Michigan Papers in Japanese Studies No. 20, Centre for Japanese Studies, University of Michigan, 1990), pp. 79–83.
24. S.C. Nixon, *Wolseley: a Saga of the Motor Industry* (London: Foulis, 1949), p. 12.
25. G. Robson, *Cars of the Rootes Group* (Croydon: Motor Racing Publications, 1990), p. 34.
26. J. Bullock, *The Rootes Brothers: Story of a Motoring Empire* (Sparkford: Haynes, 1993), pp. 181–2. The visit of Crown Prince Akihito to Coventry was opposed by local trades unions, and seems not to have gone ahead as a result. See, for example, *Coventry Evening Telegraph*, 16 May 1953; *Daily Telegraph*, 18 May 1953; *Manchester Guardian*, 18 May 1953; *Birmingham Gazette*, 18 May 1953; *Coventry Evening Telegraph*, 20 May 1953.
27. Namely *Ishikawajima Jukogyo Kabushiki Kaisha 108 Nenshi*, *Isuzu Jidoshareki* as cited above; also Isuzu Shashi Hensan Iinkai, *Isuzu Jidosha Gojunenshi* (Tokyo: Isuzu Jidosha Kabushiki Kaisha, 1988).
28. Wolseley financial and production records are held in the British Motor Industry Heritage Trust Archive and Library at Gaydon in Warwickshire. Rootes records are held in the Museum of British Road Transport Library and Archive in Coventry and in the City of Coventry Archives. I would like to thank these three organizations for making records available to me.
29. See also C. Madeley, 'Albert James Penniall: Pioneer of the Japanese Motor Vehicle Industry', in J.E. Hoare (ed.), *Britain and Japan: Biographical Portraits Volume Three* (Richmond: Curzon Press Japan Library, 1999). I am grateful to Mrs Bridget Furst and Mr Geoffrey Penniall for allowing me to quote from Albert James Penniall's diary, and for assisting with research into his life.
30. D. Coleman, 'The Uses and Abuses of Business History', *Business History*, XXIX, 2, April 1987, pp. 141–56.
31. T. Gourvish, 'Writing British Rail's History', *Business Archives*, 62, November 1991, pp. 1–9.
32. D.J. Jeremy (ed.), *International Technology Transfer: Europe, Japan and the USA, 1700–1914* (Aldershot: Edward Elgar, 1991); Jeremy, *The Transfer of International Technology: Europe, Japan and the USA in the Twentieth Century*; Yuzawa and Udagawa, *Foreign Business in Japan before World War II*.
33. M. Udagawa, 'Business Management and Foreign-affiliated Companies in Japan before World War II', in Yuzawa and Udagawa, *Foreign Business in Japan before World War II*, pp. 1–2.

34. W. Plowden, *The Motor Car and Politics 1896–1970* (London: The Bodley Head, 1971), pp. 110, 166–9.
35. Nixon, *Wolseley*, p. 97.
36. E.F.T. Crowe and H.A.F. Horne, *Report on the Commercial, Industrial and Financial Situation in Japan: 1922 and up to June 30th, 1923* (London: HMSO, 1923), p. 24.
37. R. Boulter, *Report on the Commercial, Economic and Financial Conditions in Japan: to June 30th, 1926* (London: HMSO, 1926), p. 35.
38. 'Japanese Business Men's Mission to England', *Birmingham Chamber of Commerce Journal*, 16 January 1922, pp. 28–34; 'Japanese Commercial Mission: Motor Cars and Motor Vehicles and Machine Tools', *Birmingham Chamber of Commerce Journal*, 15 February 1922, pp. 104–5.
39. This section is based on material in Genther, *The Passenger Car Industry*, pp. 18–21.
40. A table of types of subsidy and payments is set out in ibid., p. 20.
41. Ibid., p. 17.
42. This section relies on *Ishikawajima Jukogyo Kabushiki Kaisha 108 Nenshi.*
43. Y. Fukasaku, *Technology and Industrial Development in Pre-War Japan: Mitsubishi Nagasaki Shipyard 1884–1934* (London: Routledge, 1992), p. 13.
44. For a detailed account of Wolseley's early history, see Nixon, *Wolseley*. A more superficial account but one which covers the whole of the company's history until the demise of the 'Wolseley' trade mark in 1975 is in Baldwin, *The Wolseley*. For a general history see N. Georgano, Nick Baldwin, Anders Clausager and Jonathan Wood, *Britain's Motor Industry: The First Hundred Years* (Sparkford: Foulis and Company, 1995).
45. S.B. Saul, 'The Motor Industry in Britain to 1914', *Business History*, V, 1, December 1962, pp. 1–44.
46. See M. Conte-Helm, 'Armstrong's, Vickers and Japan', in Nish, *Britain and Japan: Biographical Portraits*, pp. 92–105. See also Nagura's chapter in this volume.
47. For details of this vehicle and its restoration see C. Madeley, 'Oriental Wolseley', *Old Glory: Vintage Restoration Today*, 68, October 1995, pp. 64–7.
48. *Japanese Automobile Industry*, p. 15.
49. 'An Automobile Industry for Japan', *Contemporary Japan*, 1, 4, March 1933.
50. Details are contained in *Wolseley Motors Limited Ledger General No. 4 General Ledger* (Ishikawajima Shipbuilding and Engineering Co. Ltd. 277, Ishikawajima Shipbuilding and Engineering Co. Ltd. Account), and *Wolseley Motors Ltd. Ledger General No. 5 General Ledger* (Ishikawajima Shipbuilding Co. Folio 67).
51. A brief history of each Japanese motor vehicle manufacturer still in business today is contained in Shimokawa, *The Japanese Automobile Industry*, pp. 104–40.
52. Fukasaku, *Technology and Industrial Development in Pre-War Japan*, pp. 43–61.
53. Y. Takenob, *The Japan Year Book 1923* (Tokyo: The Japan Year Book Office, 1923), p. xxxi.
54. Details of Albert James Penniall's stay in Japan and his impressions of the country and its people may be found in Madeley, 'Albert James Penniall: Pioneer of the Japanese Motor Vehicle Industry'.
55. Wolseley's Birmingham works.
56. Details in *E3 30001–30500 Order Book, A9 33001–33500 Order Book* (Gaydon).
57. Fukasaku, *Technology and Industrial Development in Pre-War Japan*, pp. 56–7.
58. The history of Rootes Motors Limited and its products is described in Robson, *Cars of the Rootes Group*, while Bullock, *The Rootes Brothers: Story of a Motoring Empire* focuses on the personalities behind the company. For a general history see Georgano et al., *Britain's Motor Industry*.

59. For a discussion of this report see ibid., p. 265.
60. Ibid., p. 106.
61. Plowden, *Motor Car and Politics*, pp. 312–15.
62. M. Udagawa, 'Historical Development of the Japanese Automobile Industry, 1917–1971: Business and Government,' *Keiei Shirin (Hosei University)*, 19, 4, January 1983, pp. 31–46.
63. Genther, *Passenger Car Industry*, p. 80.
64. Ibid., p. 81.
65. R. Barker, 'Made in Japan: 5 – Around the Isuzu, Nissan, Fuji and Toyota plants', *The Autocar*, 6 June 1958, p. 855.
66. Robson, *Cars of the Rootes Group*, p. 30.
67. Bullock, *Rootes Brothers*, p. 181.
68. Genther, *Passenger Car Industry*, pp. 69–97.
69. Ibid., p. 81.
70. Ibid., pp. 89–90.
71. Ibid., p. 90.
72. Ibid.
73. Ibid., p. 82.
74. Details of the agreement are in *Isuzu Jidosha Gojunenshi*, pp. 163–4; also in the company magazine *Isuzu*, 75, 1 March 1953.
75. Robson, *Cars of the Rootes Group*, p. 30.
76. Barker, 'Made in Japan: 5 – Around the Isuzu, Nissan, Fuji and Toyota plants', pp. 854–7.
77. Bullock, *Rootes Brothers*, p. 182.
78. Robson, *Cars of the Rootes Group*, p. 34. Detailed production figures are in Cusumano, *Japanese Automobile Industry*, p. 10.
79. Udagawa, 'Historical Development of the Japanese Automobile Industry', pp. 31–46.
80. R. Barker, 'Japan – 4: Hello Japan. A Commentary on her Car Industry – Problems and Prospects', *The Autocar*, 30 May 1958, pp. 815–18.
81. Details of the exchanges of personnel are taken from *Isuzu Jidosha Gojunen Shi*, pp. 165, 167, 169; *Financial Times*, 21 April 1953; *Isuzu*, 78, 15 April 1953; *Isuzu Shinbun* (formerly *Isuzu*), 99, 1 March 1954; *Rootes Group Review*, various issues.
82. Rhys, *Motor Industry*, p. 188.
83. See Weste's chapter in this volume.

7

British Perceptions of Japanese Economic Development in the 1920s: with Special Reference to the Cotton Industry

John Sharkey

Introduction

The study of the British and Japanese economies for the whole of the inter-war period is dominated, unsurprisingly, by the divergent trends of both economies: for Britain it was one of relative decline, while for Japan it was one of continued growth and diversification. In terms of economic growth Japan's annual average was around 2.23 per cent for the 1920s and 5.02 per cent for the 1930s; in contrast Britain's figures were a minuscule 0.55 per cent in the 1920s followed by a more impressive 3.19 per cent in the 1930s.[1] Furthermore, trading links between the two countries were not only weak, but continued to decline throughout this period. Similarly the decline in British lending to Japan, a result of internal difficulties and Japanese hostility to foreign indebtedness, argues against any complementary aspect to Anglo-Japanese economic relations through a significant British involvement in the financing of Japanese industrialization in this period.[2] Indeed, given the tenuous nature of Anglo-Japanese economic relations, the strongest academic interest derives from the juxtaposition of these parallel phenomena, so that, as testified by Kenneth D. Brown's recent and valuable study,[3] the main source of interest is in comparing and analysing the divergent economic trends between two countries whose economies, aspirations, politics, and cultures differed significantly.

In regard to the interwar British economy, and particularly the 1920s, the key academic debate centres around the idea of British economic decline and its causes. In essence much of the debate derives from divergent ideological convictions, between those who see Britain's highly 'individualistic' capitalism as the cause of decline,[4] and those who see such reasoning as somewhat spurious.[5] Naturally, this posturing has spilled over into the conscripted use of the Japanese economic model as a contrast with the British economic model. However, as an indication of the distance between the two economies, it should be noted that these comparisons have been highly selective, limited mainly to the Lancashire and Japanese cotton industries, and, more recently, to management structures.[6]

In the cotton industry debate Lars Sandberg's *Lancashire in Decline* is the touchstone for those who argue that Lancashire's decline was the product of lost comparative advantage due to external circumstance – third-market protectionism and the rise of high-tech low-wage competitors – and not of internal economic irrationality based upon the persistent use of outmoded organizational arrangements.[7] Lancashire could do nothing about its decline in the mass export markets of Asia, so its failure was not due to systemic internal irrationality. The opposite position is put forward by Yamazaki Hiroaki,[8] but is most noticeably associated with Lazonick and Mass's extension of Chandler's castigation of British management for its failure to adopt the 'visible hand'. In 'The British Cotton Industry and International Competitive Advantage: the State of the Debates', Lazonick and Mass argue that British organizational failure – the short-term adherence to nineteenth-century structures optimized for the penetration of unprotected markets with low-tech industries – led to the decline of the Lancashire cotton industry. Furthermore, this decline was reversible, or at least more manageable, since it was Lancashire's over-rigid adherence to 'individualistic' capitalism that sealed its fate against more rational Japanese competitors, while the high cost of labour in Lancashire and increased tariff protection throughout the world were of secondary importance.[9] In this case Lancashire's irrationality is not mere theory, since Japanese success serves as a concrete proof of a more rational economic model.

In contrast, for most western studies of Japan the rise of the Japanese cotton industry is of secondary importance. The main focus of attention is the continued rise and diversification of the whole Japanese economy. Economic history texts that apply positivist economic laws to Japan's economic development relate how the interaction of economic factors and political events propelled Japan's economy on an upward, though not necessarily stable, spiral. However, since the publication in 1982 of Chalmers Johnson's *MITI and the Japanese Miracle*, it has been impossible to ignore the assertion that Japan's use of 'industrial policy' provides a significantly different model from the 'orthodox' western economic model. Although Johnson sees the interwar period as one of experimentation, he still believes that the 1920s witnessed the first faltering use of industrial policy which led to the creation of the 'development state', with its greater role for state-led industrialization based upon a narrow pro-growth political consensus fostered by a centralizing elite. We can add the 'anthropological' interpretation of Japan's economic success, which, as Johnson notes, argues that 'the economic miracle occurred because the Japanese possess a unique, culturally derived capacity to cooperate with each other'.[10] Thus approaches which emphasize the orthodox application of economic factors, the innovative nature of Japan's industrial policy, and the unique nature of Japanese society, vie with each other as an explanation of Japan's economic success.

Major economic themes in the 1920s are thus Anglo-Japanese industrial competition and the economic determinants of the rise of Japan, but it is also clear that British perceptions form a central component for any understanding of the nature of British industrial decline and, to a lesser extent, the debate over Japanese economic success. In regard to the former, although the preliminary question of what Lancashire knew about Japan has received only a partial airing,[11] it is reasonable to conclude that both sides of the 'decline' debate implicitly accept that the veracity of Lancashire's understanding of the Japanese cotton industry can be determined from the degree of rationality ascribed to Lancashire's response to Japanese competition. Those, like Lazonick and Mass, who argue that Lancashire could have competed against Japan, presume that part of Lancashire's irrationality stemmed from an imperfect understanding of the Japanese cotton industry. By extension those, like Sandberg, who insist that it was rational for Lancashire to withdraw from competition with Japan, imply that Lancashire had a far better understanding of Japanese competition. However, historians such as Yamazaki, Izumi Takeo, and Alex J. Robertson who have addressed the perception question, all agree that Lancashire misperceived developments in Japan because of its dilatory exploration of the role of improved technique and organization as an explanation of Japan's competitive advances in the 1920s.

Given their inherently partial and transient nature, contemporary British interpretations of the economic rise of Japan are not in themselves any distinct source of authority. Nevertheless, it is important to recognize that such accounts may be no less authoritative than any postwar western interpretation of Japanese economic development. Furthermore, given Britain's concern over the rise of Japanese industrial competition, such accounts were of intrinsic interest to specific British industries, since British interpretations of specific Japanese industries were crucial to overall interpretations of Japanese economic development. In essence, if British industrialists were creating a wayward picture of the Japanese cotton industry, was this simply the by-product of a more fundamental misinterpretation of Japan, or did it result from a singular failure within specific British industries?

The perception of economic events in far-off places does not, therefore, stop with the acquisition of a viable amount of information and sustaining interpretation, since the function of investigating any competitor is simply as a prelude to an effective response. In this context the quality of British perceptual models of the Japanese economy and its competitive threat is measured as much by the quality of the British response as by any assessment of the information gathered and presented to the British public. In a clear echo of the Sandberg/Lazonick debate, the long-run response of specific British industries can be either to fight or flee. The rational study of

Japan could lead to industrial reorganization as a prelude to reinvigorated competition, or withdrawal from areas where Britain was at a distinct comparative disadvantage. However, assessments of the validity of such responses also require a simultaneous assessment of the capacity of a specific British industry or the entire economy to change or facilitate change. This is not merely a question of the surrounding economic environment, but also reflects the view that no firm or industry can be separated from its cultural milieu. Thus to perceive the validity of any British response to perceptions of Japan, we are again looking at not only current assessments of Britain's interwar economic dynamics, but also contemporary British self-perceptions of the same issue.

From the European armistice to the Kanto earthquake, 1918–1923

After the 1914–19 boom, Japan's economy faced serious economic problems. The impact of inflation, the return of advanced western competition, and the loss of overseas markets during the postwar slump, were all compounded by the disaster of the September 1923 Kanto earthquake. One of the key consequences of this economic sluggishness was the return of the prewar balance of payments deficit. The economic downturn resulted in a new structural economic problem, impeding the easy absorption of Japan's growing rural population within the industrial and service sectors. Moreover the 1920s witnessed the emergence of a productivity and income gap between the modern and traditional sectors.[12]

Still, the above difficulties of the Japanese economy, even during the early-1920s adjustment period, can be overstated, as the mining, manufacturing, construction, transport and utilities sectors all enjoyed substantial growth rates. In particular it was the growth of heavy industry – iron and steel, chemicals, and machinery – which was at the forefront of Japan's industrial development. Much of this industrialization translated into benefits for many factory workers who witnessed real income gains, despite the emergence of industrial dualism. Notwithstanding the trade imbalance, export earnings grew slightly faster than import expenditure, and it is strongly argued that export growth was a consequence of improved domestic productivity. In terms of industrial structure Japan was clearly established as an exporter of light manufactured goods, particularly textiles, while increased imports reflected consumer and industrial demand for foodstuffs and raw materials, the former resulting from higher real incomes, the latter from the growth of Japan's manufacturing base.[13]

However, conflicting priorities in economic policy induced a certain amount of instability in the early 1920s. In order to achieve fiscal stability successive governments pursued retrenchment in the wake of the wartime and postwar inflation, while interest rates and taxes were raised to dampen down domestic demand. At the same time the volatility in the economy led to successive interventions by the Japanese government, particularly following the 1918 rice riots and the 1920 stock market crash, as it sought to ensure cheap rice and protect the silk market and depressed firms via cheap loans from the Bank of Japan. Furthermore Japan returned to a protectionist strategy in the early 1920s as many specific duties undermined by wartime inflation were replaced by more effective *ad valorem* rates.[14]

In industrial terms the First World War had witnessed the continued development of large-scale firms and factories in Japan, particularly in the heavy industrial sector, often associated with the family-dominated structure of the *zaibatsu*. Many of these firms in the 1920s were developing techniques of business organization and management–labour relations now claimed to be the microeconomic hallmark of the 'Japanese Economic Model'. Overall Japan's large-scale manufacturers experienced 'a managerial evolution . . . based on an emphasis on industrial professionalism in top management . . . and a development of internally complex organisations'.[15] It is argued that these *zaibatsu* and large-scale firms significantly increased their control of the economy – in part through cartel operations – during the immediate postwar years, although it has been suggested that given the loose structure of the *zaibatsu* holding companies such arguments are exaggerated. However, despite the emphasis on large-scale operations small factories continued to play a critical role in the Japanese economy, in particular through subcontracting for larger firms, forming a buffer during economic downturns, and also by producing many of Japan's labour intensive products.

Many of the above features were displayed by Japan's cotton industry with its large vertically integrated combines – from the bulk purchase of raw cotton to the export of yarn and increasingly of cotton piece-goods, together with an extension of finishing plants – centred on the spinning sector. Such firms are noted for technical and managerial innovation which clearly emphasized the need to increase productivity through improved labour conditions. In contrast the more diffuse independent weaving sector retained much of its small-scale and technically backward 'Asiatic' make-up. Despite the dominance of the cotton industry by the spinning firms, and especially through the Greater Japan Spinners' Association, there is little evidence that it tried to use its dominant supply position to ensure monopsony profits, and in all probability allowed free competition as part of its strategy to drive down both yarn and piece-good prices.[16] However, in performance terms the immediate postwar period proved something of a disaster for the Japanese cotton industry, as exports declined significantly, not only as a result of the return of foreign competition but also because of the negative impact of internal reorganization and particularly wage inflation upon labour productivity and price competitiveness (see Figures 7.1–7.3).

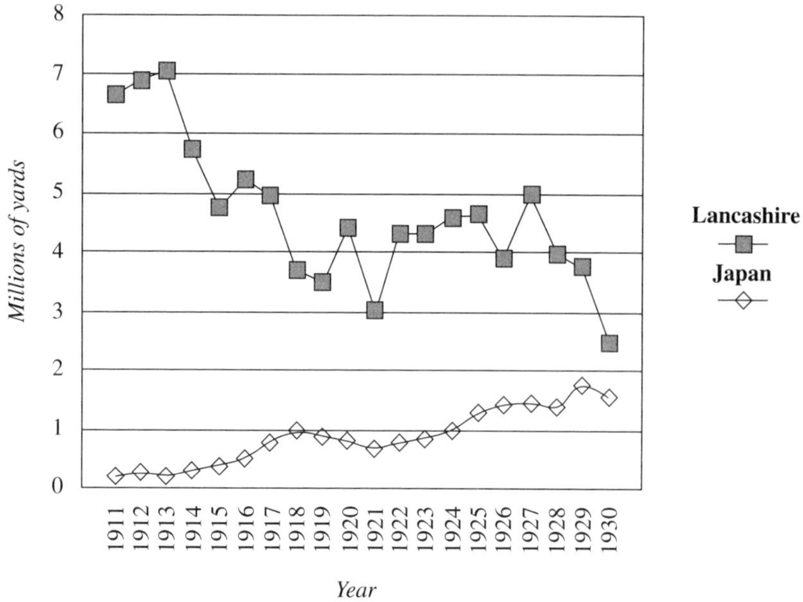

Sources: K. Seki, *The Cotton Industry of Japan* (Tokyo: Japan Society for the Promotion of Science, 1956), pp. 302–3; R. Robson, *The Cotton Industry in Britain* (London: Macmillan, 1957), pp. 332–3.

Figure 7.1 Lancashire's and Japan's cotton piece-good exports, 1911–1930 (millions of yards)

While it would be correct to argue that the immediate postwar years represented a lull in Japan's economic development, it would be wrong to suggest that such a downturn was unique to Japan. By most accounts not only was Britain's economic performance equally uninspiring, it was in all probability worse than that of Japan. In particular British exports suffered dramatically from being in areas that were losing price competitiveness in the international market – such as coal, cotton, shipbuilding, and iron and steel – and supplied markets with limited income inelasticity. In other respects there was evidence of a degree of renewed industrial dynamism in Britain through the heady postwar amalgamation boom, which was coupled with a growing interest in industrial rationalization and scientific management techniques, though there are significant disputes over the actual impact of these movements.[17] In policy terms there was a consensus over the need for a return to the prewar laissez-faire system, with a rapid dismantling of wartime economic controls and protective tariffs, coupled with Britain's announcement in April 1920 of its intention to return to the gold standard. Furthermore the government and most of the business commu-

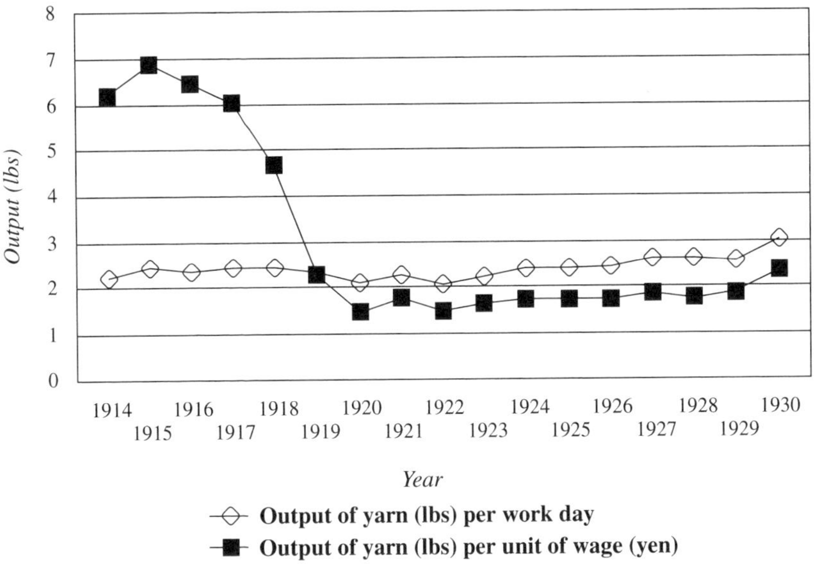

Source: S. Fujino and A. Ono, *Estimates of Long-Term Economic Statistics of Japan since 1866. Volume 11, Textiles* (Tokyo: Toyo Keizai Shinposha, 1979), tables 1, 3, 18, and 27, pp. 239, 241, 257, 266.

Figure 7.2 Changes in labour output in the Japanese spinning sector, 1914–1930

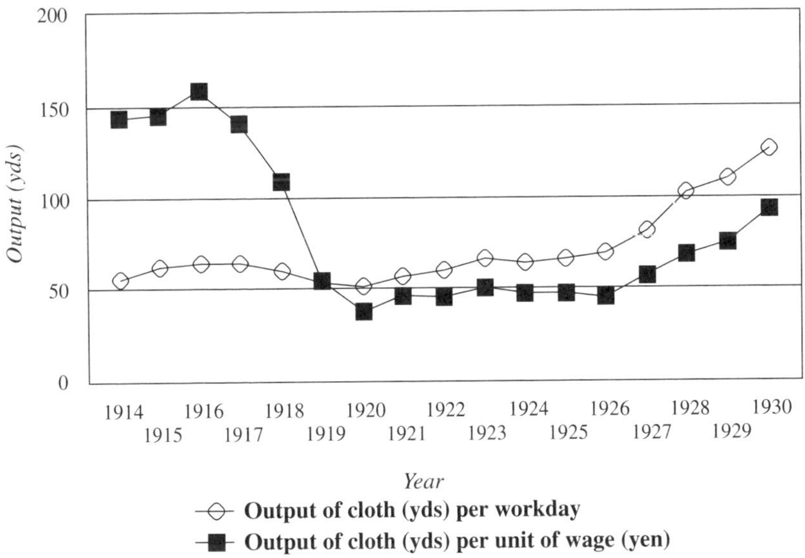

Source: S. Fujino and A. Ono, *Estimates of Long-Term Economic Statistics of Japan since 1866. Volume 11, Textiles* (Tokyo: Toyo Keizai Shinposha, 1979), tables 2, 4, 21, and 30, pp. 240, 242, 260, 269.

Figure 7.3 Changes in labour output in the weaving sector of the spinning industry, 1914–1930

nity sought to distance government from industry, especially in relation to labour questions, although there was a continuing minority interest for the development of protective tariffs.[18]

In aggregate terms most British commentators considered the position of the Japanese economy to be fairly weak. One estimate placed Japan at the bottom of an 18-country list in terms of *per capita* income and capitalization, at around $\frac{1}{10}$ and $\frac{1}{5}$ respectively of Britain's figures.[19] However, British officials argued that it was nevertheless 'safe to say that the general position of Japan is perfectly sound', and that in a comparative sense, in no way did Japan resemble 'the impoverished countries of Europe with a depreciated exchange and unstable Government'. Any current concerns over Japan's financial stability should be compared with the more precarious prewar situation, as exports were now rising faster than imports. These economic gains were in evidence throughout the economy as rising domestic prosperity was creating strong domestic demand, which in part accounted for the tail-off in exports. Indeed these officials argued that much of the pessimism about the Japanese economy stemmed from constant comparison with the wartime boom period.[20] However, they also noted that the main problems within the Japanese economy remained its overdependence upon one export – silk – and the fact that in international terms its prices were too high. In particular domestic price inflation, compared with prewar levels, remained significantly higher than that in Britain and America, and made Japanese exports uncompetitive in the world market.[21]

The major concern for British commentators at this time was the size and rapid growth of Japan's population. Even in the early 1920s few doubted the view of Trevor Johnes, who was teaching at Otaru Commercial College, that population growth necessitated the rapid industrialization of Japan.[22] This problem was intensified by foreign restrictions on Japanese emigration.[23] However, despite the recognition of population pressures within Japan, especially in exacerbating social tensions, few British officials considered these internal strains significant. They argued that incomes were rising and the depressed agricultural prices and high cost of living had not reduced domestic purchasing power.[24] Furthermore they noted the improvements which had taken place in labour conditions, particularly in the modern industrial sector, stemming from the application of rational economic laws, as Japanese employers sought to recruit and retain workers, so that:

> There has been a very great improvement of recent years in the conditions of the textile mills in Japan, and it is important to emphasise this because so many people still imagine that the conditions which prevailed ten to fifteen years ago hold good today. The change has partly been brought about by humanitarian considerations, but chiefly

> because the mills have found it increasingly difficult to get the necessary labour, and girls refused to come to mills where conditions were bad.[25]

In keeping with the perception of improved labour conditions in Japan, officials rejected reports that social unrest in Japan was significant, such as that in *The Times* indicating 'a state of social unrest more common in the West than in the East, against which the Government seems helpless'.[26] British officialdom held the line that events in Japan were being exaggerated in Britain, that there was no popular demand or pressure for universal suffrage, and that unrest stemmed from more pecuniary causes such as the need to lower the cost of living. In line with these Japan-based assessments, 1922 was reported as a quiet year in terms of labour troubles, in part because internal ideological conflicts prevented the unification of the Japanese labour movement.[27]

After initial hiccoughs British officials saw Japanese financial policy as driven by the existing international orthodoxy via retrenchment and balanced budgets. Japan proved slow to undertake such a course and officials lamented the fact that the 1920 budget included provisions for increased military expenditure and taxation, which were out of keeping with assessments that Japan faced significant domestic pressure to reduce the domestic cost of living.[28] Such uncertainty over Japan's ability or commitment to cut expenditure continued throughout the early 1920s. Although it was noticed that as military expenditure declined so too did government spending, official short-term loans and other dubious financial devices – to beleaguered industries – stoked inflation and kept interest rates high throughout the first half of 1922, as expenditure and the national debt continued to rise. Indeed it was only in the summer of 1922 – some two years after Britain – that any major attempt to reduce the money supply was noted. Once this corner had been turned officials approved of the Japanese recognition that their failure to follow America onto the gold standard in 1919 was a mistake, and that unofficial circles were disposed to return to the gold standard as soon as possible. The recent upward appreciation of the yen against the dollar indicated that this was highly possible in the near future. Despite balance of payments difficulties, the Japanese government had not sought to isolate Japan's economy from international conditions by preventing domestic companies from borrowing abroad.[29]

With regard to industrial policy, overall British concerns over the need to reduce tariff barriers focussed considerations in the early 1920s around the protectionist nature of Japanese tariff policy. In essence, and despite some quibbling,[30] the protectionist thrust of Japanese tariff policy appeared clear-cut. A detailed Department of Overseas Trade memorandum argued that Japan's postwar tariff policy was motivated 'with the object of supporting domestic enterprise and protecting home manufactures'. In particular, and despite resistance amongst industrial consumers and the general public, protection would be extended to industries which had expanded during the war, a clear application of infant industries protection after the 'German' model.[31] The geographical scope of the Japanese tariff area would be extended by Korea's incorporation from August 1920.[32] However, despite the general interpretation of Japan as protectionist British officials refused to condemn Japan for the selfishness of its actions; the main criticism was aimed at the negative effect high tariffs had upon Japan's already inflated price structure. Criticism was also extended to the fact that Japan had too many 'subsidies' for too many inefficient producers, which meant that there was no incentive to improve quality and reduce costs.[33]

Despite a general scepticism over the appropriateness of government support for industry, in terms of industrial policy British officials commented early on upon a noticeable mood swing in Japan. In November 1920 Crowe argued that there was a strong belief that there should be greater state direction of industrial policy, and in fact an Economic Investigation Committee had been established to look at this question, although no plans had been elaborated. In relation to prior and current policies, government direction was most noticeable in finance and facilities provided for distressed industries – currently the silk industry.[34] Subsequent manifestations of the government's desire to promote industry were seen in the 1922–23 economic missions to Britain, America, and South America.[35] However, much of the British concern over linkages between government and business stemmed from a fear that such linkages were primarily being used to undermine British political and economic interests in China.[36] Still others were prepared to defend Japan's desire for government–business cooperation as being neither intrinsically unethical nor threatening to British industrial and political interests. Indeed Crowe in particular was at pains to distance Japan's government–business relationships from Britain's continuing wariness of such linkages in prewar Germany, as he argued that Japan's commercial policy was not orchestrated along German lines as 'an organic whole in which every part has a definite aim'. Moreover, while in the past there had been protectionism and some indirect control of industry, to a large extent industrial development – especially that associated with the Sino- and Russo-Japanese wars – had been 'opportunistic'.[37] Such views on the piecemeal nature of government–business cooperation in Japan were supported by the failure of the fragile Japanese banking sector to respond to government encouragement to amalgamate the numerous small banks.[38]

In the immediate postwar years British officials recorded with approval the evident ambition and forward planning of the Japanese business world, particularly in relation to the international economy. Notable features included its search for cheaper foreign capital, the construction of spinning plants in China to circumvent competition from Chinese mills, and the extension of facilities in anticipation of the ban on female night shift working scheduled for the mid-1920s.[39] However, in most other respects Japanese industrial development was seen as being both weak and backward. In November 1920 Charles Eliot, the British Ambassador in Tokyo, could state that Japan did not pose a commercial threat comparable with that of Germany.[40] In particular small-scale firms acted as a drag on the economy and were feather-bedded by an inappropriate tariff structure, while Japanese firms were poorly managed and tended more to 'reckless speculation' than sound economic planning. Indeed given these overall weaknesses it was suggested that government–business cooperation was not a sign of forward dynamism but, rather, underscored the immaturity of the Japanese economy. Such were the concerns over structural weaknesses that officials approved increased concentration as something in keeping with government policy, and not as some sinister anti-competitive force.[41]

However, despite structural problems the major issue facing Japanese industrial development was identified as a failure to address the question of price and wage inflation in a low productivity economy. The comparative stickiness of prices meant that it was difficult for wages to fall into line with current levels of productivity, which would enable Japanese goods to compete in the world market, since: 'wages remain high and overhead charges are disproportionate to industrial requirements. These two factors, combined with relatively low efficiency, militate against an active export trade, which is Japan's most urgent need'.[42] Even so, Japanese wages were extremely low by British standards. One cited estimate put female daily wages at around 20 *sen* per day, whereas a similar British worker would receive over ten times this amount.[43] Despite this, recent wage rises coupled with still relatively low levels of labour productivity neutralized much of Japan's industrial potential.

In contrast with the negative portrayal of Japanese industry as a whole, by the early 1920s British officials were impressed by the Japanese cotton industry, as indicated by the recovery of yarn exports, and indications of a decline in wages. Moreover the cotton industry itself was at the forefront of attempts to increase labour productivity via improved labour conditions.[44] Interestingly, these observations were shared by many British commentators who had more direct experience of the Japanese cotton industry. In November 1920 Sir J.S. Rhodes, who had recently returned from East Asia, warned the Manchester Chamber of Commerce of Japanese mercantile ambition, while in 1921 Trevor Johnes stated that cotton was 'one of Japan's most formidable enterprises'.[45] Although positive in their assessments of the Japanese cotton industry, however, there was little to suggest that the Japanese cotton industry offered, or was developing, an industrial model which was significantly different from that of Lancashire. Indeed it would be fair to say that warnings over the potential of the Japanese cotton industry reflected the belief that it was bucking the trend over the imbalance between wages and labour productivity. Its solutions to internal efficiency problems were not novel, but were simply more rigorous than in other parts of Japanese industry.

Nonetheless, despite such positive portrayals in the immediate postwar years Lancashire tended to dismiss Japanese competition. The prime reason for this was that while Lancashire recovered some of the export trade it had lost during the First World War, difficulties in the Japanese cotton industry meant that it did not exceed its 1918 export peak until 1924. This represented something of a reversal of Lancashire's wartime fears over Japanese export penetration of the China market, and Lancashire's possible inability to compete against Japan's low wage industry.[46] By the early 1920s the slump in Japanese exports – in part due to appreciation of the yen but also because of a decline in labour productivity – led to a discounting of Japanese competition. Optimism returned in Lancashire with the belief that foreign competition posed no obvious threat, as the Japanese, American, and Italian cotton industries were all fully occupied in supplying domestic demand and had little spare capacity to supply overseas markets.[47] Further, Japanese competition had so abated that it was widely believed that Japan had squandered the opportunity of the Great War. In February 1920 E.F. Stockton, President of the Manchester Chamber of Commerce, boldly condemned the Japanese 'for instead of doing themselves credit they have done their trade enormous injury . . . they have so often failed to deliver the standard quality for which they have contracted', and he concluded that in contrast to the wartime view of the advantage of cheap labour '. . . the sweated condition of labour in Japan is not a real advantage to them'.[48] These views were not significantly out of keeping with those of British officials who had no experience of Japan, but who had witnessed the wartime expansion of Japanese cotton textile exports. In a similar vein Thomas M. Ainscough, Senior British Trade Commissioner for India, told the Manchester Chamber of Commerce that Japanese exports to India had reached their high-water mark and were now in decline.[49] Although in retrospect this initial postwar response appears complacent, it should be noted that many of the indictments of the Japanese cotton industry – particularly in terms of labour productivity – were true. Indeed similar conclusions were drawn in 1921 by the US Tariff Board, which also concluded that Japanese cotton textile exports had peaked, and that the industry was going through a process of reorganization.[50]

The postwar reversal of Lancashire's position on Japanese competition did not mean it was unaware of the deterioration in its own exports. However, this postwar decline was mainly ascribed to external factors. Lancashire condemned the high levels of postwar domestic taxation, as well as slow growth in overseas demand due to a decline in *per capita* cotton textile consumption, most noticeable in India.[51] However, it was the growth of 'native' cotton industries – such as in India and China – behind protective tariffs, which was seen as the biggest threat to Lancashire's export trade. The 1921 Indian tariff increase was roundly attacked, as not only dislocating world trade but also being a direct threat to the future of the Lancashire cotton industry.[52]

Still, despite some of the ostrich-like pronouncements on the changed world market and Japanese competition, even in the early 1920s Lancashire showed a degree of flexibility, indicating that it was conscious of changed market conditions. In an attempt to circumvent Asian competition in coarse goods Lancashire was already producing finer yarns and cloths for export, as it was noted that the Egyptian spinning section – which produced the finest quality yarns – was performing much better than the American section, which spun coarser yarns.[53] Furthermore, since the 1920 peak in wages, there had been significant declines in both nominal and real incomes amongst cotton operatives, indicating that the workforce was prepared to exhibit wage restraint in order to keep the Lancashire cotton industry competitive in world markets (see Figures 7.4–7.5).

In essence Lancashire did correctly perceive the difficulties of the Japanese cotton industry in the early 1920s. However, it appears that a certain lassitude still existed within Lancashire when it came to developing a fuller understanding of Japan's competitive potential. In part this reflected a certain generalized antipathy on the part of British industrialists towards Japan. In a tour of British industries in 1920 Crowe was shocked by the degree of hostility towards Japan. He noted that in 1911, despite substantial Japanese tariff increases, there was still a large body of business opinion favourable to Japan. However, in 1920 'there seemed to be not only distrust but dislike'. In his opinion this was a reaction to Japan's wartime commercial gains, and its reputation for sharp commercial practice – which he unequivocally rejected. Nevertheless such hostility was of deep concern because it was 'not good business to despise one's competitor'.[54] Furthermore, the combination of indifference and antipathy appears to have partly undermined Lancashire's project to investigate developments in various East Asian cotton industries – a particularly important failure given the more positive assessments which stemmed from direct observation. A mission first proposed in February 1919, and described as of the utmost importance, was quietly abandoned in 1921 because of disagreements between the Treasury and Manchester Chamber of Commerce on scale, cost and the extent to which each body would fund such a mission.[55]

To the nadir of the Great Depression, 1924–1930

The Kanto earthquake of September 1923 not only caused substantial economic damage,[56] but also epitomized a psychological paralysis which appeared to persist in economic management for the remainder of the

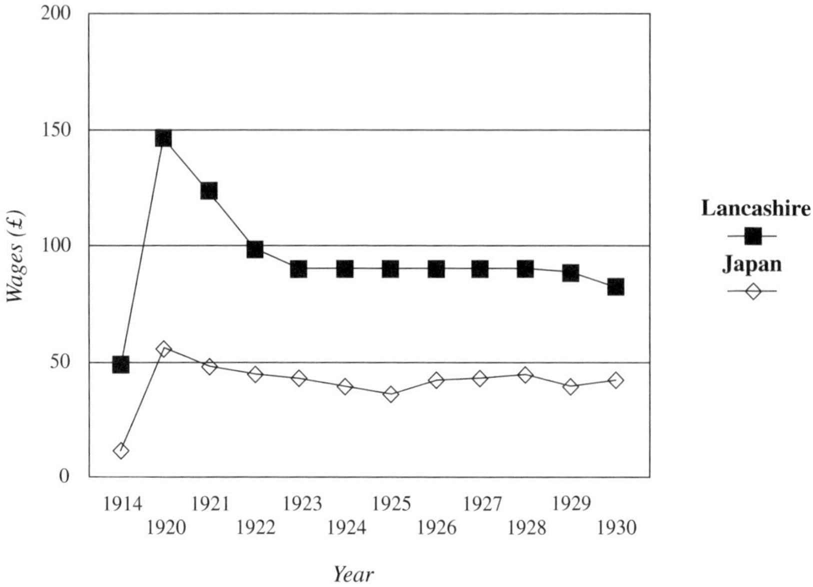

Sources: A.L. Chapman, *Wages and Salaries in the United Kingdom, 1920–1938* (Cambridge: Cambridge University Press, 1953), table 47, p. 105; *Statistical Abstract of the United Kingdom* (London: HMSO, various years): S. Fujino and A. Ono, *Estimates of Long-Term Economic Statistics of Japan since 1866. Volume 11, Textiles* (Tokyo: Toyo Keizai Shinposha, 1979), table 34, p. 278.

Figure 7.4 Annual nominal wages for operatives in the Lancashire and Japanese cotton spinning industries, 1914–1930 (sterling)

1920s. There followed the post-earthquake fiscal laxity, the 1927 Financial Panic, fiscal retrenchment in preparation for return to the gold standard, and finally the Hamaguchi cabinet's decision to return to gold after the onset of the world Depression. These vicissitudes were compounded by persistent structural difficulties. One continuing problem was population growth, as the capacity of manufacturing industry to absorb agricultural labour was essentially limited. This curb on rural out-migration threatened to exacerbate the already depressed conditions in parts of the countryside, and reinforced the dualistic income structure of the modern and traditional sectors.[57] So endemic were these difficulties that it is argued that the 1927 Financial Panic played a central role in Japan's failure to recover from the postwar depression, which 'lasted throughout the 1920s until the world depression of 1930, when it got worse'.[58]

However, this 'doom and gloom' portrait of the Japanese economy needs some qualification. In terms of growth there was a recovery during the 1920s which significantly reversed the early 1920s' stagnation. Fierce internal competition ensured that the price mechanism had a positive effect, and

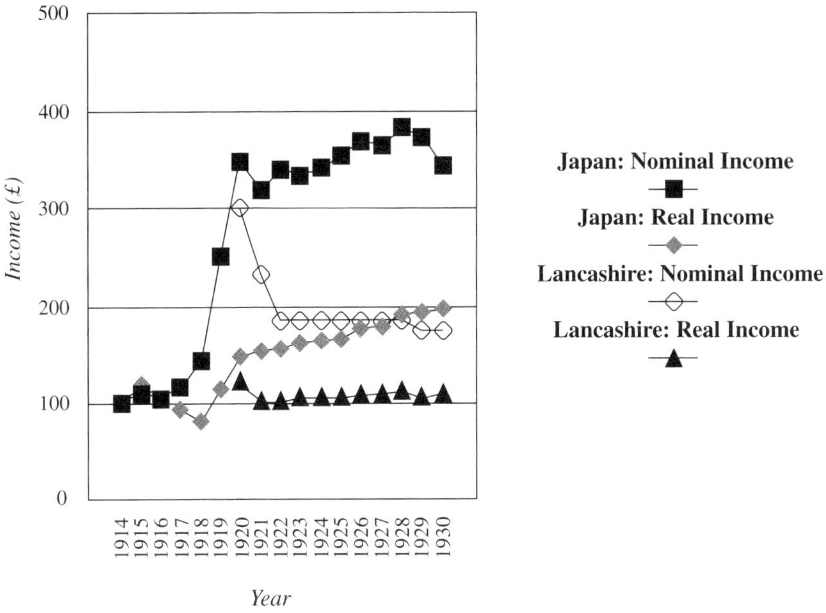

Sources: *Statistical Abstract of the United Kingdom* (London: HMSO, various years); *The Cotton Year Book* (Bradford: Textile Mercury, 1938); S. Fujino and A. Ono, *Estimates of Long-Term Economic Statistics of Japan since 1866. Volume 11, Textiles* (Tokyo: Toyo Keizai Shinposha, 1979), table 39, p. 278; T. Uyeda, *The Small Industries of Japan: Their Growth and Development* (Oxford: Oxford University Press, 1938), p. 298.

Figure 7.5 Lancashire and Japanese female operatives' nominal and real income, 1914–1930 (1914 = 100)

production was increasing through productivity gains across several sectors of the economy. Furthermore, the 1927 Financial Panic operated as a significant stimulus towards industrial reform, underlining *zaibatsu* competence, facilitating further *zaibatsu* expansion, and pushing many other firms into a closer look at rationalization. In this context exports surged from the mid-1920s and there was a significant narrowing of the trade gap. Moreover, despite social problems it was a period of rising real incomes and improved conditions for most industrial workers, particularly in *zaibatsu* firms.[59]

Although overall economic mismanagement is integral to assessments of Japan's economic development, as noted by Johnson, the mid-1920s also witnessed the arrival of industrial policy to enable the state to force the pace of industrial development. The Ministry of Commerce and Industry (MCI) was created in 1925, with the explicit goal of controlling competition, improving management, and creating economies of scale. The Export Association and Major Export Industries Laws of 1925 aimed at increasing profitability amongst small manufacturers by inducing cartelization to reduce cut-throat competition and exploitation by Japan's monopolistic trading companies. Subsequent initiatives aimed at improving industrial rationalization and assessing economic capacity in case of total war. However, the victories of the MCI were somewhat limited, as the voluntary nature of the export guilds are seen as a failure even by the champions of Japan's industrial policy.[60] Indeed the main state support for industry was through an upward revision of tariffs in 1926 – particularly in support of heavy industry – supported by more subtle policies such as a committee to promote the purchase of domestically manufactured goods.[61]

For the cotton industry, the mid- to late 1920s represents a period of significant industrial advance as leading firms were able to use their organizational structure to introduce far-reaching reforms in production technology. The rapid conversion of leading firms to new technologies stemmed from a complex interaction of internal and external factors. Aside from the profit motive, employers were faced with the need to maintain labour productivity once female night shift working was abolished in 1929, the fears raised by the 1927 Financial Panic, and the threat of emergent Chinese competition. However, one of Japan's significant advantages was continued advances within the Japanese textile machinery industry, particularly with the introduction of the impressive Toyoda automatic loom in 1924.[62] Although Japanese wage rates remained low by British standards, overall incomes and conditions continued to improve, while management continued to seek more cost-effective ways of deploying its increasingly expensive labour force.[63] Still, new technologies enabled massive productivity gains in both spinning and weaving sectors. In consequence Japanese exports of cotton piece-goods surged throughout the latter half of the 1920s.

For the British economy the mid- to late 1920s proved an undistinguished period in terms of performance and management. Problems for many staple exports, it is argued, were exacerbated by the decision to return to the gold standard in 1925 at an overvalued exchange rate, which in many ways epitomized Britain's undiminished commitment to economic 'orthodoxy'. In other respects there was substantial growth among the new industries, even if these remained small in terms of the overall economy.[64] For the Lancashire cotton industry the latter 1920s was a period of acute concern, as exports of cotton piece-goods began a steep and unrelenting decline from 1927. Recognition of these problems led to attempts to reorganize the industry, although some have argued that such attempts were hindered because they were primarily aimed at price support and because of union resistance. Nonetheless, there is some clear evidence that at the level of the firm, particularly in terms of reducing capacity, efforts were being made to reorientate the industry towards a more competitive world market.[65]

British officials continued to emphasize the progress within the Japanese economy already noted in the early 1920s. There had been a steep decline in the trade imbalance, which continued up to 1930, and imports were increasingly made up of raw materials and machinery, underscoring the progress of industrialization. Exports – particularly silk – had been stimulated by the post-earthquake depreciation of the yen, which also impeded imports of nonessential items. Rising real incomes provided a boost to manufacturers so that 'exotic' luxuries were now everyday goods, and post-1922 there had been a beneficial decline in domestic prices.[66] However, from the mid-1920s onwards officials also began to suggest more forcefully that all was not well in the Japanese economy, especially in relation to the world economy. They argued that exports were still too dependent upon silk and cotton goods, and expansion derived too much from palliatives such as a depreciating yen. The post-earthquake rise in the trade deficit indicated that prices were too high for domestic levels of efficiency, and in this regard the collapse of the yen was 'presumably a symptom of an unhealthy economic condition'.[67] In many respects the emergence of such negative assessments reflected British exasperation at Japan's tardiness in following Britain's return to the gold standard in 1925, and the 1927 Financial Panic for at least two years inspired officials' reporting to recast much of Japan's previous development in a more negative light, despite their own observations to the contrary.[68]

In contrast to the early 1920s British officials now noted Japanese concerns about the possible negative impact of rising population. However, even though this thesis was gaining international respectability, and officials accepted that this would lead to increased imports of foodstuffs,[69] they argued that rising population was not in itself to be feared. Indeed it was argued that population growth created substantial benefits, as growing domestic demand was a significant stimulant for Japanese industry. 'It must be remembered that, even in depressed times, the domestic market grows at a rapid rate, owing to increasing population and, in the case of many staple commodities, increasing consumption per head.'[70]

Similarly, given the emphasis on rising incomes, officials continued to underplay employment dualism and suggested that there was no evidence that real incomes would contract due to population pressure. One reason for the underplaying of social tensions was the awareness that in comparative terms Japan was in an enviable situation as 'the proportion of unemployed to the total population is far below that seen in Europe'.[71] However, by the mid-1920s, social tensions resulting from economic problems were increasingly noted, and other commentators began to record significant wage differentials between large- and small-scale firms.[72]

Despite the strains within Japanese fiscal policy British officials showed a high degree of sympathy towards Japan's overall plight. However, when it came to the nuts and bolts of policy, even before the 1927 Financial Panic, officials remained sceptical of Japan's unconventional policies such as the managed float of the yen, which was compounded by the slowness of the business community to write off postwar speculative losses.[73] Nevertheless, any return to fiscal rectitude was undermined by the Financial Panic, as both government and financial institutions were berated for incompetence: '. . . financial difficulties which though in part attributable to causes beyond her control, appear on the whole to be due to the fact that the financial organisation of the country is not properly adjusted to its general economic and political condition.'

Both government and business had been slow to react to the crisis, and their solution was equally ineffective, so that 'even when one makes allowance for abnormal conditions, it must be admitted that the machine has of late too frequently failed to function'.[74] Indeed, the British reaction to the Panic was so extreme that evidence that the events of April 1927 were not cataclysmic failed to modify the established perception of a malfunctioning machine. For example, the fact that the big banks not only survived but enhanced their positions was seen as a secondary consequence of the Panic, and not as an indication of these banks' inherent strength. The same officials who berated Japan in 1928 for incompetence were simultaneously recording that 'from a purely financial point of view conditions may be regarded as sounder than at any time since 1920',[75] which, given the rapid recovery, indicated the localized nature of the Panic rather then endemic incompetence. So deep-rooted was this perception that only the onset of a far graver calamity, the world Depression, facilitated abandonment of the previous charge.[76]

After the earthquake industrial promotion had less to do with innovation than the tried and trusted path of protectionism and export promotion. Despite greater public support and industrial protection, and some more subtle forms of protection through import licensing, until the mid-1920s officials argued that the Japanese government remained reluctant to extend such methods,[77] and by extension Japan's commitment to free trade. They claimed that such initiatives stemmed more from a desire to reduce the trade deficit than protect industry *per se*, since from mid-1924 the government had simply decided upon: 'a policy of reducing imports . . . and successive steps have been taken to check the import of foreign goods of a non-essential nature, to increase the consumption of Japanese manufactures, and to extend the sale of Japanese products abroad.'[78]

However, the 1926 tariff revision rendered such a sympathetic treatment of tariff policy increasingly tenuous. Officials related how the pre-1926 tariff schedule was incompatible with Japan's continued industrial development, as it was: 'considered by the Japanese Government to have become totally unsuited to prevailing conditions, whether viewed from the standpoint of important industries or from that of equilibrium between specific and *ad valorem* rates'. Other measures followed, and despite the formation of groups to support tariff reductions, officials stated that little would come of these movements; even their supporters did not want to abandon protection for infant industries.[79] Ironically enough, despite the ongoing conviction that Japan was protectionist, the events of 1930 led to a reversal of this assessment. It was argued in 1930 that in terms of import duties to import values, the Japanese 'tariff wall' was not high. However, such statistical observations ran counter to the thrust of pressures within Japan, as the immediate response of the iron and chemical industries to the Depression was to push for increased protection from foreign competition.[80]

In contrast it proved difficult for British officials to adduce any novel use of the government–business relationship during the latter half of the 1920s. Officials saw nothing original in the recommendations of the 1924 Imperial Economic Council, while even pressure to consolidate the banking system was stymied by business resistance.[81] Other more novel features, such as the 1925 Export Guilds Law, and Guilds of Manufacturers of Staple Exports Law, were treated with caution; these bodies simply extended existing legislation, and much would depend upon enforcement and operation.[82] Relief measures for small manufacturers during the Depression were 'palliatives', while the introduction of an export credit scheme was simply in keeping with the characteristics of the English Export Credit scheme.[83] Where genuine novelty was perceived it was seen as a second-best measure to address pressing industrial shortcomings. The establishment of a joint state/private purchasing and marketing organization for the iron and steel industry in 1926 was not a cause for optimism, but a response to endemic problems within the industry. Similarly a proposal for government regulation of the fertilizer industry, through controls on price and distribution, was not seen as significant.[84] While it could be argued that many of these schemes were too piecemeal to be labelled industrial policy, much of the official disregard of such developments appears to stem from ideological considerations, since Japanese criticism of the term 'rationalization' – a new name for old remedies – was used to condemn it for failing to address the problems of the Depression.[85]

Like many Japanese assessments, British officials emphasized the inherent fragility of Japanese industry, particularly compared with western standards of work organization and management. Much of this inefficiency stemmed from the relative cheapness of Japanese labour which, it was argued, acted as a significant disincentive to the introduction of modern labour-saving technology.[86] Furthermore industry was speculative and short-termist in relation to profits, features which manifested themselves in a failure to write off postwar speculative losses and the pushing up of interest rates. However, the central problem remained the high level of Japanese wages in relation to levels of efficiency. In fact the position was worsening, as wage rises were reported for early 1926, and remained difficult until the late 1920s, as prices did not fall as fast as those in Britain and America, while labour remained relatively inefficient. Even with the onset of the Depression, officials suggested that manufacturers were cautious about cutting real incomes, as they 'had hoped to be able to maintain the wage level until retail prices, always slow to respond in Japan, had followed wholesale prices'.[87]

Despite the general criticism about wage levels and efficiency many officials conceded that significant improvements were taking place in certain sectors. It was suggested that the post-earthquake crisis would be overcome, and that there was pace and variety in Japanese industrial development.[88] As the decade progressed, officials were at pains to point out the achievements of Japanese industry, and quick to recognise the limited impact of the Financial Panic on industry. Despite production curtailments the Panic had not resulted in a decline in aggregate production as 'capacity is being constantly increased at a higher rate than the rate of restriction'.[89] Indeed, such were the improvements that an explicit warning was issued to British manufacturers that Japanese competition would emerge in markets and products with which it had not hitherto been associated:

> There is no doubt, however, that she must be considered henceforth not only as an importer of manufactured products but also as a potential competitor in other markets, particularly though not exclusively in those where she has the advantage of propinquity. It behoves British manufacturers and exporters who are losing their export trade to Japan to bear these facts in mind, and to remember that Japan has already, in output of certain important commodities, developed from an importer, through an intermediate state of production for domestic needs, into an exporter. The cotton industry is the most striking example of this evolution, the woollen industry promises to furnish another, and incidental references in this report will show that the same tendency is to be discovered in other directions.[90]

Even the Depression could not shake officials from their perception of the rapid strides made by Japanese industry in the 1920s. Current industrial stagnation was due to external causes and not to any fundamental weakness of organization: 'Indeed it is probable that her industrial efficiency is at a higher point than it has ever reached before.' Furthermore, certain industries were updating technology or undertaking such improvements once business conditions picked up.[91]

In the second half of the 1920s, British officials put forward an increasingly sophisticated picture of Japanese industrial structures. The *zaibatsu* and large-scale firms had always received due attention as the most modern sectors of the economy. As in the financial sector, it was noted that large-scale firms were barely affected by the 1927 Financial Panic, since 'Exporters and importers of good standing had no difficulty in settling their exchange requirements, and merchants and manufacturers on a large scale were not much inconvenienced'.[92] However, in other respects the Panic raised the question of the negative impact of economic concentration within the Japanese economy, not through failings on the part of individual firms themselves as individual units, but through concentration and cartelization pushing up prices to the detriment as the economy as a whole. The increase in price support arrangements was noted from late 1925,[93] and such concerns post-Panic manifested themselves in ambivalence towards the degree of economic control of *zaibatsu* like Mitsubishi and Mitsui: 'The advantages of unified control over a number of inter-related enterprises are manifest; but such combinations, precisely because they are strong and far-reaching, tend to acquire an influence which is open to serious objections.'[94]

The criticism of industrial concentration may have reflected a classical antipathy to excessive economic control, but it also stemmed from increased emphasis upon the importance of small-scale manufacturers within the Japanese economy. In contrast to the early 1920s, officials now put a more positive slant upon the dynamism and importance of smaller firms, particularly in terms of their capacity to identify and respond to growing domestic demand. This happened despite many small manufacturers being hit hard by the withdrawal of credit facilities from smaller local banks during the Panic.[95]

In contrast with this fluctuating appreciation of Japanese industry, the mid-1920s onward was a period of spectacular achievement for the Japanese cotton industry. From around 1924 officials recorded its successive achievements, noting that despite a decline in labour productivity, the extension of integrated spinning and weaving operation meant that piece-good exports had actually increased and were more than holding their own against British, Indian and American goods in various East African markets.[96] Despite occasional suggestions that all was not well in the industry, officials were more likely to record Japan's ability to circumvent short-term overseas market and internal difficulties – namely the appreciation of the yen, the Financial Panic, and the abolition of female night shift working – as both production and exports continued to increase. In 1930 officials predicted that the Depression would actually intensify Japanese competition, as the exclusion of Japanese goods from Indian and Chinese markets – due to tariff increases and political disruptions – would lead Japan to seek new markets and improve the quality of its exports.[97]

Although Japan's export performance could clearly serve as a proxy for overall productivity, in the late 1920s officials were at pains to point out that it resulted from improvements within the industry, and was not the result of aggregate internal and external economic factors or unfair competitive methods. W.B. Cunningham's *Report on the Cotton Spinning and Weaving Industry in Japan, 1925–1926*, published in 1927, underlined the dynamism of the industry, and also the diversity of its constituent parts, namely a dominant spinning sector and a more heterogeneous weaving sector.[98] Subsequently other officials argued for an improvement in finished products, and a significant degree of rationalization through the introduction of labour-saving technology. In fact the Depression led to a redoubling of these trends, as every effort was made to increase efficiency through introducing more new technology and some ruthless wage cutting in early 1930.[99] The overall picture generated from official reports was of an efficiently organized industry, but one that did not possess any innovative organizational features.[100] Officials rapidly identifed the improved competitiveness of the industry during the late 1920s, which was closely related to an upswing in labour productivity and efficiency in the weaving and spinning industry.

While relative export performance may have allowed for some dismissal of Japanese competition in the early 1920s, from the mid-1920s the same criterion allowed Lancashire no such luxury. Lancashire's post-1927 export catastrophe had to contend with a doubling of Japanese cotton exports between 1923 and 1929. However, despite these divergent export trends many in Lancashire remained reluctant to concede that Japan posed a singular competitive threat. In 1925 C.W. Macara, a former president of the Federation of Master Cotton Spinners' and Manufacturers' Associations, stated that current and future developments in Japan posed no threat to Lancashire.[101] In the same year Crowe told the Manchester Chamber of Commerce that Japan was suffering not only from Chinese competition but also from wage inflation and high capital costs for land and machinery.[102] Meanwhile the joint committee of the Department of Overseas Trade and Manchester Chamber of Commerce on East Africa reported that there was no serious cause for concern over the future threat of Japanese competition in the region.[103] Over the next few years Japanese competition could still be ascribed to temporary advantages, such as the depreciation of the yen or the exceptionally low price of Indian raw cotton.[104] The final 'evidence' that Japan could only compete in the world market because of abnormal factors was the sustained charge that its cotton industry was heavily subsidized. This was the one false perception that British officials consistently tried to refute, so that even after dismissing Japanese competition Crowe was at pains to discredit to his Manchester audience the view that Japan did not run a commercial cotton industry.[105] Further, even if Japanese competition was increasing, Lancashire tried to draw comfort from the claim that its goods did not compete with those of Japan, and for most of the 1920s it insisted that Japanese goods competed more with Indian goods in the Indian market.[106] The validity of such appraisals was reinforced by the fact that as late as April 1928, Cunningham could still emphasize the pessimism existing within the Japanese cotton industry.[107]

Parallel with Lancashire's desire to discount Japan was its continued insistence that Lancashire's failings resulted from external circumstances. By extension only external solutions could alleviate Lancashire's current difficulties. Many of these problems, it was claimed, originated in Britain, including the 1926 General Strike, high taxation, and as late as 1928 the high interest rate charges in Britain.[108] However, the main concern was postwar disruption to the world economy. Proponents of this thesis argued that losses in various Asian markets – especially India and China – were due primarily to political and economic instability, and the rise of protected 'native' cotton industries, which accounted for most of Lancashire's 'lost' prewar trade.[109] From such arguments it was not illogical for Sir Ernest Thompson, President of the Manchester Chamber of Commerce, to claim in 1928 that once world demand picked up, annual exports of *c.*6000 million yards would be secure for the next six to seven years,[110] a figure far above the industry's post-1918 performance.

Given the continued post-1927 decline of Lancashire's piece-good exports in the face of near continuous Japanese advance, by the late 1920s it became virtually impossible for Lancashire to ignore its lack of competitiveness vis-à-vis Japan. The most noticeable impact of the export figures was on the Lancashire decline thesis. During the transition period Daniels, Jewkes, and the Ellinger brothers not only abandoned arguments that Lancashire's problems resulted from external factors, but also began to articulate more thoroughly Lancashire's failings, and, increasingly, to emphasize the causes of Japan's success. These British-based studies were reinforced by a number of studies conducted in Japan. The importance of Cunningham's 1927 publication was acknowledged by authorities such as Barnard Ellinger, and other commentators such as Freda Utley.[111] Equally important were the studies of Arno S. Pearse and Utley herself, which provided many much-needed factual details on the relative efficiency of the Lancashire and Japanese cotton industries. In his preface to Pearse's *Cotton Industry of Japan and China*, Frank Holroyd, President of the International Federation of Master Cotton Spinners' and Manufacturers' Associations, lauded the authoritativeness of Pearse's Japan-researched figures as proof of the competitiveness of the Japanese cotton industry.[112] Utley used her own Japanese research to refute in the *Manchester Commercial Guardian* the views of those who suggested that Japan's cheaper labour gave no advantage in production costs over Lancashire.[113] The importance of these Japan-based studies is shown by the fact that in 1928 Sir K.D. Stewart, a leading cotton merchant recently returned from Japan, still found it difficult to refute British-researched figures that purported to support such a view, since his only justification – which had no factual back-up – was first-hand experience of the efficiency of Japanese cotton mills.[114]

Even if Lancashire was willing to concede Japan's competitiveness, the root cause still had to be determined. By the late 1920s a large body of opinion believed that Japan had gained a decisive advantage through industry-level cooperation and vertical integration at the company level,[115] but not all commentators were overly impressed by the notion that such structures were inherently more efficient. Like a lot of officials, many cotton men – particularly merchants – disputed the efficiency of Japan's mass purchase of raw cotton and mass marketing methods. This general predilection for equating systemic organization with efficiency can be seen in Utley's championing of the vertically integrated American cotton industry over Lancashire. In contrast Pearse, who was later to take on board many of the organizational arguments, was on a tour of America impressed less with vertical organization and more with flexible labour practices.[116]

The central debate about Japanese competitiveness had less to do with organizational structures and was more concerned with the question of whether or not Japanese labour was more productive than in Lancashire. Even until the late 1920s, with the surge in Japanese exports many Lancashire-based experts denied that Japanese labour was more efficient. In 1928 John H. Grey argued that low wages and labour organization gave Japan no advantage in production costs over Lancashire.[117] This probably marks the final stand of those who continued to suggest that Japan's cheaper wage rates could not compensate it for its lower levels of productivity. Indeed it appears that Grey was already aware that labour productivity was improving in Japan, as his conclusion drew heavily upon evidence of continued wage inflation in Japan which rendered efficiency improvements amongst Japanese operatives less effective. To an extent this indicates how greatly the overall picture of national wage inflation influenced Lancashire's understanding of the Japanese cotton industry, so that it was possible to dismiss changes within a specific industry. However, it would be wrong to suggest that Lancashire-based commentators were prejudiced in their use of such data; within a year Grey accepted that because of relative changes in wage rates, Japanese labour was more efficient than Lancashire's.

The critical sea change in Lancashire's understanding of Japanese labour efficiency arose with the publication of Pearse's investigation into Japanese labour costs in 1929. Although no one in Lancashire had ever doubted the relative cheapness of Japanese wage rates, Pearse's conclusion left little doubt that Japanese labour was also more productive than in Lancashire. Indeed Holroyd made an explicit note of this point in his preface to the report, pointing out that while the average Lancashire weaver tended 4 power looms the average Japanese weaver tended 5.5 power looms.[118] Once Lancashire began to accept that Japanese labour productivity was comparable with Lancashire and increasing then by definition the Japanese cotton industry was more competitive than Lancashire. In fact after considering Japan's group ethos and the bulk purchase of raw cotton and mass marketing, Pearse ranked lower labour costs as Japan's other major advantage over Lancashire, while Utley drew a similar conclusion after her visit to Japan in 1929.[119] Similarly, once Japanese advantages in both labour productivity and costs were accepted then Lancashire had little choice but to address this question; in 1930 Barnard and Hugh Ellinger, both experts on the cotton industry, argued that there needed to be an immediate downward revision in Lancashire's wage rates.[120]

Although by 1930 it would be fair to say that Lancashire realized it was increasingly less competitive than Japan, there is evidence that Lancashire was responding to this loss of competitiveness. In the first place, despite criticisms of labour inefficiency, it was clear that because of wage restraint on the factory floor throughout the latter half of the 1920s, Lancashire's competitive position had been sustained by the continued stagnation of nominal and real incomes. Furthermore, even though the pace of industrial reform has been criticized, there was evidence that Lancashire was responding with greater urgency in the mid-1920s to the threat of Japanese competition and the emergence of protected 'native' cotton industries. Many commentators argued that Lancashire should switch from coarse cloth production to finer cloths where Japanese competition was still less pronounced, and indeed during this period the trend was towards finer cloths even in the American section.[121] However, what is equally noticeable is that while many within the cotton industry were prepared to fight, given the decline in investment from around 1928–29, others had already tacitly concluded that the most rational economic course for Lancashire was to flee.[122]

Conclusion

In general British officials and commentators provided both an accurate and positive interpretation of Japan's overall economic situation, from which the portrayal was one of economic growth and diversification yet without any significant social strains. These assessments are certainly in keeping with most post-1945 evaluations of the Japanese economy in the 1920s, although there would be greater dissent over the role of economic factors in domestic social and political tensions. However, it is probable that the British rejection of a fragile social structure and the question of economic causation was more accurate, since most post-1945 commentators have in effect been reinterpreting the 1920s in order to explain Japan's social and political crisis of the 1930s. Indeed while the British did note some potentially serious negative constraints within the Japanese economy – an export structure dominated by silk and high population growth – overall these were not seen as being of immediate concern since they were clearly contradicted by rising real incomes, relatively low rates of unemployment, and a lack of the impoverishment that has become the stock characterization of interwar rural Japan. Similarly the British recognition of rising real incomes allowed commentators to emphasize the role of increasing domestic demand in Japanese economic development, and escape the slanted interpretation which cannot square increased production for the domestic market with arguments for continued urban and rural impoverishment. While tensions were noted, in many respects it is fair to say that British commentators had a rather better understanding of Japan's overall economic position, an understanding that reflected a much longer time-frame on Japan's economic trajectory, more valid comparisons with similar countries, and the advantage of not having to use the 1920s to justify the 1930s. So much more valid was this perspective that British commentators were not averse to criticizing Japanese contemporaries, arguing that Japan's post-First World War pessimism stemmed from an all too frequent comparison with the wartime boom period which overplayed the problems of the 1920s, rather than drawing on an accurate comparison with the more difficult economic conditions prior to 1914.

In contrast to overall economic performance, Japan's economic policy and policy management throughout the interwar years remains one of the most contentious issues in Japanese economic and political history. Consequently how one currently interprets Japan's policy performance for the 1920s will determine how one regards the contemporary British interpretation. In regard to the latter, British officials and commentators consistently saw Japanese economic policy as both muddled and non-innovative. In particular British officials considered Japanese economic management to be incompetent, because it strayed from financial orthodoxy. Budgets remained unbalanced; there was an excess of fiscal expedients; Japan failed to re-establish itself on the gold standard; and tariffs were used too freely to support inefficient producers. Japanese flirtation with industrial policy was noted, but officials saw little evidence that it existed in practice. In effect ad hoc measures of business promotion – principally through protectionism – were being conceptually systematized under the catch-all of 'industrial policy', which may or may not be admirable, but was hardly a radical departure from established European patterns of state intervention in industry.

Although few would deny that the 1920s was an era of industrial growth and diversification, the question of industrial development showed the British to be both accurate and insightful. The British presentation of stylized strengths and weaknesses, as part of the contours of industrialization, was no mere case of orientalist stereotyping, as it represented an active engagement in the question of Japanese industrialization. The key area is the British assessment of the Japanese cotton industry. Easy as it is to focus on those who only belatedly recognized the threat of Japanese competition, it would be as well to consider the far more accurate British delineation of trends within the Japanese cotton industry. Overall, from the post-Armistice period many Japan-based commentators emphasized the competitive threat and long-term ambition of the Japanese cotton industry. However, the British also correctly identified numerous problems, particularly in labour productivity, which did undermine Japanese efficiency until the mid-1920s. Once these problems were addressed, the British were quick to record improvements in productivity and production technology, and created the dominant academic interpretation of the Japanese cotton industry which slowly penetrated business opinion. Indeed in many respects the British portrayal of the 1920s has one feature which is consistently underemphasized in postwar accounts: the question of Japanese national and entrepreneurial ambition. At times this could be caricatured as over-ambition vis-à-vis heavy industry. Yet Sansom and Macrae's 1928 warning of widening Japanese industrial competition is a reflection of a deep understanding of Japanese industrial ambition as much as a hard-headed analysis of industrial trends. Despite this, British reporting was continually peppered with a negative caricature of Japanese industry, portraying it as weak, organizationally and technologically backward, poorly managed, and on far too small a scale – in essence barely one step away from Marx's pejorative Asiatic Mode of Production. Even so many of these criticisms were valid, as the mighty cotton industry was dominated by small-scale manufacturers, and they also reflected Japanese opinion as emphasized by Japanese attempts at government-sponsored cartelization and rationalization. Furthermore British criticism of these failings contained a degree of sophistication which should be noted and respected, as they consistently argued that, coupled with historically high price and wage levels, these problems did not mean Japan's industrialization would falter within some preordained oriental de-industrial structure, but would merely inhibit Japan's ongoing penetration of the world market.

In broad terms it is quite clear that Japan-based commentators were critical in ensuring an accurate and up-to-date interpretation of economic developments in Japan. Of equal importance was not only location within Japan, but also the role of long-term residency, as an individual or corporate group, to provide a historical perspective on Japanese economic developments. But short-term contact proved equally important. The most noticeable area was in the cotton industry where the majority of people who had come into contact with this industry in Japan gained an appreciation of its competitive threat far more quickly than British-based commentators. In this regard the failure of the proposed February 1919 investigative commission, coupled with reported economic difficulties in Japan, probably ensured that the reporting of these short-term difficulties confirmed existing British-based complacency for longer than was ideally desirable. Still, these differences can be exaggerated, as they were essentially a result of timing rather than inherent prejudice. The Japanese cotton industry in the early 1920s did face significant economic problems, while by the late 1920s most British-based commentators had come around to making a radical reassessment of the competitiveness of the Japanese cotton industry. Location certainly speeded up this process, but the changing British-based interpretations, with suitable time lags, also accurately reflected the economic trajectory of the Japanese cotton industry.

If there was any area which ensured a continuing blind spot towards interpretations of Japanese economic development, then it stemmed from economic ideology. The British, and particularly official, preference for fiscal orthodoxy – balanced budgets and low tariffs – to an extent led to stronger charges of economic incompetence than was just. The most noticeable case was the 1927 Financial Panic, in which officials were quick to condemn Japanese policy management, and then equally quick to concede its limited impact upon industry and the economy in general. Furthermore, it is probable that officials consistently ignored the positive effects of tariffs on Japanese industrial development, a surprising feature since commentators were always bemoaning the negative impact of such tariffs on British exports. Similarly it could be argued that economic orthodoxy led officials to underplay the role of industrial policy. However, it is fair to say this was not the case as their examinations of the wider shores of industrial policy noted how it remained more a piece of rhetoric than as yet a tool for industrial development.

Overall it can be argued that whatever racial stereotypes the British held of the East, and of Japan in particular, these had little impact upon interpretations of Japanese economic development. Officials, commentators, and eventually the business community had at hand a robust and accurate model of Japanese economic and industrial developments. Thus the British failure to compete against Japan – essentially the Japanese cotton industry – was not intrinsically due to British misperceptions, but had more to do with failures within the British cotton industry. These in turn could be said to be due to the rigidities of 'individualistic' capitalism, but it would be more correct to agree with Sandberg's argument that the British cotton industry's loss of any comparative advantage against Japanese and colonial competitors meant that no amount of industrial reorganization could have reversed this process. If British misperceptions did exist, then it was a case of underestimating Japanese competition as a prelude to fleeing more quickly than it did. Indeed, those, like Lazonick and Mass, who insist that the Lancashire cotton industry could have competed against Japan, show a degree of misunderstanding about the economic circumstances of the Lancashire and Japanese cotton industries which suggests that ideologically-driven reinterpretations of historical circumstances are as prone to misperceptions as those charges made against their historical objects.

Notes

1. R. Minami, *The Economic Development of Japan: a Quantitative Study* (Basingstoke: Macmillan – now Palgrave, 1986), pp. 43, 54.
2. P.J. Cain and A.G. Hopkins, *British Imperialism: Crisis and Deconstruction, 1914–1990* (London: Longman, 1993), pp. 44–8; F. Warner, *Anglo-Japanese Financial Relations: a Golden Tide* (Oxford: Basil Blackwell, 1991), ch. 8; R.P.T. Davenport-Hines and G. Jones, 'British Business in Japan since 1868', in R.P.T. Davenport-Hines and G. Jones (eds), *British Business in Asia since 1860* (Cambridge: Cambridge University Press, 1989), p. 230; Minami, *Economic Development of Japan*, pp. 201–10.

3. Kenneth D. Brown, *Britain and Japan: a Comparative Economic and Social History since 1900* (Manchester: Manchester University Press, 1998).
4. D.H. Aldcroft and H.W. Richardson, *The British Economy, 1870–1929* (London: Macmillan, 1969); D.S. Landes, *The Unbound Prometheus* (Cambridge: Cambridge University Press, 1969).
5. D. McCloskey and L. Sandberg, 'From Damnation to Redemption: Judgements on the Late Victorian Entrepreneur', *Explorations in Economic History*, 5, 9, Fall 1971.
6. J.F. Wilson, *British Business History, 1720–1994* (Manchester: Manchester University Press, 1995).
7. L. Sandberg, *Lancashire in Decline: a Study in Entrepreneurship, Technology and International Trade* (Columbus: Ohio State University, 1974).
8. H. Yamazaki, 'Nihon Mengyo Kozoron Josetsu', *Keiei Shirin*, 1968; Wilson, *British Business History*, pp. viii, 5–8.
9. W. Lazonick and W. Mass, 'The British Cotton Industry and International Competitive Advantage: the State of the Debates', in M.B. Rose (ed.), *International Competition and Strategic Response in the Textile Industries since 1870* (London: Frank Cass, 1991). For a summary of this view in Japanese see T. Abe, 'Mengyo – Senkanki ni okeru Boseki Kogyo no Tenko o Chushin –', in H. Takeda (ed.), *Nihon Sangyo Hatten no Dainamizumu* (Tokyo: University of Tokyo Press, 1995), pp. 36–7.
10. C. Johnson, *MITI and the Japanese Miracle: the Growth of Industrial Policy, 1925–1975* (Stanford: Stanford University Press, 1982), p. 8.
11. T. Izumi, '"Igirisu Mengyo Hokoku" o toshite Mita 1930-nen Zengo no Igirisu Mengyo no Jijo no Kyoso', *Shakai Kagaku Nenpo*, 1984; T. Izumi, 'Senkanki Sekai Mengyo Shijo ni okeru Nichi-Ei Mengyo no Kakushitsu ni tsuite no Josho', *Senshu Keizaigaku Ronshu*, 1993; T. Izumi, '1930-nendai Sekai Mengyo Shijo ni okeru Nichi-Ei Kakushitsu', *Shakai Kagaku Nenpo*, 27, 1993; A.J. Robertson, 'Lancashire and the Rise of Japan, 1910–1937', in Rose, *International Competition and Strategic Response in the Textile Industries*; Yamazaki, 'Nihon Mengyo Kozoron Josetsu'.
12. Brown, *Britain and Japan*, pp. 35–9, 48–9, 60–1; T. Nakamura, *Economic Growth in Prewar Japan* (New Haven: Yale University Press, 1983), pp. 116–17, 119–20; S. Sugayama, 'Work Rules, Wages and Single Status: the Shaping of the "Japanese Employment System"', in E. Abe and R. Fitzgerald (eds), *The Origins of Japanese Industrial Power: Strategy, Institutions and the Development of Organisational Capability* (London: Frank Cass, 1995), pp. 120–40; Minami, *Economic Development of Japan*, pp. 42–3, 47–8, 102, 116–18, 225, 259, 265–7, 288–90.
13. Brown, *Britain and Japan*, pp. 37–8, 60–1.
14. Nakamura, *Economic Growth in Prewar Japan*, pp. 116, 119–20, 126; Minami, *Economic Development of Japan*, pp. 250–1, 332–3, 340–1, 356; Brown, *Britain and Japan*, pp. 39, 114.
15. T. Yui, 'Development, Organisation, and Business Strategy of Industrial Enterprises in Japan (1915–1935)', *Japanese Yearbook on Business History* 5, 1988. See also Brown, *Britain and Japan*, pp. 40, 44–5; Nakamura, *Economic Growth in Prewar Japan*, pp. 119–20, 127; T. Okazaki, 'The Japanese Firm under the Wartime Planned Economy', in M. Aoki and R.P. Dore (eds), *The Japanese Firm: Sources of Competitive Strength* (Oxford: Oxford University Press, 1994), p. 359; S. Yonekura, *The Japanese Steel Industry, 1850–1990: Continuity and Discontinuity* (Basingstoke: Macmillan – now Palgrave, 1994); Minami, *Economic Development of Japan*, pp. 126–7, 148, 315, 318.

16. Abe, 'Mengyo – Senkanki ni okeru Boseki Kogyo no Tenko o Chushin –', pp. 38–40, 44–7, 55–7, 60–1; Minami, *Economic Development of Japan*, pp. 127–8.
17. Brown, *Britain and Japan*, pp. 41–3; Wilson, *British Business History*, p. 143.
18. Brown, *Britain and Japan*, pp. 50, 105, 107, 109–10; A.J. Marrison, *British Business and Protection, 1903–1932* (Oxford: Clarendon Press, 1996).
19. J.C. Stamp, 'The Wealth and Income of the Chief Powers', *Journal of the Royal Statistical Society*, July 1919, p. 491.
20. E.F.T. Crowe and H.A.F. Horne, *Report on the Commercial, Industrial and Financial Situation in Japan: 1922 and to June 30th, 1923* (London: HMSO, 1923), pp. 5–8, 16, 29, 34–5.
21. Ibid., pp. 8–13, 29.
22. T. Johnes, 'Notes on the Social and Economic Transition of Japan', *Economic Journal*, 1921, pp. 55–6.
23. H. Wright, *Population* (London: Nisbet, 1923), pp. 122–3.
24. Crowe and Horne, *Report on Commercial, Industrial and Financial Situation* (1923), pp. 12–13.
25. Ibid., pp. 20–1.
26. 'Japan at a Crisis', *Times*, 8 March 1920.
27. Alston (Tokyo) to the Foreign Office, 15 March 1920, FO371/5351, F172/41/23; Eliot (Tokyo) to the Foreign Office, 26 and 5 November 1920, FO371/5361, F2758, and F3350/199/23; Crowe and Horne, *Report on Commercial, Industrial and Financial Situation* (1923), p. 44.
28. Alston (Tokyo) to the Foreign Office, 15 March 1920, FO371/5351, F172/41/23.
29. Crowe and Horne, *Report on Commercial, Industrial and Financial Situation* (1923), pp. 9–13.
30. Johnes, 'Notes on the Social and Economic Transition of Japan', p. 55.
31. Department of Overseas Trade memorandum, 'A Brief Review of the Causes and Provisions of the Recent Amendments to the Tariff Law', 6 August 1920, FO371/5351, F2037/41/23; Crowe, 'Memorandum on Economic Conditions in Japan', November 1920, FO371/5361, F3350/23.
32. Minute by Bentaelle, 26 April 1920, FO371/5351, F642/56/23.
33. Johnes, 'Notes on the Social and Economic Transition of Japan', p. 58.
34. Crowe, 'Memorandum on Economic Conditions in Japan', November 1920, FO371/5361, F3350/23.
35. Crowe and Horne, *Report on Commercial, Industrial and Financial Situation* (1923), p. 37.
36. Eliot (Tokyo) to the Foreign Office, 26 June 1920, FO371/5355, F1868/41/23; Minute by Vailui, 16 June 1920, FO371/5335, F114/60/23; Tsian and Tsingtao British Chambers of Commerce to the Association of British Chambers of Commerce (Shanghai), 4 June 1920, FO371/5361, F3350/199/23.
37. Crowe, 'Memorandum on Economic Conditions in Japan', November 1920, FO371/5361, F3350/23.
38. Crowe and Horne, *Report on Commercial, Industrial and Financial Situation* (1923), p. 12.
39. Ibid., pp. 12, 20, 29; Crowe, 'Memorandum on Economic Conditions in Japan', November 1920, FO371/5361, F3350/23.
40. Extract from private letter, Eliot (Tokyo) to Wellesley, 8 November 1920, FO371/5361, F3341/199/23.
41. Crowe and Horne, *Report on Commercial, Industrial and Financial Situation* (1923),

pp. 11–12, 19–20, 42; Crowe, 'Memorandum on Economic Conditions in Japan', November 1920, FO371/5361, F3350/23.

42. Crowe and Horne, *Report on Commercial, Industrial and Financial Situation* (1923), pp. 8–13, 29–30.
43. Ibid., p. 20.
44. Ibid., pp. 16–17, 32–3.
45. Johnes, 'Notes on the Social and Economic Transition of Japan', p. 56. See also *Manchester Chamber of Commerce, Monthly Record* (hereafter *MCC, MR*), December 1920, p. 365.
46. *MCC, MR*, March 1915, p. 70; March 1918, p. 75.
47. *MCC, MR*, December 1921, p. 427.
48. *MCC, MR*, February 1920, p. 57.
49. *MCC, MR*, July 1920, p. 216.
50. United States Tariff Commission, *Report of Japanese Cotton Industry and Trade, 1921*, cited in G. Hubbard, *Eastern Industrialisation and its Effect on the West: With Special Reference to Great Britain and Japan* (Oxford: Oxford University Press, 1935), p. 53.
51. *MCC, MR*, July 1922, p. 229; October 1923, p. 339.
52. Ibid., July 1921, p. 253.
53. O. Jones, 'Lancashire Cotton Industry', *Harvard Business Review*, 2, 4, July, 1924, p. 448.
54. Memorandum by Crowe, 'Feeling of Commercial Community in Gt. Britain towards Japan', 26 May 1920, FO371/5359, F971/119/23.
55. *MCC, MR*, July 1919, pp. 186–7, August 1919, p. 237, October 1919, pp. 267, 278, September 1920, p. 263, and February 1921, p. 63.
56. Nakamura, *Economic Growth in Prewar Japan*, pp. 120–1.
57. Ibid., pp. 121–3, 127–9; Brown, *Britain and Japan*, pp. 35–6, 52, 60–1, 72; M.J. Ramseyer and F. Rosenbluth, *The Politics of Oligarchy: Institutional Choice in Imperial Japan* (Cambridge: Cambridge University Press, 1995), pp. 106–17; Minami, *Economic Development of Japan*, pp. 288–90, 341, 344–5, 356.
58. B. Gao, *Economic Ideology and Japanese Industrial Policy. Developmentalism from 1931 to 1965* (Cambridge: Cambridge University Press, 1997), pp. 71–2; Johnson, *MITI and the Japanese Miracle*, pp. 96–7, 100.
59. Brown, *Britain and Japan*, pp. 35, 40, 45, 61; Nakamura, *Economic Growth in Prewar Japan*, pp. 123–5, 128; Minami, *Economic Development of Japan*, p. 43; Johnson, *MITI and the Japanese Miracle*, pp. 102–4.
60. Brown, *Britain and Japan*, pp. 49, 78; Ramseyer and Rosenbluth, *Politics of Oligarchy*, pp. 139–43; Johnson, *MITI and the Japanese Miracle*, pp. 98–9, 102–4, 118.
61. Nakamura, *Economic Growth in Prewar Japan*, p. 126; Minami, *Economic Development of Japan*, pp. 250–2; Johnson, *MITI and the Japanese Miracle*, p. 99.
62. Abe, 'Mengyo – Senkanki ni okeru Boseki Kogyo', pp. 40–2, 51–9; Mass and Lazonick, 'The British Cotton Industry and International Competitive Advantage', pp. 40–5.
63. Abe, 'Mengyo – Senkanki ni okeru Boseki Kogyo', pp. 55–7, 60–1.
64. Brown, *Britain and Japan*, pp. 43–4, 110–11.
65. Mass and Lazonick, 'The British Cotton Industry and International Competitive Advantage', p. 41; J.H. Bamberg, 'The Rationalisation of the British Cotton Industry in the Interwar Years', *Textile History*, 1988, pp. 88, 90–4; M.W. Kirby, 'The Lancashire Cotton Industry in the Inter-War Years: a Study in Organisational Change', *Business History*, 1974, p. 159.

66. G.B. Sansom and W.J. Davies, *Report on the Commercial, Industrial and Financial Situation in Japan and her Dependencies in 1923 and up to June 30th, 1924* (London: HMSO, 1924), pp. 9–10, 15, 17–18, 28–9; R. Boulter, *Report on the Commercial, Economic and Financial Conditions in Japan: to June 20th, 1926* (London: HMSO, 1926), pp. 9–10, 14–15, 26–7; G.B. Sansom and H.A. Macrae, *Report on Economic Conditions in Japan: to 30th June, 1928* (London: HMSO, 1928), pp. 12–13; G.B. Sansom and R. Boulter, *Economic and Financial Conditions in Japan: to June 30th, 1929* (London: HMSO, 1929), pp. 10, 16–18.
67. Sansom and Boulter, *Report on Commercial, Economic and Financial Conditions* (1929), pp. 14–15, 17–19; Sansom and Macrae, *Report on Economic Conditions in Japan* (1928), pp. 10, 16, 18–21, 25–6; Boulter, *Report of Commercial, Economic and Financial Conditions* (1926), pp. 9–11, 18–19; Sansom and Davies, *Report on Commercial, Industrial and Financial Situation* (1924), pp. 9–11, 14–16.
68. Sansom and Boulter, *Economic and Financial Conditions in Japan* (1929), pp. 7, 14–15, 17; Sansom and Macrae, *Report on Economic Conditions* (1928), pp. 11–12, 22; Boulter, *Report on Commercial, Economic and Financial Conditions* (1926), pp. 9–11, 18–19.
69. Sansom and Macrae, *Report on Economic Conditions* (1928), p. 131. See also I.H. Nish, 'Britain's View of the Japanese Economy in the early Showa Period', in R.P. Dore and R. Sinha (eds), *Japan and World Depression, Then and Now: Essays in Memory of E.F. Penrose* (Basingstoke: Macmillan – now Palgrave, 1987), p. 140.
70. Sansom and Boulter, *Economic and Financial Conditions in Japan* (1929), p. 16.
71. Boulter, *Report on Commercial, Economic and Financial Conditions* (1926), p. 72. See also Sansom and Davies, *Report on Commercial, Industrial and Financial Situation* (1924), pp. 15–16.
72. A.S. Pearse, *The Cotton Industry of Japan and China: Being the Report of the Journey to Japan and China* (Manchester: International Federation of Master Cotton Spinners' and Manufacturers' Associations, 1929), pp. 27, 91; Sansom and Boulter, *Economic and Financial Conditions in Japan* (1929), pp. 16–17; Boulter, *Report on Commercial, Economic and Financial Conditions* (1926), p. 72.
73. Boulter, *Report on Commercial, Economic and Financial Conditions* (1926), pp. 8–13, 15–17, 20–6; Sansom and Davies, *Report on Commercial, Industrial and Financial Situation* (1924), pp. 12–14, 17.
74. Sansom and Macrae, *Report on Economic Conditions* (1928), pp. 7–8, 11–18.
75. Ibid., pp. 15–20.
76. G.B. Sansom and H.A. Macrae, *Economic Conditions in Japan: To 30th June, 1930* (London: HMSO, 1930), pp. 8–9, 11–14.
77. Sansom and Davies, *Report on Commercial, Industrial and Financial Situation* (1924), pp. 40, 53–4, 57–8.
78. Boulter, *Report on Commercial, Economic and Financial Conditions* (1926), p. 8.
79. Sansom and Macrae, *Economic Conditions in Japan* (1930), pp. 9–10; Sansom and Macrae, *Report on Economic Conditions in Japan* (1928), pp. 33, 72–3; Boulter, *Report on Commercial, Economic and Financial Conditions* (1926), pp. 32, 35, 58–9, 61–4.
80. Sansom and Macrae, *Economic Conditions in Japan* (1930), pp. 16, 39, 48.
81. Boulter, *Report on Commercial, Economic and Financial Conditions* (1926), pp. 9–10, 25–6; Sansom and Davies, *Report on Commercial, Industrial and Financial Situation* (1924), pp. 43, 53.
82. Boulter, *Report on Commercial, Economic and Financial Conditions* (1926), pp. 59–61.

83. Sansom and Macrae, *Economic Conditions in Japan* (1930), pp. 10–11.
84. Sansom and Boulter, *Economic and Financial Conditions in Japan* (1929), pp. 36, 51; Boulter, *Report on Commercial, Economic and Financial Conditions* (1926), pp. 34–5.
85. Sansom and Macrae, *Economic Conditions in Japan* (1930), p. 15.
86. Ibid., p. 38; Boulter, *Report on Commercial, Economic and Financial Conditions* (1926), pp. 43–4; Sansom and Davies, *Report on Commercial, Industrial and Financial Situation* (1924), p. 49.
87. Sansom and Macrae, *Economic Conditions in Japan* (1930), pp. 25, 28, 34. See also ibid., pp. 25, 34; Sansom and Macrae, *Report on Economic Conditions in Japan* (1928), pp. 11, 26; Boulter, *Report on Commercial, Economic and Financial Conditions* (1926), pp. 11, 17–20; Sansom and Davies, *Report on Commercial, Industrial and Financial Situation* (1924), pp. 15–17, 43.
88. Sansom and Macrae, *Report on Economic Conditions in Japan* (1928), pp. 7–11, 34; Boulter, *Report on Commercial, Economic and Financial Conditions* (1926), pp. 46–7; Sansom and Davies, *Report on Commercial, Industrial and Financial Situation* (1924), pp. 10–11, 16.
89. Sansom and Macrae, *Report on Economic Conditions in Japan* (1928), p. 22.
90. Ibid., p. 34.
91. Sansom and Macrae, *Economic Conditions in Japan* (1930), pp. 11, 15, 26–7, 31, 38.
92. Sansom and Macrae, *Report on Economic Conditions in Japan* (1928), pp. 17–18, 23.
93. Boulter, *Report on Commercial, Economic and Financial Conditions* (1926), p. 11.
94. Sansom and Macrae, *Report on Economic Conditions in Japan* (1928), p. 21.
95. Ibid., pp. 17–18, 21–3; Sansom and Davies, *Report on Commercial, Industrial and Financial Situation* (1924), pp. 28–9.
96. Sansom and Davies, *Report on Commercial, Industrial and Financial Situation* (1924), pp. 46–8.
97. *MCC, MR*, July 1925, p. 219; Sansom and Macrae, *Economic Conditions in Japan* (1930), pp. 23–8; Sansom and Boulter, *Economic and Financial Conditions in Japan* (1929), p. 16; Sansom and Macrae, *Report on Economic Conditions in Japan* (1928), pp. 9, 22, 61–3; Boulter, *Report on Commercial, Economic and Financial Conditions* (1926), pp. 10–11, 27, 43–4.
98. W.B. Cunningham, *Report on the Cotton Spinning and Weaving Industry in Japan, 1925–1926* (London: HMSO, 1927).
99. Sansom and Macrae, *Economic Conditions in Japan* (1930), pp. 23, 26–7; Sansom and Boulter, *Economic and Financial Conditions in Japan* (1929), pp. 22–6.
100. Sansom and Macrae, *Economic Conditions in Japan* (1930), p. 27; Sansom and Boulter, *Economic and Financial Conditions in Japan* (1929), p. 24. Indeed officials argued that in many respects the Japanese spinning sector was excessively vertically integrated, as the bulk purchase of raw cotton led to speculative losses as raw cotton prices moved against Japanese bulk imports.
101. C.W. Macara, *Trade Stability and how to Obtain it* (Manchester: Sherrat and Hughes, 1925), p. 37.
102. *MCC, MR*, July 1925, p. 219.
103. *MCC, MR*, January 1925, pp. xii–xxiii.
104. *MCC, MR*, June 1925, pp. 174–7; July 1925, p. 202; April 1926, p. 114; July 1926, p. 205; February 1927, p. 42.
105. *MCC, MR*, July 1925, p. 219.

106. *MCC, MR*, February 1927, p. 42; July 1926, p. 205; April 1926, p. 114; December 1925, p. 384; July 1925, p. 202.
107. *MCC, MR*, April 1928, pp. 112–13.
108. B. Ellinger, 'Lancashire's Declining Trade with China', *Transactions of the Manchester Statistical Society* 1928, pp. 30–8; *MCC, MR*, July 1926, pp. 198, 205.
109. G.W. Daniels and J. Jewkes, 'The Comparative Position of the Lancashire Cotton Industry', *Transactions of the Manchester Statistical Society*, 1926–27, pp. 72–8; *MCC, MR*, December 1924, pp. 443–5; July 1924, p. 253; February 1924, pp. 60–1; July 1923, p. 244; February 1923, p. 61.
110. *MCC, MR*, July 1928, pp. 210–11.
111. F. Utley, *Lancashire and the Far East* (London: George Allen & Unwin, 1931), p. 51; B. Ellinger, 'Lancashire's Declining Trade with China', *Transactions of the Manchester Statistical Society*, 1928.
112. Preface to Pearse, *The Cotton Industry of Japan and China*.
113. Cited in Robertson, 'Lancashire and the Rise of Japan', pp. 95–6.
114. Cited in Daniels and Jewkes, 'The Comparative Position of the Lancashire Cotton Industry'.
115. Utley, *Lancashire and the Far East*, pp. 83–5; B. and H. Ellinger, 'Japanese Competition in the Cotton Trade', *Journal of the Royal Statistical Society*, 1930, pp. 196–201, 207–18; Pearse, *Cotton Industry of Japan and China*, pp. 18, 25–9; J. Ryan in Ellinger, 'Lancashire's Declining Trade with China', p. 33.
116. Utley, *Lancashire and the Far East*, p. 61; A.S. Pearse, 'Efforts to Rationalise the Cotton Industry of the U.S.A.', *Transactions of the Manchester Statistical Society*, 1928–29, pp. 81–92.
117. J.H. Grey, 'Memorandum on Relative Costs of Manufacture in Lancashire and Japanese Weaving Sheds', pp. 45–9.
118. Holroyd in Pearse, *The Cotton Industry of Japan and China*, p. 5.
119. Ibid., pp. 141–2; Utley, cited in Robertson, 'Lancashire and the Rise of Japan', pp. 95–6.
120. Ellinger and Ellinger, 'Japanese Competition in the Cotton Trade', p. 188.
121. J. Jewkes, 'Factors in the Cotton Industry', *Quarterly Journal of Economics*, 1930, p. 36; E.P. Learned, 'Mergers in the Cotton Industry', *Harvard Business Review*, 1930, pp. 501–12; D.J. MacGregor, 'Problems of Rationalisation', *Economic Journal*, 1930, pp. 251–358; J. Ryan, 'Machinery Replacement in the Cotton Industry', *Economic Journal*, 1930, pp. 633–7; Daniels and Jewkes, 'Comparative Position of the Lancashire Cotton Industry', pp. 64–7; G.W. Daniels and J. Jewkes, 'The Post-War Depression in the Lancashire Cotton Industry', *Journal of the Royal Statistical Society*, 1928, pp. 162–8.
122. Kirby, 'The Lancashire Cotton Industry in the Interwar Years', p. 159.

8

Facing the Unavoidable – Great Britain, the Sterling Area and Japan: Economic and Trading Relations, 1950–1960

John Weste

Introduction

In October 1948, for the benefit of the annual Conservative Party Conference, Winston Churchill spoke assuredly of the 'Three Circles' upon which Britain's future as a world power was based. British links with each circle of Commonwealth and Empire; the English-speaking dominions, Great Britain and the United States; and a United Europe purportedly reinforced British might in the remaining two. Indeed, if one were to envision the three interlocking circles, it would become immediately apparent that Britain was 'the only country which has a great part in every one of them'.[1] While not equal to the superpowers, the United Kingdom's global interests would at least partially compensate for diminished capabilities. With Churchill's return to power in 1951, this concept was installed as the basis of the Conservative government's foreign policy and even used in the publicity of diplomatic missions.[2] Equally, given this almost celestial self-appointment as 'the very point of junction',[3] it was inevitable that the impact of Japanese economic resurgence and trade would also have to be faced in each circle. The needs and direction of the recovering Japanese economy over the 1950s affected significantly British connections with Empire and Commonwealth (English-speaking or otherwise), the crucial relationship with the United States, and, naturally, relations between the British and Japanese home islands themselves.

Anglo-Japanese trade in the 1950s covered a broad variety of goods, ranging from textiles and glassware to iron and steel. While potentially politically emotive, such items were also in a way quite mundane when compared to the more exciting and adventurous avenues of trade in nuclear technology and jet engines. In these two fields, Britain could still claim to match, if not exceed, American capabilities. Successfully developing these markets in Japan would confirm British technological and engineering prowess, and loosen Japanese dependence on the United States in such areas then held as vital to the continued development of a modern industrial power of the first rank. Secondly, it was the 1950s which saw the return of Japanese sovereignty, the Cold War entrenched in East and Southeast Asia, and the subsequent increased American involvement in the region, as well as British attempts to utilize Washington's financial might in the regional struggle against communism and to prolong London's indirect political influence over the decolonizing Southeast Asian members of the Commonwealth. The question of Japan's future economic security, social stability and continued alliance with the capitalist bloc was as intimately linked to all these concerns as the stance of the United Kingdom was important.

British perceptions of the challenges, threats or even the opportunities posed by the Japanese economy are not limited to any one period of modern Anglo-Japanese relations. Images of cheap labour and sweatshops were evoked by interwar Lancashire in response to the perceived unfairness of Japanese competition. Similarly, the late 1960s, and especially the 1970s and 1980s, saw the sweatshops of the 1930s merged with the wartime Greater East Asia Co-prosperity Sphere to depict a new economic animal: a Japan at war with the West with *sarariman* as the modern-day incarnation of the Imperial Japanese Army.[4] However, the emphasis on the contemporary should not distract from 1950s economic and trading relations between Great Britain, the sterling area and Japan.

British imperial possessions and Commonwealth in Southeast Asia were held as indispensable to a continued global role in an international environment dominated by the two superpowers. Although postwar American pre-eminence, the Cold War, anti-colonialism and relative British decline ensured the failure of such policies, this was not at all clear in the early 1950s. Whilst aware of complexities and potential damage from Japanese trade, UK officials saw a guided Japanese economic return to the region as a means of promoting local economic development. In turn, this measure would more tightly link both Japan and British possessions to the capitalist bloc in the crusade against communism. This decision was made in full knowledge of the long history of Anglo-Japanese trade friction. Indeed, British business was often puce with rage over government policy regarding Japan, and its representatives, such as chairman of the Cotton Board, Sir Raymond Streat, regularly reached back in time before the War to find evidence supporting their views of a renewed Japanese trading threat to Great Britain. Wartime imagery and Japanese atrocities could provoke useful hysteria and doubtlessly reinforced many perceptions held with regards to Japan, but were not an esssential component of the business case against expanded Japanese trade.

Also of significance to British policy was Japan's close relationship with the United States in the context of the Cold War, as well as London's own treasured version of an American alliance. The United Kingdom could not but pay a great deal of attention to American policy for East and Southeast

Asia. The British Embassy in Washington, sensitive to American criticism of the sterling bloc and colonial policy, observed many complaints that the UK was squeezing Japan out of Southeast Asia. The feared effect was a Japanese return to prewar patterns of trade with Northeast Asia, a region controlled by communist powers.[5] Concern over the interests of the more powerful American partner is immediately apparent. Of equal importance, however, is the simple fact that British trading actions vis-à-vis Japan and Southeast Asia were held to be of such significance to American policy success.

American officials in occupied Japan, such as Kenneth Morrow of SCAP's (Supreme Commander of Allied Powers) Economic and Scientific Section,[6] vigorously promoted Southeast Asia as a key source of raw materials for Japanese manufacturers and a logical market for the resultant products. Anything less would harm Japanese potential as the 'Workshop of Asia'. The 1950s also saw the initial interest of certain Japanese businessmen and bureaucrats in developing a Southeast Asian supply base and market. Clearly, Japan's reparations programme informed this early concern for Southeast Asian economic development. No doubt so did the anticipated economic and political returns of cooperating with United States anti-communist policy in the Far East.

Naturally, the Southeast Asian connection does not represent the sum total of Anglo-Japanese economic relations. Particularly, in the context of the retreat from empire in the latter half of the 1950s, further aspects of the trading relationship become apparent as the importance of the colonies began to fade. British technological prowess, as seen through jet engines and airframes, and atomic power, would hopefully serve to guarantee a leading position for the UK commensurate with its assumptions of status. Even so, Britain failed to make significant long-term inroads into the Japanese market in such narrow specialist fields. Aspirations that excellence in technology alone would ensure perpetual success were sorely misplaced as British weakness east of Suez was as apparent as American dominance. A jet engine, equal to any American product, proved to be of limited worth when backed up neither by liberal financial loans to aid exports and licensed manufacture, nor by the will to risk an outright challenge to US assumptions of dominance, nor by the clout necessary to persuade Japanese bureaucrats, politicians and businessmen of the desirability for manufacture in the first instance. Washington held both financial might and influence in abundance and still found encouraging the Japanese import and manufacture of American jet engines and aircraft an entirely unexpected trial.

The respective balance of the UK and Japanese economic presence in postwar Southeast Asia neatly demonstrates the many complications Britain faced in re-establishing international standing, power and prestige. The 1941–45 Far Eastern military conflict ensured American succession as the dominant western power in East Asia and the ongoing search of indigenous peoples for independence from the ties of empire. Increasingly over the

1950s, the pattern of Anglo-Japanese business and trading relations confirmed this fact politically and economically both within the decolonizing empire in Southeast Asia and in specific attempts to rival the United States in the domestic Japanese market.

Anglo-Japanese trading relations and Southeast Asia

Numerous studies have examined the US–Japanese relationship in the context of the Cold War in Asia.[7] Their focus lies on American support for the 'Workshop of Asia' and its sponsorship of a Japanese economy redirected away from Northeast to Southeast Asia as a source of raw materials and a market for Japan's manufactures. This approach, however, neglects the fact that Britain retained considerable economic and political influence in Southeast Asia, and not merely within the formal empire. Recent scholarship emphasizes the vitality of British policy initiatives and regional planning to combat the Cold War in Asia. American weight behind Japan was crucial, but equally so was London's attitude towards a reinvigorated Japanese economic presence in Southeast Asia.[8] As the British Embassy in Thailand correctly observed to the Foreign Secretary, Anthony Eden, Japan's attempts to develop its export market in Southeast Asia relied much upon British cooperation.[9]

The revival of Japanese interest in promoting an economic return to Southeast Asia following defeat and occupation was both rapid and logical. The region represented a valuable source of non-dollar imports. Further, the developing Cold War in Asia (symbolized by the 1949 communist victory in China and the June 1950 outbreak of the Korean War), combined with the gradual removal of Allied restrictions following the 1951 San Francisco Peace Treaty with Japan, provided additional motivation for a Japanese southwards economic expansion.

In 1953, the career bureaucrat and Keidanren[10] vice-president, Uemura Kogoro, publicly lambasted the Japanese government for failing to conclude Treaties of Navigation and Commerce with Southeast Asian governments. He regarded the region as resource-rich and its development essential to ensure Japan the supply of cheap raw materials crucial to lowering the costs of manufactured goods.[11] Other Keidanren officials followed suit and demanded the settlement of reparation payments as a further means of spearheading Japanese economic penetration of the region. Payments, ideally in the form of goods and services, would raise the level of the region's economy, which in turn would lead to new markets for Japanese goods and demands for investment. One response of the Japanese government came in June 1953 with the formation of the Southeast Asia Council within the Ministry of Foreign Affairs. At its head sat Hara Yasusaburo, a long-time exponent of expanded trade with Southeast Asia and president of Nippon Kayaku.[12] Depending on the method, Hara reasoned that reparations payments would, from an economic perspective, 'create a favourable relationship of inseparability [thus] opening a permanent market for Japanese goods'.[13] Quite simply: 'We shall be able to turn misfortune into fortune'.[14]

Other Japanese paid attention to the matter of aid. Clearly, any assistance Japan could offer in the short term was limited as domestic reconstruction absorbed the bulk of Japan's scarce resources. Nonetheless, Fukushima Masao, a member of the Keidanren secretariat, argued that technical and economic aid would stimulate Southeast Asian economic development and heighten the region's purchasing power. In the process, Japan might create competitors in the field of cotton yarn exports, for example, but Fukushima considered the long-term gains to be worth the risk.[15] Finally, it is worth noting the military context of Japan's economic interests in Southeast Asia. Former president of Mitsubishi Heavy Industries and chairman of the Keidanren-connected Defence Production Committee, Goko Kiyoshi, anticipated American offshore procurement and mutual security assistance could fund $10 million worth of military sales to Indo-China alone.[16] In March 1956, Keidanren dispatched a goodwill mission to Southeast Asia with the hidden aim of exploring the potential market for Japanese munitions.[17] One direct result of this goodwill mission was the September 1956 formation of Japan Technical Co-operation Co. Ltd, which oversaw the dispatch of several teams of Japanese technicians under the command of former Rear Admiral Shimizu Fumio to repair South Vietnamese naval dockyards and military facilities.[18]

However Japan approached the region, though, the legacy of bitterness and anti-Japanese sentiment caused by the disastrous occupation of much of Southern Asia in the Second World War could not be avoided. Fukushima called for sensitivity: desire for raw materials should not blind the Japanese to alternative Southeast Asian visions of development. Cooperation was the key: 'I desire that we be more humble and prudent.'[19] Toshiba president, Ishizaka Taizo, was more blunt in calling for Japan to 'reject egoism: we must not fail twice.'[20]

Purged of egoism or otherwise, by the mid-1950s Japanese failure in Southeast Asia was appearing most unlikely. From the late 1940s onwards, Japan entered into trade agreements with Burma and began exchanging manufactured goods, such as rolling stock, for rice with Thailand.[21] Within British territories, too, Japan's presence was soon felt. In 1948, Japanese imports from Malaya and Singapore amounted to *c.*£2.5 million, and exports *c.*£1.65 million. By 1951, trade growth, fuelled by the Korean War, was phenomenal, with the level reaching *c.*£19.6 million and *c.*£30.46 million respectively.[22] Over January to May 1954, the International Bank for Reconstruction and Development surveyed Malaya with an eye to advising on economic development, and concluded that, given Malayan iron ore mining's dependency upon exports for survival, Japan constituted the logical market. In 1954 Malayan iron ore production totalled 1 212 780 tons, of which 1 039 430 was exported to Japan. Bauxite mining at Telok Ramunia,

Johore provided a similar example where again the bulk of monthly production of 20000 tons was shipped to Japan.[23]

By 1952, Japan's trade with the whole of Southeast Asia accounted for 15 per cent of exports as compared to 12 per cent in 1937. The same year imports from Southeast Asia accounted for 11 per cent of Japan's total imports, representing a slight increase over the 1937 figure of 10 per cent. Demonstrative of such trends, Japan participated in international bodies such as the Economic Commission for Asia and the Far East (ECAFE), the International Rice Commission and the Food and Agriculture Organization to further promote regional economic influence. In October 1954, Japan was granted membership in the Colombo Plan sponsoring South and Southeast Asian economic development.[24]

Japan's rapid economic return to Southeast Asia, and its powerful American support, provoked mixed reactions on the part of the British government, bureaucracy and commercial interests. A gallimaufry of responses was employed, from cautious encouragement, suspicion, and resignation, to the September 1952 anti-Japanese campaign of the *Daily Express*.[25] While an absolute distinction is impossible, generally British manufacturing concerns and some local colonial administrators identified Japan as a rival and dangerous economic competitor to be compelled and repelled with high tariffs, and strict controls and quotas. Despite such fears, Westminster and Whitehall tended to support, albeit with care and often distaste, Japanese economic recovery and its push into Southeast Asia.

This response is not necessarily a puzzling one. Certainly, Japan's almost casual military humiliation of Britain in Southeast Asia, coupled with the brutal treatment of POWs, created a bitter legacy which, as Japanese imperial visits show, remains to this day. Further, in the late 1940s and early 1950s, Britain's Southeast Asian territories and dependencies were held as indispensable to United Kingdom economic recovery, and to global strategic interests. Nonetheless, British officials were not intent upon 'selling-out' British interests to the Japanese, or necessarily to the United States, for that matter. Instead, if properly harnessed, Japanese economic strength could contribute to regional living conditions and hence help fulfil British plans for regional security and the defeat of communism. In addition, wanted or otherwise, Tokyo's economic contribution soon proved essential given the difficulties London found in persuading UK financial and business concerns to provide for Southeast Asian development.[26] In this context, Japan's return to Southeast Asia reflects British decolonization and the growth of more attractive non-imperial markets for UK enterprises as much as it does desire to cooperate with the United States in the Cold War.

Non-metropolitan views were made clear at least as early as October 1949 when R. F. Hollyer of the British Embassy, Washington, informed the Foreign Office with cautious optimism of increased potential for multilateral cooperation and American aid to Southeast Asia. Less buoyantly, however, he recorded American references to Southeast Asia as a market and supplier of raw materials to Japan and called for vigilance 'over the extent to which the Americans seek to expose Southeast Asia to Japanese penetration'.[27] Local British officials in Malaya made similar observations. Malayan iron ore was an imperial resource with never again 'any question of its export . . . to Japan'.[28] In 1953, General Sir Gerald Templer, high commissioner to the Federation of Malaya, portrayed Japanese economic interests as a revival of the Co-prosperity Sphere under different garb; a claim others were destined to repeat.[29]

UK enterprises also moved quickly to warn against Japanese economic activities. Fears of unscrupulous business practices, such as dumping, prevailed, only to be reinforced by the January 1954 Anglo-Japanese Payments and Trade Agreement which removed most colonial restrictions on imports of Japanese products. Lancashire, home of Britain's textile industries, protested tonitruously and, as the *Economist* observed, 'when trade with Japan is under discussion all kinds of emotion are bound to be unleashed'.[30] To many, it was certainly preferable to give full rein to passion rather than Japan. Few forgot that the Japanese percentage of textiles imported into Malaya had risen mortifyingly quickly from 24 per cent in 1929 to 48 per cent in 1933.[31] As early as September 1946, Lancashire began warning of the threat posed by Japan and, over the late 1940s and early 1950s, continually implored the British government to impose quota and import restrictions on the Japanese.[32] These concerns were frequently channelled through Sir Raymond Streat, chairman of the Cotton Board 1940 to 1957, whose diaries demonstrate the extent to which Japan dominated the minds of British cotton and textile interests.

Streat, and many of his contemporaries, did not seek to deny Japan a right to exist and trade. They readily acknowledged that Japan, like Great Britain, had to export to survive, and that like it or not 'Japan existed and would exist, with all its talents and its terrifyingly large population – still increasing'.[33] An outlet was necessary. China was considered the rational market, but discounted through communist victory. At the very least that implied 'acute discomforts for somebody', exacerbated by American failure to understand the problems 'posed by the proposition of Japan in a free world'.[34] Streat sought to curtail Japan, and buy time for Lancashire's programme of domestic investment and modernization which he believed could easily be undone through low-wage Japanese competition. It was imperative to convince the 'capitalist and entrepreneur in the East that if he enlarged his bid for world trade to unreasonable proportions he would meet with such counter-action (import quotas or prohibitions) as to make his bid highly unprofitable.'[35]

It is crucial to remember that Streat was not protesting simply against unfair Japanese trading practices, but against the sum total of potential Japanese trade in textiles (and other sectors too, such as shipping), regardless of its fairness. At an October 1954 meeting in London between Streat and Japan's conservative prime minister, Yoshida Shigeru (to whom Streat referred as 'His squeaky little Excellency'), economic matters inevitably dominated the conversation. Yoshida observed that if Japan were to remain a bastion against the spread of communism, economic strength was essential. Unfair competition should be combated and solved, but fair competition was, quite simply, 'fair'. In reply, Streat merely conceded the difficulties of competition were great, but in his diaries added 'I left out the adjective [that is, fair] but I doubt if he observed the implication of the omission'.[36]

In order to push forward the views of Lancashire, Streat vigorously lobbied the British and American governments, but also the Supreme Commander of Allied Powers (SCAP), General Douglas MacArthur, directly. In this context, he represents a further dimension to UK–Japan economic and political relations beyond bureaucrats and politicians. In May 1950, Streat headed a joint Anglo-American Cotton Mission to Japan to assess his rivals in more detail and impress his concerns upon MacArthur.[37]

MacArthur, initially suspicious of the joint mission, met Raymond Streat and Sir Alvary Gascoigne, head of the British Liaison Mission to Japan, on 8 May 1950. Perhaps forewarned of the General's legendary ego, Streat slotted his own concerns within the larger framework of MacArthur's profound impact on twentieth-century history, which might well 'give a new moral and spiritual force to the eastern half of the world's population'.[38] Acknowledging the need for economic growth to maintain Japan's viability, Streat nonetheless spoke against exports for exports' sake and explained that exporting goods rampantly would only attract hostility, lead to increased tariff barriers and thus detract from long-term economic growth. The purpose of his visit, therefore, was to ascertain the extent to which such principles were understood and accepted, and how far Japanese intentions conformed to policies of 'mutual respect and toleration'.[39] MacArthur offered little. He did promise to eradicate unfair trade should it appear, but as to Sir Raymond's greater concern of the total volume of trade, rather than its fairness, no concessions were to be made. As Streat quoted MacArthur in early 1949, 'Japan must either export to pay her way or the US taxpayer must keep Japan at his expense: what I want is more Jap goods sold anyhow they can be sold.'[40]

Other than discomforting guided tours of Japanese mills which proved to be all too modern and efficiently managed, Streat gained little from his mission in terms of concrete assurances and promises to limit Japanese trade. This was not unexpected and matched his suspicions of limited sympathy for cotton in Whitehall and the press.[41] In such beliefs Streat was, of course, almost entirely correct.

London was, naturally, mindful of American policy for occupied Japan and the ramifications such policy held for economic relations between the sterling area and Japan. Inevitably, Southeast Asian members of the Empire and Commonwealth figured in such calculations as Britain worked to balance the American alliance with its Commonwealth interests.

The Occupation of Japan began in August 1945. Although termed an Allied occupation, American interests usually overruled those of the allies who held limited and indirect powers to guide its course.[42] SCAP's initial aims were to demilitarize and democratize Japanese society and the economy. The Imperial Army and Navy were abolished, war-crime trials conducted and a purge of prewar and wartime leaders enacted. Further, land was redistributed, plans were drawn up to break the dominant industrial groupings, and a reparations programme was introduced to dismantle Japan's industrial might and shift it abroad to aid the industrialization of the victims of Japanese wartime aggression. Not only would Japan's capacity to wage aggressive war be removed for all time, but so would the militarist and economic forces which promoted it in the first instance. However, over 1948 and 1949, there appeared a gradual and irregular shift in the Occupation as SCAP moved from reform to reconstruction. This change is known as the 'reverse course' as the United States worked to redevelop the Japanese economy and prepare for Japan's return to the international order as an American capitalist ally.[43] Urgency was granted by successful communist revolution in China and the Korean War as *zaibatsu* dissolution was watered down and reparation payments ceased. Special procurement orders (*tokuju*) on behalf of United Nation forces fighting on the Korean Peninsula from June 1950 to July 1953 led to Japan's first postwar economic boom as orders and dollars flooded in.

Korean War procurement visibly demonstrated Japan's industrial capacity and its value as the key Asian ally in the Washington-led capitalist bloc. SCAP, and other American agencies, turned their attention to further enlisting Japanese economic might in the struggle against communism. Southeast Asian markets and resources were essential to this process and the need to link the region with the Japanese economy strongly emphasized.

In October 1951, Kenneth Morrow, chief of SCAP's Economic and Scientific Section's (ESS) Programs and Statistics Division, drew up a report outlining how Japan 'as the most important workshop of the Far East [could] make its optimum contribution to the Free World'.[44] Japan's own economic growth would improve conditions throughout Southeast Asia by increased productivity, production and levels of trade.[45] In this manner, Japan could contribute to the regional economic battle against communism 'as the principal processing nation in the area'.[46] The goal of Japanese economic development was clear given the extant model of Northeast Asia:

> in the years before World War II nearly one fifth of Japan's exports to Korea and China were in the form of equipment and machinery neces-

> sary to produce raw materials contributory to Japan's own development. This same kind of development must be repeated, this time in another part of the Far East.[47]

To this end, joint SCAP–Japanese missions toured through South and Southeast Asia to promote Japanese access to raw material supplies and markets. A SCAP-prepared report of April 1950 proudly explained that Japan held the 'capacity to produce all types of the capital goods and equipment required . . . without impairment of her domestic economy'. Eagerly, the report projected Japanese exports to Southeast Asia to exceed $710 million by 1955.[48]

Open American calls for a regional linking of the Japanese and Southeast Asian economies continued over the 1950s.[49] Inevitably, Great Britain's interests, as witnessed by Sir Raymond Streat amongst many others, would suffer. However, it is unnecessarily simplistic to dismiss Britain as a desiccated imperial power too bereft of vision and will to design and implement policy for Japan and Southeast Asia. In many instances, a controlled Japanese economic resurgence in Southeast Asia complemented British planning; American support for these aims could be supportive as well as destructive.

Official British policy sought to eradicate Japan's ability to mobilize industrially for war but equally, as Sir Stafford Cripps, president of the Board of Trade, stated in October 1946, Japan must be left 'internationally solvent'. The alternative was the need for 'permanent foreign support', which was clearly beyond the United Kingdom's resources.[50] Japan was held to be incapable of withstanding anything matching British economic policy for occupied Germany, and any attempt to apply it would devastate the country, leading to impoverishment, unemployment and unrest. By way of contrast to initial SCAP and Washington planning for the Japanese economy, Great Britain actually appeared quite generous.[51] Enlightened self-interest was clearly important, but concern that Japan not be economically crippled remained. In May 1948, Foreign Secretary Ernest Bevin spoke out against leaving Japan and its 'ninety millions of people . . . in a cesspool of poverty', and was supported in Japan by members of the UK Liaison Mission such as Sir Esler Dening.[52]

British industry feared it, too, was heading for the cesspool and continued to press, via the Board of Trade, for the imposition of quotas and restraints upon Japan. Raymond Streat rejoined that Britain could not have full employment, social security and exports if Japan were free of restraints.[53] In July 1948, a Lancashire delegation insisted upon seeing Bevin to demand that Japanese spindles be restricted to 3.5 million, fewer than one-third the prewar number. Bevin declined to see the delegation and made clear his views in a letter to Harold Wilson, president of the Board of Trade and important ally to Lancashire. Restrictions were beyond unacceptable; they were a

> reversal of the policy towards Japanese industry hitherto advocated. On the grounds of economic principle, political possibility and administrative expediency, H.M. government have always maintained that no proposal for restricting the development of Japanese consumption goods industries should be put forward.[54]

Without doubt, the 'reverse course' and the extent to which the United States was willing to remove Japan's economic fetters concerned the British government.[55] Nonetheless, it held firmly to the line that British industry would have to embrace competition and survive through higher efficiency and more 'derring-do' in international markets.

To explain the refusal to entertain industrial demands for protection, one cannot deny the overriding importance of the Anglo-American alliance to British policy. Over-antagonizing the Americans could promote an outright assault on the sterling area and Britain's regional position to ensure Japanese economic penetration. Apart from being humiliating, such a step would also have threatened Britain's own recovery given Malaya's status as the major dollar earner of the sterling area. Further, it was increasingly apparent over 1949 that initial American hostility to the survival of the sterling area and British colonialism in Asia had waned and would even be reversed in the face of the United Kingdom's imminent economic collapse. Washington understood the link of Imperial and Commonwealth trade to the postwar recovery of the United Kingdom, and hence its ability to resist communism in Western Europe. While the protectionist arrangements of the 1930s were rejected, America would nonetheless come to the assistance of Great Britain and the sterling area.[56] Washington agreed to aid London re-establish the prewar system of triangular trade, whereby UK dollar deficits were partially balanced by surpluses in trade with Malaya, and Malayan surpluses with the United States.[57]

Growing American support for the sterling area aside, it is also true that by the end of the 1940s, Britain had independently come to acknowledge that domination of Southeast Asia was no longer possible. Nonetheless, political and economic influence could be maximized through general intra-regional cooperation and economic growth. Such development would lead to new British markets and guarantee raw material supplies, with the huge dollar-earnings of Malayan natural rubber being the prime example. The corollary was the economic and social stability deemed essential if the region were to be successfully inoculated against the dangerous allures of communism. Inevitably, the problems were enormous. The colonial attitudes of European allies, namely the Netherlands and France, were regarded as more obstructive than enlightened. More importantly, Britain blatantly lacked the resources necessary to implement grandiose policies of aid and trade development.[58] Attracting American interest and cash was of paramount importance. While perhaps not quite so emphatic, to many Japanese involvement was also desirable and more than likely inevitable, even if occasionally repugnant.

The 1949–50 sterling area trade agreement, itself a great expansion upon the 1948 agreement, emphasized this point through permitting $400 million in Japanese–sterling area trade.[59] Similarly, Malcolm MacDonald, the Commissioner-General of the United Kingdom in Southeast Asia 1948–55, strongly promoted these aims of expanded Anglo-Japanese trade in his capacity as commissioner-general and chairman of the Far Eastern Defence Co-ordination Committee. Other UK officials, such as Esler Dening, provided support from within Japan.

The 1949 defeat of the Guomindang in China confirmed in MacDonald's mind the dangers posed by the spread of communism in Asia, and in May that year he returned to London to partake of an interdepartmental meeting with representatives from the Foreign, Colonial and Commonwealth Offices. MacDonald spoke emphatically on the danger of communist contagion; success in China was but the beginning. He predicted most of Indochina would fall within six months, to be followed by Thailand and Burma. With the buffers gone, Malaya and India would be left to face directly the communist threat. As a counter-measure, MacDonald proposed a regional political, economic and defence policy to convince Southeast Asians of their and Britain's ability to resist.[60] Allowing Japan a role could be deftly used to the advantage of the United Kingdom in its international relations with America, Japan and Southeast Asia.

MacDonald's several visits to Japan and the annual regional conferences held at Bukit Serene and then Mallaig,[61] make clear his concern for improved Japanese relations and trade. Japanese technical ability, consumer and capital goods, and even influence, were most likely a potential boon to the development and stability of Southeast Asia. Japan's return, therefore, 'should be viewed with friendly understanding'.[62] The gains for all were likely to be great. Japan must at all costs be kept within the capitalist camp and helped to avoid the economic and social decay, in addition to rising nationalism, born out of international isolation. By all accounts, MacDonald believed communism to be Japan's greatest peril and stated there was a real danger that Tokyo would succumb to this threatening ideology by the early 1960s. This would be an untenable 'blow to our [British] security in the Pacific and in Asia' in light of Japan's 'strategic land area, . . . the potential industrial power of this populous nation and . . . its energetic, efficient and aggressive military capacities'.[63] The Foreign Office concurred that Japan was a particularly important anti-communist bastion to the UK and a possible threat to British Far Eastern colonial and economic assets should the communists take hold. That Japan be prosperous was of cardinal importance and it should be made plain to Tokyo that cooperation would be made worth its while.[64] So important was retaining Japan for the free world that not only was a Japanese economic presence in Southeast Asian made acceptable, but

Japan should be pressed and aided to purchase even more. Malayan iron ore and rubber were good examples.[65] After all, one definite means of redressing the Southeast Asian imbalance of trade with Japan was to increase the overall volume of trade and promote Japanese purchases in the region.

East Asians, not that they were necessarily being asked, were also expected to gain under this system. The expansion of trade would maintain the Japanese standard of living as well as catering to the poorer sections of the populations in Southeast Asia who needed cheap consumer goods.[66] Exposing populations to the immediate gains derived from free trade within the capitalist bloc was the most effective means of denying communist propaganda a foothold in the region. MacDonald argued that economic suasion was a far more subtle means of winning hearts and minds than the Americans' ready turn towards military solutions. An overbearing western military presence only made easier communist appeals to nationalism.[67]

Finally, MacDonald argued that expanded regional trade with Japan was also to the greater benefit of British trade as a whole. Firstly, British territories would remain free of communism and thus open to British interests. Secondly, trade with Japan would increase the region's standard of living, the purchasing power of the rather large populations, and therefore stimulate further the expansion of international trade from which Britain could only gain.[68] This vision would not be without its short-term costs to British industry, but, echoing Whitehall and Westminster, MacDonald advised that manufacturers would do better to maintain quality, study special regional needs and improve upon delivery dates, than to demand protection.[69] Others added their voices to MacDonald's. The British Embassy in Thailand also supported a Japanese economic return to Southeast Asia as valuable, arguing that 'long term benefits of this prosperity will be reflected in the long-term benefits to British trade'.[70] The Treasury, too, sought to maximize trade between the colonial empire and Japan as without it Britain could 'hardly hope to induce her not to switch trade to the dollar area'.[71]

Positive encouragement from MacDonald aside, to a very real degree Japanese imports into Southeast Asia were needed to replace British exports. The United Kingdom's ill-affordable Korean War-led rearmament programme directed industrial production away from exportable consumer goods. Lancashire might have complained about Japanese textiles penetrating the Malayan market, but was in any case frequently unable to meet local demand. Equally, the costs of informal influence proved high and, over the early 1950s, doubts arose as to Great Britain's ability to sustain the necessary effort into the future. Public funds soon proved insufficient to meet the needs of colonial investment programmes. Alternative private sources of capital failed to materialize in sufficient quantity, as the City found more profitable avenues in Western Europe and North America than in grand plans for Empire and Commonwealth development. The Treasury, unconvinced of the economic grounds for colonial development, in its way also declined to prime the pump. For example, it proved highly unwilling to surrender 'double taxation', whereby a UK company gained relief neither from UK income tax nor colonial government levies.[72] Tellingly, from conception the Colombo Plan, regardless of its Commonwealth origins and symbolic value as evidence of UK commitment to colonial development, was reliant upon the United States for funds. From 1950–61, American aid to Southeast Asia through the Colombo Plan totalled $8.3 billion in comparison to the UK sum of £250 million over the same period.[73] In this context, decolonization and relative British decline also helped ease acceptance of the Japanese economic presence in Southeast Asia.

British sentiment towards Japan might thus appear rather benign, even indulgent. Malaya, Britain's dollar basket of the early Cold War, was apparently sufficiently juicy to share, textile and shipping industries could go on unprotected and Whitehall was imbued with the spirit of MacDonald's 'friendly understanding'.[74] Inevitably, there is a need for caution. Despite a remarkable generosity, Britain maintained significant fears as to the depth and longevity of a potential Japanese economic assault on UK interests. The 1949 Dodge Plan for Japanese stabilization is often held to have dramatically undervalued the yen in order to boost Japan's Asian and Pacific exports. While not nearly so apparent at the time, Britain and Australia were both sufficiently concerned to defy intense American pressure, refusing to agree to most-favoured-nation trading arrangements for Japan.[75] Indicative of long-term British fears, once more against powerful US pressure, London opposed Japanese admission to GATT until 1955. The Foreign Office was sufficiently wary of domestic opposition and feared that calls for protection would only increase as the Japanese economy grew. Further, the Commonwealth connection preyed upon Whitehall's mind. New Zealand, Australia, South Africa and other colonies discriminated against Japan to the United Kingdom's advantage; if Great Britain scaled down its economic discrimination against the Japanese, it could tempt others to do likewise to even greater UK detriment.[76]

In Southeast Asia, too, Britain sought to temper an open-armed embrace with a narrower doorway. MacDonald might well have viewed Japan as being worth some 'calculated risks',[77] but he always qualified his remarks. The British were not 'going to be "mugs"' and negotiate unfavourable disagreements; nor would the Japanese be permitted to 'advance their selfish interests to our own prejudice'.[78]

Britain accepted a renewed Japanese presence, but on the proviso the '*process is gradual*'.[79] Graduality was often relatively easy to enforce. For example, when Japan's Kokan Mining Company requested permission to recommence activities at Malaya's Temangan Mine, it was advised by British representatives that UK and Malayan partners would increase its chances. Furthermore, Commonwealth partners were to have a controlling interest; Japanese employees were not to exceed 100, among whom 'any subversive activities . . . could be controlled by normal Special Branch methods'; and a one-third minimum of technicians had to hold a Commonwealth nationality.[80] Other means were also open: visas could be restricted and in the case of Singapore commercial travellers were limited to one month; Malaya would admit no one who had been resident prior to or during the war (Tokyo's first nominated vice consul to Singapore, Oda Masakazu, was also rejected on these grounds),[81] and even the Raffles Hotel refused to accept bookings for Japanese consular officials in search of lodgings and offices on the 'grounds that their staff would object strongly'.[82] In Southeast Asia, Britain was 'at home' to the Japanese, but equally determined to retain the rights and will to exercise control over the nature of the visit.

The world of the mid- to late 1950s, however, was much changed even when compared to a mere five years previous. Weaponry and political developments rendered many colonial bases far less strategically useful than imagined. The Commonwealth shrank and became increasingly incohesive and impotent: Burma left in 1948, the Federation of Malaya gained internal self-government in 1955 as did Singapore in 1959. Increasingly, Southeast Asians wrested control over economic decision-making from the British. The United Kingdom also looked to the United States and an incrementally uniting Western Europe as the key sources of economic prosperity and military security.

The high-tech option: jet engines and atomic power

Anglo-Japanese economic and trading relations did not fall away with the retreat from empire. The 'Three Circles' ensured the United Kingdom itself held direct interests in trade with Japan and not merely through colonial and Commonwealth partners. Trade continued on a broad front, but of particular interest are the British attempts to forge within Japan a market for jet engine technology and nuclear reactors. The attempt testifies to British determination to remain an engineering and industrial power of the first rank, and a measured willingness to challenge American predominance in Japanese markets. Despite the implications such technologies held for the globally sensitive issue of Japanese rearmament, Britain's manufacturers nonetheless steadfastly pursued the growing Japanese market.

A jet engine remains to this day a highly complicated piece of machinery, whose manufacture requires sophisticated technological application. While its romantic grandeur and value as a status symbol has, for the most part, fallen away to be replaced by a search for the perfect garlic crusher, previous generations saw things rather differently. Sir Raymond Streat, borne down upon by postwar austerity and a Britannia no longer laughing foes to scorn, soothingly reflected that 'in the midst of all these indications of retreat our leadership in the jet aeroplane brought comfort to the heart of our meanest citizen'.[83] A rather less phlegmatic industrialist, Okano

Yasujiro, grandiloquently claimed that 'nations which cannot carry out the planned manufacture of such [jet aeroplanes] will fall from the ranks of civilisation'.[84]

Japanese and British aviation interests were quick to explore mutual interests as the Occupation came to an end and Japan regained its sovereignty in April 1952. Japanese orders for civilian aircraft were immediate, and numerous UK aircraft and engine manufacturers, such as De Havilland, Rolls Royce and Percival Aircraft, reported Japanese inquiries and sales of aircraft and engines.[85] Neither was passivity a characteristic of the UK aviation sector and its ambitions in the Japanese marketplace. De Havilland exploited its representatives in Japan (Cornes and Co.) to negotiate the possible licensed manufacture of the Vampire jet trainer. Further, in November 1952, Auster Aircraft dispatched its chief test pilot, Ronald Porteous, to demonstrate its wares to a thrilled Japanese public. While the Crown Prince's attendance was gratifying, it was Porteous' display at Hamamatsu, Headquarters of the National Police Reserve (NPR), which better indicated the potential future of Anglo-Japanese aviation links.[86]

April 1953 saw Baron Okura [*sic*], head of the Okura Trading Company, visit the United Kingdom to sound out the acquisition of manufacturing rights for helicopters and fighters. The visit was purely a private commercial one, although Okura discussed his visit with the commercial secretary of the British Embassy in Tokyo, who recommended he be given all reasonable assistance.[87] Okura lost no time in catching up with old chums, including Lord Brabazon of Tara, to whom he was affectionately known as Ping Pong. Brabazon invited Okura for dinner, where the latter elaborated upon the purpose of his mission. Okura explained that Japan was not permitted armaments, but showing a deft understanding of language, he voiced a hope that, given the acceptability of a National Police Reserve, a National Police Fighter Force might be possible. A sympathetic Brabazon proffered advice on how to visit Hawker for fighters; visits to Westland and Bristol had already been arranged.[88]

There are no records of any concrete results from the Okura visit, but further proof of Japanese military interest came with the August 1952 formation of the Japanese National Security Force (NSF), whose officials approached De Havilland with a view to purchasing 100 Vampires at a cost of £4 million.[89] Again, while large-scale orders failed to materialize, it did provide evidence to the British of Japanese willingness to seek non-American suppliers. London was quite happy to assist this process. British assistance to Japanese rearmament was tricky given public opinion, but politically speaking the Foreign Office and Ministry of Supply held no objections; if Japan did not purchase military aircraft from the UK she would merely go elsewhere, namely the United States. The potential economic gains were such it would have been foolish to lose out.[90]

In the long run, however, Britain did most definitely lose out, as industrialists and officials were forced to accept drastically reduced circles of influence. Arming East Asia was an American preserve; British intervention was at best irritating and certainly not acceptable. In this instance, concern over the Anglo-American alliance and the fragility of British power east of Suez severely limited military sales. Ironically, it was the very enormity of the potential Japanese market that tempered manufacturers' grand schemes, as they calculated the degree of offence British success would cause the United States was too great. Despite many positive signs, De Havilland held back from exploiting Japanese demand, as they did not 'wish to risk a rebuff administered by the Americans to the Japanese supporters of our products'.[91]

In reality, the American position was unassailable and the UK lacked the economic and political leverage to make any dramatic difference. Aeroplane manufacture is incredibly expensive and Japanese development programmes of the 1950s were totally reliant upon American financial and technological support.[92] Malignant neutrality alone was sufficient to demolish Japanese plans to 'Buy British', because all the United States need do was refuse to fund it. The Japanese Ministry of Finance fought fiercely against paying for the full cost of jet aeroplane manufacture and the UK lacked the resources to match American generosity.[93] The close US–Japanese military alliance, the extent of American funding and insistence on hardware compatibility (enforced through large-scale American military aid in kind) thus blocked British military sales to Japan. Little could be done to redress the imbalance, and privately the Foreign Office admitted that it used many of the same measures itself to ward off American aid proposals to designated areas of British influence, such as Iraq and Pakistan.[94] To challenge the United States in the Far Eastern military market could very easily prove counterproductive to Britain's larger strategic and economic concerns.

The nuclear industry represented a further aspect to Anglo-Japanese relations. While important from an economic perspective, atomic energy held far more promise to both nations than simply trading balances and monetary returns. Great Britain hoped to reaffirm its prestige in East Asia as a great power with technology and industry as good as, if not better than, anywhere else. In turn, the Japanese conservative elite found in British science and energy concerns a useful ally in the campaign to dispel the persistent 'nuclear allergy' derived from Hiroshima and Nagasaki. Britain once again challenged entrenched American and Japanese business interests, but strove to extend market share in a leading-edge industry with enormous potential for growth. Opportunities for Japan to play each western power off against the other no doubt proved attractive, as did the chance to attract sources of nuclear power and technology external to the United States. In April 1959, the Japan Atomic Power Corporation (JAPC) agreed that Japan's first atomic reactor would be British.

Industrial atomic power in Britain commenced on 16 October 1956 at Calder Hall, Cumbria, with a royal tug of a lever sending atomic reactor-generated electricity coursing through the National Grid. It was preceded, nearly four years to the day, by Britain's first explosion of an atomic bomb in the Monte Bello island group lying off Australia's western coast. In both civil and military applications of atomic energy Britain was thus a leading power. Control over how best to develop these capacities for the future was entrusted to the United Kingdom Atomic Energy Authority (UKAEA).[95] In Japan, atomic energy research was administratively framed by the 27 December 1956 Basic Atomic Energy Law, to promote research, development and utilization of the atom for peaceful purposes, and the simultaneous establishment of the Japan Atomic Energy Commission (JAEC). The Commission was under the immediate control of Shoriki Matsutarô, former proprietor of Yomiuri Newspapers.

One of JAEC's more immediate tasks was to address the negative image of nuclear energy in Japan. Shoriki, with his media links, was by all accounts a 'forceful and energetic businessman . . . closely associated with the swing of public opinion in favour of atomic energy development'. In the eyes of the Foreign Office, much of the credit was also due to 'Mr Nakasone Yasuhiro . . . one of the most prominent younger Diet members'.[96] Keen to get the show (quite literally) on the road, Shoriki helped arrange for a touring exhibition, based upon the enormously successful 1955 Geneva-based International Conference on Peaceful Uses of Atomic Energy, to visit Japan. British interest was strong, and despite some financial difficulties, London stressed the need to participate 'to counteract United States preponderance in this field'.[97] A March 1956 request by Yomiuri for either Sir John Cockcroft or Sir Christopher Hinton, both leading British atomic scientists, to visit Japan and lecture provided the perfect opportunity.

Eventually, Sir Christopher Hinton took up the offer and travelled to Japan in May 1956. The entire visit was carefully stage-managed and as much a propaganda coup, to the advantage of all concerned, as an economic opportunity. Hinton elected to travel by liner, but before he could sail into Yokohama, he was intercepted by a private launch filled to the brim with such notables as the first secretary of the British Embassy, the vice president of Yomiuri and approximately 40 journalists and photographers. Should, heaven forbid, the boffin prove staid and life grow dull, Miss Yokohama 1956 was strategically placed to add glamour to the proceedings. Hinton was later introduced to Emperor Hirohito, and escorted to the Diet, where he faced yet another barrage of television cameras and studio lights. The prime minister, Hatoyama Ichiro, mixed explanation with apology: 'I hope you do not mind all of this, it is democracy.'[98]

Hinton spent the next fortnight lecturing in Japan's major conurbations and being wooed by 'democracy'. He gleefully noted the British Embassy's comment that 'no individual had so great an effect on British prestige in

Photograph 8.1 Examining the University of Kyoto's cyclotron

Japan on any previous occasion except possibly that of the Prince of Wales in the late 1920's [*sic*]'.[99] The visit pleased all, including Shoriki, who 'knew how to squeeze every penny worth of value from what he spent to give publicity to atomic energy'.[100] Confirming heightened British status in Japan scientific circles, the Howell Reactor School agreed to accept two Japanese students in July 1956.

As to future market share, Hinton was confident of British success and stated the Japanese market was potentially the biggest and most important in the world after Great Britain. He reiterated that the Americans were also most likely of a similar mind and busily cultivating the Japanese. Finally, he reported an approach by the JAEC to purchase a Calder Hall-type reactor.[101] Sir Esler Dening confirmed as much from within the British Embassy, but also added that while the Japanese were interested he suspected they would 'try to derive the maximum advantage from our knowledge and experience and to give us as little as possible in return'. He predicted a similar policy towards the Americans.[102]

Nonetheless, the British Embassy in Tokyo lobbied hard to promote the sale of atomic reactors to Japan. It acknowledged that Britain was pressed to

Photograph 8.2 Sir Christopher Hinton takes part in a panel discussion sponsored by *Yomiuri Shinbun* on 'History and Future Prospects of British Atomic Power' – *left to right*: Kojima Fumio, *Yomiuri* Managing Editor; Dr Fushimi Koji, Chairman of Japan Science Council's Special Committee on Atomic Energy; Ishikawa Ichiro, Member of the Atomic Energy Commission; Sir Christopher Hinton; Dr Fujioka Yoshio, Member of the Atomic Energy Commission; and Komagata Sakuji, Director of the Atomic Energy Research Institute

supply the equipment and fuel for its own commitments, and that conventional thinking had surrendered Japan to the Americans. However, Japan was held to be a special case, worth an extra effort and far too valuable to be given over so readily to US interests. The attraction again lay in Japan being the 'Workshop of Asia'. Japan was already an advanced industrial nation with a developed electricity power industry. This was not a market that needed to catch up with the West, but rather one that could immediately and on a large-scale absorb British nuclear talent and exports.[103] Britain, being the first nation to feed nuclear-generated electricity into a national grid, was in the prime position to lead the way in the peaceful application of atomic energy.

As 1956 progressed teams of Japanese scientists visited Calder Hall and negotiations over the purchase of an atomic reactor continued. Initially,

British business followed nicely the official lead. Babcock & Wilcox (London), and its numerous subsidiaries (not all of which were British), demonstrated ready interest in the Japanese energy market.[104] The English Electric Company moved with alacrity and dispatched its Far Eastern representative, a Mr Thompson, to Tokyo with instructions to stay for an indefinite period and nurture the market. The British Embassy was delighted, and reported back that this 'kind of vigorous follow-up action . . . helps to keep the pot boiling for us'.[105] Painfully cognisant of deficient British resources, the Embassy also considered the best means for Britain to penetrate the Japanese market and successfully see off American competition. Under UKAEA rules, groups of manufacturers were required to tender for the construction of an entire reactor which led to four, later five, consortia. In effect, each one of these consortia could therefore bid to manufacture nuclear reactors for Japan. To the Embassy's consternation, the consortia could be led into cut-throat bidding against each other, rather than concentrating resources to face the true rival, that is the United States. The need to consider how effectively to deploy limited resources was crucial.[106]

Thompson and Babcock, however, were more prominent in Japan through being few in number rather than startlingly active. Contrary to urgings from the Embassy's commercial section, compared to the US, British business' 'manifestations of interest [were] pathetically inadequate'.[107] This was despite individual Japanese firms approaching UK manufacturers directly (much to the annoyance of the Japan Atomic Energy Commission).

One major block on British activities was the American dominance in key areas. Technical tie-ups between US and Japanese industrial concerns helped render many market areas impenetrable. Tokyo Electric, for example, held links to America's General Electric; similarly Kansai Electric used only Westinghouse equipment. American moves to dominate the Japanese market were well supported and the US Export–Import Bank announced it would lend the Japanese 80 per cent of the funds necessary to purchase a nuclear reactor. Finally, the United States simply had significantly more cash available to promote its products. For example, Great Britain could only sit and enviously watch the May 1957 Joint US–Japan Industrial Forum. Over 40 American industrial representatives from Detroit, Edison, Westinghouse and so on assembled in Japan to advertise their wares. Participants were invited from all over South and Southeast Asia (including many Commonwealth countries), lavishly entertained and showered with glossy promotional literature at American expense. The United Kingdom was horrified, but powerless, as the Forum degenerated into thuggery and the Americans used it as a public platform to insult British reactors as 'just plain amusing', 'a poor attempt' and 'inefficient'. It later became apparent these responses were stimulated by an earlier press conference at which the aircraft magnate, Okano Yasujiro, told the waiting reporters that the Americans were far behind the British.[108]

The approach of the British nuclear industry to Japan was in turn largely coloured by suspicion of Japanese intentions. Businessmen tended to side more with Dening's earlier statement that Britain would end up giving a great deal of aid and advice for very little long-term gain. The Nuclear Power Plant Company (NPPC) made clear its lack of interest from the outset. Its chairman, Sir Claude Gibb, evoked textile manufacturers' fears of Japanese design theft, and stated that Japan was simply out to copy British equipment and methods.[109] Reluctant to sponsor an East Asian rival, NPPC doubts as to Japanese business morality grew throughout the early months of 1957 and the board decided that Japanese visitors took up too much time, other pressures were great, and that consequently it did not 'wish to receive any more visitors from that country'.[110] Doubts within the official nuclear establishment also grew. UKAEA grew more convinced the Japanese were simply trying to squeeze information from the UK as in a 12-month period alone it hosted over 70 Japanese visitors without any sign of business.[111]

Such suspicions may well have had some foundation, but Japan itself was hardly in a position to make snap decisions. Inevitably, the Japanese needed to settle upon policy and decide the direction they wished their newly-born nuclear industry to take. The Japanese were split, as the British well knew, into rival factions. Generally, manufacturers wished to import reactors as opposed to the scientists who preferred a 'ground-up' approach of developing technique through basic experimentation performed in Japan.[112] The Joint US–Japan Industrial Forum, if nothing else, made clear that at best Japan would import only one or two British atomic reactors.

This reduced promise was fulfilled in April 1959 when Britain's General Electric Company, in conjunction with Fuji Denki, made a successful tender to build Japan's first nuclear reactor at Tokai Mura, Ibaragi Prefecture. The experience came to symbolize the UK's sinking fortunes in the Japanese energy sector. According to Christopher Hinton, 'the contract was disastrously managed and . . . the job did untold harm to the prestige of British heavy engineering in the Far East'.[113] Design specifications were revised, work went poorly and the project was late and over budget. On-site construction fared little better because of endless delays. British-supplied steel plates were defective and had to be replaced by plates rolled in Japan. Once the plant was started up the boiler tubes vibrated until they broke. Indeed, the experience had not been 'a happy one'.[114]

Conclusion

1950s Anglo-Japanese trade and economic relations does not consist merely of balance sheets and figures. The perceptions and imageries held and employed by the British as the postwar economic relationship redeveloped reveal much of how Great Britain viewed Japan and, even more, its own position in the new world order.

Churchill's placing of Britain in the very juncture of the 'Three Circles' itself speaks volumes on an elite unwilling to conceive of a role less than central to international affairs. This is not to say that awareness of overwhelming American power, projected both globally and within Japan, had not seeped into British consciousness. The 1956 Suez Crisis ensured that no British prime minister would again directly defy the wishes of the United States. Nevertheless, Britain could still seek to mediate and balance the two superpowers. Experience with a global empire, supposed diplomatic prowess, and lengthy familiarity with the Far East was meant to count for something. As the ditty has Lord Halifax whispering to Lord Keynes 'it's true they have the money bags, but we have all the brains'.[115]

As a self-appointed tutor and mediator, Britain's first task was to 'encourage the Japanese in their present tendency to look to Great Britain as the greatest stabilising influence in international affairs'.[116] This mission held as true for trade as anything else. Through proper guidance, the Japanese could be educated out of their wicked interwar commercial habits and learn to participate responsibly in the international economy. Trade malpractices were intolerable, but entering into honest arrangements could help teach the Japanese to appreciate the obligations as well as the benefits of international cooperation and provide instruction in the standards of behaviour becoming to an important member of the Free World.[117] Benevolence could ease this process: not only would Japanese participation in Southeast Asian trade be of monetary value, but Britain could encourage it before Japan had time 'to reassume the garb of the truculent and embittered outcast'.[118]

Wartime bitterness also influenced British images of Japan with a resultant negative effect on economic relations. Stereotypes were reinforced and no doubt, subconsciously or otherwise, guided policy-makers and businessmen in their commercial dealings with Japan. Writing in 1950, Erick Pollock, a partner in Matheson & Co., felt as though the British were 'still at war', with negative attitudes towards the Japanese giving Britain the air of a vindictive nation to its long-term economic cost.[119] Foreign Secretary Anthony Eden spoke for many when he confessed 'it is not easy to like the Japanese, but clearly they count for a great deal and will count for more'.[120] Malcolm MacDonald, a man who saw himself as a good friend of the Japanese and keen to involve them in Southeast Asian economic development, readily lapsed into stereotypes to support policy recommendations. Again, the 'Japanese are an unsatisfactory people' whose desire to economically, if not politically, dominate the Far East had been tempered merely by the enormity of defeat.[121] Japanese characteristics had not changed and, in fact, one of the key reasons for their apparent susceptibility to communism was a liking for authoritarian rule (by the Right or Left, it mattered little lest the Japanese appear fussy), and possessing a dictatorially authoritarian nature.[122] With such honesty apparently being the basis of friendship, MacDonald added, 'as friends of both the Americans and the Japanese we can make a considerable contribution to the solution of the problem between the Western democracies and Japan'.[123]

Sir Christopher Hinton, holder of the Order of the Rising Sun, provides a further example of both the flexibility of perceptions and the potential impact on Anglo-Japanese economic relations. According to Hinton, the sale and construction of the atomic reactor was a disastrous episode. At least indirectly, Hinton attributes some of the difficulties to racism and hatred of the Japanese. Sir Claude Gibb, chairman of the Nuclear Power Plant Company, is given as a prime example: a man who would have nothing to do with the Japanese to the long-term detriment of Britain's business relations. Cynically, Hinton added that 'this carry-over of wartime Australian hatred for the Japanese evaporated after 1962 when Britain made her unsuccessful attempt to get into the Common Market and Japan became one of Australia's biggest customers'.[124] With no sense of irony or inconsistency, Hinton then likened the Japanese, as many have done before, to children. Like children 'they are slow to take strangers to their heart but once they [trust you] their reliance . . . and friendship . . . is enduring'. The child-like nature of the Japanese explained their quick intelligence, ability to learn and receptiveness to new ideas. The war, of course, gave a new twist to an old tune: 'And like children, when they were cruel, as they were during the War, they are really cruel and who can be as cruel as a cruel child?'[125]

Trading and economic relations between Great Britain, the Commonwealth and Empire and Japan over the 1950s succinctly demonstrate the problems facing the United Kingdom as it sought to affirm its position in the postwar economic and political order.

The manner of Japan's economic return to Southeast Asia tells heavily of Britain's limited ability to defy the United States and unwillingness to sacrifice the American alliance. The protectionist calls of British manufacturers were generally discounted and colonial economic links gradually withered. However, the retreat was neither chaotic nor immediate. British policymakers did envision a Japanese economic role in the region that flattered their own long-term interests in a managed withdrawal. To an extent, Whitehall and Westminster were able to limit and define the nature of Japanese economic activities in Southeast Asia. Other markets and possibilities attracted British industry and finance away from Empire and thus inevitably made room for Japanese counterparts. Nonetheless, British political influence was clearly eroded in East Asia. Atomic reactors and jet aeroplanes and engines were a showcase of UK talent with great commercial opportunities in Japan. However, the British remained wary. Profit and the chance to weaken American predominance were attractive and reflect interest in the Japanese market and mutual Anglo-American rivalries and jealousies. The resources necessary to overturn the American position and ignore the subsequent political ramifications did not always reflect aspirations. Daily, the oscillations of the 'Three Circles' grew more difficult to synchronize.

Acknowledgements

The author would like to thank archivisits and staff at the Institute of Mechanical Engineers (Christopher Hinton Papers), Palace Green Library, University of Durham (Malcolm MacDonald Papers) and the Public Records Office, London.

Notes

1. W. Churchill, *Europe Unite: Speeches 1947 and 1948* (London: Cassell, 1950), p. 417.
2. On Churchill's 'Three Circles' concept, see J. Frankel, *British Foreign Policy 1945–1973* (London: Oxford University Press, 1975), pp. 157–60.
3. Churchill, *Europe Unite*, p. 418.
4. E. Wilkinson, *Japan versus Europe: a History of Misunderstanding* (Harmondsworth: Penguin Books, 1983), pp. 68–77.
5. Public Record Office, London (hereafter PRO), FO 371/105386 'British Embassy Washington to John Boyd, Information Office, Foreign Office', 30 November 1953.
6. Supreme Commander for Allied Powers. This title refers both to General Douglas MacArthur, who directed the Allied occupation of Japan until his dismissal in 1951, and also to the bureaucratic organization as a whole which oversaw occupied Japan 1945–52.
7. See, for example, W. Borden, *The Pacific Alliance: United States Foreign Economic Policy and Japanese Trade Recovery, 1947–1955* (Madison: University of Wisconsin Press, 1984); J. Dower, *Empire and Aftermath: Yoshida Shigeru and the Japanese Experience, 1898–1954* (Cambridge, Mass.: Harvard University Press, 1979); and J. Dower, 'Occupied Japan and the Cold War in Asia', in J. Dower, *Japan in War and Peace: Selected Essays* (New York: New Press, 1993).
8. See, for example, T. Remme, *Britain and Regional Cooperation in South-East Asia, 1945–49* (London: Routledge, 1995); and N. White, 'Britain and the return of Japanese economic interests to South East Asia after the Second World War', *South East Asia Research*, 6, 3, 1998, pp. 281–307.
9. FO 371/99439, British Embassy, Bangkok to Anthony Eden, FO, 23 December 1951.
10. *Keizai Dantai Rengokai* (Federation of Economic Organisations). Pressure group representing the interests of Japan's heavy and chemical industrial sector formed in August 1946. See C. Yanaga, *Big Business in Japanese Politics* (New Haven and London: Yale University Press, 1968), passim.
11. K. Uemura, 'Nankan Nihon Keizai no Dakaisaku', *Jitsugyo no Sekai*, 50, 8, 1953, pp. 24–5.

12. Nippon Kayaku manufactured gunpowder, but changed production to fertilizers after Japanese defeat in 1945.
13. Y. Hara, 'Baisho Mondai to Tonan Ajia Shokoku no Doko', *Keidanren Geppo*, 3, 1953, p. 7.
14. Ibid., p. 7.
15. M. Fukushima, '"Tonan Ajia Kaihatsu" to iu koto no Kangaekata', *Keidanren Geppo*, 3, 1953, pp. 2–4.
16. 'MSA Enjo to Boei Seisan', *Keizai Orai*, August 1953, pp. 12–13.
17. K. Kondo and H. Osanai (eds), *Sengo Sangyoshi e no Shogen*, vol. III (Tokyo: Mainichi Shinbunsha, 1973), pp. 251–3.
18. (Asano) Keidanren Jimukyoku, 'Nihon Gijutsu Kyoryoku Kabushikikaisha no Setsuritsu Keika ni tsuite', *Keidanren Geppo*, 9, 1956, pp. 45–7; T. Senga (Chiga), 'Betonamukoku to no Gijutsu Kyoryoku Keiyaku Teiketsu no Keii', *Keidanren Geppo*, 1, 1958, pp. 57–9; Keidanren, *Boei Seisan Iinkai Tokuho*, 58, 25-5-58, 'Boei Sangyo Seibi ni kansuru Kenkyu Hoshin o Kettei', pp. 1–4.
19. Fukushima, '"Tonan Ajia kaihatsu" to iu koto no Kangaekata', p. 5.
20. Cited in K. Shoda (ed.), *Kindai Nihon no Tonan Ajiakan* (Tokyo: Ajia Keizai Kenkyujo, 1978), p. 135.
21. A. Rotter, *The Path to Vietnam: Origins of the American Commitment to Southeast Asia* (Ithaca and London: Cornell University Press, 1987), pp. 130–1.
22. Malcolm MacDonald Papers, University of Durham (hereafter MMC), 19/7/13, 'Press Release on Third Visit to Tokyo', 8 July 1952. The actual figures are originally given in Malay dollars (Malay $19 700 000; $13 200 000; $157 000 000; $243 700 000 respectively). As of 1906, the pound sterling–Malay/Straits dollar exchange rate was set at the constant level of 2s 14d to the dollar, that is nearly 12 new pence or one-eighth of a pound.
23. International Bank for Reconstruction and Development, *The Economic Development of Malaya* (Baltimore: John Hopkins University Press, 1955), pp. 352–3.
24. White, 'Britain and the Return of Japanese Economic Interests', p. 283. On the Colombo Plan, see A. Porter, 'Colombo Plan', Note by Secretary of State for Foreign Affairs and other Ministers, 20 December 1951, CAB 129/48, in A.N. Porter and A.J. Stockwell (eds), *British Imperial Policy and Decolonisation 1938–64*. vol. 2, *1951–64* (London: Macmillan – now Palgrave, 1989), pp. 115–26; Remme, *Britain and Regional Cooperation*, pp. 200–16.
25. M. Dupree (ed.), *Lancashire and Whitehall: the Diary of Sir Raymond Streat*, vol. 2, 1939–57 (Manchester: Manchester University Press, 1987), pp. 646–50.
26. Remme, *Britain and Regional Cooperation*; N. Tarling, *The Fall of Imperial Britain in Southeast Asia* (Kuala Lumpur and London: Oxford University Press, 1993); White, 'Britain and the Return of Japanese Economic Interests', p. 286.
27. Cited in Remme, *Britain and Regional Cooperation*, p. 206.
28. White, 'Britain and the Return of Japanese Economic Interests', p. 287.
29. Ibid., p. 287.
30. Cited in Dupree (ed.), *Lancashire and Whitehall*, p. 699.
31. Ibid., p. 289.
32. G. Daniels, 'Britain's View of Post-war Japan, 1945–9' in I. Nish (ed.), *Anglo-Japanese Alienation, 1919–1952* (Cambridge: Cambridge University Press, 1982), pp. 273–4.
33. Dupree (ed.), *Lancashire and Whitehall*, p. 737.
34. Ibid., p. 737.
35. Ibid., p. 552.

36. Ibid., pp. 730–1.
37. British members included Raymond Streat (chairman), Cuthbert Clegg (president of the British Employers Confederation), Haygarth Jackson (Cotton Board member and textile employer), Ernest Thornton (trade unionist and Labour MP for Farnsworth 1952–70), Air Vice-Marshal Bouchier (Federation of British Industries representative, Japan) and Cotton Board staff, James Broatch, T. D. F. Powell, R. Robson and Miss Morris (ibid., p. 540).
38. Ibid., p. 541. Once removed from MacArthur's presence, Streat's opinion of the man altered rapidly. By the time of the General's dismissal in 1951, Streat held that his 'philosophy, his experience and his egotism make him too narrow to wield all the influence he has been wielding' (p. 578), and by December 1954, MacArthur's ideas were decidedly more 'infantile' than profound (p. 736).
39. Ibid., p. 541.
40. Ibid., p. 581.
41. Ibid., p. 711; Daniels, 'Britain's View of Post-war Japan', pp. 274–5.
42. For example, through the Allied Council of Japan (ACJ) and the Far Eastern Commission. On the British role in the occupation, see R. Buckley, *Occupation Diplomacy: Britain, the United States and Japan 1945–1952* (Cambridge: Cambridge University Press, 1982).
43. On the occupation of Japan, see, for example, M. Schaller, *The American Occupation of Japan: the Origins of the Cold War in Asia* (New York and Oxford: Oxford University Press, 1985). The 'reverse course' is a generally accepted term in discussing the Occupation of Japan, however, debate still remains as to what exactly constitutes the 'reverse course' and even as to the date at which it can be said to have commenced.
44. GHQ/SCAP Records, RG 331, Box No. 6194, Folder No. (1) 004.03, Jan. 1951–Nov. 1951, ESS Programs and Statistics Division, 12 October 1951, *Administration of Japan's Industrial Mobilization*, p. 2.
45. Ibid., p. 2.
46. GHQ/SCAP Records RG 331, Box No. 7498, Folder No. (1), *Japan's Industrial Potential, Volume II*, October 1951, p. 1.
47. Ibid., p. 3.
48. GHQ/SCAP Records (RG 331, Box No. 6714, Folder No. 5, 'South East Asia, 1951 – Japan's export potential with specific reference to the economic development of the countries of South and Southeast Asia', p. 1.
49. See, for example, Borden, *The Pacific Alliance*.
50. Cited in Daniels, 'Britain's View of Post-war Japan', pp. 260–1.
51. Buckley, *Occupation Diplomacy*, pp. 123–5.
52. Cited in Daniels, 'Britain's View of Post-war Japan', pp. 262–3. As Japan was not a sovereign nation it was unable to officially be accredited with embassies, hence the designation 'Liaison Mission'. On Dening, see R. Buckley, 'In Proper Perspective: Sir Esler Dening (1897–1977) and Anglo-Japanese Relations 1951–1957', in H. Cortazzi and G. Daniels (eds), *Britain and Japan 1859–1991: Themes and Personalities* (London: Routledge, 1991), pp. 271–6.
53. Dupree, *Lancashire and Whitehall*, p. 441; Buckley, *Occupation Diplomacy*, p. 168.
54. Cited in Dupree, *Lancashire and Whitehall*, pp. 460–1.
55. For example, in 1948 the Draper Mission, led by William Draper, a former Wall Street banker and then under-secretary of the Army in charge of German and Japanese occupation policy, slashed reparations, watered down *zaibatsu*-dissolution plans and called for an 800 or 900 per cent increase in Japanese

exports (Borden, *Pacific Alliance*, pp. 77–83). On British concerns, see Buckley, *Occupation Diplomacy*, pp. 163–70.
56. White, 'Britain and the Return of Japanese Economic Interests', p. 295.
57. Rotter, *The Path to Vietnam*, p. 141 and Chapter 7, passim.
58. Remme, *Britain and Regional Cooperation*, pp. 195–9.
59. Buckley, *Occupation Diplomacy*, p. 169; Rotter, *The Path to Vietnam*, p. 129.
60. Remme, *Britain and Regional Cooperation*, p. 190.
61. Bukit Serene was MacDonald's first official residence in Malaya, with Mallaig being the second upon Bukit Serene's return to the local sultan. The major annual conferences, held annually over the period of MacDonald's appointment, to review Southeast Asian affairs and British policy for the region took their names from the respective residences.
62. MMC, 18/4/15, 'Bukit Serene Conference 1951 – Japan', 28 November 1951.
63. MMC, 33/2/85–7, MacDonald report to Anthony Eden, Foreign Secretary, 'Note on Japan', 26 July 1952.
64. FO 371/110435, 'Foreign Office Minute on Draft Paper on Policy Affecting Commercial Relations with Japan', July 1954.
65. MMC, 33/2/89, Ibid.; MMC 18/7/13, 'Mallaig Conference 12 December 1953 – Japanese Economic Expansion'.
66. MMC, 33/2/89, MacDonald report to Anthony Eden, Foreign Secretary, 'Note on Japan', 26 July 1952; MMC, 18/5/13, Bukit Serene Conference 1952 – Trade', 9 December 1952. On East Asian resentment and suspicion of such goals see Borden, *The Pacific Alliance*, p. 79. The Nationalist Chinese, for example, objected to Chinese gold looted by the Japanese being used by the US to promote Japan's emergence at the centre of the East Asian economy. General Romulo of the Philippines likewise feared Japan was being built up to again dominate the Far East.
67. MMC, 33/2/86, MacDonald report to Anthony Eden, Foreign Secretary, 'Note on Japan', 26 July 1952. On this point at least, MacDonald would have enjoyed Japanese support. In preparing for a doomed November 1954 visit to Washington to request a Marshall Plan for Asia, Yoshida Shigeru and his advisers also observed that 'the test of fighting communism lies as much, if not more, in the political and economic fields as in the military'. Cited in Dower, *Empire and Aftermath*, p. 473.
68. MMC, 33/2/90, MacDonald report to Anthony Eden, Foreign Secretary, 'Note on Japan', 26 July 1952.
69. MMC, 18/5/13–14, 'Bukit Serene Conference – Trade, 9 December 1952'; MMC 18/5/17, 'Bukit Serene Conference – Japan, 9 December 1952'.
70. FO 371/99439, British Embassy, Bangkok to Anthony Eden, FO, 23 December 1951.
71. Cited in White, 'Britain and the Return of Japanese Economic Interests', p. 296.
72. Porter and Stockwell (eds), *British Imperial Policy*, pp. 25–32.
73. Remme, *Britain and Regional Cooperation*, pp. 214–15.
74. MMC, 18/4/15, 'Bukit Serene Conference 1951 – Japan', 28 November 1951.
75. Buckley, *Occupation Diplomacy*, p. 193.
76. FO 371/110436, 'Problems Affecting UK Relations with Japan – Memorandum: Commercial Policy of the United Kingdom Towards Japan', 1954. On Japan and GATT, see G.C. Allen, *The Japanese Economy* (London: Weidenfeld & Nicolson, 1981), p. 168.

77. MMC, 33/2/92, MacDonald report to Anthony Eden, Foreign Secretary, 'Note on Japan', 26 July 1952.
78. MMC, 33/2/85 and MMC, 33/2/92, Ibid.
79. MMC, 18/4/15, 'Bukit Serene Conference 1951 – Japan', 28 November 1951. Underlined in the original.
80. FO 371/107003, 'Secretary for Defence, Defence Department, KL, Federation of Malaya – Japanese Iron Mining – Malaya', 5 September 1953. Even here, while the Board of Trade did not welcome any scheme that increased Japanese competitiveness through access to cheaper raw materials, it accepted the development as inevitable and offered no objections as long as there was no unfair depression of price. FO 371/107003, 'S. H. Levine (Board of Trade) to R. W. Selby (Foreign Office)', 12 December 1953. The Kokan Mining Company was represented in Malaya by Metal Exports Inc., an American firm based in Japan. It was soon apparent that Metal Exports was merely a front and full control rested with Kokan, itself closely linked to Japanese steel combines. On British attempts to limit the Japanese in Southeast Asia, especially with regards to iron ore and banking, see also White, 'Britain and the Return of Japanese Economic Interests', pp. 299–304.
81. MMC 19/7/16–17 'Consular Appointments', 25 July 1952; MMC 19/1/49–50, 'Entry of Japanese Nationals into the Malayan/Borneo Territories'.
82. MMC, 19/7/21, 7 October 1952.
83. Dupree (ed.), *Lancashire and Whitehall*, p. 706.
84. Mitsubishi Jukogyo, *Nagoya Kokuki Seisakujo Ni-jugonenshi* (Nagoya: Mitsubishi Jukogyo, 1983), p. 41. Okano was a wartime president of Mitsubishi's Nagoya Aircraft Works and lobbied vigorously for the postwar resumption of jet aircraft manufacture in Japan.
85. For example, in 1952, De Havilland confirmed Japanese orders for two Comets II, four Doves (a twin-engine monoplane), and three Herons (a four-engine version of the Dove which sat 14 passengers), worth £1.5 million – 'Comets for Japan', *Flight*, LXII, 2271, 1 August 1952, p. 135. De Havilland also formed links with Shinmeiwa to service and overhaul its Gipsy engines (used principally in Herons and Doves) (*Flight*, 67, 2410, 1 April 1955, p. 413).
86. *Flight*, 62, 2288, 28 November 1952, p. 693. The National Police Reserve, a 75 000-strong force formed in August 1950 under the orders of SCAP as the American occupying army and dispatched to the Korean conflict, represented the first stage in open Japanese rearmament. From its postwar inception to the current day, the greater percentage of Japanese aviation production has been directed towards the military.
87. FO 371/105409 'Visit of Okura to England to obtain manufacturing rights for helicopters and fighter aircraft for Japan – Tokyo to Foreign Office', 10 May 1953. Despite the Occupation-inspired removal of such titles as baron for all bar immediate members of the imperial family, official British correspondence maintained use of the title. Okura was very familiar with the United Kingdom, having received his education in an English 'crammer' and at Cambridge.
88. Ibid., 'Letter from Lord Brabazon of Tara to Sir William Strang, Permanent Undersecretary of State, Foreign Office', 16 April 1953.
89. FO 371/110467 'De Havilland Aircraft Company Ltd – letter to J. L. Thorne (Ministry of Defence), 19 February 1954; Ibid., 'Sale of De Havilland Vampires to Japan', 16 September 1954.

90. FO 371/105408 'Supply of Airplane Parts to Japan', undated (but certainly early 1953).
91. FO 371/110467 'De Havilland Aircraft Company Ltd – letter to J. L. Thorne of MoD', 19 February 1954.
92. For example, in order to make the first round (1956–8) of the North American F-86 Sabre production economically and politically acceptable, the United States had to promise $32 million in assistance as opposed to the Japanese contribution of $21.7 million (*Nihon Keizai Shinbun*, '2 nenkan ni 194ki', 16 March 1955.
93. FO 371/110467, p. 169.
94. FO 371/110467 'From F.O. to MoD', 9 April 1954.
95. Calder Hall was the world's first commercial nuclear power station. For the official history of Britain's atomic energy programme, see M. Gowing, *Independence and Deterrence: Britain and Atomic Energy, 1945–1952* (2 vols, London and Basingstoke: Macmillan – now Palgrave 1974).
96. FO 371/123155 Atomic Energy – Japan, 1956.
97. Ibid., 'Permanent under-secretary Foreign Office to Information Office, UK Embassy, Japan', 26 January 1956.
98. Hinton Papers, Institute of Mechanical Engineers (hereafter, HP), A6, *The Memoirs of Christopher Hinton* (unpublished, 1970), p. 346.
99. Ibid., p. 347. Bright, but prickly, Hinton was apparently known to his colleagues as 'Sir Christ' (T. Hall, *Nuclear Politics* (Harmondsworth: Penguin Books, 1996), p. 77). He made several later visits to Japan and in 1966 was awarded the Imperial Order of the Rising Sun. Such favours were reciprocated – for example, one of Hinton's Japanese colleagues, Dr Ipponmatsu Tamaki, received the honorary insignia of the Commander of the Order of the British Empire in 1977.
100. HP, *Memoirs*, p. 346.
101. FO 371/123156 Atomic Energy 'Visit of Sir Christopher Hinton to Japan (from Sir Christopher Hinton to Sir Edwin Plowder)', 18 May 1956. Calder Hall was an air-cooled reactor (ACR).
102. FO 371/123156 Atomic Energy 'Visit of Sir Christopher Hinton to Japan (from Sir Esler Dening, Tokyo)', 4 June 1956.
103. FO 371/123156 Atomic Energy 'British Embassy, Tokyo to S.H. Levine, Commercial relations and Exports Department, Board of Trade, London', 14 March 1956.
104. Babcock & Wilcox is a good example of the complexity in Anglo-American–Japanese business relations. Babcock & Wilcox (London) as Babcock & Wilcox and Taylor Woodrow joined with the English Electric Company to form one of the initial four consortia charged with constructing Britain's nuclear programme. There was also a Babcock & Wilcox (United States) which eventually manufactured the pile at Three Mile Island. Further complicating matters was Babcock & Hitachi (represented in Japan by Jock Shearer). Through the Hitachi link, Babcock was also able to enjoy a business relationship with Shibaura and then the Tokyo Electrical Company (which later merged with Shibaura to form Toshiba), to whom Babcock supplied American equipment through Babcock & Wilcox (USA) (Hall, *Nuclear Politics*, pp. 50, 174; FO 371/123157 Atomic Energy 'Letter from W. Harpham, British Embassy Tokyo to S.H. Levine, Commercial Relations and Exports Department, Board of Trade', 14 September 1956.
105. FO 371/129293 Atomic Energy 'letter from W. Harpman, British Embassy, Tokyo to P.G.F. Dalton, Foreign Office', 28 December 1956.

106. Ibid.; The consortia were AEI and John Thompson; the English Electric Company, Babcock & Wilcox and Taylor Woodrow; the Nuclear Power Plant Company; and the General Electric Company.
107. FO 371/129294 Atomic Energy 'Anglo-Japanese Co-operation', 8 February 1957.
108. FO 371/129295 Atomic Energy 'Japan/US Atomic Industrial Conference', 13 May 1957 and 'Japanese Atomic Development, William Hoplin (British Embassy, Tokyo) to Robin Hooper (Foreign Office). The list of nations which attended the Forum are as follows (number of attendees in parentheses): Afghanistan (1), Australia (4), Burma (9), Ceylon (4), India (1), Indonesia (7), Iran (1), Korea (10), The Lebanon (2), Pakistan (1), Philippines (11), Taiwan (18), Thailand (2), and Vietnam (1).
109. FO 371/123158 Atomic Energy 'Anglo-Japanese Co-operation', September 1956. Gibb was in fact an Australian.
110. FO 371/129298 Atomic Energy 'Letter from A.I. Scott, UKAEA to S.H. Levine, Board of Trade' (undated, but early 1957).
111. FO 371/129297 Atomic Energy 'Anglo-Japanese Atomic Co-operation', 3 July 1957.
112. FO 371/123156 Atomic Energy 'Visit of Sir Christopher Hinton to Japan (from Sir Esler Dening)', 4 June 1956.
113. HP, A6, *The Memoirs of Christopher Hinton*, p. 350.
114. Ibid., p. 347.
115. M. Hogan, *The Marshall Plan: America, Britain, and the Reconstruction of Western Europe, 1947–1952* (Cambridge: Cambridge University Press, 1987), back cover.
116. MMC 18/8/30 'Mallaig Conference 1955', 5 March 1955. The United States, incidentally, was also in need of British guidance as 'over and over again in Asia they do the right thing in the wrong way . . . we must do all we can to "educate" the Americans so that they make a more subtle understanding and wise approach to the Japanese'. MMC, 33/2/86 MacDonald report to Anthony Eden, Foreign Secretary, 'Note on Japan', 26 July 1952.
117. MMC 18/5/17 'Bukit Serene Conference – Japan', 8 December 1952.
118. FO 371/99439 Japan's Trade Relations with South-East Asia 'British Embassy, Bangkok to Anthony Eden, Foreign Office', 23 December 1951.
119. FO 371/83844 'Anglo-Japanese Relations', 9 March 1950.
120. MMC 22/10/24 'Anthony Eden to Malcolm MacDonald', 23 May 1952.
121. MMC 33/2/92 MacDonald report to Anthony Eden, Foreign Secretary, 'Note on Japan', 26 July 1952.
122. MMC 33/2/84 MacDonald report to Anthony Eden, Foreign Secretary, 'Note on Japan', 26 July 1952.
123. MMC 33/2/86 MacDonald report to Anthony Eden, Foreign Secretary, 'Note on Japan', 26 July 1952.
124. CH, *Memoirs*, p. 349.
125. Ibid., pp. 347–8.

9
Anglo-Japanese Investment in the Postwar Period*

Marie Conte-Helm

Introduction

The paths of British investment into Japan and Japanese investment into Britain in the postwar period have been alternately strewn with opportunities, obstructions and incentives. Fluctuating economic climates and government policies have dictated the pattern and direction of investment flows, as have the global ambitions of certain UK and Japanese firms. Against this broad picture, the much-observed asymmetrical relationship between British and Japanese direct investment can be seen as a phenomenon of only the last few decades. While Britain became the favoured destination for Japanese manufacturing investment in Europe in the run-up to 1992 and the formation of the Single European Market, Japan proved a more elusive goal for British manufacturers seeking to expand their interests abroad. The Anglo-Japanese trade imbalance has focused attention on bilateral disparities in general without considering the specific roots of the investment gap. In tracing the investment links forged by Britain and Japan in the postwar period, it is instructive to reflect back upon the case of a British multinational pioneer investor in Japan, to review the circumstances through which the history and pattern of Anglo-Japanese investment first evolved.

Dunlop Rubber Company established its factory at Kobe in 1909, initially motivated by the fear of tariffs and Japanese plans to launch their own rubber mills. Specializing in tyres for rickshaws and then cars, Dunlop maintained a dominant position in this industrial sector until the Second World War. It resumed operations at the Japanese plant following the war and, in 1963, transformed the company into an Anglo-Japanese joint venture, Sumitomo Rubber Industries (SRI). Dunlop's 40% stake in the firm was acquired by SRI in 1984; SRI then proceeded to purchase Dunlop's loss-making tyre factories in Britain, France and Germany for £45 million. In claiming to have

* Particular thanks are due to my Research Assistant on this project, Anna Spadavecchia.

'changed the master/student relationship,[1] SRI's chairman summoned up a legacy of Anglo-Japanese trade, technology transfer and economic relations which dated back to the Meiji period (1868–1912). The signing of the Anglo-Japanese Alliance in 1902 and its renewal in 1905 and 1911 marked the culmination of a half-century of diplomatic efforts and emerging business ties which saw firms such as Dunlop enter into the Japanese sphere. It is this historical perspective which lends such resonance to the postwar investment relationship between Britain and Japan.

This chapter will provide an overview of Anglo-Japanese investment in the postwar period but will do so in the context of changing economic imperatives and government policies. It will consider the framework, nature and scope of investment in Britain and Japan and the response that has been elicited by the presence of Japanese companies in Britain and British firms in Japan. The 1984 Sumitomo/Dunlop takeover represents an intriguing episode in the Anglo-Japanese relationship which cannot simply be explained away by 'coming-of-age' rhetoric, but derives from a complexity of factors central to the evolution of both countries' postwar economies. How this Edwardian investor in Meiji Japan became part of the postwar Japanese investment presence in Britain can be viewed as a subtext to the chapter or, in a sense, the 'ghost at Mrs Thatcher's table'. The transition from Dunlop in Japan to Sumitomo in Britain goes beyond the fortunes of a single company or industry to relate to patterns of international business activity in the pre- and postwar periods.

Britain's early business interests in Japan

Following Japan's reopening to trade in the 1850s, British business interests became centred on the merchant houses, shipping companies and banks which served this outward-reaching sector of the Japanese economy.[2] Foreign direct investment (FDI) was permitted initially only in the treaty ports, but the revision of the Commercial Code in 1899 paved the way for a wider spread of investment prospects in subsequent years. As a result, over the next three decades, a total of 21 joint British operations were established in Japan; this, in comparison with the 36 American and 17 German joint ventures formed by 1932.[3] It was during this period, in 1909, that Dunlop Rubber Company (Far East) Ltd was opened in Kobe.

Other British multinational investments in Japan prior to 1914 included the Japan Explosives Company Ltd, a cordite manufacturing firm established in 1905 by Armstrong-Whitworth, Chilworth Gunpowder Company and Nobel's Explosives. (Nobel's merged with several other firms in 1926 to form ICI.) In 1907, Nihon Seikosho (the Japan Steelworks), a steel and armaments factory, was established at Muroran on Hokkaido through a joint venture between Vickers, Armstrong-Whitworth and the Hokkaido Coal and Steamship Company.[4] In other sectors of industry, J & P Coats launched their Teikoku Cotton joint venture in 1907 and Babcock & Wilcox formed its Japanese joint venture, Toyo-Babcock, in 1910. In that same year, Lever opened a soap factory near Kobe. 'There is no doubt', wrote William Lever of this venture, 'that whoever enters into Japan in its development state will greatly benefit by having a secure foothold in the early days.'[5] There were, in addition, instances of British technology licensed to Japan, as with the supply of Parsons turbines to Mitsubishi from the early 1900s, a reflection and extension of the significant shipbuilding links between Britain and Japan. By and large, however, after 1918, the transfer of technology from Britain to Japan and commercial ties dwindled. One exception was the large chemical-importing business established by the British alkali-maker, Brunner Mond, in 1920, another antecedent to ICI links.[6]

Britain's already limited industrial presence in Japan declined further following the First World War. As Japanese competition increasingly threatened British markets in the East, few British multinationals sought to develop business ties in Japan. By 1940, British companies retained investments in just seven Japan-based manufacturing operations, three of these 100 per cent owned and four with some Japanese capital. The British multinationals' neglect of Japan over this period was documented in a 1934 report by the Federation of British Industries: 'If tariffs or cost of production prevent certain goods from being imported, British manufacturers should consider having their products manufactured in co-operation with Japanese concerns. For some reason British manufacturers have lagged behind their American competitors in this respect.'[7]

While British firms were thus characterized as reluctant in their pursuit of Japanese business, it has been argued that British industry in the interwar period in fact had little to offer a Japan eager for new skills and technology and locked into advantageous partnerships with American firms. It was only in certain sectors, such as the import and refining of petroleum, as in the case of the Rising Sun Petroleum Company, a subsidiary of the Anglo-Dutch Shell Group, that the British were able to compete effectively with American interests in Japan. The sequestering of all British assets in Japan during the Second World War brought an end to this phase of British investment and, in principle, allowed for new relationships to emerge in the postwar period.[8]

The Japanese business presence in Britain pre-1941

The nineteenth-century trade with Britain also resulted in the first direct investments from Japan in London. As elsewhere in Europe, the earliest Japanese affiliates were established in the fields of trade, banking, shipping and insurance.[9] Through their local offices, Japanese trading companies performed an important function in the late Meiji period, both as importers of European goods and technology into Japan and exporters of Japanese products to Europe. The most important of these, Mitsui & Co., established its London office in 1879. Others soon followed, along with representative offices of Japanese banks, such as the Yokohama Specie Bank, which opened its first European branch in London in 1884. The Yokohama Specie Bank, as the Japanese government's overseas agent, took on the responsibility for servicing Japan's foreign loans, raised on the London capital market. Britain's contribution to the modernization of Japan can also be calculated in this significant financial underpinning which saw, between 1897 and 1910, some £200 million raised by the Japanese government via the City of London.[10] London's importance as a financial centre was once again to exert an impact upon Japan's investment relationship with Britain in the postwar period.

Trade activities with Europe contributed a further Japanese presence in the form of shipping and insurance companies. Nippon Yusen Kaisha (NYK), Japan's premier shipping concern, established its European line service, operating between Yokohama and Antwerp, from 1896. It formed particular links with London, its port-of-call on the westbound route, and Middlesbrough-on-Tees, where it loaded goods for the return journey to Japan.[11] Meanwhile, various Japanese insurance companies set up London branches to supply shipping and insurance services to cover the cargo being transported between Japan and Europe. Tokio Marine Insurance Company dominated the field and established a London base in the 1890s. While such ventures were important to the servicing of trading links with Britain, the overall level of Japanese direct investment in this early period was relatively low.

Changes in the pattern of trade following the outbreak of the First World War in 1914 initially had an adverse effect upon the European operations of Japanese companies. The subsequent increase in the trade with Europe, however, led to the further expansion of the Japanese presence in Britain in the interwar period. By the mid-1920s, in addition to Mitsui & Co., a number of other leading trading firms, including Nihon Menka, Mitsubishi Shoji, Suzuki Shoten, Iwai Shoten, Okura Shoji, Takashimaya Iida and Ataka Shokai, had gravitated to London and were diversifying their trading operations, as well as serving as sources for market intelligence.[12]

Other Japanese service organizations moved to Britain in the aftermath of the First World War. The Sumitomo Bank established its London branch in 1918 and was followed by the Mitsubishi Bank and Mitsui Bank. Further Japanese shipping companies similarly set up agencies in Britain to support expanded services as Japanese overseas trading links flourished. As for the insurance sector, it has been calculated that, led by Tokio Marine, some ten Japanese insurance companies operated offices in Britain in the interwar period.[13] Despite these developments, Japanese investment in Britain prior to the Second World War remained limited in scope and served as an infrastructure for trade. When Japan's British assets were frozen on 26 July 1941, estimates placed their total value at less than £1 million, a sum that was later utilized to compensate former Allied prisoners of war.[14] By 1951, the slate was literally wiped clean with respect to Japanese direct investment in Britain, and a new pattern was set to emerge in line with changing economic circumstances in Britain and Japan.

Postwar foreign direct investment and policy initiatives in Japan

In the immediate aftermath of the war, a range of opportunities existed for British firms to resume earlier business connections in Japan. During 1946–47, for example, British shipping temporarily took up its former lead in the transport of commercial cargo to Japan. The resumption of Britain's investment interests was led by the banks and multinational firms with a prewar presence in Japan.[15] The Hong Kong and Shanghai Bank reopened its branches in Yokohama and Kobe in 1948, specialising in trade-related finance and catering to foreign customers. It was only in 1947 that British traders and businessmen were allowed to return; Foreign Office correspondence records an approach made to General MacArthur in that year by three of the largest prewar British investors, Babcock & Wilcox, J&P Coats and Dunlop, who were seeking to re-establish their Japanese operations. The armaments' manufacturer, Vickers, in contrast, chose for political reasons to decline a favourable offer, made in 1952, to restore its shares in the Japan Steel Works.[16]

The most notable and frequently-quoted instance of technology transfer from Britain to Japan during this period was in the motor industry. With the encouragement of the Ministry of International Trade and Finance (MITI), Nissan Motor Company entered into a technical agreement with Austin Motors in 1952, initially for the assembly and later the full production of Austin cars in Japan. Nissan's redesign and adaptation of Austin models remedied the lack of medium-sized cars in its product range, while earning royalties for the British firm of ¥600 million (about £600 000) between 1954 and 1959.[17] In another Anglo-Japanese automotive collaboration from these years, Isuzu licensed the technology from Britain's Rootes Group to assemble the Hillman Minx in Japan.[18] Overall, however, Britain's role as a purveyor of technology to Japan in the postwar period was limited in scope and greatly outpaced by Japan's American involvements. As Tsurumi has documented, of the international licensing agreements concluded between 1950 and 1964 which lasted over twelve months, Britain's share was 5.3% as compared to the 60% share held by US firms.[19] Over this same period of high growth in the Japanese economy, Britain's contribution of 1.5% to Japan's imports in 1954 had risen to only 2% in 1965.[20]

The small amount of British foreign direct investment in postwar Japan can be partly explained in relation to Japanese government policy between the 1950s and 1970s. Following the establishment of the Ministry of International Trade and Industry (MITI) in 1949, the enactment of the Foreign Exchange and Foreign Trade Control Law in 1949, and the Foreign Investment Law in 1950, international licensing agreements and foreign direct investments were strictly screened to protect Japan's indigenous industries from foreign competition. In sanctioning this legislation, the Occupation authorities were subsequently described as having presided over 'the institutionalization of the most restrictive foreign trade and foreign exchange control system ever devised by a major free nation'.[21] Certainly, until the liberalization of investment policy following Japan's admission to the Organization of Economic Cooperation and Development (OECD) in 1964, such legislation provided a disincentive for British and other foreign firms seeking to invest in Japan.[22] It has been argued that this 'negative legacy' affecting FDI in Japan extended to the post-1964 'slight liberalization', which continued to place the interests of Japan's infant industries above those of foreign investors, thus hindering their entry into the Japanese market at the most opportune time.[23]

Until the 1970s, applications for imports of technology and inward direct investment were carefully screened by the Foreign Investment Council. Only officially approved projects were guaranteed access to foreign exchange for the repatriation of dividends or capital and official approval was contingent on a breadth of vaguely-worded criteria. A US Senate Report (1975) underlined the oppressive spirit of this screening process that operated in the 1950s and 1960s:

> the process of obtaining validation was cumbersome and time consuming, characterised by ambiguity, uncertainty, red tape and protracted delay. Formal submission of the application was often preceded by lengthy informal negotiations with the authorities, who would insist on 'improvements' that could render the undertaking to be less attractive to the investor.[24]

While licensing agreements were the favoured form of transaction, in practice, approval might be more readily given to direct investment projects involving technology that could not be otherwise obtained.[25] In such cases, foreign ownership was limited to a maximum of 50 per cent with the Japanese joint venture partner always in control. Only yen-based investments allowed for full ownership by a foreign firm, though access to foreign exchange in such cases was not guaranteed. The priorities of government were clearly stated in the preamble to the Foreign Investment Law:

> The purpose of this law is to create a sound basis for foreign investment in Japan: by limiting the induction of foreign investment to that which will contribute to the self-support and sound development of the

> Japanese economy and to the improvement of the international balance of payments by providing for remittances arising from foreign investment, and by providing for adequate protection for such investment.[26]

Not suprisingly, the early postwar legislation and the procedures used to implement it led to little British foreign direct investment in Japan in the decades following the war.[27] Prior to 1970, there were just 16 wholly-owned British companies in Japan and 31 joint ventures, 29 in the manufacturing sector and 18 in service-related fields. The British companies which did succeed in penetrating the Japanese market during this period were mainly small. Two-thirds of the total capital of British manufacturing operations in Japan before 1970 can be attributed to just four Shell companies. Beyond these, there were few instances of British joint ventures in the manufacturing sector which were of significance to Japan's postwar development. Dunlop, as previously noted, was one. Having reacquired its Kobe factory in the late 1940s, it entered into a 40 per cent-owned joint venture with Sumitomo Rubber Industries in 1963. The partnership was sustained until the late 1970s by SRI's heavy dependence on Dunlop's technology. As Dunlop foundered in the early 1980s, its joint venture partner gradually assumed a different relationship with the UK tyre industry through its own foreign direct investment in Britain.

Japan's technological needs very much governed the implementation of trade and investment policy in the postwar period. This was particularly the case in the pharmaceutical sector where British expertise helped to fill a significant gap in the Japanese market. The story of Glaxo's long-term success in Japan[28] dates back to the 1950s, and illustrates the importance of links forged in the aftermath of the Allied Occupation following the Second World War. A marketing agreement concluded between Glaxo Laboratories and Shin Nihon Jitsugyo in 1954 for the sale of Dionosil in Japan resulted in the securing of exclusive agency rights for all Glaxo products in 1955. Shin Nihon's first joint venture company, the 40% British-owned Glaxo-Fuji Pharmaceutical Laboratories, was established in 1968, in the aftermath of the 1965 liberalization of trade. A further development led to the promotion and marketing of Glaxo products in Japan through the formation of Nippon Glaxo Ltd, a 50/50 joint venture company, in 1973. Between 1975 and 1976, Glaxo raised its stake in Glaxo-Fuji to 50 per cent and in Shin Nihon to 44%, leading to the growth of the firm's Japanese sales from £15 million in 1976 to £70 million in 1986. Such were the fortunes of one British manufacturer, perhaps battling against the legislative odds, but with a leading edge product base which was marketed effectively in Japan.

With Japan's admission to the OECD in 1964 and acceptance in 1963 of Article 8 of the Agreement of the International Monetary Fund (IMF), forbidding recourse to import restrictions for reasons of imbalance in international payments, a series of liberalization measures was set in place.

An official four-round Liberalization Programme began in July 1967 and was completed in 1971 with a fifth round initiated in 1973. The government announcement made on 1 May 1973 that Japan was '100 per cent liberalized' was received with scepticism by some, however, for in practice there were still protected industries, still prohibitive rules governing joint ventures and subsidiaries and still administrative restrictions on trade and capital transfer.[29] The screening of investment applications also continued beyond liberalization. It was, however, the start of an ongoing process which led the OECD, drawing on statistics from 1975–77, to conclude in 1979 that 'restrictions on inward direct investment have been progressively relaxed . . . such investments are fully liberalised'.[30]

As Dunning has noted, until the late 1970s British foreign direct investment in Japan exceeded that of Japanese firms in the UK.[31] Just as the Foreign Investment Law and FEFTCL inhibited British involvements in Japan, so too, reflecting the balance of payments situation, did it provide for tight controls on Japanese outward investment in the early postwar period. Investment applications were individually screened through MITI, with no published criteria for approval, and a Ministry of Finance permit was required for any direct outward investment.[32] This, combined with restrictions on outflows of foreign reserves, greatly curbed overseas investment initiatives. It was not until the end of the 1960s that the rising value of the yen, as well as shortages and increased costs for labour and raw materials, began to alter government policy in this respect and to stimulate foreign investment from Japan.

Postwar Japanese FDI in Britain prior to 1980

The relationship between trade and foreign direct investment forms part of the underlying history of Japanese firms in the UK following the Second World War. Just as technological needs influenced the pattern of approval for foreign investors in Japan, so too was overseas direct investment in the aftermath of the war geared to the procurement of raw materials to aid in Japan's reconstruction and development and the re-establishment of a marketing network to facilitate trade. It was in the latter sphere that Japan looked to the UK in the 1950s.

Japan's trading companies began to return to Britain soon after the Occupation ended, led by Mitsui & Co.'s London branch office which re-opened in 1953. Kawasaki Steamship Co. arrived in 1956 and Takaraisu Sales launched its London operation in 1959. The Ministry of Finance gave approval to a limited number of Japanese banks to establish representative offices overseas during this same period. The Bank of Japan returned to London in 1951, Fuji Bank and Teikoku Bank opened London branches in 1952 and Mitsubishi Bank and Sumitomo Bank resumed operations in 1956. Various services organizations, including airlines, travel agents and restaurants, later arrived in London to support the growing Japanese community and business links.

A number of joint ventures were established by the trading firms with Japanese manufacturers seeking to break into European markets during the 1960s, as with the tie-up of electrical goods manufacturer, Sanyo, with Marubeni (Sanyo Marubeni (UK) Ltd) in 1969. It was in Shannon, Ireland, however, that the first postwar direct manufacturing investment in Europe by a major Japanese firm was established, with the opening of a Sony production facility for transistor radios in 1959. Sales and distribution outlets for Japan's major manufacturing firms helped to create a UK network for Japanese exports in the 1960s. Honda opened its British sales operation in London in 1962 to expand further its motorcycle trade; Toyota's UK marketing organization was established in 1965 and a similar Nissan operation was opened in the same period. Japan's FDI outflows to Europe from 1951 to 1970 have been calculated at $636 million and were concentrated in the UK, West Germany and France, among the larger domestic markets for Japanese goods in Europe.[33] Yet Japanese manufacturing investment in the UK at the end of this period was so small that separate figures do not even appear in the industry analyses of investment flows.[34]

Changes in Japanese government policy on outward investment, paralleling the liberalization measures on inward investment, were initiated in 1969 with a five-stage process deregulating existing controls. While the final implementation of this process did not occur until 1978, by mid-1971 a key policy shift saw the Ministry of Finance automatically granting approval to Japanese companies seeking to establish greenfield investments overseas without financial limit.[35]

Rising balance of payments surpluses and increasing pressures from Japanese industry lay behind this significant volte-face which dramatically altered Japan's investment profile overseas. Among the factors influencing government policy from the late 1960s were the rising value of the yen as well as shortages and increased costs for labour and raw materials in Japan. Reflecting the immediate impact of this shift in policy, 1972 came to be known as the '*gannen*' (the first year of a new imperial reign) of Japanese foreign direct investment.[36] Certainly, the postwar pattern of Japanese investment into the UK was to alter markedly from 1972 as Japanese manufacturers responded to this long-awaited opportunity to gain direct access to some of their leading export markets through the establishment of production facilities in Europe. Britain's admission to membership of the EEC in 1973 heightened Japanese interest in the UK as an entry point to continental markets.

YKK Fasteners (UK) Ltd was the first Japanese manufacturer to invest in Britain. Its assembly operation for zip fasteners (one of a number of investments across Europe), established at Runcorn in Cheshire in December 1966, was transformed into a full manufacturing facility in 1972. In the aftermath of the key deregulating controls on outward investment, Sony Corp was to make its landmark decision to invest in the UK. The establishment of its £4.64 million colour television factory at Bridgend in South Wales in May 1973 helped to redefine Wales's economic identity with respect to Japanese foreign direct investment. The factors that determined Sony's decision in favour of the UK and Wales lend insight into the inward investment process and the cross-cultural balancing of global and regional interests.

Until its abolition in 1979, the Exchange Control Act of 1947 was the only British legislation which specifically addressed foreign investment, requiring all potential investors to obtain permission from the Bank of England and/or the Treasury (largely a formality) in consultation with other government departments.[37] Hodges notes that between 1964 and 1970 foreign investment was not considered to be 'a salient policy issue' by the British government which offered a 'qualified welcome' to foreign investors, treating them much the same as indigenous firms.[38] A gradual yet significant shift occurred from the early 1970s, from a position of passive acceptance to the more proactive encouragement of inward investment. The formation of the Invest in Britain Bureau (IBB) in 1977 officially heralded this change in outlook. The subsequent establishment or reorganization of territorial agencies in Northern Ireland, Scotland and Wales, and English regional development bodies, the latter part-funded by the IBB, provided a framework for the coordination and promotion of inward investment into the UK. Such developments went hand-in-hand with contemporary moves in Japanese industrial policy. As one Japanese scholar observed in 1979:

> For Japan . . . overseas production has suddenly emerged as a national requirement encompassing practically the entire spectrum of her industries and enterprises, small and large alike. The segments of industrial activities that are no longer suitable, environmentally or otherwise, for the Japanese economy need to be transplanted abroad, and overseas resources must now be developed more directly to insure [sic] supplies . . . Furthermore, overseas investment is now viewed as an essential device by which to upgrade Japanese industry.[39]

This forward-looking approach to overseas investment was encapsulated in the experience of Sony in South Wales. While Takiron, a small producer of PVC corrugated sheet, was in fact the first Japanese manufacturer to establish a base in Wales in 1972, Sony, the second, as a major multinational corporation and household name, was to attract attention on an altogether different scale. By 1970, Sony had established a network of regional sales offices in the UK and a distribution and service centre at Hounslow, near London's Heathrow Airport. The rationale behind opening its manufacturing plant in Britain was later described by the Chairman of Sony, Akio Morita:

> It was in an era before trade frictions had begun . . . We could see our UK business growing, and in 1971 we projected that we might get our share of the market up to 7 or 8 per cent. Together with other Japanese importers we could conceivably reach 10 per cent or more by 1975 or 1976, and that could mean trouble from domestic makers and politicians.[40]

The decision to invest in the UK prompted a feasibility study that took in sites in Scotland, the North of England, East Anglia and Wales. The considerations and inducements that influenced Sony ranged from plant locations, financial incentives, and infrastructural advantages to the fact that the Prince of Wales, according to Morita, 'had urged me to look at Wales when and if we decided to manufacture in Britain'.[41]

Labour relations were inevitably of concern to Sony at a time when Britain's reputation for militant trade unionism was well known. Asked by fellow businessmen at a Tokyo seminar in November 1976, 'But what about *eikoku byo* (the British disease)? How did you cope with it?', Sony's Director of European Operations, Hiroshi Okochi, described the firm's negotiation of a single union agreement with the Amalgamated Engineering Union as follows:

> We told them that we were only willing to negotiate through one designated trade union. Of course, we assured them that they could belong to any union of their choice, but if that particular union was not the designated trade union, it would have to negotiate with the company's trade union. We made this clear from the start and we have not experienced problems.[42]

That Sony's industrial relations arrangements, despite trade union power, generated relatively little public outcry at the time may have been due to the underestimation of the future impact of Japanese investment in Wales:

> Few people predicted, and even fewer acted upon, the dramatic transformation of Wales's political economy during the next decade . . . Nor was it conceived that the early Japanese investments in Wales were to be only the first among many, and that Japanese-generated employment was to become so important.[43]

Debates about Japanese investment in the UK have centred upon such issues as labour relations and the transferability of Japanese styles of management. The case of Sony and other pioneer Japanese investors in Britain in the 1970s also provides a focus for the consideration of the transformation of regional economies in this period through the effects of FDI. The success of Sony has been measured with respect to its continued expansion and diversification, to the employment it has generated (as the largest Japanese employer in Wales) and to its excellent record on labour relations. It is also acknowledged that Sony's smooth integration into the UK has attracted further Japanese investors to Wales and to other parts of Britain. As Munday has pointed out:

> the experiences of the first few Japanese 'pathfinder' manufacturing investments was very important in framing the wider impression of Japanese businessmen towards the UK operational environment . . . Sony proved that a large Japanese company could operate successfully in an environment of uncertainty that other Japanese businessmen may have feared.[44]

The concentration of Japanese affiliates in Wales from the early 1970s can, in part, be attributed to the example set by Sony, to the ongoing efforts of the Development Corporation for Wales (now the Welsh Development Agency), and to a host of site-specific factors. Matsushita Electric (UK) Ltd subsequently established its production facility for CTVs and microwave ovens at Cardiff in August 1974; Sekisui (UK) Ltd set up its polyethylene foam factory at Merthyr Tydfil in Mid Glamorgan in September 1975; Hitachi formed its (ill-fated) joint venture with GEC, GEC-Hitachi Television Ltd for the production of CTVs, VCRs and microwave ovens at Aberdare in Mid Glamorgan in December 1978; and Aiwa (UK) Ltd established its manufacturing operation at Crumlin in Gwent for the production of audio/hi-fi equipment, VCRs and CD players in October 1979. While Wales thus secured its place in the early history of Japanese manufacturing investment in Britain, other major Japanese companies turned to North East England and Scotland in the 1970s to establish production bases.

On the last day of his visit to Japan in January 1974, Christopher Chataway, Britain's Minister for Industrial Development, announced the decision by NSK, Japan's largest manufacturer of ball bearings, to establish NSK Bearings Europe Ltd at Peterlee in County Durham. Investment in the UK, NSK's largest market for bearings in Europe, was an obvious choice for the Japanese firm. Chataway, perhaps reflecting the UK government's 'qualified welcome' approach to foreign investment, noted that it was 'better for Britain that we should have investment in the UK serving the European market, rather than investment in Europe, from where the goods would be exported to Britain'.[45] After consideration of some 18 sites within development areas in North East England, Scotland and Wales, NSK's decision to invest in County Durham was based on a complex range of factors including the availability of government grants and loans amounting to some £1.4 million, the competitive wage levels in the region, the availability of a suitable factory site, access to skilled labour, a good communications network and local amenities. The North of England Development Council (NEDC) (later NDC),[46] which opened one of the first UK regional offices in Japan in 1975, worked in close collaboration with the Department of Trade and Industry (DTI) and other local agencies to secure this first major investment from Japan for North East England. As with Sony in South Wales, the 'follow-the-leader' factor would work to the region's advantage in attracting other investments from Japan during the next decade.

The concentration of Japanese manufacturing investment in the electronics sector in Scotland dates back to the late 1970s. The birth of 'Silicon Glen' took place with the establishment of Mitsubishi Electric (UK) Ltd in East Lothian in January 1979. Mitsubishi Electric acquired a defunct factory site at Haddington, vacated by a Norwegian firm, and upgraded it for the production of CTVs and microwave ovens. The company later opened a second factory at Livingston in West Lothian, a greenfield development, for the production of VCRs and VCR components. From this period onwards, Scotland, like South Wales and North East England, was fixed on the map of Japanese investment in Britain.

These early Japanese manufacturing investments in the UK were made against the backdrop of mounting trade frictions and an ever-widening trade gap. The devaluation of the dollar in 1971 and the imposition of import restrictions by the US refocused Japanese interest on the opportunities offered up by European markets. Between 1970 and 1980, exports to the European Community increased 10 times in value while EC exports to Japan rose by only 5 times over this same period.[47] Despite the introduction of voluntary export restraints and the launching of a series of anti-dumping investigations, the flow of exports from Japan to the EC increased fourfold between 1970 and 1976.[48] The oil shocks of the 1970s exacerbated these trends until, in an EC Commission Report, leaked to the press in the spring of 1979, the trade debate was personalized with its unfortunate characterization of the Japanese as 'workaholics' living in 'rabbit hutches'. In this climate, the alleviation of trade frictions and access to European markets increasingly influenced the path of Japanese overseas direct investment.

The 'bubble economy' years: foreign business in Japan in the 1980s

The 'closed door' image which Japan maintained until the 1970s with respect to potential investors from abroad has been likened to the wary 'welcome' extended to Commodore Perry's 'black ships' in the 1850s. The programme of liberalization measures begun in 1967, while gradually opening up investment opportunities, continued to be viewed with scepticism by foreign firms, for it did so against the backdrop of the spectacular MITI-led growth of the Japanese economy. One Japan-based European executive, quoted on the subject, described investing in Japan as 'rather like being invited to the cinema when all the best seats have been taken'.[49]

Speaking at the Third Pacific Trade and Development Conference held in Sydney in August 1970, another commentator compared the ongoing Japanese debate on FDI to the alternative French approach: '. . . France always talks about keeping foreign investment out and in practice has let it in, while Japan always talks about letting foreign investment in and in practice has kept it out'.[50]

The gradual implementation of liberalization measures nonetheless culminated in the reform of the Foreign Exchange and Foreign Trade Control Law in 1980. This altered the foreign direct investment process, replacing screening and approval mechanisms with 'prior notification' and allowing for full ownership by foreign firms. While certain industries were exempted and the Japanese government retained the ultimate right to prohibit foreign investments impinging upon national security and other interests, the new legislation represented a significant relaxation of control. 'Prior notification' procedures required only the submission of a set of forms to the Bank of Japan. In routine cases, if no objections were raised by the Ministry of Finance or other relevant industrial ministries, the project could commence without delay. The formerly-applied rule of 'prohibition in principle' was amended to 'liberalization in principle', but 'prohibition in an exception'.[51] The subsequent upward trend in FDI projects, recorded by Ministry of Finance statistics, would seem to indicate a positive response by foreign investors to this 're-opening' of Japan. While only 196 FDI projects were initiated in Japan in FY1976, the accumulated total of FDI projects by the end of FY1987 was 27 124.[52]

Foreign direct investment in Japan grew by 54 per cent between 1979 and 1984 but nevertheless remained small by world standards. The European share of the total accumulated direct investment in Japan to 1984 was 26.3 per cent, as compared to the US share of 59.3 per cent; British investment amounted to just 5.8 per cent overall.[53] In 1986 one writer noted that investment by Japanese companies in the UK (excluding financial services and energy production) had by 1981 exceeded the value of net assets of UK firms in Japan.[54] Few British companies were engaged in manufacturing activity in Japan in the 1980s; Ohmari recorded just eight British factories in Japan in 1986.[55] Compared with Britain's performance in other markets over a similar period (1975–83), sales arising from licensing in Japan greatly exceeded those arising from either exports or FDI.[56] Thus, while the environment for FDI in Japan had improved by the 1980s, Britain's investment levels still remained low, with the joint venture route as the preferred form of market entry for investors, and Japanese FDI in the UK concurrently on the rise.

There are various reasons for the limited attraction of foreign direct investment into Japan during the 1980s. While controls over FDI were considerably relaxed in 1980, many other government regulations existed to inhibit foreign ownership in various sectors, such as the banking, insurance and distribution industries.[57] Market conditions inevitably contributed to the reticence of foreign firms with regard to investment in Japan. While the massive appreciation of the yen following the Plaza Accord in 1985 provided the impetus for the Japanese to invest abroad, its domestic impact, including rising wages, land prices and rental costs, was to adversely affect the inward flow of foreign direct investment. In the second half of the 1980s, the international liberalization of financial markets led to an increase in FDI internationally. While Japan shared in that increase, the ratio of FDI inflow to GNP was just one-tenth that of the US, UK and France.[58] Other factors that affected FDI in Japan during this period included the difficulties in penetrating the Japanese market posed by *keiretsu* relationships, the nature of the Japanese distribution system, and different corporate strategies determining long- versus short-term outlooks. A variety of non-tariff barriers further contributed to the image of Japan as an impenetrable market for foreign business.

Exports to the US and the EC continued to grow after 1985, despite the appreciation of the yen, intensifying trade frictions. The Maekawa Report, released in April 1986, addressed 'the harmonization of Japan's economic relations with other nations' through its policy recommendations.[59] While no specific measures were proposed in support of FDI, its general tone put internationalization on the national agenda and generated considerable debate both at home and abroad. The launching of Prime Minister Nakasone's *Action Programme for Improved Market Access* in July 1985 had acknowledged the need for increased foreign participation in Japanese markets. The active promotion of inward direct investment similarly became an aspect of Japan's changing world view in the mid-1980s.[60] May 1984 saw the establishment within MITI's Industrial Policy Bureau of an Office for the Promotion of Foreign Investment in Japan. The Japan Development Bank (JDB), a government-affiliated lending institution, meanwhile, established a loan programme in 1984 for foreign firms seeking to set up operations in Japan. The role of the Japan External Trade Organization (JETRO), founded in the 1950s to promote Japan's exports abroad, underwent a shift of emphasis in line with these initiatives. JETRO became proactive, at this point, in the pursuit of inward investment through overseas promotional missions and other networking activities. In the latter half of the 1980s, the scale of FDI in Japan increased significantly to about $3000 million, reflecting the growth of interest by foreign firms. The concentration of this investment in manufacturing and commerce, as well as banking and insurance, constituted a departure from earlier patterns.[61]

How, then, did these various developments and initiatives affect British interests in Japan in the 1980s? Nakasone's *Action Programme* may have served as the model for a series of parallel Department of Trade and Industry (DTI) campaigns, aimed at increasing opportunities for British business in Japan. The aptly-named *Opportunity Japan* campaign, which sought to double Britain's flow of goods into Japan over a three-year period, was launched by Trade and Industry Secretary, Lord Young, in 1988. Its successor campaigns, *Priority Japan* in 1991 and *Action Japan* in 1994, focused again on increasing exports but also British investment in Japan. *Opportunity Japan* responded to the inflationary mood of Japan's late 1980s' 'bubble economy', promoting British high-quality consumer goods as well as a range of other industrial products. The ethos of the campaign, later summed up by Michael Perry, was to stop treating Japan 'as a problem' and to start treating it 'as an opportunity'.[62] Perry, as chairman of both Unilever plc and the subsequent *Priority Japan* campaign, was an appropriate spokesman for British interests in Japan. Unilever's investment in Japan dated back to 1965 (though Lever first operated in Japan from 1910), and its three factories there employed over 1000 people by the early 1990s.

The *Opportunity Japan* campaign did result in the near-doubling of British exports to Japan and witnessed increased investment by British firms. Wedgwood, for example, set up a fully-owned subsidiary, Wedgwood Japan, to import and sell Wedgwood products in Japan in 1983. Japanese sales, as a percentage of total sales, rose from 11 per cent in 1987 to 13 per cent in 1989.[63] The Rover Group also established its Japanese subsidiary, Rover Japan, in 1983. Its struggles, over the next ten years, to sell foreign models in an increasingly depressed market proved worthwhile; Rover Japan's sales as a percentage of total imported car sales grew from 4.5 per cent in 1985 to 7.6 per cent in 1990.[64] The President of Rover Japan, Peter J.Woods, summed up the obstacles posed by the conservatism of Japanese dealers and customers, despite the gradual opening up of the Japanese market in the 1980s: 'As far as our industry's case, the Japanese market is not closed anymore because most barriers came down six or seven years ago. But it is protected by such people's conservative mind-set, which frustrates many Americans and Europeans.'[65]

Dunhill Holdings, the British luxury consumer goods manufacturer, another British success story from this same period, was also forced to adapt to the Japanese 'mind-set'. As recounted in *The Financial Times*:

> At one stage Dunhill started buying shirts manufactured in Hong Kong. These were not intended for distribution in Japan, only in other parts of the world; yet still their Japanese buyers objected. They complained that the practice was likely to undermine the company's image as a purveyor of quality European merchandise and, although there was nothing wrong with its Hong Kong shirts, Dunhill reverted to manufacturing in Europe.[66]

While not all British firms have so flexibly adjusted to the requirements of the Japanese market, Japanese buyers and distributors can also be seen to have placed unreasonable demands on their overseas business partners. In

Table 9.1 Foreign direct investment in Japan, by key countries (Numbers of cases, Value in US$, Share of Total)

Fiscal year/country	*1994*			*1995*			*Cumulative 1950–1995*		
	Cases	*Amount*	*Share*	*Cases*	*Amount*	*Share*	*Cases*	*Amount*	*Share*
USA	347	1596	38.4	463	1843	48.0	10381	15613	41.2
Canada	15	319	7.7	12	14	0.4	816	1663	4.4
North America Total	362	1915	46.1	475	1857	48.4	11197	17276	45.6
United Kingdom	40	123	3.0	64	117	3.0	4371	1643	4.3
Germany	49	502	12.1	57	167	4.4	2802	2062	5.3
France	49	66	1.6	29	114	3.0	2911	777	2.1
Switzerland	31	154	3.7	40	101	2.6	3030	2250	5.9
Netherlands	63	523	12.6	58	561	14.6	3623	3361	8.9
Others	81	144	3.5	82	258	6.7	2493	1696	4.2
Europe Total	313	1512	36.4	330	1318	34.3	19130	11653	30.7
Hongkong	51	77	1.9	52	26	0.7	4821	747	2.0
Singapore	9	58	1.4	26	6	0.2	–	–	–
SouthKorea	20	66	1.6	36	94	2.4	–	–	–
Taiwan	72	25	0.6	51	104	2.7	–	–	–
China	46	7	0.2	44	13	0.3	–	–	–
Others	35	23	0.6	33	14	0.4	–	–	–
Asia Total	233	256	6.2	242	257	6.7	–	–	–
Japan	163	310	7.5	162	242	6.3	5360	3951	10.4
Others	64	162	3.9	63	163	4.2	–	–	–
Total	1135	4155	100.0	1272	3837	100.0	52097	37925	100.0

Source: Ministry of Finance, Japan.

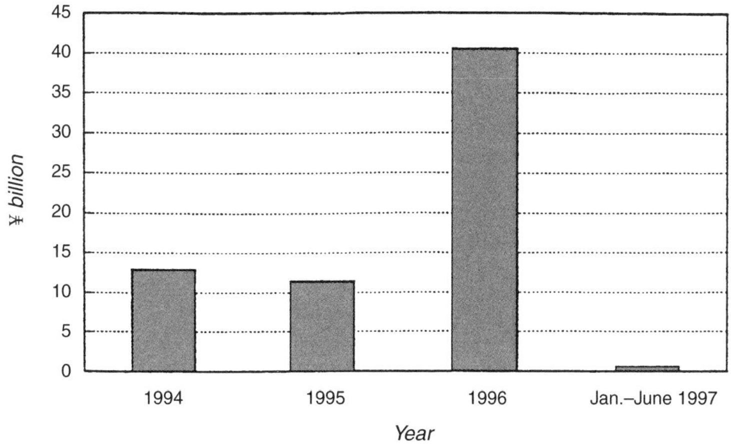

Number of cases reported:

1994	1995	1996	Jan.–June 1997
40	64	59	23

Value (¥ billion):

1994	1995	1996	Jan.–June 1997
12.9	11.4	40.5	0.6

Source: Ministry of Finance, *Direct Investment In and Out of Japan.*

Figure 9.1 British direct investment in Japan, 1994–1997

attempting to penetrate the Japanese market in 1987, the chief negotiator for Cable & Wireless finally concluded: 'We are as different as *sake* and hot water. You just can never tell what they are thinking'.[67]

It can certainly be argued that at least some of the cultural mist began to clear during the 1980s as Japan's internationalization drive and market-opening campaigns were matched by a more proactive stance on the part of the British government and business. By the end of the 1980s, British FDI in Japan had not greatly increased but exports had risen and new outlooks emerged which, combined with other factors, paved the way for increased business collaboration and investment in the 1990s.

1992 and the 'great wave' of Japanese investment in Britain

Trade frictions and the impact of the appreciation of the yen following the Plaza Accord of 1985 greatly accelerated Japanese foreign direct investment. The recommendations of the 1986 Maekawa Report included the reduction of Japan's dependence on exports by the more than doubling of outward

Table 9.2 Trend in investment by Japanese-affiliated companies (manufacturers) in Europe (by country) (Companies with production bases, excluding independent R&D bases and design centres)

Time of investigation Country	*1983 End of Dec.*	*1984 End of Dec.*	*1985 End of Dec.*	*1986 End of Dec.*	*1987 End of Dec.*	*1988 End of Dec.*	*1989 End of Dec.*	*1990 End of Dec.*	*1991 End of Dec.*	*1992 End of Dec.*	*1993 End of Dec.*	*1994 End of Dec.*	*1995 End of Dec.*	*1996 End of Dec.*
United Kingdom	34	39	48	56	77	98	129	158	180	191	199	203	214	223
France	20	25	30	37	47	56	69	79	88	92	94	100	108	114
Germany	35	38	39	45	53	58	72	80	88	95	98	98	100	101
The Netherlands	14	16	18	19	22	25	30	30	37	41	44	45	48	52
Belgium	15	16	17	20	21	24	29	36	38	41	42	43	43	43
Luxembourg	–	–	–	–	–	–	1	1	2	2	2	2	2	2
Ireland	8	8	8	10	11	13	17	23	25	27	30	30	35	36
Spain	21	23	23	26	30	35	43	47	52	54	55	58	59	60
Italy	10	11	12	13	18	24	29	32	36	37	38	40	43	45
Finland	2	2	2	2	2	3	3	3	3	4	4	5	6	6
Norway	–	–	–	–	–	–	–	–	1	1	1	1	1	1
Sweden	3	3	3	3	4	4	6	7	8	10	12	12	13	16
Denmark	1	1	1	1	1	1	2	2	2	2	2	2	2	2
Austria	1	2	3	6	7	7	8	9	9	11	11	11	11	11
Portugal	4	4	4	5	5	7	9	11	11	11	12	13	15	15
Switzerland	2	2	2	4	5	5	5	6	6	7	7	7	7	7
Greece	3	3	3	3	3	3	3	3	3	3	3	3	3	3
Iceland	–	1	1	1	1	1	1	1	1	1	1	1	1	1
Total	173	194	214	251	307	364	456	528	590	630	655	674	711	738
Annual change (number)		21	20	37	56	57	92	72	62	40	25	19	37	27
Annual change (%)		12.1	10.3	17.3	22.3	18.6	25.3	15.8	11.7	6.8	4.0	2.9	5.5	3.8

Note: These statistics show the trend of 738 Japanese-affiliated manufacturing companies which are currently operating (including those established, but not yet operating).
Source: JETRO, *The 13th Survey of European Operations of Japanese Companies in the Manufacturing Sector* (Sept. 1997).

direct investment as a percentage of gross domestic product (GDP) by 1992.[68] Between 1970 and the end of 1980, Japanese outflows had increased at an annual rate of 7.4 per cent but, from 1981 to 1986, the rate of increase surged to 13.4 per cent per annum.[69] The signing of the Single European Act in 1985 gave a particular boost to Japanese manufacturing investment in Europe and, within Europe, the UK. Successful investments by such pioneer companies as Sony in South Wales and NSK in North East England during the 1970s began to signpost Britain as a 'springboard', 'hangar' and 'launching pad' for Japanese investment into Europe. The critics reverted to more historical analogy, likening Japanese investment to the legendary Trojan Horse, penetrating the walls of 'Fortress Europe'.

Throughout the 1980s, Britain attracted the highest percentage of Japanese manufacturing investment as well as cumulative investment in Europe. The UK's substantial financial and services infrastructure accounted for its 8.6 per cent global share of Japanese cumulative FDI as calculated in 1992.[70] London's 'Big Bang' of 1986 was a spur to financial investment from Japan in the late 1980s while an over-inflated domestic economy increased the purchasing power of Japanese real estate investors overseas. Indeed, Japan's investment position in finance, insurance and real estate in 1986 alone almost doubled.[71] In the era of conspicuous consumption, *sushi* and *karaoke* bars sprang up all over London and British golf courses and department stores were bought up by Japanese entrepreneurs. The high visibility of such investments met with criticism from some quarters and the lack of reciprocity elicited official warnings as when, in March 1987, an irate Mrs Thatcher threatened to revoke the licenses of Japanese banks and insurance companies in the UK if the Japanese did not yield more seats to British firms on the Tokyo Stock Exchange and open their market to scotch whisky.[72]

By contrast, Japanese manufacturing investment in Britain met with relatively little opposition through the 1980s. Employment opportunities and exposure to new technologies and management methods represented the positive face of Japanese investment at a time when the decline of traditional heavy industries was impacting severely on the UK's regional economics. Government policy followed the path of renewal rather than resuscitation and promoted inward investment in unemployment blackspots through regional development grants, tax incentives and infrastructural support.

The pattern of Japanese manufacturing FDI in the UK was set by the Japanese consumer electronics firms which arrived in the 1970s, first producing colour televisions and then diversifying in the 1980s into the manufacture of videocassette recorders, compact disc players and microwave ovens.[73] Component suppliers followed in their wake as Japanese firms, bound by European regulations on local sourcing, sought to match the quality of their home manufactures in the UK. Japanese office equipment manufacturers also established UK operations in the 1980s for the production of electronic typewriters, photocopiers, facsimile machines, mobile telephones, and dot-matrix and daisy-wheel printers. Other companies introduced a diverse range of products from machine tools to batteries to optical lenses via their particular regional operations. After Sony, further key investments in Wales during the 1980s included the establishment of Sharp Manufacturing (1984), Brother Industries (1985), Orion Electric (1986), Diaplastics UK (1987), Tsuda UK (1987) and GKK Plastics (1989). Elsewhere in the UK, Toshiba Consumer Products (UK) was launched at Plymouth in Devon in 1981, Sanyo Industries (UK) at Lowestoft in Suffolk in 1982, NEC Semiconductors (UK) at Livingston in West Lothian in 1981, Maxell (UK) in 1980 and Ricoh UK Products in 1983 at Telford in Shropshire, Tabuchi Electric at Thornaby in Cleveland in 1984, Komatsu (UK) at Birtley, Tyne & Wear in 1985, NEC Technologies (UK) at Telford in 1986 and Epson Telford in 1987, Citizen Manufacturing (UK) at Scunthorpe in South Humberside in 1987, JVC Manufacturing (UK) at East Kilbride, Strathclyde in 1987, and Sanyo Electric Manufacturing (UK) in County Durham and Cleveland in 1988.[74] The increasingly wide regional spread of investment reflected the efforts of the different regional development agencies to attract Japanese firms, and also the increasing sophistication, local knowledge, and changing priorities of Japanese investors, not all of whom were influenced by the 'follow-the-leader' factor as a locational incentive.

FDI by Japanese motor vehicle manufacturers during the 1980s helped to diversify the industrial base of the UK regions with which it became associated. Nissan Motor Co., Japan's second largest auto manufacturer, which made Austin cars under license in early postwar Japan, announced its decision in January 1981 to build a major car production facility on a greenfield site in Britain. An extensive feasibility study followed which took the Nissan team to a range of 'special development areas' where automatic grants of 22 per cent were being offered.[75] In the North East of England, the company met with local officials, union representatives and NSK managers to gauge the prospects for a successful venture. Ongoing deliberations through 1982 and 1983 centred on concerns over the recession, local content requirements, union representation and Britain's continued membership of the EEC. Nissan's decision in favour of a site near Sunderland was finally announced in March 1984. It was reported that Japan's Prime Minister, Nakasone, having had 'both ears bent' by Mrs Thatcher at the Williamsburg summit, prompted Nissan's president, Takashi Ishihara, to 'get on with the job'.[76] Lord Marsh, a senior UK adviser to Nissan and a leading member of the negotiating team, described the investment as 'one of the last opportunities to revitalize the economic base of the region . . . [giving] a new lease of life to a part of the country which has had little to cheer it for a long time'.[77]

The significance of Nissan lay in its scale (both in investment and employment terms),[78] in its contribution to the industrial diversification of the North East, and in its impact on the UK and European motor industries. As with the consumer electrical sector, Nissan's investment also led to an influx of Japanese automotive supplier firms. It has recently been calculated that, of the 34 Japanese manufacturing companies and R&D facilities in the North East, more than half operate (either wholly or partly) in the automotive sector.[79] These include: Ikeda-Hoover, Calsonic Exhaust Systems, and SMC Pneumatics (all established in 1986), Nissan Yamato (now Unipress) and Llanelli Heater Systems (both established in 1987), and Hashimoto Ltd, Marley Kansei and Mi-King (established in 1989). Not all of the Japanese automotive suppliers sprang from the Nissan connection. As previously noted, Sumitomo's takeover of Dunlop's UK factories, including its Washington-based tyre plant, led to one of Britain's earliest investor firms in Japan becoming part of the 1980's 'great wave' of Japanese investment into Britain. Similarly, while NSK Bearings predated Nissan in the North East by some ten years, this first Japanese manufacturer in the region went on to open a steering components plant at Peterlee in 1990. Both firms became suppliers to Nissan.

Three of Japan's leading automakers, Nissan, Toyota and Honda, had all established plants in Britain by the end of the 1980s. Honda's links with the UK began in the 1960s with the opening of a sales and distribution outlet for its thriving motorcycle trade. The company moved into car production, forming a series of technical collaboration agreements with British Leyland (later Rover) from 1979 for the production of Honda models in the UK. Honda later opened a car engine plant with Rover in 1987 and an assembly plant at Swindon in Wiltshire in 1992. It has been claimed that 'Rover benefited from the Honda link not only by saving development costs but also by oberving and imitating the Japanese company's approach to designing and making cars'.[80] The Honda–Rover partnership nevertheless foundered in 1994 when the German car giant, BMW, took over the majority share in the British firm. Severing its financial links with Rover, Honda chose to expand its production base rather than to consider withdrawal from the UK. As the President of Honda Motor Europe, Miyake Shojiro explained: 'Honda has had a long history in Europe and has established a very good relationship with European people and society. We have already established our own manufacturing facilities . . . nothing will affect our commitment to European and British industry. That commitment will not change.'[81]

The collapse of the Honda–Rover relationship, while arising from a corporate takeover rather than an unworkable alliance, raises the issue of ownership advantages in relation to FDI. While the majority of Japanese manufacturing investments in the UK in the 1980s were wholly-owned subsidiaries, the experiences of such unsuccessful joint ventures as those of Rank–Toshiba and GEC–Hitachi in the late 1970s led some to conclude that: 'the UK [partner] companies had little to contribute in terms of technical expertise, marketing ability or the development of new products'.[82] Transformed into wholly-owned enterprises in the early 1980s, both companies transcended their earlier difficulties.[83]

Toyota Motor Company's greenfield investment, in a £700 million car production facility at Burnaston, Derbyshire in April 1989 and a car engine factory at Deeside in North Wales in July 1989, brought the largest Japanese auto manufacturer to the UK. Toyota's investment decision loomed as a dispute raged in Europe over the local content ratio of Nissan cars made in Washington. The strong stand taken by the British government in defence of Nissan reassured Toyota and was applauded by Japanese firms throughout the UK who recognized the strength of Anglo-Japanese mutual investment interests.[84]

By the late 1980s, Japanese manufacturing FDI in the UK encompassed a diverse locational and sectoral spread. The announcement in April 1989 that Fujitsu, the Japanese electronics manufacturer, was investing £400 million in a semiconductor plant in County Durham was followed by the Fujitsu takeover of the British computer company, ICL, in November 1990. As the 'bubble economy' passed into history, these two high-technology investments came to represent the legacy of the 1980s Japanese investment boom in Britain. An over-inflated economy and an undervalued indigenous producer were set to undergo change in the following decade. Through the 1980s, Britain's share of Japanese cumulative investment in Europe rose to over 40 per cent. In the period from 1983 to 1990, the number of Japanese manufacturers operating in the UK nearly quadrupled.[85] Meanwhile, the increase in Japanese R&D and design facilities over this same period served as evidence of the deepening investment links between Britain and Japan.

The approach of 1992, accelerating trade frictions and the high value of the yen provided the impetus for Japanese companies to establish production bases in Europe. Britain's attractions as a base for that investment range from the infrastructural to the cultural. Along with the availability of labour, competitive wage rates and a good industrial relations record in recent years, the English-language factor and the welcome extended both nationally and regionally to Japanese firms have been repeatedly cited as informing and influencing Japanese decisions to invest in the UK. Despite the general standardization of financial and other inducements across Europe, Britain has continued to dominate Japan's investment interests in the EC.

Recent developments in Anglo-Japanese investment

Japan's economic ascendancy in the 1980s and growing international links were paralleled by pressures from American and European trading partners to address imbalances in trade and investment. The Uruguay Round of multilateral trade negotiations, initiated under the auspices of the General Agreement on Tariffs and Trade (GATT) in 1986, was concluded in 1993. It contextualized the 'liberalising deregulatory emphasis of the Single Market'[86] by seeking to break down trade and investment barriers. The Structural Impediments Initiative (SII) negotiations of 1989–90 provided a further US–Japan platform for considering the obstacles to greater market access, from the role of *keiretsu* groupings to retail practices.

The programme of measures instituted to liberalize and deregulate the Japanese economy from the 1980s has derived from domestic as well as external forces. The 'boom and bust' scenario of the 'bubble economy' focused attention on the need for a reassessment of the banking system as well as more deep-seated structural reforms. 1990s' Japan has seen banking collapses, tumbling land and share prices, corporate restructurings and a rise in unemployment. The Asian financial crisis and depreciation in the value of the yen in 1998 have contributed to a recession in Japan while reducing the cost of Japanese exports abroad and potentially exacerbating conflicts over trade. Throughout such turmoil, a process has been set in train which has inevitably moved the Japanese economy toward greater openness.

While foreign investments in Japan declined overall in fiscal 1997, falling 12 per cent from the previous year to 678.2 billion yen, foreign financial firms increased their presence in preparation for the 'Big Bang' reform and internationalization of Japan's financial market by 2001.[87] The growth in financial investment has been accompanied by an increase in real estate investment and some instances of mergers and acquisitions, traditionally difficult areas for foreign penetration. The expansion of Japanese sales networks by foreign retailers and manufacturing initiatives have both been aided by the recent deregulatory measures and the burgeoning network of both local and national agencies acting in support of foreign direct investment.

Amendment of the 1980 Foreign Exchange and Foreign Trade Control Law in 1991 replaced the former 'prior notification' requirement with regard to FDI by an 'ex post facto notification' requirement for investment in non-restricted industries. The Inward Investment Law, established in March 1992, extended preferential tax treatment to eligible investors, designated as 'inward investors'. The need to improve Japan's investment climate was acknowledged by the formation of the Japan Investment Council in 1994. Chaired by the Prime Minister, it has initiated Cabinet-level discussions on investment-related issues. Meanwhile, a further easing of investment controls took place with the completed formulation of the government's three-year *Deregulation Action Plan* in March 1997. This addressed deregulation in the areas of housing, land zoning, financial services, employment services and telecommunications, while setting an agenda for the future.

An organizational framework in support of potential FDI has developed alongside of these deregulatory measures. JETRO, the MITI-led, trade-related body, with offices worldwide, has taken on an increasingly active role in this regard. The Japan Development Bank has expanded its low-interest loan programmes, begun in the 1980s, for the benefit of foreign-affiliated firms. In addition, in June 1993, the Foreign Investment in Japan Development Corporation (FIND), chaired by Akio Morita, Chairman of Sony, was established to advise foreign firms and coordinate investment opportunities. At the local level, a range of investment promotion programmes has evolved with the regional Japan Investment Council centrally facilitating links throughout Japan. Twenty-two Foreign Access Zones (FAZs) provide an infrastructural base for foreign firms.

The wide-ranging policy changes and implementation measures that have been set in place are aimed at narrowing the gap between inward and outward investment flows. That gap has most recently been quantified by 1996 statistics which value Japan's overseas FDI at $50 billion US while inward investment has been calculated at just one-seventh of that amount.[88] Comparative UK–Japan investment figures for FY1995 show that Japan's direct investment in Britain amounted to more than twenty times that of Britain's investment in Japan; Japanese FDI in the UK was set at US$37 244 million while UK direct investment in Japan totalled US$1643 million.[89] This differential, combined with the £5.2 billion trade imbalance (as of December 1997), has intensified the British export and investment drive in Japan and highlighted the importance of Japanese attempts to encourage FDI.

The relaunch of the DTI's *Action Japan* campaign in 1998 coincided with a fall in the value of the yen against the dollar and the consequent reduction in the cost of Japanese exports. For British firms seeking to make inroads into the Japanese market, this has escalated the existing difficulties. Waterford Wedgwood, winner of the *Opportunity Japan 'Award for Consumer Success in Japan'*, built on its success in Japan by opening a retail outlet in Tokyo in 1995. The economic downturn has caused a 2–3 per cent drop in sales volume, but a more significant decrease in the value of the goods being sold, matching the decline in consumer confidence and interest in foreign luxury products in Japan.[90] Yet British exports to Japan, valued at £4.3 billion in 1996, have increased nearly $2\frac{1}{2}$ times in the last decade and some 400 British companies, in a wide variety of sectors, are currently operating in Japan.

Some of the major British investors in Japan can look back to prewar business connections. ICI plc, through its constituency companies, was one of the first British investors in Japan. It now operates from nine manufacturing sites in different parts of Japan and has research facilities in Tokyo, Osaka, Ibaraki and Mihara.[91] Glaxo began marketing its products in Japan in the 1950s, before moving into manufacturing and the establishment of a research and development centre at Tsukuba Science City. BP, Rover, Unilever and many other large British and joint-British firms have established extensive interests in Japan, but small and medium-sized enterprises (SMEs) in the industrial, retailing, R&D and services sectors have also made inroads into the Japanese market and are being officially encouraged in this process. The British Industry Centre at Yokohama Business Park was formally opened in January 1998 by Prime Minister Tony Blair. A cooperative venture between the British government, the Yokohama City government, the Nomura Real Estate Company and the British Chamber of Commerce, it offers office space and support for investment by UK SMEs. The Yokohama base may have been chosen for its reflection of past British ties with the former treaty port, but it nevertheless represents a concrete union of interests, aimed at increasing British industry's present-day associations with Japan.

The charting of Anglo-Japanese trade and investment links has become a phenomenological mire. While British investors such as The Body Shop, Culpepper, HMV, Laura Ashley and Virgin Megastore provide 'a shop window for British goods and British style' in Japan, British motor vehicles, including Primeras built at Nissan's Sunderland plant, have become the UK's single-largest export item to Japan.[92] British car components also feature prominently in the trade figures; for example, £6.2 million worth of automobile components were supplied to Japan in 1993, some of these by Nissan's and Honda's UK supplier of air filters, Coopers Filters of Abergavenny, which also exports filters to Honda's plants in Japan.[93] Third-country business links between British and Japanese firms have resulted in collaborative projects throughout the world in such areas as environmental monitoring, power generation, telecommunications and civil engineering. Ove Arup, one of the UK's largest independent firms of consulting engineers, has developed extensive partnerships with Japanese industry and operates its own office in Japan. In addition to Japan-based commissions such as its fire design work for the Kansai International Airport,[94] it has designed a car plant for Toyota in Turkey and worked on other Japanese projects in Germany, Malaysia and China.[95] Research and development (R&D) has become a further area of mutual involvement by investor companies in both the UK and Japan. It has characterized the deepening of investment links in the 1990s and reflects the ethos of long-termism so often associated with Japanese firms.

Japanese direct investment in the UK in the last decade can be seen as the second of two consecutive waves. The first peaked at the end of the 1980s, leaving a spread of 129 Japanese-affiliated manufacturers and 52 R&D and design facilities (11 of these independently-owned) across the UK.[96] Deflationary pressures, but also prior investment commitments made in the UK by Japan's leading international firms, signalled a decrease in new projects and an inevitable levelling-off of Japanese investment in the run-up to 1992. The second wave, of less dramatic proportions, has consisted of some investment by SMEs, the elaboration of existing projects by previous investors, and the increased establishment of R&D and design centres.[97] Britain's share of Japanese manufacturing investment in Europe at the end of 1996 was 30.2 per cent and, of R&D investment, 36 per cent.[98]

Table 9.3 Number of Japanese companies with R&D and design facilities in Europe, 1989–1996 (Figures in parentheses ( ) indicate the numbers of independent R&D facilities)

Time of investigation *Country*	*1989* *End of Dec.*	*1990* *End of Dec.*	*1991* *End of Dec.*	*1992* *End of Dec.*	*1993* *End of Dec.*	*1994* *End of Dec.*	*1995* *End of Dec.*	*1996* *End of Dec.*
United Kingdom	52 (11)	70 (15)	86 (17)	96 (20)	105 (23)	108 (25)	112 (27)	118 (28)
France	18 (3)	24 (5)	27 (5)	32 (6)	34 (7)	36 (8)	41 (12)	44 (13)
Germany	27 (8)	35 (10)	45 (12)	53 (16)	56 (17)	58 (18)	61 (20)	63 (22)
The Netherlands	7	8	15 (3)	16 (3)	18 (3)	18 (3)	18 (3)	18 (3)
Belgium	11 (3)	15 (3)	16 (3)	18 (3)	18 (3)	18 (3)	18 (3)	18 (3)
Luxembourg								
Ireland	4 (1)	6 (2)	6 (2)	6 (2)	9 (3)	9 (3)	9 (3)	9 (3)
Spain	14	17	22	23 (1)	24 (1)	26 (1)	28 (1)	28 (1)
Italy	8 (2)	8 (2)	10 (3)	10 (3)	12 (4)	13 (4)	14 (4)	16 (4)
Finland								
Norway			1	1	1	1	1	1
Sweden	6	6	7	8	10	10	10	11
Denmark								
Austria	2	2	2	3	3	3	3	3
Portugal	1	1	1	1	1	1	1	1
Switzerland		1 (1)	1 (1)	1 (1)	1 (1)	1 (1)	1 (1)	1 (1)
Greece								
Iceland								
Total	150 (28)	193 (38)	239 (46)	268 (55)	292 (62)	302 (66)	317 (74)	331 (78)
Annual change (number)		43 (10)	46 (8)	29 (9)	24 (7)	10 (4)	15 (8)	14 (4)

Source: JETRO, *The 13th Survey of European Operations of Japanese Companies in the Manufacturing Sector* (Sept. 1997).

The impact of Anglo-Japanese investment cannot only be measured in statistically-quantifiable terms. The historic pattern of trade and investment has adapted to the demands of a differently-orientated marketplace in which cross-cultural boundaries are ceasing to exist. The nature of this dynamic was addressed in 1994 by Sir Paul Girolami, the then Chairman of Glaxo:

> . . . international trade and investment is increasingly conditioned by global investment and trading strategies and multi-faceted international relationships. We have advanced a long way from the simple exchange of goods for money and from the exchange of primary materials for manufactured goods . . . The UK and Japan have, for different but complementary reasons, a crucial part to play in the working of this complex world-wide pattern of investment.[99]

Postwar Japanese investment in Britain gathered momentum in the context of trade imbalance, currency fluctuation, and the micro-climates of European union and inflationary pressures in Japan. Its value and effects have been diversely assessed and debated from international, national and regional perspectives. Britain's investment presence in Japan is of a different order and on a dissimilar scale, yet it has its roots in years of alliance and business collaboration from the start of the present century. At the time of the Dunlop takeover by Sumitomo Rubber Industries, the company Chairman, Yokose Kyohei, looked back to his boyhood in Kobe where he grew up within sight of the belching chimneys of the Dunlop plant and used the company's rubber water bottles stamped with the bearded portrait of Sir John Boyd Dunlop.[100] The sense of the past informing the present echoed through his recollection. A few years after Lever's established its soap factory in that same part of Japan, Sir William Lever addressed the company AGM (1914) on the long-term view required of overseas investments: 'When we go to a country and put up works there, we cannot immediately get a return on that capital. Trade is small, advertising and other expenses are large and it takes some little time.'[101]

As Britain and Japan seek to balance their bilateral interests in a changing economic climate, the lessons of the past and the appreciation that 'it takes some little time' provide a useful perspective on the future.

Notes

1. 'Breaking The Mould of Old Practices: Japanese Tyre Group Sumitomo Rubber's European Operation', *Financial Times*, 7 March 1986.
2. R.P.T. Davenport-Hines and G. Jones, 'British Business in Japan since 1868', in

R.P.T. Davenport-Hines and G. Jones (eds), *British Business in Asia since 1860* (Cambridge: Cambridge University Press, 1989), pp. 224–5. This source has furnished considerable detail of company links in the pre- and postwar periods. See also the chapter by Ishii in this volume.

3. Ibid., pp. 225, 272.
4. See Nagura's chapter in this volume.
5. C. Wilson, *The History of Unilever: a Study in Economic Growth and Social Change*, vol. 1 (London: Cassell, 1954), p. 191.
6. W.J. Reader, *Imperial Chemical Industries: a History*, vol. I, *The Forerunners 1870–1926* (London: Oxford University Press, 1970), p. 335.
7. Davenport-Hines and Jones, *British Business in Asia*, p. 231.
8. Ibid., p. 234.
9. M. Mason, 'Historical Perspectives on Japanese Direct Investment in Europe', in M. Mason and D. Encarnation (eds), *Does Ownership Matter? Japanese Multinationals in Europe* (Oxford: Oxford University Press, 1994), pp. 6–7.
10. P. Newall, *Japan and the City of London* (London: Athlone, 1996), p. 10. See also Suzuki's chapter in this volume.
11. W.D. Wray, *Mitsubishi and the NYK, 1870–1914: Business Strategy in the Japanese Shipping Industry* (Cambridge MA: Council on East Asian Studies, Harvard University, 1984), p. 318.
12. Mason and Encarnation, *Does Ownership Matter?*, p. 11.
13. Ibid., pp. 12–13.
14. Ibid., p. 15.
15. Davenport-Hines and Jones, *British Business in Asia*, p. 234.
16. R.W. Buckley, 'British Diplomacy and the Allied Control of Japan, 1945–1946', in *Proceedings of the British Association for Japanese Studies*, vol. 2 (1977), p. 167; Davenport-Hines and Jones, *British Business in Asia*, p. 234.
17. Ibid., p. 236.
18. 'Nissan Shifts Gear', *The Economist*, 29 October 1983. See also Madeley's chapter in this volume.
19. Y. Tsurumi, *Technology Transfer and Foreign Trade: the Case of Japan, 1950–1966* (New York: Arno Press, 1980), p. 246.
20. Davenport-Hines and Jones, *British Business in Asia*, p. 235.
21. C. Johnson, *MITI and the Japanese Miracle: the Growth of Industrial Policy* (Stanford CA: Stanford University Press, 1982), p. 195.
22. While US firms were also affected by this legislation, business links established in the immediate postwar period and subsequent Japanese reliance on American technology laid the groundwork for the greater dominance of US investors in Japan.
23. R.Wakasugi, 'Why Foreign Firms' Entry has been Low in Japan: an Empirical Examination', in M. Yoshitomi and E.M. Graham (eds), *Foreign Direct Investment in Japan* (Cheltenham: Edward Elgar, 1996), pp. 116–17.
24. D. Bailey, G. Harte and R. Sugden, *Transnationals and Governments: Recent Policies in Japan, France, Germany, the United States and Britain* (London: Routledge, 1994), p. 12.
25. C. Higashi and G.P. Lauter, *The Internationalization of the Japanese Economy* (Boston MA: Kluwer, 1990), p. 222.
26. Tsurumi, *Technology Transfer and Foreign Trade*, p. 136.
27. See Davenport-Hines and Jones, *British Business in Asia*, pp. 236–41.
28. Ibid., p. 242.

29. Johnson, *MITI and the Japanese Miracle*, p. 302.
30. Bailey, Harte and Sugden, *Transnationals and Governments*, p. 27.
31. J.H. Dunning, *Japanese Participation in British Industry* (London: Croom Helm, 1986), p. 10.
32. Bailey, Harte and Sugden, *Transnationals and Governments*, pp. 13–14.
33. Mason and Encarnation, *Does Ownership Matter?*, p. 21.
34. R. Strange, *Japanese Manufacturing Investment in Europe: Its Impact on the UK Economy* (London: Routledge, 1993), pp. 109–10.
35. Mason and Encarnation, *Does Ownership Matter?*, p. 21.
36. Ibid., p. 24.
37. Quoted in Strange, *Japanese Manufacturing Investment in Europe*, p. 114.
38. Ibid.
39. T. Ozawa quoted in P. Dicken, 'The Changing Geography of Japanese Foreign Direct Investment in Manufacturing Industry', in J. Morris (ed.), *Japan and the Global Economy: Issues and Trends in the 1990s* (London: Routledge, 1991), p. 30.
40. A. Morita, *Made in Japan* (London: Collins, 1987), p. 298.
41. Ibid.
42. 'Sorting out Britain Japanese Style', *The Times* 15 November 1976, pp. 1, 8.
43. J. Morris, M. Munday and B. Wilkinson, *Working for the Japanese: the Economic and Social Consequences of Japanese Investment in Wales* (London: Athlone, 1993), p. 96.
44. M. Munday, *Japanese Manufacturing Investment in Wales* (Cardiff: University of Wales Press, 1990), pp. 39–40.
45. *Financial Times*, 24 January 1974.
46. As of spring 1999 the NDC has been replaced by a new regional agency entitled 'One Northeast'.
47. E. Wilkinson, *Japan versus Europe: a History of Misunderstanding* (Harmondsworth: Penguin, 1981), pp. 189–90.
48. Strange, *Japanese Manufacturing Investment in Europe*, p. 89.
49. P.J. Buckley, H. Mirza and J.R. Sparkes, 'Direct Foreign Investment in Japan as a Means of Market Entry: the Case of European Firms', in P.J. Buckley and P. Ghauri (eds), *The Internationalization of the Firm: a Reader* (London: Academic Press, 1993), p. 126.
50. Hugh Patrick quoting Stephen Hymer, in R. Komiya, 'Direct Foreign Investment in Postwar Japan', in P. Drysdale (ed.), *Direct Foreign Investment in Asia and the Pacific* (Canberra: Australian National University Press, 1972), p. 168.
51. Yoshitomi, *Foreign Direct Investment in Japan*, p. 117.
52. Higashi and Lauter, *Internationalization of the Japanese Economy*, second edition, p. 223.
53. JETRO statistics quoted in Buckley and Ghauri, *Internationalization of the Firm*, p. 127.
54. Dunning, *Japanese Participation in British Industry*, p. 10. Since Dunning is primarily concerned with production bases his figures exclude oil, insurance and banking, which are, of course, significant.
55. Quoted in Buckley and Ghauri, *Internationalization of the Firm*, p. 129.
56. P.J. Buckley, *Foreign Direct Investment and Multinational Enterprises* (Basingstoke: Macmillan – now Palgrave, 1995), pp. 91–2.
57. Yoshitomi, *Foreign Direct Investment in Japan*, p. 117.
58. Ibid., p. 116.
59. Higashi and Lauter, *Internationalization of the Japanese Economy*, p. 125.

60. Strange, *Japanese Manufacturing Investment in Europe*, pp. 72–3.
61. Ibid., pp. 73–4.
62. 'UK Businesses Target Japan', *The Japan Times*, 19 September 1993, p. 6.
63. The company's name was changed to Waterford Wedgwood in 1986 following its acquisition by Waterford. See DTI, *Twelve of the Best* (London: Department of Trade and Industry, 1991), p. 7.
64. Ibid., p. 3.
65. 'British Firms Cracking into Japan's market', *The Japan Times*, 19 September 1993, p. 6.
66. 'Breaching a Cultural Barrier – How Japan Came to be Dunhill's Most Successful Export Market', *Financial Times*, 25 June 1987.
67. 'Try Hard to Take the Terror out of That Kamikaze Trip to Tokyo', *The Guardian*, 17 August 1987, quoted in Davenport-Hines and Jones, 'British Business in Japan Since 1868', p. 243.
68. Strange, *Japanese Manufacturing Investment in Europe*, p. 52.
69. S.E. Thompson, 'The Growth of American, British and Japanese Direct Investment in the 1980s', *RIIA Discussion Papers* 2, 1988, p. 21.
70. JETRO/Ministry of Finance statistics.
71. Thompson, 'The Growth of American, British and Japanese Direct Investment in the 1980s', p. 31.
72. T. Jackson, *Turning Japanese: the Fight for Industrial Control of the New Europe* (London: Harper Collins, 1993), p. 216.
73. Strange, *Japanese Manufacturing Investment in Europe*, p. 132.
74. This listing provides only a representative sample of some of the larger Japanese investments in the UK during the 1980s.
75. *The Financial Times*, 8 April 1981.
76. 'Nissan Shifts Gear', *The Economist*, 29 October 1983, p. 88.
77. *Sunderland Echo*, 2 April 1984.
78. In 1998, NMUK was valued at £1.2 billion and employed 4500 people, making it the largest single investment by a Japanese company in Europe.
79. K. Burge, 'Japanese Manufacturing Investment in Europe – Recent History and Future Prospects', *Business Review North* 8, 4, Spring 1997, p. 17.
80. G. Owen, 'From Mass-Market Manufacturer to Niche Player: Product and Marketing Strategy at British Leyland/Rover from 1968 to 1995', in E. Abe and T. Gourvish (eds), *Japanese Success? British Failure? Comparisons in Business Performance Since 1945* (Oxford: Oxford University Press, 1997), p. 229.
81. 'Honda to Carry on in the UK', *Japan Contact*, 27 April 1994.
82. Strange, *Japanese Manufacturing Investment in Europe*, p. 199.
83. Ironically, it was the British government which pressed for the ill-fated GEC–Hitachi tie-up in the 1970s while allowing Britain's last major domestic car producer – with its successful Japanese links – to pass into foreign ownership.
84. H. Kitamura, 'The Subtlety and Tenacity of British Diplomacy: Lessons for Japan', *Japan Echo* 19, 3, Autumn 1992, pp. 63–4.
85. JETRO, *The 13th Survey of European Operations of Japanese Companies in the Manufacturing Sector*, September 1997, p. 5.
86. D. Hurd, 'The 1990s: Challenges for Trade', *Anglo-Japanese Journal*, 4, 1, April–June 1990, p. 5.
87. 'Foreign Investors Attracted to Japan's Market', *The Nikkei Weekly*, 29 June 1998.
88. *Bank of America Trade Directory*, http://www.tradeport.org/ts/countries/japan/climate/shtml, pp. 1–2.

89. JETRO, *White Paper on Foreign Direct Investment*, 1997.
90. 'The Vanishing Yen', *The Sunday Times*, 14 June 1998, p. 7.
91. *ICI Fact Book*, 1998, pp. 42–3.
92. DTI, *Japan: an Overseas Trade Supplement*, May 1997, p. 4.
93. D. Wilson, 'Economic Links: Britain's Partner in the East', in Anglo-Japanese Economic Institute (eds), *Anglo-Japanese Collaboration: On to Global Partnership* (London: Anglo-Japanese Economic Institute, 1995), pp. 42–3.
94. The airport project involved a total of 13 British firms.
95. N. Khosla and J. Locke, 'Partnerships with Japan on Major Projects Worldwide', in Daiwa Anglo-Japanese Foundation (ed.), *Managing Across Borders: Culture and Communication Issues for British and Japanese Businesses* (London: The Daiwa Anglo-Japanese Foundation, 1996), pp. 99–111.
96. JETRO, *White Paper on Foreign Direct Investment*, 1997, pp. 5, 7.
97. At the time of writing, the latest available statistics indicated the establishment of a total of 243 Japanese-affiliated manufacturers and 130 R&D facilities in the UK as of the end of 1998 (JETRO, *The 15th Survey of European Operations of Japanese Companies in the Manufacturing Sector*, September 1999, appendices 1 and 2).
98. JETRO, *White Paper on Foreign Direct Investment*, 1997, pp. 5, 7.
99. P. Girolami, 'Britain's Worldwide Trading Interests', Speech delivered at 'Britain and Japan – the New Era' Conference, London, 17 January 1994.
100. *The Financial Times*, 7 March 1986.
101. Sir William Lever at the AGM of the Shareholders, 5 March 1914, quoted in Wilson, *The History of Unilever*, vol. 1, p. 188.

Index